Transnational Theatre Histories

Series Editors
Christopher B. Balme
Institut für Theaterwissenschaft
Ludwig-Maximilians-Universität
Munich, Germany

Tracy C. Davis
Northwestern University
Evanston, IL, USA

Catherine M. Cole
College of Arts and Sciences
University of Washington
Seattle, WA, USA

Transnational Theatre Histories illuminates vectors of cultural exchange, migration, appropriation, and circulation that long predate the more recent trends of neoliberal globalization. Books in the series document and theorize the emergence of theatre, opera, dance, and performance against backgrounds such as imperial expansion, technological development, modernity, industrialization, colonization, diplomacy, and cultural self-determination. Proposals are invited on topics such as: theatrical trade routes; public spheres through cross-cultural contact; the role of multi-ethnic metropolitan centers and port cities; modernization and modernity experienced in transnational contexts; new materialism: objects moving across borders and regions; migration and recombination of aesthetics and forms; colonization and decolonization as transnational projects; performance histories of cross- or inter-cultural contact; festivals, exchanges, partnerships, collaborations, and co-productions; diplomacy, state and extra-governmental involvement, support, or subversion; historical perspectives on capital, finance, and administration; processes of linguistic and institutional translation; translocality, glocality, transregional and omnilocal vectors; developing new forms of collaborative authorship.

Series Editors
Christopher B. Balme (LMU Munich)
Catherine M. Cole (University of Washington)
Tracy C. Davis (Northwestern)

Editorial Board
Leo Cabranes-Grant (UC Santa Barbara, USA)
Khalid Amine (Abdelmalek Essaadi University, Tétouan, Morocco)
Laurence Senelick (Tufts University, USA)
Rustom Bharucha (JNU, New Delhi, India)
Margaret Werry (University of Minnesota, USA)
Maria Helena Werneck (Federal University of Rio de Janiero, Brazil)
Catherine Yeh (Boston University, USA/ University of Heidelberg, Germany)
Marlis Schweitzer (York University; Canada)

More information about this series at
http://www.palgrave.com/gp/series/14397

Rashna Darius Nicholson

The Colonial Public and the Parsi Stage

The Making of the Theatre of Empire (1853–1893)

palgrave
macmillan

Rashna Darius Nicholson
University of Hong Kong
Hong Kong S.A.R., China

This book is the revised version of a doctoral thesis entitled 'The Theatre of Empire' submitted to the Faculty of History and the Arts, Ludwig Maximilian University of Munich, Germany.

Transnational Theatre Histories
ISBN 978-3-030-65835-9 ISBN 978-3-030-65836-6 (eBook)
https://doi.org/10.1007/978-3-030-65836-6

Cover image: 'An Actress in a Fine Company. India.', H. C. White Company, 1996.0009.WX25689, Keystone-Mast Collection, UCR/California Museum of Photography, University of California at Riverside.

This Palgrave Macmillan imprint is published by the registered company Springer Nature Switzerland AG
The registered company address is: Gewerbestrasse 11, 6330 Cham, Switzerland

Acknowledgments

As this work formally began in 2010, the debt that I owe to several individuals and institutions is significant. The first draft of this book was completed as a doctoral thesis entitled *The Theatre of Empire* at the DFG-Graduiertenkolleg Globalisierung, Ludwig Maximilian University of Munich. I thank first and foremost Christopher Balme, Christoph Neumann, and Robert Stockhammer, who taught me my first lessons in history-writing.

Research for this book was conducted at the following private and public archives: the J. N. Petit Institute, Mumbai; the K. R. Cama Oriental Institute, Mumbai; the National Centre for the Performing Arts, Mumbai; the Alexandra High School, Mumbai; the Maharashtra State Archives, Mumbai; the Unesco Parzor Foundation, New Delhi; the Sangeet Natak Akademi, New Delhi; the National School of Drama, New Delhi; the National Archives of India, New Delhi; the Natarang Pratishthan, New Delhi; the Calcutta Parsi Amateur Dramatics Club, Kolkata; the National Library, Kolkata; the Natyashodh Sansthan, Kolkata; the British Library; and the New York Public Library. The generosity of Muncherji Cama, Nawaz Mody, Shernaz Cama, Bahadur and Ratan Postwalla, and the staff of the J. N. Petit Institute cannot be overstated.

This book is undergirded as much by anecdotes, family photographs, and memories as by archival research; I am grateful to the late Noshir Gherda, the Khatow family (Vinci Khatow, Percy Khatow, Aspi Khatow, Tony Parr), the Madan family (Rustom Bharucha and Gool Ardeshir), the

Khambatta family (Shirin Vakil, Rukshan Vakil, and Daulat Mewawala), the Marzban family (Ardeshir Dubash), the Kabraji family (the late Rusi Vaccha and Jal Mehta), and the Sethna family (Ms. Raja).

For their continued intellectual support, special acknowledgement is due to the IFTR Historiography Working Group. Claire Cochrane is singled out for her counsel and encouragement. For pointing me in unseen directions, I thank my colleagues at the Institute of Theatre Studies at the LMU, Munich: Judith Rottenburg, MeLê Yamomo, Nic Leonhardt, Anirban Ghosh, Gero Toegl, and my friends Carla Nobre Sousa, Jo Tyabji, Simin Patel, Saachi Chitkara, Danilo Spanicciati, and Richard Bösel. The courage and strength of my colleagues and students and the institutional support from the School of English at the University of Hong Kong made the revisions of this book possible. I am grateful to Otto Heim, Jessica Valdez, Julia Kuehn, Janny Leung, the anonymous reviewers, Catherine M. Cole, Jessica Hinds-Bond, Jack Heeney, and especially Tracy C. Davis for their advice during the publishing process.

The copyright of images from *Pārsī Nāṭak Takhtānī Tavārīkh* belongs to the K. R. Cama Oriental Institute. These images cannot be used in any other form or publication or for any other purpose without the written permission of the institute. The cover image, 'An Actress in a Fine Company. India', is from the Keystone-Mast Collection, UCR/California Museum of Photography, University of California in Riverside. Excerpts from this book have appeared in different forms in *Ethnic and Racial Studies*, *Nineteenth Century Theatre and Film*, and *The Methuen Drama Handbook of Theatre History and Historiography*.

Finally, there are few words to express my gratitude towards my family in Mumbai, Vicenza, and New York. I am particularly indebted to my mother, who taught me how to read Gujarati between 2010 and 2014, and to Giovanni, for all that he has given.

This book is for Soona and Jehangir.

Glossary

nāṭak	theatre
maṇḍalī	club/company
seṭh	wealthy merchant leader/man of high social standing
nazar	sight/vision/surveillance/evil eye
kalyug	Hindu mythological age of discord or downfall

Transliteration Note

All translations are my own unless specified otherwise.[1] I have used the ALA-LC transliteration system. Pha has been replaced with Fa in keeping with the Parsi model of transliterating names. Additionally, the more commonly used 'za' in Hindi and Urdu has been replaced with 'ja' or 'jha' when translating from Gujarati in keeping with the original character in the source text (e.g. Marajbān̄). However, I have retained the 'za' in common Hindustani terms such as 'nazar'. Variations in the spelling of the names of actors, managers, and directors have been mentioned in the endnotes. I have adopted as the standard spelling the version that was used by the person or company themselves. In the absence of this information, the most commonly used spelling between the nineteenth and early twentieth centuries has been cited. The names of famous personalities (e.g. Dadabhai Naoroji) have been spelled according to popular usage. Colonial Anglicized spelling has been used for city names and for theatre productions primarily described in English newspapers.

Note

1. For a more elaborate description of the transliteration system, see Rashna Darius Nicholson, 'What's in a Name? The Performance of Language in the Invention of Colonial and Postcolonial South Asian Theatre History', in *The Methuen Drama Handbook of Theatre History and Historiography*, eds. Claire Cochrane and Jo Robinson (London: Bloomsbury, 2019), 199–209.

Contents

1 Introduction 1

Part I Discipline

2 Parsi Compradors and the Public Sphere 23

3 Social Reform, Lawmaking, and the Origins of the Parsi Theatre 43

4 Corporeal Discipline 89

Part II Re-Enchantment

5 Science, Secular Mythology, and the Professionalization of the Parsi Theatre 129

6 The Expansion of the Parsi Theatre 175

Abbreviations

BG	Bombay Gazette
BT	Bombay Times and Journal of Commerce
KIH	Kaysare Hinda
NA	Ek Jāṇītā Pārsī Ekṭarno Ardhī Sadī Uparno Nāṭakī Anubhav
PNTT	Pārsī Nāṭak Takhtānī Tavārīkh
RG	Rāst Goftār
	Rāst Goftār tathā Satya Prakāś
STOJ	Straits Times Overland Journal
TOI	Times of India

List of Figures

Fig. 2.1	'Bombay Play-house, 1810' (*Source* British Library, File number D40013-09, © British Library Board. All Rights Reserved/Bridgeman Images)	24
Fig. 2.2	'The Entertainment given to C. Forbes Esquire, in the Theatre at Bombay, on the Night of 16th Oct. 1811' (*Source* British Library, File number D40013-27, © British Library Board. All Rights Reserved/Bridgeman Images)	25
Fig. 3.1	Naśarvānjī Dorābjī Āpakhatyār (*Source* Paṭel, *PNTT*, 49. Courtesy: The Trustees, The K. R. Cama Oriental Institute, Mumbai)	51
Fig. 3.2	Kuvarjī Sorābjī Nājar, member of the Elphinstone Theatrical Club (*Source* Paṭel, *PNTT*, 7. Courtesy: The Trustees, The K. R. Cama Oriental Institute, Mumbai)	58
Fig. 3.3	Dhanjīśāh Navrojī Pārakh, member of the Elphinstone Theatrical Club (*Source* Paṭel, *PNTT*, 9. Courtesy: The Trustees, The K. R. Cama Oriental Institute, Mumbai)	60
Fig. 3.4	Naśarvānjī Navrojī Pārakh, member of the Elphinstone Theatrical Club (*Source* Paṭel, *PNTT*, 36. Courtesy: The Trustees, The K. R. Cama Oriental Institute, Mumbai)	61
Fig. 4.1	Dādābhāi Ṭhuṭhī (*Source* Paṭel, *PNTT*, 158. Courtesy: The Trustees, The K. R. Cama Oriental Institute, Mumbai)	94
Fig. 4.2	Farāmjī Dalāl (*Source* Paṭel, *PNTT*, 285. Courtesy: The Trustees, The K. R. Cama Oriental Institute, Mumbai)	95

Fig. 4.3 Farāmroj Jośī (*Source* Paṭel, *PNTT*, 38. Courtesy: The Trustees, The K. R. Cama Oriental Institute, Mumbai) 96

Fig. 4.4 Kekhuśro Kābrājī (*Source* Tārāporvāḷā, Pe. Kha. *Kābrājī-Smruti*. Bombay: 'Sāñj Vartamān' Press, 1905, n.p. Courtesy: The J. N. Petit Institute, Mumbai) 97

Fig. 4.5 Austen Henry Layard, 'Hall in Assyrian Palace, Restored', 1849. From General Research Division, The New York Public Library, New York Public Library Digital Collections. Accessed July 15, 2020, http://digitalcollections.nypl.org/items/510d47dc-46e4-a3d9-e040-e00a18064a99 102

Fig. 4.6 Dhanjībhāi Rūstamjī Kerāvālā (*Source* Paṭel, *PNTT*, 330. Courtesy: The Trustees, The K. R. Cama Oriental Institute, Mumbai) 104

Fig. 4.7 Kāvasjī Naśarvānjī Kohīdārū (*Source* Paṭel, *PNTT*, 286. Courtesy: The Trustees, The K. R. Cama Oriental Institute, Mumbai) 105

Fig. 4.8 Dādābhāi Sorābjī Paṭel (*Source* Paṭel, *PNTT*, 95. Courtesy: The Trustees, The K. R. Cama Oriental Institute, Mumbai) 106

Fig. 5.1 Nāhānābhāi Rūstamjī Rāṇīnā (*Source The Calcutta Parsi Amateur Dramatic Club Golden Jubilee Souvenir Volume. 1907–1947*, Calcutta, 1957. Courtesy: The Calcutta Parsi Amateur Dramatic Club) 136

Fig. 5.2 Advertisement for *Dāde Darīāv* by the Victoria Nāṭak Maṇḍalī. This advertisement was the first in the Parsi theatre's history to include a picture (*Source RG*, 22 May 1870, 342. Courtesy: The J. N. Petit Institute, Mumbai) 138

Fig. 5.3 Khurśedjī Mervānjī Bālīvālā (*Source* Gulfām, *Bhamto-Bhut*, Bombay: Fort Printing Press. Courtesy: The PARZOR Foundation, New Delhi) 152

Fig. 6.1 Edaljī Dādābhāi (*Source* Paṭel, *PNTT*, 274. Courtesy: The Trustees, The K. R. Cama Oriental Institute, Mumbai) 182

Fig. 6.2 Ḍosābhāi Fardunjī Mogal (*Source* Paṭel, *PNTT*, 159. Courtesy: The Trustees, The K. R. Cama Oriental Institute, Mumbai) 183

Fig. 6.3 Jamśedjī Farāmjī Mādan (*Source The Calcutta Parsi Amateur Dramatic Club Golden Jubilee Souvenir Volume. 1907–1947*, Calcutta, 1957. Courtesy: The Calcutta Parsi Amateur Dramatic Club) 189

Fig. 6.4 Farāmjī Dādābhāi Apu (*Source* Paṭel, *PNTT*, 160. Courtesy: The Trustees, The K. R. Cama Oriental Institute, Mumbai) 190

Fig. 6.5 The Pandal under construction in Mysore of the Parsee Victoria Theatrical Company of Bombay, 1st July 1902 (Courtesy: Shirin Vakil) 192
Fig. 6.6 Grandpa Jehangir (Courtesy: Shirin Vakil) 195
Fig. 8.1 Photograph of the Kābrājī family with Bahmanjī standing at centre (Courtesy: Rusi Vaccha) 268
Fig. 8.2 Portrait of Mary Fenton in Parsi dress (*Source* Paṭel, *PNTT*, 308. Courtesy: The Trustees, The K. R. Cama Oriental Institute, Mumbai) 270
Fig. 8.3 'Scene in a tragedy by Famous Troup[e] [Bālīvālā's company]', H. C. White Company, 1996.0009.WX25692, Keystone-Mast Collection, UCR/California Museum of Photography, University of California at Riverside 278

CHAPTER 1

Introduction

This book is a history of the Parsi theatre. No sentence could be more deceptive in its apparent simplicity. Originating in Bombay, the colonial Parsi theatre, performed in Gujarati, English, Farsi, and Hindustani, and comprising Hindu, Muslim, Jewish, Parsi, and Anglo-Indian personnel, rapidly became South Asia's primary form of entertainment during its eighty-year existence (1853–ca. 1933). The Parsis, today considered an ethno-religious Indian minority of Iranian origin, created this sophisticated, commercial theatre industry that played a formative role in Asian cultural history. Emerging with the rise of colonial *entrepôts* and modern forms of cultural consumption, Parsi theatre was highly syncretic; its plays amalgamated Indo-Persian and Hindu mythological stories, *Arabian Nights* lore, Shakespearean tragedy, English melodrama, and Western and Hindustani music. Described as the 'Indian equivalent of Victorian spectacular theatre',[1] it introduced European stagecraft, forms of theatrical management, and spectacle in a recognizable idiom across South and Southeast Asia. As the precursor of numerous influential

The original version of this chapter was revised: At the end of the first paragraph "West Africa" was corrected to "East Africa". The correction to this chapter is available at https://doi.org/10.1007/978-3-030-65836-6_10

R. D. Nicholson, *The Colonial Public and the Parsi Stage*, Transnational Theatre Histories,
https://doi.org/10.1007/978-3-030-65836-6_1

cultural forms such as Komedie Stamboel, Bangsawan, Yemeni drama, the autochthonous regional theatres of India, and South Asian cinema, Parsi drama's impress was significant. As Matthew Isaac Cohen argues, 'much of the theatrical history of South and Southeast Asia is cloaked in mystery. ... But the history of the popular theatre movement can be traced more or less precisely to a point of origin, the Parsi ... minority of Bombay during the 1850s'.[2] Consequently, the title of this book alludes to the Parsi theatre's vast cultural influence during the colonial period, as well as the 'unselfconscious provincialism', noted by Claire Cochrane, that has skewed theatre history towards the belief that everything significant in British theatre happened in London.[3] The Theatre of Empire, I propose, was not located in the capitals of Western Europe but instead circulated in the mediated form of Parsi theatre, from Bombay—*Urbs Prima in Indis*, the First City of India—across South and Southeast Asia, East Africa, and beyond.

While the broad lineaments of the story of Parsi theatre are well-known, detailed histories are nonexistent. Despite the temporal and geographic scale and long-term impact of this cultural phenomenon, the inaccessibility of its primary sources has led to the historiographic omission of its leading figures, landmark productions, and catalytic events in existing Asian cultural histories. This book offers foundational primary source information that is almost entirely absent from existing scholarly literature. It is the first comprehensive appraisal of the origins and early development of this pan-Asian theatrical form between 1853 and 1893, a forty-year span that covers the first half of the commercial Parsi theatre's existence and that encompasses three key moments of rupture in India's history: the 1865 share crash, the 1874 Parsi-Muslim riots, and the 1893 cow-killing Hindu-Muslim riots. The year 1893, with which this book concludes, was a watershed year for South Asian society and theatre alike, as it also marked the birth of cinema, which spelled the end of the theatre's transregional popularity.[4] By delimiting the chronological frame to a forty-year period, I am able to unravel in detail such critical, hitherto unanswered questions as which troupes existed when; who were their star actors and playwrights; what were the theatre's significant plays and productions; what scenography, performance conventions, and organizational structures were appropriated, adapted, and/or created; and when and how did the theatre professionalize and diffuse across the urban and semi-urban areas of the subcontinent to present-day Singapore, Indonesia, and Burma? In sum, the book delineates the complex institutional history of a dramatic phenomenon that originated among an intrepid minority community and yet became the British Empire's most influential cultural commodity of the nineteenth and early twentieth centuries. To fill the historiographic black hole of the colonial Asian theatrical past and ease the work of future scholarship through the positivist accumulation of data is a function of this book.

Simultaneously, the title *Theatre of Empire* functions as a double entendre, analyzing not only the object itself (Parsi theatre) but also a meta-theatre of imperialism and nationalism, of which the proscenium stage was an active participant and a passive index. Parsi theatre is usually described as sensational entertainment, insulated from the protracted, contentious sociocultural debates and political developments that culminated in the birth of the nation. By drawing on a large body of literature (advertisements, newspaper articles, autobiographies, and not least the plays themselves) in Gujarati, English, and Hindustani, this book contests the dismissal of the composite, often thorny relationship between Parsi theatre and the many communities that it attempted to please. The unpredictable, ambiguous Parsi performance world of fluttering fairies, sinking ships, and man-eating demons limning illusion and reality, dreams and moral certitude, the known and the unknown, half-light and half-truth, was not without logic. On the empire's stage, customs and values were disenchanted, legitimized, and disputed, hopes and dreams were conceived and challenged, loyalty and revolution were intoned, and, above all else, a relative cultural homogeneity was established.

As the aesthetic glue that bound together disparate regional, linguistic, and ethnic constituencies, the Parsi theatre was foundational to the interpretation of the South Asian past and present and was therefore the single most important aesthetic formation to create the conditions for the birth of competing visions of nationhood. Through its pivotal role in the Parsi reform movement, its appropriation of designations such as the Victoria, Ripon, Elphinstone, Imperial, and Alfred Theatrical Companies, and its elaborate demonstrations of loyalty, Parsi drama was initially an influential site for the translation of the imperial project in Bombay. However, after its professionalization in the 1870s, a corpus of spectacular, mythological, and melodramatic plays offered romanticized visions of ancient pasts, organized and disseminated a moral economy that functioned as a counterpoint to colonial bourgeois thought, and propagated racial theories in popular form. In so doing, the theatre curated, indexed, and distributed highly charged symbols that were eventually adopted by nationalist movements in the early twentieth century for ritual stagings of political legitimation and sovereignty. In the absence of the clear narrative direction characteristic of novels, journalistic reportage, and travelogues, audiences drew on their own explanatory frames, crafting Parsi mythological and spectacular drama into a deliciously subversive site for the accumulation and transmission of a constellation of contrasting worldviews and beliefs. The theatre's unparalleled reach to the masses across the Indian subcontinent and Malay Peninsula—populations who had little access to print—further consolidated its position as a sociopolitical powerhouse during the period of high colonialism. The book shows how shifts in visual signage, the rehearsal of allegorical codes and figurative themes, and especially the spectacular delineation of the origins and efflorescence of classical genus enabled the invention of tradition. From the *Arabian Nights* expanse of Turkey to China, from a mythical Ancient Persia and a similarly mythical Sanskrit 'India', to the village idyll of Navsari and contemporaneous colonial Bombay, audiences imagined themselves inhabiting specific places. Spaces and places began to serve narratological functions, thus becoming meaningful. Touring companies dotting the landscape functioned as polyvocal sites of meaning-making, drawing on colonial knowledge systems and material flows of capital, goods, and labour in order to make and unmake topographies of religious, ethnic, and linguistic identities. By tracing how the incongruous, often ambiguous, and multivocal Parsi theatre imaged and reinforced communal and national forms of belonging and exclusion, the book attempts to uncover the incipient possibilities in the nineteenth century of nations unformed, repressed, or to be dreamed into being.

The Cultural Comprador

The trajectory of the book begins with the Parsis (Parsees), followers of Zoroastrianism, who fled for the coast of Gujarat between 8 and 10 CE to escape religious persecution in the aftermath of the Arab conquest of Persia. The community remained on the periphery of Gujarat for approximately eight hundred years, until the first Portuguese and British mercantile settlements in Western India were established in the sixteenth and seventeenth centuries. The Parsis thrived in these transformed political environs because, as Amalendu Guha explains, they had been relatively uninvolved in previous Muslim and Hindu administrations, had greater occupational mobility, and were as a community disconnected from the sociopolitical power struggles that characterized the first phase of the consolidation of colonial rule.[5] Migrating in droves to the emerging colonial *entrepôt* of Bombay, which would soon overrun Surat as the capital of Western India, the community made a swift occupational shift, from agriculture and artisanry to international trade and shipping. During the colonial reconfiguration of trade networks from the export of finished products to raw cotton and opium, Parsis joined existing European firms, becoming indispensable in such occupations as brokerage, banking, and shipbuilding.[6] Jürgen Osterhammel clarifies that in Asia, Europeans required an extended period of time to adapt to conditions that were foreign and seemingly impenetrable.[7] Collaborators not only helped manage the colonial trade but also developed joint Indo or Sino-European ventures and new commercial routes that actuated the rise of port cities and the development of new forms of consumption. In their capacity as 'go-betweens', gatekeepers, and knowledge brokers, these 'compradors' (as the Portuguese first designated them) thus facilitated the global flow of capital through translation. The common Parsi surnames Dalal (broker) and Dubash (two languages or translator) reference the community's privileged diplomatic role in controlling the movement of goods, information, and forms of knowledge between diverse constituencies. The book demonstrates how Parsis as compradors were the lifeblood of the British Empire, actuating the formation of not only a global capitalist economy but also a cross-cultural conceptual economy characterized by processes of interpretation, legitimation, and diffusion.

Colonialism, as has frequently been noted, was realized not merely through a coercive machinery of military, economic, and political phenomena, but also through cultural technologies of power such as literature, journalism, and theatre. The comprador trader, the first *burgher* or bourgeois, herein played a decisive role. Yet several studies have also argued that compradorial complicity was not wholly unalloyed; there was a considerable overlap between national and comprador elements, between early national industrialization and colonial capital.[8] Doubly peripheral, belonging neither to the worlds translated from nor to the worlds translated to, Parsis as compradors negotiated zones of difference, inhabiting a grey area of constant ambiguity. The book traces how the Parsis not only domesticated the imperial project through acts of translation but also created sites for self-representation and subsequently for sedition and subversion through their critical role in the development of the vernacular public sphere.

The Public Sphere

In Jürgen Habermas's formulation, the public sphere, 'a theater in modern societies in which political participation is enacted through the medium of talk', arose in the eighteenth century in Europe. Distinct from the state, the economy, and the family, the public sphere was a discursive arena for deliberation and debate where the state was brought into contact with the needs of society. According to his Westphalian account, the public sphere was a mechanism for shaping state policy and exercising political sovereignty through rational-critical discourse.[9] Although the concept has attained remarkable critical currency across disciplinary and geographic boundaries over the last few decades, it has also generated criticism for its universalism, normativity, and exclusivity, especially in view of intuitively common-sense concepts that do not align with the borders of territorial states, such as Islamic public spheres, transregional public spheres, and the global public sphere. Nancy Fraser's 'Transnationalizing the Public Sphere' neatly summarizes the problematic of theorizing a mediated, plural, multilevel, and networked public sphere in a post-Westphalian, globalizing world by delineating six assumptions that Habermas's model takes for granted: the correlation of the public sphere with the modern territorial state; the association of the public with the citizens of a democratic state; the public sphere's location in a capitalist market economy established by and subjected to state regulation; a tacit emphasis on national media; linguistic transparency; and the public sphere's roots in eighteenth- and nineteenth-century bourgeois literary forms that also gave rise to the imagined nation.[10] Although Fraser delineates these assumptions to chart the limits of Habermas's frame in a neoliberal globalizing present—in which modes of deliberation, politics, publics, and administrative policy-making bodies have become dispersed, infrequently halting at the frontiers of territorial states—the problematic is much older. The unique developmental account and historic specificity of the Westphalian frame has been the thorn in the side of most attempts to map the public sphere onto colonial and postcolonial territories where linguistic plurality, distinctive subjective formations arising from religious, regional, and ethnic affiliation, and not least the importation of rational-liberal debate within the colonial legacy of undemocratic, state-based oppression, pre-empt glib translation. Fraser's (and Habermas's) blind spot is, as Kimberly Hutchings points out, the 'before and after' narrative: a Westphalian and post-Westphalian frame of the 'present' experienced as novel, premised on the sovereign experiences of imperial and post-imperial welfare states that are unknown to postcolonial subjects and incompatible with their civil societies and public spheres.[11] Hutchings interrogates whether globalization in the 'Global South' marks a novel, epochal shift from the norm of Westphalian sovereignty. For most civil societies 'outside of the perspective of the "metropole"', she argues, domestic administrative bodies consistently lacked the authority to efficiently manage the lives of their subjects, and consequently, dispersed interlocutors did not share common concerns, a joint understanding of the present, or universally legible claims to justice.[12]

In nineteenth-century British India that witnessed the efflorescence of journalism, literature, public associations, and modern ticketed theatres, the vernacular public sphere was not coeval with a profoundly unequal, undemocratic, and economically exploitative colonial state that elided the possibility of parity of publics, negotiation with public authority, constitutional safeguards concerning freedom of expression, and popular sovereignty. The term 'colonial subjects' implies subjection, not citizenship. Dipesh Chakrabarty has described how the British, swayed by their own liberal theories of self-governance, introduced highly regulated and limited forms of representation in the colonial administration. Colonial governance was characterized by profound ambiguity due to its negotiation between an altruistic limited franchise and a more potent authoritarian dominance.[13] As there existed no common sphere of constitutional politics in which publics could directly participate, this limited legislative representation was viewed as elite politics, and colonial Indian deputies were deemed to be unrepresentative of the masses that they claimed to represent. In pursuit of popular sovereignty, local leaders (national, regional, and communal) had to devise other, instantly discernable, visual ways of asserting their right to represent the public that bypassed the conceptual and inegalitarian apparatus of legislative representation and the Anglophone press. Consequently, the colonial public sphere, to use Arvind Rajagopal's term, was 'split',[14] functioning not only as an interlocutory realm of rational-critical debate between influential indigenous authorities and the colonial state but also as a discursive site where hitherto disconnected peoples were imagined, interpellated, and forged on multiple scales: intra-communal, inter-communal, regional, and protonational. Emerging from the oppressive sociopolitical and market conditions of colonialism, these 'multiple, parallel, segmented publics defined by community, political persuasion, religion, and caste' were characterized by differing subjectivities, social imaginaries, political orientations, and understandings of the now, as well as by an untranslatability of 'common concerns' and segregated modes of deliberation.[15]

Religion and Revolution

Central to the public sphere's fragmentation was the universalizing category of 'religion', which, as this book demonstrates, generated the colonial public. While with the European Reformation the status of the Church changed and religion became a private matter, in colonial India, missionary activity allied with colonial legal and educational policy rendered religion contestable and open to dispute that is, representative and 'public' thus prompting religious reformations, forms of sociocultural relativism, and the formation of new discursive realms for social contestation. Part I of this book ('Discipline') demonstrates how the vernacular bourgeois public sphere was the primary arena for the disenchantment of hitherto equivocal customs on the basis of post-enlightenment bourgeois-rationalist conceptions of civilization and progress. Colonial domination was exercised through an epistemic and moral framework that delimited 'authentic', 'discovered' non-Christian religions as dissimilar yet structurally equivalent to Christianity, and the press, reform association, and modern Parsi theatre were core instruments in this process. In the place of interlocution with the state, the Parsi theatre functioned in its early years to distinguish an authentic, stable textual core of Zoroastrianism from ritual accretions, myth, and magic, thereby converting unruly communities into law-abiding subjects. Plays that depicted local superstitions, corrupt priests, and a de-allegorized Persian past in homogenous empty time reconfigured a spiritual economy of representation in line with colonial ideals of morality and virtue, spurred 'rational' debate on the most intimate elements of social life, and generated new forms of intracommunal conflict. An important feature of the colonial reform of Indian religions was, as Tanika Sarkar has noted, its publicness or theatricality.[16] This book shows how Bombay's public sphere initially functioned as a coercive theatre in which practices hitherto deemed 'private' were made unreservedly visible, integrated into knowledge of social, communal, and ethnic groups, and subjected to colonial jurisdiction and control.

Gradually, however, the vernacular public sphere—hitherto an observatory where customs and traditions were disciplined through rational-critical debate within a complex architecture of power—transformed into an intimate arena for introspection, imaginative play, and world-making. Part II ('Re-Enchantment') details how Parsi theatre professionalized, transforming from morally upright amateur amusement for the reformation of Bombay's Parsi community to commercial entertainment for the subcontinent's masses. From the late 1860s onwards, plays that combined Victorian mechanical scenery and spectacular effects with Persian myths and *Arabian Nights* themes not only offered a form of escapism from the didactic project of colonial morality and virtue but also facilitated the development of an autonomous, antidisciplinary public domain that troubled post-Enlightenment conceptions of civilization and progress. No longer a panoptical tribunal, the spectacular Parsi theatre transformed into an inclusive sphere marked by self-contemplation and meditative conservatism, confusing conventional distinctions between technology and superstition; a progressive, scientifically advanced Europe and the tyrannical, unchanging orient; and the political logic that underpinned these differences. The heterogeneity of themes and incongruous merging of Indo-Persian mythical landscapes with flying fairies, demons, panoramas, sinking ships, and magic lanterns were not due to simplistic cultural syncretism or innocent amusement as scholars have previously deemed. Rather, these changes were the result of the theatre's exploration of phenomenological and ideological issues: the relationship between seeing and believing and the nature of truth. The disorienting Parsi spectacular play implicitly enunciated the revolutionary idea that self and other were not comprehensibly knowable and therefore could not be subjected to a totalitarian epistemological power. Through its dissemination of a new, common aesthetic vocabulary across South and Southeast Asia, appropriation of the imperial perspective, and interrogation of the moral economy of colonial reason, the Parsi theatre created an imaginative sphere of sovereignty for the development of alternative networks of authority, political mobilization, and new group solidarities that were imagined in arenas both wider and narrower than the nation-state.

Part III ('Revolution') traces how from the 1870s onwards the *tour du monde* of the spectacular, *Arabian Nights*-inspired Parsi theatre was circumscribed through the ancient Indian dramaturgy of the Hindu mythological play, whose cultural universe alluded to an 'inherently limited and sovereign' ideological and geographic whole.[17] Hindu deities onstage disclosed elegiac truths, articulated new messianic visions of the past and dystopic understandings of the present, disseminated a corpus of populist symbols, and helped formulate a new regime of knowledge in the form of Hindu revivalism across a confoundingly complex, segmented polity. The colonial state's formulation of individuals' legal identities on the basis of religion, as well as widespread propagation of Indo-Aryan theory, had created a strong feeling of kinship to a homogeneous religious group. 'Hindu' plays tapped into this new sphere of intimate belonging, using glittering javelins, vermilion garments, and Sanskritized terminology to choreograph the dramaturgy of political congregations, anticolonial demonstrations, and the movement for self-government into a righteous combat of cosmic proportions. The Parsi theatre thus provided, for the first time in modern Asian history, a common arena for individuals of disparate language, caste, and ethnic affiliation to congregate and partake in informal, delicately dissident dialogue. The Parsis, middlemen between the rulers and the ruled, had involuntarily created wide-ranging networks for the development and diffusion of a deep, heavily inflected, populist vocabulary that skirted more prolonged, elite discourses of national awakening. Simultaneously, however, the Parsi community—alienated from both a seemingly 'Hindu' ethno-nationalist movement and the now 'Hindu' Parsi theatre—articulated anxieties of its diminutive population and diminishing political and cultural strength through the Parsi social drama, a genre that exemplified the vernacular public sphere's broadening fissures along religious and linguistic lines. Plays performed in Parsi Gujarati on Parsi domestic themes for the Parsi community of Bombay served not only to distinguish the Parsi public sphere from the seemingly 'Hindu'-Indian nationalist domain proper but also reflected Parsis' mixed allegiance to the emerging project of Indian nationalism and conflicted yearnings for a distinct self and nationhood.

The vernacular public sphere was therefore multiply segmented, demonstrating both the creation, dissemination, and advocacy of a majoritarian 'Hindu' ethnonationalism and a minoritarian resentment of 'Hindu' culture and publics. This vernacular public sphere was in sharp contrast with Habermas's Westphalian incarnation, in which the modern state and capitalism facilitated the rise of bourgeois literary forms, which fostered a self-reflexive subjectivity that in turn enabled communicative rationality in economic and sociopolitical arenas. Only *modern* subjects, according to Habermas, could recognize the particularity of the present as modern and comprehend belonging to a unified community. In British India, however, the influence of gods and religious observances in the kairotic time of Hindu mythology was magnified through the ubiquitous Parsi theatre, which gestated mythical perceptions of historical development and common fate, affective modes of deliberation, and agonic, non-textual claims to justice, even as other social imaginaries contested this 'Hindu' conceptual frame.[18] Long before the advent of the 'network society', the colonial public sphere exceeded normative, Westphalian understandings of the world, facilitating fissured expressive economies and disparate forms of ethnonational belonging such as pan-Islam, Hindu fundamentalism, and Parsi proto-nationalism.

The Colonial Public and the Parsi Stage describes this long, intricately interwoven history of nationalism and communalism, complicating the dominant perception of the nationalist struggle (as something that began in 1885 with the founding of the Indian National Congress) by recourse to the reformist period. It demonstrates how conflicting understandings of nationalist and sectarian thought in moderate and extremist avatars were cultivated through the hazy silhouette of the proscenium, eventually spilling into the interlocutory realms of political negotiation, anticolonial agitation, and inter-communal conflict. In sum, the book pieces together how religion generated not only the colonial public sphere but also the concepts of anticolonial resistance and nationhood through the complex re-arrangement in the theatre of the taxonomies of morality and degeneracy, truth and falsehood, the prosaic and poetic, rational-critical discourse and spiritual performance, the modern time of the colonial state and the mythical time of a nation to be born.

Women

At the heart of this rapid reconfiguration of the vernacular epistemological field was the ever-evolving 'women's question', which, as Lata Mani first demonstrated, was not about women.[19] Rather it constituted the most important site for the sociocultural encounter between colonizer and colonized: an essential discursive mechanism for colonialism's affirmation of its moral authority and, subsequently, the articulation of nationalism. During the period of social reform, women were posited through the vernacular public sphere and the theatre as the sign of the intrinsic despotism and civilizational backwardness of Parsi society. Plays that depicted the evils of 'timeless' customs such as child marriage empowered English-educated reformists to determine what constituted authentic Zoroastrian tradition, assert their sociocultural and political superiority, and re-engineer the self-definition of Parsi society through the drafting of personal law. Simultaneously, by distinguishing itself from precolonial forms of amusement such as the nautch, the Parsi theatre not only self-reflexively marked itself as 'honourable amusement' but also defined respectable middle-class Parsi women, who attended the theatre, in contradistinction to women of the 'lower orders'. Accordingly, the reformist reconfiguration of indigenous values and traditions undergirded the reorganization of forms of leisure according to the values of the ruling class and the terms governing women's appearance in public—a subtle disciplinary mechanism for policing female bodies.

In the 1860s, however, both the dramatic motif of the tyrannized female as metonym for a tyrannical indigenous society and the freedoms enjoyed by women in the playhouse underwent changes. A surfeit of plays with titular female characters that protected their chastity and escaped from or slaughtered malevolent rulers pervaded the commercial Parsi theatre, marking the beginnings of an autonomous subjectivity in the vernacular public sphere.[20] Female characters, symbols of indigenous tradition, were here conceptualized as a crucible of indigenous power insusceptible to colonial intervention. A decade later, this motif of the inviolate indigenous woman would metamorphose into Hindu goddesses and pure, loyal, submissive, ritual-abiding women, indicating the first phase of Hindu revivalist nationalism. These female icons that embodied not only voluntary suffering and servility but also martyrdom, ideological superiority, and triumphal power, constituted representational figures for *Bharatmātā* (the motherland) and mnemotechnic devices for the willing self-sacrifice that would distinguish anticolonial Hindu militancy and Gandhian pacifist nationalism. The gendered imagery of the late nineteenth-century Parsi theatre—outwardly an unassuming visual manifestation of religious orthodoxy and ruminative conservatism—was therefore in truth the hallmark of growing insurgence.

Yet, even as the Hindu mythological play's valorous Vedic heroines reversed the colonial trope of the orient (oppressed woman to be liberated by the gallant, hyper-masculine occident), the Parsi social drama depicted mothers who were both loyal and disloyal to their husbands, families, and communities—an enigmatic motif that epitomized the comprador community's confused loyalty between colonial rule and a seemingly exclusivist Hindu ethno-nationalist movement. This equivocality of allegiance was also expressed through anxieties of mixing with 'the children of the soil' and fears of ethnic defilement and degeneration; women were cast either as mothers who would secure the perpetuity of the Parsi race or as miscreants guilty of racial atrophy. In the theatre, actresses—who infringed prescriptive bourgeois separations between public and private spheres and whose talents of masquerade and coquetry undermined public affirmations of sexual *naïveté*[21]—were the most palpable personifications of the potential for racial deterioration and the devastation of the communal body. Female performers, many of whom were compelled to find occupational refuge in the Parsi theatre after its professionalization, thus became the sites for corporeal surveillance, the enunciation of desires for ethnic renewal, and the conceptualization of a biopolitical understanding of the social organism. From the reformist emblem of woman as the body of law of a despotic society to her iconization as a repository of national strength to her incarnation of the possible degradation of the larger ethnic body, women served diverse narratological functions, articulating the conflicting political aspirations and slippery claims of a rapidly mutating social order. This book shows how the public sphere both reflected and reinforced these shifting taxonomies of women as metaphors of universalizing totalities (community, nation, and *volk*), archiving on behalf of the 'women's question' the terms of legibility of self, truth, and home—even as women's own voices were elided.

The Archive

Women's bodies thus functioned as sites of both intervention and inscription, registering the metamorphosis of the public sphere, evolving social formations, and contestations over ideals, desires, law, and power. This book, however, does not simply map the shifts that took place through the theatre between physical and discursive bodies, between the construction and deconstruction of women as repositories of communal and national values; it also interrogates how these rhetorical manoeuvres are rendered legible by the material yet hidden body of the archive. Over and above theoretical orientations of postcolonial, gender, and performance studies—implicit therefore in the methodological framing of this historical investigation—are affective and aesthetic questions of the body of/as archive: its relationship to performance, power, and violence, the question of home, and the desire for amnesia and annihilation.

Due to its scale, influence, and significant role in the indexing of the linguistic, ethnic, religious, and territorial fractures of colonial modernity, the Parsi theatre has amassed a dense and highly contested interpretive legacy. The problematic of historicizing and interpreting an eighty-year-long, pan-Asian cultural phenomenon has most comprehensively been examined by Kathryn Hansen, who describes how secondary literature on Parsi theatre in Hindi, Urdu, and Gujarati is characterized by communal and linguistic bias that postdates the theatre's prime.[22] While Urdu scholars lay claim to Parsi theatre as 'Urdu theatre' by favouring Muslim dramatists and belittling the Parsis, histories in Hindi and Gujarati discount the Muslim contribution or commend the Parsis as outstanding reformers and pioneers of the modern drama.[23] According to Hansen, as Parsi theatre was a 'site of communal harmony' and part of a 'cosmopolitan entertainment economy' created at a historical juncture when 'linguistic and communal identities were fluid and overlapping', a partial presentation of information hinders a precise appraisal of the theatre's composite, plural character.[24] Hansen thus not only alludes to the necessity of deliberation and transparent accountability in the treatment of historical documents but also hints at the silences, losses, and absences that must urgently be remedied in the reconstitution of the past in order to resolve the serious ethical, political, and juridical problems of the present.

What, however, are the specific problems or losses that the historian should attempt to redress? Who is the historian responsible towards, and what are the implications of historical responsibility on archival (il)legitimacy? Against the backdrop of the 1990s rise of totalitarian group identities such as Hindutva in South Asia, Hansen's cosmopolitan thesis of the Parsi theatre pegs the historical conversation on Parsi theatre to a pluralist, universalist framework underpinned by a liberal politics of diversity, inclusivity, and equal recognition. The risk however of a panoptical archival cosmopolitanism is a doctrinaire, aspatial, and potentially hegemonic perspective, one that supports the myth that equitable representation results in historical objectivity and neutrality and obfuscates the microphysics of contextual politics, the complex inter-mediation between culture and identity, and the localized effects of aesthetic phenomena and their archival traces on composite forms of social belonging, deep collective memory, and acutely disputed, intersubjective historical knowledge. The progress and decline account of a rational-universalist cosmopolitan culture preceding an irrational, excessive, and divisive national and communal politics in transparent, linear time, not only flattens the rocky socio-political topography of a theatrical phenomenon that unsettled, modified, and reinforced antagonistic conceptions of ethnic, communal, and linguistic identities from its beginning but also obliquely narrows the scope of eligible sources and trails for historical study, privileging distant readings of secondary, easily accessible literature, discouraging ambient, embodied forms of archival discovery, and inhibiting the intricate, subtle elucidations that therein ensue. The mining of primary source data within linguistic, regional, and/or communal registers allows for thick, compound understandings of the interwoven filaments of nationalism, communalism, and cosmopolitanism; reveals the cosmopolitan entertainment economy of Parsi theatre and the theatre's communalization of knowledge to be the common products of cultural, political, and social interaction; and makes clear how the untidy boundaries of 'place' and 'identity' were conceptualized, deliberated, and transgressed through theatrical publics and counterpublics within convoluted constellations of power. But this sort of work also interrogates the power structures *within* archives: their privileging of dominant languages and cultures and their othering of peoples and forms of knowledge.[25]

Embedded in the writing of this book is an interrogation of how knowledge, the archive, and the historian are co-constitutive of one another in representing the past: a complex synthesis of the receiver and received that occurs within socially constructed, ideologically charged frameworks. With its choice of unmodernized transliteration, extensive reference to seldom-examined newspapers and plays in the now-dead language of nineteenth-century Parsi Gujarati, inclusion of moth-eaten photographs culled from family albums belonging to Parsi theatre stars' descendants—whose vocal timbre, bone structure, and recollections unanesthetize history, rendering palpable embodied intermediations between past and present only dimly suggested in documentary records—the book probes how scientific 'objectivity' obscures power struggles over memory and identity innate in archives. Archives, in the book's methodological purview, are unstable, active sites of sociopolitical contestation where the production, preservation, and destruction of material and discursive records have physical consequences on the disappearance or ghosting of peoples, memories, and truths. Women's bodies, an inadvertent subject of this book, is therefore accompanied by the retrieval, preservation, and legitimation of feminized, intellectually specious, hidden away, and physically jeopardized bodies of textual and non-textual, official and unofficial evidence. The pluralization of archivally available voices by scaling down instead of up, shifts the tenor of the conversation on the historicization of South Asian culture from a liberal politics of inter-religious inclusivity to questions of structural power imbalances, the necessity of an archival self-reflexivity (one conscious of the effacement of its own history), and the enmeshments in the archive of memories and imaginative figments, enunciative possibilities and impossibilities, and the yearning for memorialization and obsolescence. In the constitution of knowledge, as Hansen suggests, memory accompanies amnesia, voices beget silences, and erasure and loss pivot conscious recall.[26] The endangerment of bodies of Parsi-Gujarati historical evidence due to their delegitimization is not distinct from the endangerment of the Parsi communal body politic, which, with a steadily declining population of fewer than fifty thousand members in the twenty-first century, 'appears bound for extinction'.[27] The spectralization of the Parsis in India's urban landscape—embodied by the haunting marble busts of the old Parsi colonial comprador class littering every street corner of old Bombay—is not distinct from the spectralization in societal memory of unresolved nineteenth-century debates on identity, race, nationhood, and women's bodies, an archival violence that this book has unwittingly sought to reckon with.

Notes

1. Aparna Bhargava Dharwadker, *Theatres of Independence: Drama, Theory, and Urban Performance in India Since 1947* (Iowa City: University of Iowa Press, 2009), 39.
2. Matthew Isaac Cohen, 'On the Origin of the Komedie Stamboel. Popular Culture, Colonial Society, and the Parsi Theatre Movement', *Bijdragen tot de taal-, land-en volkenkunde/Journal of the Humanities and Social Sciences of Southeast Asia* 157, no. 2 (2001): 315.
3. Claire Cochrane, *Twentieth-Century British Theatre: Industry, Art and Empire* (Cambridge: Cambridge University Press, 2011), 2–3.
4. The kinetoscope, the precursor to the motion-picture film projector, was first demonstrated to the public at the Brooklyn Institute of Arts and Sciences on 9 May 1893.
5. Amalendu Guha, 'The Comprador Role of Parsi Seths, 1750–1850', *Economic and Political Weekly* 5, no. 48 (1970): 1935. See also Christine E. Dobbin, *Asian Entrepreneurial Minorities: Conjoint Communities in*

the Making of the World-Economy, 1570–1940 (Richmond: Curzon Press, 1996), 2.

6. Amalendu Guha, 'Parsi Seths as Entrepreneurs, 1750–1850', *Economic and Political Weekly* 5, no. 35 (1970): M107.
7. Jürgen Osterhammel, 'Semi-colonialism and Informal Empire in Twentieth-Century China: Towards a Framework of Analysis', in *Imperialism and After: Continuities and Discontinuities*, eds. Wolfgang J. Mommsen and Jürgen Osterhammel (London: Allen and Unwin, 1986), 305.
8. See Robert Vitalis, 'On the Theory and Practice of Compradors: The Role of Abbud Pasha in the Egyptian Political Economy', *International Journal of Middle East Studies* 22, no. 3 (1990): 292–93.
9. Jürgen Habermas, *The Structural Transformation of the Public Sphere: An Inquiry into a Category of Bourgeois Society* (Boston: MIT Press, 1989), 51–55.
10. Nancy Fraser, 'Transnationalizing the Public Sphere: On the Legitimacy and Efficacy of Public Opinion in a Post-Westphalian World', in *Transnationalizing the Public Sphere*, ed. Kate Nash (Cambridge: Polity Press, 2014), 11–12.
11. Kimberly Hutchings, 'Time, Politics, and Critique: Rethinking the "When" Question', in Nash, *Transnationalizing the Public Sphere*, 101.
12. Hutchings, 'Time, Politics, and Critique', 102, 107.
13. Dipesh Chakrabarty, '"In the Name of Politics": Sovereignty, Democracy, and the Multitude in India', *Public Culture* 19, no. 1 (2007): 41.
14. Arvind Rajagopal, *Politics After Television: Hindu Nationalism and the Reshaping of the Public in India* (Cambridge: Cambridge University Press, 2001), 24–26.
15. Thomas Blom Hansen, 'Whose Public, Whose Authority? Reflections on the Moral Force of Violence', *Modern Asian Studies* 52, no. 3 (2018): 1078.
16. Tanika Sarkar, *Hindu Wife, Hindu Nation: Community, Religion, and Cultural Nationalism* (New Delhi: Permanent Black, 2017, first published 2001), 74.
17. Benedict Anderson, *Imagined Communities: Reflections on the Origin and Spread of Nationalism* (London: Verso, 2006, first published 1983), 6.
18. For a comprehensive analysis of the development of a new scopic regime in colonial India, see Christopher Pinney, 'The Nation (Un)Pictured? Chromolithography and "Popular" Politics in India, 1878–1995', *Critical Inquiry* 23, no. 4 (1997); and Christopher Pinney, *'Photos of the Gods': The Printed Image and Political Struggle in India* (London: Reaktion Books, 2004).
19. Lata Mani, *Contentious Traditions: The Debate on Sati in Colonial India* (Berkeley: University of California Press, 1998).

20. For a description of how this process took place in Bengal, see T. Sarkar, *Hindu Wife, Hindu Nation.*
21. Tracy C. Davis, *Actresses as Working Women: Their Social Identity in Victorian Culture* (London: Routledge, 2002), 3.
22. Kathryn Hansen, 'Parsi Theater, Urdu Drama, and the Communalization of Knowledge: A Bibliographic Essay', *Annual of Urdu Studies* 16 (2001): 59; and Kathryn Hansen, 'Languages on Stage: Linguistic Pluralism and Community Formation in the Nineteenth-Century Parsi Theatre', *Modern Asian Studies* 37, no. 2 (2003).
23. Hansen, 'Parsi Theater', 44–45.
24. Hansen, 'Parsi Theater', 43; and Hansen, 'Languages on Stage', 383.
25. See Benjamin Zachariah, 'Travellers in Archives, or the Possibilities of a Post-post-archival Historiography', *Práticas da História*, no. 3 (2016).
26. Hansen, 'Languages on Stage', 383.
27. Amrit Dhillon, 'The Parsis Fighting to Stop Their Culture Dying Out, and Why It Appears Doomed', *South China Morning Post*, 8 December 2016.

PART I

Discipline

In the essay 'State and Its Margins', Veena Das and Deborah Poole complicate the idea of the state as a rational, centralized sociopolitical organization with fixed boundaries. Instead, they suggest that the state is produced along its margins where forms of illegibility, partial belonging, and disorder legitimize its modes of order and lawmaking.[1] The state is brought into being through invocations of the anarchy, wilderness, and barbarism that exist beyond its authority but also challenge it from within. Following this conception, Part I demonstrates how religion, as the most significant social margin of secular governance, was essential to the formation of the modern colonial state and at the centre of an epistemic rupture in a shifting landscape of economic and political power. Envisioned by East India Company officials, missionaries, and orientalists as the locus for the development of rational subjecthood, religion was the site for the establishment of a new moral economy that aligned with the norms of the colonial state. However, as the East India Company was at pains to demonstrate its religious neutrality, the location of religion had to shift, as Peter van der Veer notes, from being part of the state to being part of an incipient bourgeois public sphere.[2]

Chapters 2, 3, and 4 illustrate how religion created the colonial public. Opinion was moulded, diversified, and fissured by the reorganization of religion through the orientalist and juridical emphasis on textual authority for Indian customs, missionary proselytism, and new opportunities for social mobility. The vernacular public sphere was not primarily an interlocutory realm with the state. Instead, it functioned as a conduit for the reconfiguration of ephemeral, figurative, and allegorical custom into disenchanted and indisputable detail, thereby interanimating several complex overlapping movements: the reformation of Hinduism, Islam, and Zoroastrianism and the coinciding development of a religious orthodoxy; the marginalization of precolonial forms of knowledge and shifts in conceptions of historical time; the rise of a bourgeois, middle-class intelligentsia and the formulation of colonial masculinity as normative. In order to demonstrate an intellectual equivalence with Christianity, the ritual incantations of Hinduism and Zoroastrianism were deontologized; a phenomenology of faith contingent on literalism, utilitarianism, and a historically specific mode of inquiry stemming from capital accretion emerged; and a rational, true religious core that was textually discernable was unhinged from mystery, superstition, miracles, and magic.

In the colonial formation, religion facilitated 'rational' debate because it required adherents to consent to fixed doctrines that could be evaluated and scientifically compared. Aligned with secular capital accumulation, law, science, and universal history in homogenous time, reformed religion signified an entitlement to citizenship, scientific rationality, and modernity. Part I traces how a hegemonic textuality characterized by evidence gathering, documentary proof, and post-Enlightenment forms of intellectual inquiry reconfigured ritual performance and spurred new forms of intra- and inter-communal conflict. It delineates how the rapidly growing colonial *entrepôt* Bombay functioned as a pluralistic, religious marketplace where faith had to be plied to a discriminating audience. Missionaries, colonial officials, and orientalist scholars were competing agents who used new channels such as the vernacular press to create a competitive religious environment where communities could no longer rely on the unwavering adherence of their members.[3]

The Parsis—followers of Zoroastrianism—were loyal comprador subjects who swiftly took to English models of administration, jurisprudence, and education. During the first half of the nineteenth century they established the *Mumbai Samācār*, the first Gujarati-language newspaper in Western India, in order to deliver market rates and news quickly and cheaply. Chapter 2 demonstrates how missionary attacks on the Zoroastrian religion in this newspaper prompted both the flourishing of a bourgeois public sphere and religious conversions. Conversion here is to be understood in manifold ways. Specific cases of Parsi conversion to Christianity in the 1830s paralleled broader transformations in a spiritual economy of representation where religion was distinguished from magic, and where unruly populations were converted into law-abiding subjects. The illegibility of Parsi customs under English law—and the incompatibility of Parsi religious prescriptions and proscriptions with colonial capitalist morality—underscored their civilizational otherness. Through the press and theatre, these customs were reformed in line with colonial ideals of civilization and progress and an emerging global order of transaction, value, and desire. A characteristic feature of the colonial reform of religion was its visibility or publicness and correspondingly its theatricality. As Tanika Sarkar notes in the context of Hindu debates on sati and widow remarriage, popular discourse and official legal proceedings on the most intimate aspects of religious custom could be followed through newspapers, reports, and popular texts. 'The structures governing one's innermost beliefs, closest relationships and everyday practices ... were now being dragged out, debated and contested in the public eye. In the process, the ideological basis of prescription and common sense was demystified and made transparent'.[4]

Chapters 3 and 4 demonstrate how the Parsi theatre, as an integral component of the vernacular public sphere, functioned in its infancy in the 1850s and 1860s on multiple scales. Parsi dramas on Bombay's stages that depicted 'illogical' superstitions, the emptiness of rituals performed by an ignorant priesthood, corrupt communal leaders, and a new deallegorized Persian history stripped of myth and magic were subplots in a larger performance of the reconfiguration of 'tradition'. Appropriating orientalist and Christian missionary distinctions between ritual accretions and a true faith discernible in Zoroastrian scripture, Parsis performed new understandings of ethics and paganism, the sacred and profane, private morality and public ceremony. In seeking to fashion Zoroastrianism as a legitimate, rational, monotheistic religion, reformists policed traditional performative modes involving ghosts, spirits and demons, shamanic rituals, and idol worship—beliefs that provided alternative epistemological frameworks to the colonial order. Bodies were disciplined according to a Victorian ethos of bourgeois propriety; hitherto unquestioned customs were interrogated, cast off, or aggressively codified; and communities were pushed into history. In the process, new social hierarchies materialized, and monolithic imaginations of community with hard boundaries took shape. Religion thus not only shaped but was also shaped by the emerging vernacular public sphere.

Notes

1. Veena Das, Deborah Poole, 'State and its margins: comparative ethnographies', *Anthropology in the margins of the state,* (Oxford: Oxford University Press, 2004), 7–11.
2. Peter van der Veer, *Imperial Encounters: Religion and Modernity in India and Britain* (Princeton, NJ: Princeton University Press, 2001), 27.
3. See Nile Green, *Bombay Islam: The Religious Economy of the West Indian Ocean, 1840–1915* (Cambridge: Cambridge University Press, 2011).
4. Tanika Sarkar, *Hindu Wife, Hindu Nation: Community, Religion, and Cultural Nationalism* (New Delhi: Permanent Black, 2017, first published 2001), 74–75.

CHAPTER 2

Parsi Compradors and the Public Sphere

The English Theatre

In the first years of the nineteenth century, Bombay was described as notoriously dull, a condition aggravated by the tottering state of the town's theatre.[1] Bombay's first theatre, the Bombay Amateur Theatre, had been built in 1770 at the old Bombay Green. As Bombay possessed no town hall at the time, the theatre hosted significant social events for the local English community.[2] It then served a 'society' that was demographically small and quite exclusive, the narrow and intimate sphere of East India Company officials and their relations (Figs. 2.1 and 2.2). However, as Bombay grew from fishing village to colonial *entrepôt*, the theatre grew apace. In 1818 its managers circulated a subscription to pay off the theatre's mounting debts, repair its stage, and enlarge and improve its accommodation due to the growth of the settlement.[3]

These repairs contained the germ of the Bombay Amateur Theatre's eventual destruction. In 1819 the newly renovated theatre opened with Thomas Holcroft's suitably entitled *The Road to Ruin* and a debt of approximately Rs. 17,000.[4] From this period this liability progressively increased due to the excessive extravagance of the stage management. When the theatre's last manager, William Newnham, retired to England, its debt amounted to upwards of Rs. 33,000. He was held accountable for the debt and was therefore constrained to safeguard himself from loss by applying to the Bombay Government for relief. While the latter

R. D. Nicholson, *The Colonial Public and the Parsi Stage*, Transnational Theatre Histories,
https://doi.org/10.1007/978-3-030-65836-6_2

Fig. 2.1 'Bombay Play-house, 1810' (*Source* British Library, File number D40013-09, © British Library Board. All Rights Reserved/Bridgeman Images)

was conceded, the fate of the theatre was sealed. Initially its properties, library, scenes, and furniture were auctioned off and sold piece meal for Rs. 2,133, and soon after the edifice shared the same fate, being 'knocked down' for about Rs. 52,000 in 1835.[5]

The Parsi *seṭhs*, who had begun to enjoy positions of significant influence in South Asia due to their indispensable role in the colonial cotton and opium trade, wielded a strong hand in the theatre's fate.[6] One large motivating factor was the theatre's strategic location in the commercial centre of Bombay. Bomanjee Hormusji Wadia, descendant of the Parsi master builders of Bombay's dockyards, owned a house in the theatre's immediate vicinity and was anxious to gain the ground on which it stood. Nevertheless, on 16 June 1835, he refused the government valuation of the plot as disproportionate, and the theatre was put up for public auction. On 30 October 1835 the Bombay Theatre was sold for fifty thousand rupees to the Parsi tycoon Jamsetjee Jeejeebhoy, who controlled the opium market with Jardine Matheson and Co. through the Malwa Opium Syndicate. The actual deed of sale was, however, niftily made

Fig. 2.2 'The Entertainment given to C. Forbes Esquire, in the Theatre at Bombay, on the Night of 16th Oct. 1811' (*Source* British Library, File number D40013-27, © British Library Board. All Rights Reserved/Bridgeman Images)

out to a purchaser by the name of 'Bomanjee Hormusjee', by request of Jeejeebhoy so that Wadia could procure the coveted plot.[7] At this decisive juncture in the theatre's history, the *Bombay Gazette* decried:

> If (when Bombay becomes the Theatre of British enterprise, colonization, manufactures and wealth) an Indian Shakespeare should arise, shall there be no *stage* to call forth the creations of his fancy?, shall his genius sleep, and its fruits be lost to his country, for the sake of the paltry consideration for which that house is now to be consigned to a fate, which has hitherto overtaken such edifices, only in the days of Gothic and Vandal barbarism? Forbid it shame! Forbid it Pride! Forbid it Wisdom![8]

The *Bombay Gazette's* plea for a stage for Bombay, the 'Theatre of British enterprise [and] colonization', centres this figure of an 'Indian Shakespeare' and thus reflects a more significant aspect of Parsi interest in the Bombay Theatre: Parsi *seṭhs* had by this time become active theatregoers.

A survey of Parsi involvement in the theatre in the decade preceding its demise makes this theatrical interest clear. On 13 December 1822 two Parsis, Hormusjee Bomanjee and Sorabji Framji, purchased two tickets each for a performance of Richard Brinsley Sheridan's *The Rivals* (1775)—the first known attendance of Parsis at the theatre. A few years later, in 1830, the Parsi Manockjee Cursetjee was given 'a silver ticket of perpetual free admission' to the theatre as a token for work he had conducted there.[9] That same year, when the theatre's management petitioned for funds, eleven Indians—of which six were Parsi—featured among a group of fifty donors. By 1833, Gujarati-language advertisements of English-language performances, translations of English theatre reviews, and miscellaneous items of theatrical news were carried in Gujarati newspapers such as the *Halkārū*. And in January 1840, five years after the Bombay Theatre had been torn down, the erstwhile theatre manager A. W. Elliot, keenly aware of the changing composition of Bombay's theatre audience and the importance of wooing 'our Native Friends, our great millionaires of Bombay', addressed 'all classes of [Bombay's] increasing community' for the restoration of the late theatre.[10] Funds were procured; a committee was formed comprising Europeans, Hindus, and Parsis; and a plot in Grant Road in the heart of the 'Native Town' was gifted by the Hindu merchant-philanthropist Jagannath Shankarsheth as the site for the new theatre.[11]

However, not everyone was happy about this new development or the promise of more mixed audiences, as an 1845 letter to the *Bombay Times*, signed 'Old Bombay Drury', makes clear:

> SIR.—Although not very wise perhaps to enter the Lists where the Combatants are all on one side, yet I have no doubt, … you will allow me to ask two questions.
>
> 1st.—Is the Bombay Theatre to be an Amateur one?
>
> If so, allow a very old Amateur to assure you it will be a failure.
>
> I cannot think that Amateur can be found who would perform to such an audience, one of so general and mixed a character as that of Bombay in the present day.
>
> 2nd—Or is the Theatre to be sustained by a paid company?
>
> I would put it to yourself, Sir, advocate as you are for the Theatre, do you believe that the present feeling of our Society is such as would be likely to support a paid company? … I remain, one who voted for a Ball-room and against the Theatre, and *once* of the
>
> OLD BOMBAY DRURY[12]

Despite Old Bombay Drury's fears of the 'general and mixed character' of Bombay's audiences, in November 1845 Mrs Deacle, an English actress engaged at Calcutta's San Souci theatre, formally consented to perform with her paid company at the Grant Road Theatre for a year, rent-free.[13] In its first months, the new theatre witnessed several changes: from amateur to semi-professional entertainment, from an alignment with 'society' to the more inclusive 'public', and from English patrons to local spectators that 'crammed the pit and filled it to crushing'.[14] Soon after the theatre's opening, rumours were rife that Mrs Deacle intended to reserve the front row of boxes for the sole use of Europeans. This was 'partly to do' with the fact that 'several gentlemen' complained of the obstruction 'occasioned by the bulky and extensive turbans of the Parsees'.[15] Sensitive to these overtures, Parsis boycotted the theatre. Mrs Deacle, attuned to the decline in box office figures, promptly sought to appease her Parsi patrons and announced a performance exclusively for their benefit.[16]

What does this brief history of Bombay's first theatre tell us about the microphysics of power that had begun to play out on the larger stage of the 'Theatre of British enterprise'? What does the warp of the lexical transition of theatre audiences from 'society' to the 'public' tell us about the woof of the civilizing reveries of East India officers, comprador merchants, and a growing Indian middle class? How did seemingly 'innocent' forms of entertainment reflect and shape larger factors, among them the radical overhauling of regional and global trading and finance; the growth of distinct moral economies and disciplinary networks; the engineering of new thresholds of legibility (of modernity and tradition, religion and science, progress and delinquency); the organization of new technologies of power over the body; and the development of normative spheres of interaction, self-representation, and debate? And what cog did the Parsis—negotiating audience seating in the new, highly stratified Grant Road Theatre and subsequently harkening to calls for an 'Indian Shakespeare'—constitute in the complex clockwork of colonial dominion?

Parsi Compradors, Colonial Education, and the Anatomy of Discipline

By the end of the eighteenth century numerous Parsi *seṭhs* enjoyed positions of significant influence in India due to the fortunes that they had amassed in the colonial trade. While Banaji Limji opened up the Burmese market for Parsi trade, the Readymoneys and Camas established extensive mercantile operations in China, and by 1809, the Chinese city of Canton was home to several Parsi *seṭhs* and only one English trader. The Wadias (who had a hand in the destruction of Bombay's first theatre) were famous as shipwrights, even as the Modis won their riches through contracts with the English for sourcing provisions to the troops in the garrison. The business of importing wines, liquors, and other European goods was especially lucrative due to the upsurge in the English population of Bombay, and the Modis were followed by other Parsi families such as the Jasavalas, Pochajis, and Panthakis, who worked as both agents and bankers for their customers.[17] In 1813 the chief Parsi traders were closely affiliated with all of Bombay's European agencies in most of their foreign speculations, advancing large sums of money to enable these houses to trade.[18] In 1820 Walter Hamilton described the docks as 'entirely occupied by Parsees, who possess an absolute monopoly in all the departments; the person who contracts for the timber being a Parsee, and the inspector on delivery of the same caste'.[19]

Parsi comprador success has been attributed to their occupational mobility; their double peripherality, role ambiguity, or obscure political allegiance (they were relatively uninvolved in previous Muslim and Hindu administrations); and their ability to ensure that their commerce was not straightforwardly opposed to that of English merchants.[20] On the contrary, they managed to entrench themselves in existing European trading structures, rendering themselves indispensable in such occupations as brokerage and banking.[21] Between the Revolutionary and Napoleonic Wars (1793–1815) and the Opium War (1839–1842), Parsi trading firms experienced unprecedented growth from the exportation of raw cotton and opium.[22] However the Opium War stalled this development: several Parsi opium traders committed suicide, and the rest became increasingly dependent on Jardine Matheson and Co., which enjoyed a close partnership with the Parsi merchant-prince of Bombay, Jamsetjee Jeejeebhoy. Jeejeebhoy, who at one time held deposits of thirty million rupees in the Bank of Bombay, thus became the most affluent of his co-religionists.[23] Parsi firms dealing with shipbuilding and the export of raw cotton also faced setbacks, the former due to the exclusion of indigenous ships from European waters and the introduction of steam power and the latter due to export duties.[24] In addition, other communities such as the Ismailis and Bombay Jews began to seriously challenge the Parsis' trading monopoly. These changes stimulated a structural change in Parsi commerce, from trade to the development of industry through the modicum of the joint-stock company.

Nevertheless, these early and extensive mercantile pursuits left an indelible mark on the community. A new class of Indian collaborators with European capitalism had emerged, prospered, and established themselves as people of significant economic and political clout within both the Parsi community and the close-knit group of East India Company officials. This new Indian urban elite, according to Jesse Palsetia, epitomized the conversion of private capital interests into political authority and influence both within and outside their community.[25] Accordingly, Parsi *seṭhs* who had extensive business interests with the English rapidly assumed leadership positions in Bombay's Parsi Panchayat, the governing body of the Parsi community.[26] The Panchayat, which had been established circa 1725 but was not officially recognized by the British government until 1 January 1787, typified British attempts to integrate the Parsis into the political system through 'indirect rule', delegating community-specific matters to self-administration.[27] While the *seṭhs* assiduously served the interests of their own community, often against British interests (as evinced by Jeejeebhoy's purchase of the Bombay Amateur Theatre), they desired and doggedly courted recognition from colonial officials through Western-style social gatherings and prodigious philanthropic schemes.[28] Jeejeebhoy, who was the first Indian to be bestowed with knighthood and baronetcy, was memorialized as the benefactor of the infrastructural development of Bombay, Parsi communal institutions, British patriotic and military funds, and European-style pedagogical projects. By allowing charitable *seṭhs* to serve in the municipal administration as justices of the peace and in the Supreme Court of Bombay as grand jurors, the British government fostered an imperial culture of cooperation that enabled Indian elites to further raise their social standing even as they were progressively and unknowingly socialized to colonial values.

This conversion to colonial values is to be understood as both a protracted process and an event (as in the case of proselytism). To begin, the compradorial necessity of logistical coordination of manufacture, trade, and distribution across continents compelled a temporal shift: from the inexact, dissimilarly experienced time of dawn and dusk, tides and seasons, to the precise, universal frameworks of the Gregorian calendar and international standard time.[29] Against the expansion of colonial domination, modern market relations, and global capital, the temporal markers of days, months, and years were institutionalized and reified, thereby disciplining duration through seriation, steering and anchoring knowledge, and transforming lived experience. World time functioned as an instrument of discipline; it enabled heterogenous activities such as risk-taking, the development of wage labour, markets and industrial forms of production, the reading of the newspaper, and the formation of a modern individual subjectivity as exemplified by the novel. By pursuing profit, accumulating capital, and controlling activity, labour, and bodies, colonial power articulated onto time, extended from the Parsi steamship and factory to the temple, Panchayat, and schoolroom.

At the beginning of the nineteenth century, during the height of Parsi mercantile prosperity, Parsi families awakened to the economic advantages of an English education,[30] and sent their children by the droves to a growing crop of evangelical schools. The advent of modern education in Bombay is largely a monument to the Christian missionary enterprise. In 1813 government funds were allocated for Indian education, and controls over proselytism relaxed. Two years later, the American Marathi Mission set up the first Western-style school in Bombay.[31] By 1826 nine girls' schools attended by 240 pupils operated under this first mission alone. Similarly, the Church Missionary Society opened its first school in 1820. Among these societies, the Scottish missionary John Wilson, considered 'the best-hated European in India' due to his efforts to proselytize the local population, was a relative latecomer. However, within a year of his arrival he had established six schools for local girls, and in 1832 he opened a school for boys.[32] Aware of the financial and political clout wielded by the Parsis as well as the 'filtration principle' (that intervention in Indian society had to happen from the top), Wilson chose localities for his schools that suited the convenience of the Parsis.[33] The curriculum of his schools—of mathematics, astronomy, geography, moral philosophy, and not least history—was as crucial to the missionary enterprise as Christian instruction itself. 'Homogenous, secular, calendrical time', which was measurable, infinitely divisible, and ostensibly neutral, was integral not only to the organization of capitalist economic relations and Parsi compradorial activity, but also to scholastic disciplines such as history.[34] Seemingly innocuous, repetitive, ritualized disciplinary practices common to compradorial labour and European pedagogy: notation; seriation; the accumulation, categorization, and classification of documents; and the organization of information, allowed missionaries, orientalists, and colonial officials to examine communities on a linear, civilizational continuum as objective, comparable bodies of knowledge for easily controlled administration. A great empirical knowledge, 'orientalism', thus linked the formation of knowledge to the exercise of a particular power.

The Birth of the Vernacular Public Sphere

On his arrival in Bombay, Wilson had acquainted himself with orientalist scholarship on the religious tenets and history of the Parsi community. After a protracted study of Anquetil du Perron's 1771 translation of the Parsi prayer-book, the *Zend Avesta* and the linguistic and orientalist works of Rasmus Christian Rask, Eugene Burnouf, Franz Bopp, William Erskine, Thomas Hyde, and Niels Ludwig Westergaard, he published a critical account of Zoroastrian theology in the *Oriental Christian Spectator* in July 1831. Wilson, who according to the orientalist Martin Haug was the first to write a 'work written in English which shows any acquaintance with the original Avesta texts', contended that the divine mission of Zoroaster was destitute of divine authority. He further averred that the ecclesiastical code, the *Vendidad*, was 'a highly irrational account of ... good and evil' and 'directly opposed to morality', and that the religion was polytheistic, taught and recognized the deification of elements and other inanimate objects, contained gross scientific blunders, and comprised an immense number of absurd ceremonies.[35]

Wilson's arguments in the English and subsequently Gujarati press marked 'Disenchantment' (*Entzauberung*), a widespread epistemic rupture in the self-definition of Indian society. Drawing on Max Weber's thesis, scholars such as Talal Asad, van der Veer, and Robert Yelle have demonstrated how the Protestant iconoclastic conceptualization of religion as distinct from magic was a salient feature of the modern age and of colonial rule.[36] In British India, the distinction between religion and myth was projected onto the distinction between the backward East and the modern West.[37] Orientalist scholars and missionaries functioned as 'legislative intellectuals', purifying 'discovered' non-Christian religions of myth that was defined as the human capacity for (mis)representation and false science.[38] Consequently, as Lata Mani notes, the regenerating mission of colonization had been conceived not as the enforcement of a Christian moral order but as the recovery of the lost truths of authentic religion.[39] Religion was a source of morality unopposed to scientific knowledge,[40] whereas myth comprising 'irrational accounts', 'gross scientific blunders', devil worship, and idolatry was a sign of barbarity, otherness, and civilizational backwardness. As, according to the colonial purview, religion had to be purified of mythic accretions for civilizational advancement, 'myth' as a discursive category authorized intervention in the beliefs and customs of the world's ostensibly primitive peoples.

Shortly after Wilson's piece in the *Oriental Christian Spectator*, a letter was published by a Parsi in the Gujarati-language *Mumbai Samācār*, condemning the *Samācār* editor's silence on the subject and soliciting assistance in 'forming an opinion' to counter Wilson's criticisms.[41] Subsequently, Wilson submitted several letters to the *Mumbai Samācār* on the falsehoods of the Zoroastrian religion in the hope that a direct attack would trigger a response.[42] Instead of responding, however, the editor of the *Mumbai Samācār* attempted to 'drop the undertaking'.[43] The *Mumbai Samācār*, the first vernacular newspaper of Western India, had been founded on 1 January 1822 by Fardunji Marzban with financial assistance from the Parsi opium tycoon Jamsetjee Jeejeebhoy.[44] Marzban had previously operated a private postal service that had delivered prevailing market rates between Bombay, Surat, Navsari, and Bharuch faster than government postage.[45] His success with the post prompted him to publish the first issue of the *Mumbai Samācār* in July 1822 to convey news cheaply and more efficiently. In 1832 the newspaper was bought by the Chinese trading Cama family after one of Marzban's mercantile ventures failed; Parsi mercantile capital thus financed the perpetuation of the Gujarati press.[46] As an organ of Western Indian commerce for Bombay's Gujarati-speaking communities, the *Mumbai Samācār* was ill equipped to deal with Wilson's arguments; Parsi readers had never been petitioned to speak their mind on their own religion by a Gujarati-speaking European missionary. The 'forming of an opinion' through the medium of the newspaper on the truth and falsehoods of a religious 'history' that was protean in form, combining moral instruction, theology, poetry, and mythology, was not only unprecedented but also deemed by the *Samācār* editor to be a 'private' matter.[47] However, the editor's entreaties to drop the subject went unheeded as, according to Wilson, the Parsis had to 'devote themselves … to the pursuit and practice of truth'.[48]

Van der Veer describes how Indians 'were quite literally converted to modernity by the efforts of missionary Christianity, especially in its nineteenth-century Protestant incarnation'.[49] While Veer and Gauri

Viswanathan emphasize the importance of education in conversion, I contend that the burgeoning public sphere played an equal role.[50] With Wilson's criticisms, the *Mumbai Samācār* inadvertently transitioned from an intimate arena of interaction between members sharing common commercial interests to an observatory, where Parsis, Banias, Bohras, Christian missionaries and East India officials, converts and non-converts, and outsiders and insiders could see and be seen within a complex architecture of power. Wilson's comments in the *Mumbai Samācār* thus mark the beginning of a protracted series of public disputes with Bombay's Hindu, Muslim, and Parsi communities. In 1830, Hindu scholars such as Laxman Shastri and Mora Bhat Dandekar engaged in public debates on the merits of Hinduism with Wilson and the convert Ram Chandra.[51] These heavily attended public events, accessible to people of varied caste and religious denominations, constituted a great tribunal, a sphere of extensive, omnipresent surveillance within which communities were subjected to a compulsory visibility. As Tanikar Sarkar notes, 'the structures governing one's innermost beliefs, closest relationships and everyday practices ... were now being dragged out, debated and contested in the public eye'.[52] Increasingly, local intellectuals functioned as witnesses and instruments of a non-corporeal power that was organic rather than imposed, operating on the underside of the law. A host of new vernacular newspapers began to function as minor theatres where—through a complex network of gazes and writings, observations, comparisons, debates, and the fixing of truths—power asymmetries were reproduced, a mechanism of universal juridicism was generalized, and a disciplinary society was born.

The first of these newspapers, the *Bombay Vartaman*, was a weekly journal founded on 1 November 1830. Navrojī Dorābjī Cāndāru (1807–59), 'the first independent native journalist of Western India', founded the journal in order to offer 'a fair field and no favour' for a discussion based on Wilson's criticisms. The *Bombay Vartaman*, re-entitled *Bombay Halkaru and Vartaman* (henceforward *Halkārū*) in November 1832 and subsequently known as the *Cābuk* (*Whip*), spurred the Parsi reform movement that was frequently and perhaps candidly dubbed the 'Protestantization' of the community. Spearheaded by the *Halkārū*, a new class of indigenous intellectual elites deployed religion as a site for self-representation and self-surveillance, interiorizing the orientalist differentiation between a true religious core and mythical accretions. Religious tradition thus opened up to widespread debate began to generate a public. Print progressively amassed and organized plural, stratified, and contradictory opinions on the most intimate features of communal life, thereby interanimating numerous parallel developments that irrevocably transformed everyday habits, discourses, and social identities.[53]

One such development was the progressive vilification of traditionally dominant groups. The *Halkārū's* insults were directed primarily at the allegedly 'immoral' and 'undisciplined' Parsi priesthood that uncomprehendingly muttered prayers by rote and the Parsi Panchayat. Although the Panchayat had consolidated its authority during the height of Parsi compradorial success in the eighteenth century, by the nineteenth century it had declined in power due to its inconsistency in dispensing justice, the hereditary assumption of its membership, the impropriety of some of its members, and the mounting sense that its dominance was based on custom rather than the written word of law.[54] As the *Halkārū's* public assaults increased in fervour, the Panchayat founded what would be the second longest running newspaper in South Asia after the *Mumbai Samācār*, the *Jāme Jamśed*.[55] First published by Māṇekjī Pestanjī Motīvālā on 12 March 1832, the *Jāme* fervently defended Panchayat members and the priestly classes when they were attacked by the *Halkārū*.[56] Motīvālā's relationship with the comprador leaders of the community, especially the cotton and opium magnate Jeejeebhoy, was tightly knit from the start. Jeejeebhoy provided substantial financial backing to the *Jāme* in order to 'render public the workings of the Panchayat' due to the 'weakening of its leaders' rights and powers … in the face of attacks by the *Mumbai Samācār* and *Halkārū*'.[57] If the opium trade indirectly financed the birth of Parsi journalism, so also did it provide the material basis for the formation of a Parsi 'public sphere'; it is with the *Jāme*'s inauguration that the term 'Parsi public' gained currency, a term that was paradoxically first used by Wilson himself.[58]

From the very beginning, therefore, the Parsi public sphere was not completely inclusive. Parsis solicited the necessary start-up capital to fund their journalistic ventures from wealthy merchants; thus the public sphere established itself institutionally—at least in the beginning—as a beneficiary of mercantile patronage. Additionally, because discursive interaction was limited to religious reform, its character was a necessarily communal one, a sociological arrangement that would only be strengthened with the elaboration of British demographic systems that heightened communal identities. Consequently, the Parsi literary public sphere was formally exclusionary from the beginning, its organizational structure not merely marginalizing but completely eliding questions of ethnically, linguistically, and religiously diverse publics.

Conversion

Wilson had thus prompted new imaginations of community that were characterized by harder boundaries and more unified identities than were older social formations that faced limited external contestation. The social debates that he spurred may be perceived as evidence not merely of the fracturing and pluralization of opinion but also of a politics of time. In the mid-nineteenth century, the Parsis, confronted with Wilson's effusions—on truth and falsehood, textual proof, sceptical inquiry, and civilization—faced plural, conflicting conceptualizations of time: ostensibly neutral, homogeneous chronologic time, the discriminatory time of colonial civilization and progress and colonized savagery and backwardness, the hierophantic time of tradition and the uneven, immanent 'becoming' of a globalizing modernity birthed in Europe and swelling out to the rest of the world. His public, inter-religious debates prompted a composite revolution in Indian social life through the development of Hindu, Muslim, and Zoroastrian reformist and traditionalist presses (e.g. the *Halkarū* and the *Jāme*), theatres, and publics that dissimilarly regulated regimes of truth, discipline, and spiritual and material consumption. By 1855 the vernacular press would grow to include ten Gujarati, three Marathi, one Hindustani, and one Farsi newspaper.[59] Moreover, the same impetus behind the creation of Parsi journalism led to the 1831 creation of the Mulla Firoz Library, which housed manuscripts dealing with the Zoroastrian religion, and the 1837 establishment of the Jijibhoy Dadabhoy Parsi Madressa for the teaching of Zoroastrian scriptures in Zend and Pahlavi.[60]

Despite these large-scale forms of conversion, both traditionalists and reformists considered the actual proselytism of a Parsi to Christianity inconceivable as 'even a Pársí babe, crying in the cradle, [was] firmly confident in the venerable Zartusht'.[61] Consequently, when on 1 May 1839 two Parsi students of Wilson's school were baptized at the Scottish Mission House, the Parsi community immediately attempted 'to seek their serious injury', withdrew their children from missionary schools, applied for a writ of habeas corpus for their return to the Parsi fold, and prosecuted Wilson for contravening the conditions under which the students had been put in his charge. According to Palsetia, by requesting the writ of habeas corpus and Wilson's trial, the Parsis became the first community in Western India to use the law to confront missionaries.[62] However, the court case worked against the Parsis as, according to the defendants and a long line of colonial administrators before them, the community had no codified law. In the landmark judgement, the boys, established as being of age according to Parsi and Hindu custom, were pronounced by the chief justice as being at liberty to choose their religion. Any attempt to interfere with their freedom was punishable. In response to a subsequent appeal known as the 'Anti-Conversion Memorial', the governor in council argued that while the government observed strict neutrality towards missionary labour, 'the course of argument and fair reason [could not] be impeded, since its progress [was] a necessary consequence of the extension of education, for which, in the abstract, [the Parsis were] justly so anxiously solicitous'.[63] If an English secular education characterized by the organization of time through segmentation, seriation, and totalization was indispensable for Parsis to remain a competitive force in their mercantile and industrial ventures—and if mathematics, geography, moral philosophy, and history were a necessary scholastic program for their offspring—the 'serious blunders in chronology, history, and geography' of their own religious scriptures had become impossible to overlook not merely in the informal, minor tribunal of the vernacular public sphere but also in the institutionalized courtrooms of Bombay. Through the conversion cases, a time lag in the coexistence of local-indigenous and centralized-European forms of governance, in communal practice and secular law, and in the separation of 'private' and 'public' spheres was indubitably laid bare.

The conversion cases thus reveal on the part of the British government a composite set of administrative, legal, and cultural mechanisms developed for the coordination of a complex disciplinary regime. Although the British had instituted a dual system in India whereby issues pertaining to religious custom were deliberated on the basis of local rules distinct from civil law, both long-drawn-out processes and explicit incidents of conversion reveal a complex web of entanglements between the state, religion, and the public. The colonial state drew its legitimacy from the assertion that it was merely recognizing and implementing prevailing indigenous law. However, as indigenous law itself was fragmented, plural, and contradictory—and in the Parsi case based on variable custom rather than unwavering written tenet—the state repeatedly arbitrated and legislated on what was 'religion' by ascertaining whether a particular custom or text was authentic. Paradoxically, then, as Barton Scott and Brannon Ingram show, religion could only be liberated from state interference once it acquired the state's imprimatur.[64] Consequently, although religion in England had been situated outside the remit of public discussion, such a stance was implausible in the colonies. While in Europe, according to Jürgen Habermas, 'the status of the Church changed as a result of the Reformation; the anchoring in divine authority that it represented—that is, religion—became a private matter', in colonial India missionary activity and the ensuing processes of conversion rendered religion contestable and open to public dispute.[65] Despite British law's conception of religious belief as existing outside the jurisdiction of secular courts and therefore on the margins of state, the conversion cases bestowed new authority on the colonial state. By adjudicating and determining what constituted authentic religious law, the colonial disciplinary apparatus reached deep into the heart of indigenous families and homes, transmuting the most cherished features of communal life.

For the Parsis of Bombay, it abruptly became imperative to write their collective world down—to pin, as Sudipta Kaviraj says, 'every practice down on paper, to give it a reliable image, a fixity required for subsequent reflection'.[66] The social world, hitherto characterized by a variability of local practices, had to be written down. Lawmaking would thus rapidly become the 'vehicle for the expression of collective identity', while granting an extraordinary level of intra-group power to a class of elites deeply involved in the colonial state.[67] Split in the double time of modernity and tradition, the Theatre of Empire thus began to take shape as a moral representational economy through invocations of anarchy and wilderness, reason and citizenship, and the overriding necessity of pigeonholing the flux of community life into immutable word and doctrine. As the next chapter demonstrates, law, theatricalized in the estranged half-light of Bombay's stages, bespoke the desire to discipline non-disciplinary spaces, reinforcing through rationalization and historicization, acts and scenes, a society of interminable surveillance.

Notes

1. 'The Old Bombay Theatre', *TOI*, 31 July 1886, 4.
2. Untitled, *BT*, 8 January 1842, 21; 'The Old Bombay Theatre', *TOI*, 31 July 1886, 4; Kumudini A. Mehta, 'English Drama on the Bombay Stage in the Late Eighteenth Century and in the Nineteenth Century' (PhD diss., University of Bombay, 1960), 1, 11.
3. 'The Old Bombay Theatre', *TOI*, 31 July 1886, 4.
4. 'The Old Bombay Theatre', *TOI*, 31 July 1886, 4.
5. Untitled, *BT*, 8 January 1842, 21. See also Samuel Townsend Sheppard, *The Byculla Club, 1833–1916, a History* (Bombay: Bennett, Coleman, 1916), 9–10.
6. 'Seṭh' or 'sett' is the Gujarati term for an individual of high social standing. It also specifically denoted a class of wealthy comprador leaders. Jesse S. Palsetia, *Jamsetjee Jejeebhoy of Bombay: Partnership and Public Culture in Empire* (Oxford: Oxford University Press, 2015), 63.
7. Genl. Dept. Vol. 38-A/370A for 1836, 89–91, 116, 120, cited in Mehta, 'English Drama on the Bombay Stage', 96–97.
8. Untitled, *BG*, 12 September 1835, cited in Mehta, 'English Drama on the Bombay Stage', 99.
9. Mehta, 'English Drama on the Bombay Stage', 46. Also spelled 'Manackjee Cursetjee Shroff', 'Māṇekjī Kharśedjī Śaraf' and 'Maneckji Cursetji'.
10. A. W. Elliot, 'Correspondence', *BT*, 25 January 1840, 59.
11. Untitled, *BT*, 8 January 1842, 21. Born on 10 February 1803 to a wealthy mercantile family, Shankarsheth was the first Indian member of the Asiatic Society of Bombay, advanced Hindu reforms such as the abolishment of sati, and played a key role in the Elphinstone Fund, which eventually led to the foundation of the Elphinstone School, the Elphinstone College, and the University of Bombay.
12. Old Bombay Drury, 'The Theatre', *BT*, 22 October 1845, 692.
13. Untitled, *BT*, 19 November 1845, 754; and *BT*, 26 November 1845, 770.
14. Mehta, 'English Drama on the Bombay Stage', 116.
15. Untitled, *BT*, 25 February 1846, 124.
16. 'The Theatre', *BT*, 30 May 1846, 352.
17. Dosabhai Framji Karaka, *History of the Parsis: Including Their Manners, Customs, Religion, and Present Position*, volume 2 (London: Macmillan, 1884), 47–90.
18. John Hinnells, 'Anglo-Parsi Commercial Relations in Bombay Prior to 1847', *Journal of the K. R. Cama Oriental Institute*, no. 46 (1978): 15.
19. Karkaria, *The Charm of Bombay*, 533.

20. Amalendu Guha, 'The Comprador Role of Parsi Seths, 1750–1850', *Economic and Political Weekly* 5 (1970): 1935; and Christine E. Dobbin, *Asian Entrepreneurial Minorities: Conjoint Communities in the Making of the World-Economy 1570–1940* (Richmond: Curzon Press, 1996), 2.
21. Guha, 'The Comprador Role of Parsi Seths, 1750–1850', 1935.
22. Amalendu Guha, 'Parsi Seths as Entrepreneurs, 1750–1850', *Economic and Political Weekly* (1970): M109.
23. Guha, 'The Comprador Role of Parsi Seths', 1933; and Guha, 'Parsi Seths as Entrepreneurs', M114.
24. Guha, 'The Comprador Role of Parsi Seths', 1933.
25. Palsetia, *Jamsetjee Jejeebhoy*, 55.
26. Bombay's first recognizable Parsi Panchayat, established c. 1725, comprised members that had extensive business interests with the English. Over the eighteenth century it consolidated its authority, implementing communal rules that were approved and disseminated at public meetings. John Hinnells, 'Bombay Parsi Panchayat', *Encyclopædia Iranica*, online edition, Vol. IV, Fasc. 4, https://www.iranicaonline.org/articles/bombay-parsi-panchayat-the-largest-zoroastrian-institution-in-modern-history. See also Jesse S. Palsetia, *The Parsis of India: Preservation of Identity in Bombay City* (New Delhi: Manohar, 2008), 95–97.
27. Sohrab P. Davar, *The History of the Parsi Punchayet of Bombay* (Bombay: New Book, 1949), 1; and Eckehard Kulke, *The Parsees in India, A Minority as Agent of Social Change* (Bombay: Vikas, 1974), 64.
28. Palsetia, *Jamsetjee Jejeebhoy*, 64.
29. For analyses of historical time see Kimberly Hutchings, *Time and World Politics: Thinking the Present* (Manchester: Manchester University Press, 2013); and Victoria Browne, 'Feminist Historiography and the Reconceptualisation of Historical Time' (PhD diss., University of Liverpool, 2013).
30. Guha, 'Parsi Seths as Entrepreneurs', M107.
31. Eugene Stock, *One Hundred Years: Being the Short History of the Church Missionary Society* (London: Church Missionary Society, 1899), 27.
32. John Murray Mitchell, *In Western India: Recollections of My Early Missionary Life* (Edinburgh: D. Douglas, 1899), 72.
33. John Wilson, *The Pársí Religion: As Contained in the Zand-Avastá* (Bombay: American Mission Press, 1843), 82–83; and 'Missionary Efforts in India', *Asiatic Journal* 21 (April 1826): 450.
34. See Dipesh Chakrabarty, 'Postcoloniality and the Artifice of History: Who Speaks for "Indian" Pasts?' *Representations*, 37 (1992): 1–26.
35. Wilson, *The Pársí Religion*, 67.
36. Talal Asad, *Formations of the Secular: Christianity, Islam, Modernity* (Stanford: Stanford University Press, 2003), 13–14; Peter van der Veer, *The Modern Spirit of Asia: The Spiritual and the Secular in China and India*

(Princeton: Princeton University Press, 2014), 115–18; and Robert A. Yelle, *The Language of Disenchantment: Protestant Literalism and Colonial Discourse* (Oxford: Oxford University Press, 2013), 12–15.
37. Peter van der Veer, *The Modern Spirit of Asia: The Spiritual and the Secular in China and India* (Princeton: Princeton University Press, 2014), 116.
38. Mitch Numark, 'Translating *Dharma*: Scottish Missionary-Orientalists and the Politics of Religious Understanding in Nineteenth-Century Bombay', *Journal of Asian Studies* 70, no. 2 (2011): 473–75.
39. Lata Mani, 'Contentious Traditions: The Debate on Sati in Colonial India', *Cultural Critique* 7 (1987): 127.
40. Van der Veer, *The Modern Spirit of Asia*, 115.
41. Kustí-bandni, *Bombay Samáchár*, 18 July 1831, cited in Wilson, *The Pársí Religion*, 27, 17.
42. *Bombay Samáchár,* 1 August 1831 cited in Wilson, John. *The Pársí Religion*, 29.
43. *Bombay Samáchár*, 18 July 1831, cited in Wilson, *The Pársí Religion*, 28.
44. Also spelled 'Furdoonji Marzban', 'Fardunjī Marajbān'.
45. Hormazdyar Shahpurshah Dalal, *Adi Marzban—A Gentle Genius* (Bombay: R. K. Anklesaria), 13–17. See also B. K. Karanjia, 'Parsi Pioneers of the Press (1822–1915)', in *A Zoroastrian Tapestry: Art Religion & Culture*, eds. P. J. Godrej and F. Punthakey Mistree (Ahmedabad: Mapin, 2002), 479–82.
46. J. R. B. Jeejeebhoy, 'Historical Survey of Bombay Journalism', in *Jāme Jamśed Centenary Memorial Volume* (Bombay: Messrs Jehāṅgīr Be. Marajhbānnī, 1932), 272–87, 279–80.
47. *Bombay Samáchár*, 1 August 1831, cited in Wilson, *The Pársí Religion*, 29.
48. Wilson, *The Pársí Religion*, 67.
49. Van der Veer, *The Modern Spirit of Asia*, 90.
50. See Gauri Viswanathan, *Masks of Conquest: Literary Study and British Rule in India* (New York: Columbia University Press, 2014).
51. Jesse Palsetia, 'Parsi and Hindu Traditional and Nontraditional Responses to Christian Conversion in Bombay, 1839–45', *Journal of the American Academy of Religion* 74, no. 3 (2006): 619.
52. T. Sarkar, *Hindu Wife, Hindu Nation*, 74–75.
53. See Sumit Sarkar and Tanika Sarkar, eds., *Women and Social Reform in Modern India: A Reader* (Bloomington, IN: Indiana University Press, 2008), 2.
54. Wilson, *The Pársí Religion*, 64.
55. Jeejeebhoy, 'Historical Survey of Bombay Journalism', 280; and Dr. Śamsul Olmā Modī and Sir Jīvanjī Jamśedjī, 'Jāme Jamśed, tenā e nām māṭenā sababo', in *Jāme Jamśed Centenary Memorial Volume*, 42.

56. Jeejeebhoy, 'Historical Survey of Bombay Journalism', 280.
57. *Jāme Jamśed Centenary Memorial Volume* (Bombay: Messrs Jehāṅgīr Be. Marajhbānnī Co., 1932), 3; and Modī, Śamsul Olmā Dr. Sir. Jīvanjī Jamśedjī, 'Jāme Jamśed, tenā e nām māṭenā sababo', in *Jāme Jamśed Centenary Memorial Volume* (Bombay: Messrs Jehāṅgīr Be. Marajhbānnī Co., 1932), 42–43.
58. Wilson, *The Pársí Religion*, 69.
59. Untitled, *RG*, 22 July 1855, 231.
60. Stephen Meredyth Edwardes, *The Gazetteer of Bombay City and Island* (Bombay: Times Press, 1910), 3:143–44.
61. Wilson, *The Pársí Religion*, 74.
62. Palsetia, 'Parsi and Hindu Responses', 623.
63. Wilson, *The Pársí Religion*, 92–93.
64. J. Barton Scott and Brannon D. Ingram, 'What Is a Public? Notes from South Asia', *South Asia: Journal of South Asian Studies* 38, no. 3 (2015): 367.
65. Jürgen Habermas, *The Structural Transformation of the Public Sphere: An Inquiry into a Category of Bourgeois Society*, trans. Thomas Burger and Frederick Lawrence (Boston: MIT Press, 1989), 11.
66. Sudipta Kaviraj, 'Modernity and Politics in India', *Daedalus* 129, no. 1 (2000): 147.
67. Mitra Sharafi, *Law and Identity in Colonial South Asia: Parsi Legal Culture, 1772–1947* (Cambridge: Cambridge University Press, 2014), 165.

CHAPTER 3

Social Reform, Lawmaking, and the Origins of the Parsi Theatre

Reformists

The first available issues of the chief reformist organ of the Parsi community, the *Rāst Goftār* (instituted on 15 November 1851 by the leading lights of Parsi social reform: Dadabhai Naoroji, Naoroji Fardunji, Jehangir Burjorji Vaccha, and Sohrabjee Shahpurjee Bengalee),[1] abound with visual terms and phrases: 'finding God by opening one's eyes', 'seeing one's faults before the *juddins* [non-Parsis] do', 'being observed by other communities', 'the blind justice of the Panchayat', and *jāher mat* (public opinion; *jāher* means 'being in public view').[2] The term *nazar* (observation/gaze), previously linked to devotional practices, pan-Asian beliefs in the evil eye, and shamanic rituals, assumed new meaning in the period of social reform. Signifying the cultivation of discrimination and judgement through the study of English literature and history and rational and intellectual amusement, *nazar* in the mid-nineteenth century implied the ability 'to see' between pure and impure custom, history, law, and language on the basis of reason. The reformists—or 'Young Bombay', the first fruits of the English education given at Bombay's Elphinstone College (est. 1856)—appropriated the colonial conceptions of religious syncretism as falsehood, of long-standing customs as devoid of divine agency and therefore subject to critical inquiry, and of the quest for truth discernible through the diligent study of scripture. Concurrently, this surfeit of optical terms rendered conspicuous the new vernacular

R. D. Nicholson, *The Colonial Public and the Parsi Stage*, Transnational Theatre Histories,
https://doi.org/10.1007/978-3-030-65836-6_3

public sphere's spatial configuration as an observatory that permitted a class of local elites closely linked to the colonial state apparatus, an articulated form of intra-group control and intergroup self-representation. That the introduction of print and the colonial idea of the public opened up domestic issues for the first time to widespread judgement is epitomized by the Gujarati term for publicity, *jāher*, which corresponds with the German *Öffentlichkeit*. The most intimate features of community life were now exposed to new forms of address and deliberation that effortlessly inserted themselves into the everyday activities of students, businessmen, clerks, intellectuals, and a small group of educated housewives. It was possible, as Tanika Sarkar notes, to follow from journals and printed reports not only what rules were approved, but also what people thought of them.[3]

'News' was of secondary concern to the vernacular press, a characteristic compounded by the one-month journey for English mail to reach India through the P. & O. Co. steamer.[4] Instead, newspapers such as the *Rāst* functioned in tandem with the Society for the Diffusion of Knowledge (Dnyān Prasārak Maṇḍalī); the Religious Reform Association (Rāhnumāi Mājdayaśnī Sabhā); and the Bombay Association, the first indigenous political organization in Western India, as pedagogical tools, elaborating on themes such as the monotheism of Zoroastrianism; the ideas of sin, repentance, and fear of God; the evils of gambling dens, opium, child marriages, dowry and the 'prevailing belief in ghosts, devils, spells … [and] the custom of contracting alliance by betrothal and marriage from a consultation of the horoscope'[5]; the search for 'truth' based on the discovery of non-Hindu or *aslī keānī revāj* (authentic Kayanian rites); the absurdity of Parsi women wailing at funerals; inordinate wedding expenses (such as that of the Petit and Wadia families); the ugliness and futility of the *ḍaglī* (Parsi robe) and *pāghḍī* (Parsi hat) for protecting the body and brain properly; the impropriety of women wearing sandals during the monsoons; quack doctors; and the need for the standardization of individual and collective identities through the introduction of Parsi surnames, birth and death announcements, and a communally organized census. Many articles threw a spotlight on particular individuals (for example, the Petit and Wadia families) as 'the responsibility of the native press was to punish delinquents through *prajānī inśāf ane dhīkār* [public justice and abhorrence]'. Although letter writers contended that many of these ostensibly questionable behaviours took place in 'private' gatherings and were therefore private matters, the *Rāst* defended its name-taking stance.[6]

Bombay's Parsi public sphere had therefore become a coercive theatre in which individuals, actors on a stage, were perfectly visible and therefore subject to a particular economy of power. Affairs deemed intimate a few decades ago were thrown open to the public, debated, integrated into knowledge of social, communal, and ethnic groups, and transformed into the exercise of authority. Iteration functioned as persuasion; the repetitive imposition of micro-penalties—of corporeal norms (clothing and jewellery), customs (gambling and dowries), and character (the officialization of identities)—introduced new registers of normality, changed criteria for membership in the communal body, orchestrated obedient bodies, and developed the middle classes (*vacle vāndhenā loko*) who 'possessed neither wealth nor pride enabling them to engage rapidly in reforms'.[7] This juridical-theatrical characteristic of the developing vernacular press was imaged in the newly founded Parsi theatre, which appeared, at first glance, as a courtroom where individuals were tried, penalties were dramatized, and law was reproduced. On Saturday, 29 October 1853, a 'Parsi Theatrical Committee' comprising a number of the reformists that founded and supported the *Rāst* (including Dadabhai Naoroji, Jehangir Burjorji Vaccha, Kharshedji Nusserwanji Cama, Ardeshir Framji Moos, and Bhau Daji) announced the performance at the Grant Road Theatre of a play based on a celebrated Persian legend, *Roostum Zabooli and Sohrab* (*Ruśtam Jabulī*). This play, which will be discussed in the next section, was accompanied by the 'local drama' or 'farce' *Dhanji Garak* (*Dhanjī Garak*).[8]

The plot of *Dhanji Garak* is as follows: a Portuguese butler gives his watch to a Parsi watchmaker, Dhanji, for repair. Dhanji promises to return it shortly but instead 'garaks' (sells; lit. swallows) it and absconds to Poona on the pretence of his grandmother's funeral. The butler is put off each day and finally quarrels with the boy in charge of the shop, but due to the dishonesty of the sepoy stationed in the division, he is obliged to await the watchmaker's arrival. On the latter's return, despite numerous complaints, the butler is further stalled; consequently, he issues a warrant against Dhanji. At the Police Court, Dhanji promises the magistrate to return the watch in two days, but before leaving, he bribes a policeman, moving him to declare that the order of the sitting magistrate was that the watch should be returned in two weeks. A second summons is served by the butler, the case comes on for trial a second time, and Dhanji in his defence lays all the blame on the butler himself, saying that the plaintiff's frequent interruptions prevented him from attending to his work or repairing the watch. Nevertheless, the trying officer, in his 'magisterial wisdom', is not fooled by this 'lame excuse'. Dhanji is sentenced to pay a fine of fifty rupees or to be confined in the House of Correction with hard labour for three months.[9]

Significantly, *Dhanji Garak* comprised 'exact personifications of some of that class of men who might be met with in all parts of the island', with the character of Dhanji 'fail[ing] not to remind one of some of the Parsi tradesmen about the town'.[10] The Parsi actor Jahāṅgīr Pestanjī Khambātā recalled a real Parsi watchmaker named Dhanji who would fill watches with snuff and subsequently tell his customers, 'look here, there is so much dirt in the watch'. According to Khambātā, due to the success of the play many of the real Dhanji's clients boycotted him and his business failed.[11] Khambātā also recalled a songstress named Tīrīrām who allegedly tricked boys from well-to-do families, convincing them that she would teach them how to sing. After plying them with spirits she would steal their possessions and send them off in a rented carriage to the *maidan* (esplanade) well. After the Pārśī Nāṭak Maṇḍalī (Parsi Theatrical Club) performed a farce by the name of *Tīrīrām*, 'people were made aware of her trickery'.[12] In a similar vein, *Bad ilat no Gofo* depicted the evils of alcoholism, opium, and gambling; *The Alchymist* showcased native superstitions; and *Bejun Soortee* (*Ūṭhāūgīr Śurtī*) cautioned against 'a Parsee ... who made his profession one of continued and interrupted cheating and cunning'. Other farces, among them *Deśī Pantujīo* (*Native Teachers*), *Badkārokī Maktab* (*The School for Scandal*), *Bāl Vīvā* (*Child Marriages*), and the farce of 'the dangerous practice of loading children with ornaments' carried their warnings in their titles. All of these plays played on themes that were extensively elaborated in the *Rāst*'s front pages.[13]

Thus begins 'the theatrical era among the Parsis', hailed as 'an era in the history of that enterprising race, [that] will ever point to the young men who have enlisted themselves in this glorious cause, as the Cynosure of wondering posterity'.[14] It was however crucial that in the development of a taste 'for the Noble and the Beautiful', the Parsi theatre be 'kept in subordination to Morality and Virtue'.[15] Likewise the *Bombay Gazette* proclaimed that Parsi 'genius, freed from the shackles of superstition and prejudice, shall have to own no restraints but those imposed upon it by morality and virtue'.[16] The consistent reference to 'morality and virtue' is noteworthy. Traditional custom was rapidly giving way to a new set of prescriptions undergirded by universal reason that seemingly emancipated peoples from despotism and false belief. Significantly, literacy in 'morality', as the Parsi reformist Manockjee Cursetjee noted, could not be brought about merely by education. As morality was the result not of a slow historical process but of a sudden, forceful rupture, the book and lecture readings in schools and colleges were deemed by Cursetjee and other reformists as insufficient to bring up moral development to the English standard.[17] Central to Adam Smith's 1759 *Theory of Moral Sentiments*, a foundational text in British India's curriculum, is the role of the 'spectator' who views his own behaviour through a looking-glass to judge the propriety of his own conduct.[18] The farce functioned not dissimilarly, reflecting appropriate and inappropriate manners for the many Indians for whom European-styled educational institutions and the press were inaccessible.

Uncoincidentally, the founders of the Parsi Theatrical Committee were reformists, and its actors Pestanjī Dhanjībhāi Māsṭar, Nāhānābhāi Rūstamjī Rāṇīnā, Dādābhāī Elīaṭ (Eliot), Mancerśāh Be. Meharhomjī, Bhīkhājī Kha. Mus (Moos), Kāvasjī Ho. Bīlīmorīyā, Rū. Ho. Hāthīrām, and Kāvasjī Naśarvānjī Kohīdārū were students educated in English who would subsequently become teachers, physicians, and playwrights.[19] Similarly, one of the group's frontrunners, Edaljī Naśarvānjī Majgāmvāḷā (Edaljī Prussia), was not only a teacher at the Elphinstone College but also editor of the *Rāst*. Consequently, the Parsi reform movement not only comprised a tightly knit group of Elphinstone College graduates but also functioned as a coherent ideological apparatus for sociocultural transformation. From the beginning, therefore, the Parsi theatre functioned as a node in a larger disciplinary network comprising school, press, and courtroom. Like the press, the theatre—which would rapidly become an integral component of the new vernacular public sphere—had become a panoptical field where individuals were subjected to compulsory visibility and examination. Farces dramatized social deviants such as Dhanji as precisely legible, enabling literate and illiterate audiences to adjudicate, much like the sitting magistrate, on morality and virtue or 'truth'. Through indirect carceral mechanisms—the vilification of characters (indigenous teachers), customs (child marriages), and beliefs (superstition)—bodies were disciplined, their gestures, activities, and postures becoming the objects of impalpable forms of coercion. All individuals—actors and audiences—witnessing and judging, arbitrating and disputing, were thus gradually transformed through a play of personages, lines, screens, and scenes. Innocuous caricatures exercised a subtly corporal power on Bombay's new theatre public, dramatizing how actors offstage were infinitely visible, knowable, and subjected to judgement, penalty, and possibly eventual redemption. Despite the introduction of the proscenium in the indigenous theatre, the observed had become infinitely observable and the borders between stage and public had been compositely blurred. With these hundreds of eyes, ever watching-judging-knowing, a violent colonial theatre came into being.

Persian Myth

The farce *Dhanji Garak* accompanied the three-part Persian mythological play *Roostum Zabooli and Sohrab*. 'Crowned with complete success', according to the *Bombay Gazette*, the first part of the drama began with a clown cutting vegetables and singing a country song in a field on the confines of a Persian jungle. Subsequently, Rustom, the hero of the play, is seen hunting at a distance in the jungle. Approaching the clown, Rustom commands him to roast his chase. The clown cooks the meat, which Rustom swallows in a few bites, confirming the clown's belief that he is superhuman. Rustom then goes to sleep, leaving his horse, Raksh, to roam in the fields while charging the clown to take care of the animal. However, the clown falls asleep; some 'Turks' attempt to steal the horse, but in the ensuing conflict the animal kills two of them. Consequently, on waking the clown finds two dead men and a missing horse and hence comes up with the excuse that strangers took the horse away and killed the men. Rustom, aggrieved on waking to see his horse gone, takes off for the plains of Tartary, tracing the footsteps of his creature. After his arrival at Summungan in Tartary, Rustom is invited by the king to reside in his palace as a guest. One night Teminee, the king's daughter, goes to Rustom, describes his heroic deeds, and 'unbosome(s) in enchanting language, the long-cherished love she bore for him', imploring him to take her as his partner. The play ends with the celebration of their marriage and Rustom's departure for Zabulistan.[20] Part II, performed on 12 November, begins with news of the birth of a son, Sohrab, who eventually grows into a robust boy, the 'prototype of his father in strength and proportions'. While playing one day, he is taunted by his friends of his illegitimate birth. Enraged, Sohrab sets off towards Zabulistan in search of his father against his mother's wishes. Meanwhile, Afrasiab, the tyrant of Turan, hears tales of Sohrab's strength and courage and sends a message couched in flattery to him to win him over to the Turanian side. Sohrab receives Afrasiab's message and joins the 300,000 strong army against the Iranians. During an expedition, the army besieges the Iranian fortress Soofed Dej; here Sohrab fights with Goordafreed, the daughter of the guardian of the fortress who is disguised as a man. On revealing herself as a woman, she falsely declares that she is in love with him and begs of him to marry her and set her free. Sohrab, deceived by her apparent sincerity is locked within the fortress by Goordafreed while her father sends a dispatch to Kykaoos, King of Iran. On receipt of the dispatch, Kykaoos convenes a council of warriors who decide that Rustom was indispensable to win the war. Eventually Rustom returns and unknowingly prepares himself for battle with his son. Here Part II ends.[21]

If the absence of a chronological history within Zoroastrian scripture was a troubling theme debated in the Parsi press, the theatre was not far behind. In the Grant Road Theatre, Persian history that was previously protean, comprising poems, myths, and moral instruction, was radically overhauled. *Rustom Zabooli and Sohrab* was a first tentative step towards the process of rediscovering a sequential narrative of the ancient Persian past based on European forms of scholarship, a theme that would reach its climax with the establishment of the Victoria Club in 1868. As religious authority was relocated from the temple and Panchayat to the press, reform association, and theatre—institutions that were ideologically and administratively allied as evinced through the play's advertisements[22]—the Persian mythological story began to serve a narratological function, transmuting into a chronicle for intellectual pursuit predicated on 'the exercise of reason rather than unquestioning faith'.[23] If Wilson's chief argument against the inaccuracies and fabrications of Parsi scripture was due to the admixture of history and myth, Parsi historical narrative had to bring itself to intellectual maturity through a process of demystification and, subsequently, insertion in evolutive time. Through the introduction of clowns and blind men within the plot, *Rustom Zabooli and Sohrab* rendered the legend mundane and therefore public, thus permitting criticism and contestation as it could no longer claim to provide divine revelation. Many plays based on Persian myths were performed in the early years of the Parsi theatre, among them *King Jamshed and the Tyrant Zokah* (1854), *The Defeat of Zohak and Accession of Furredoon to the Throne (Faredun)* (1855), and *King Afrasiab and Rustom Pehlvan* (1857). Like the press, therefore, the Parsi theatre was grounded within a religious sphere that had now become public—that is, visible and open to 'reform' within the three walls of the proscenium.[24]

Traditionalists

Intriguingly, the Parsi theatre's very first performance was described by the *Bombay Gazette* as 'a complete success [that] ... dissipated from [spectators'] minds the unfounded fears ventilated by false rumours against the amateurs'.[25] While the theatre was counselled by and shared members with the *Rāst*, its reformist zeal was consistently tempered by 'false rumours' advanced by a counterpublic of other, competing Parsi journals such as the *Cābuk*, *Āpakhatyār*, and the traditionalist *Jāme Jamśed*. The Pārśī Nāṭak Maṇḍalī was met with apprehension, suspicion, and even boycott. The editor of the *Cābuk*, Naśarvānjī Dorābjī Āpakhatyār (1835–78) (Fig. 3.1), accused the club of frivolity, aping of *śuratmā bhavaio tathā malārāo* (base Hindu theatre groups) and destructive potential, and complained of its farcical and deceitful portrayal of the community before an audience of Englishmen.[26]

These complaints amplified after the Pārśī Nāṭak Maṇḍalī produced *Nādarśānā Lagan* (*The Marriage of Nādarśā*) on 21 February 1857. An inebriated Parsi, Kāvaśśā Seṭhnā, agrees to wed his little boy Nādarśā to the daughter of a friend. A woman, bribed by the girl's mother, convinces Kāvaśśā of the girl's beauty; consequently, although the young girl has never been seen by her future in-laws, wedding arrangements are made. Kāvaśśā borrows thousands at exorbitant rates of interest, feasts transpire for weeks on end, and the marriage day finally arrives. The priests prepare to fasten the matrimonial tie, yet the bride has not been seen by the bridegroom or his family. An hour later, the mistake is unravelled. Little Nādarśā is wed forever to a one-eyed bride.[27] 'But', proclaimed the *Bombay Times* in its review of the performance, 'Kavassha is not a solitary fool of his race—his error may have been committed even yesterday by dozens. This is indeed a stigma upon the Parsees, who presume to the credit of initiating among themselves, all that is noble, good, and praiseworthy in the European element'.[28]

The *Bombay Times*' criticisms of child marriage, hitherto one of the most intimate social customs of a community that, in the reporter's words, prided itself on imitating all that was 'praiseworthy in the European element', gestated a special anxiety, one that would culminate in 1865 through the creation of 'The Parsi Marriage and Divorce Act' and

Fig. 3.1 Naśarvānjī Dorābjī Āpakhatyār (*Source* Paṭel, *PNTT*, 49. Courtesy: The Trustees, The K. R. Cama Oriental Institute, Mumbai)

a special Parsi legal regime. The Parsi theatre had inadvertently, unofficially, publicly, and not uncontroversially begun to assume a legislative function by taking over the role of administrative bodies such as the Parsi Panchayat that adjudicated on the legitimacy of custom. Audiences—lay and priestly, Parsi and non-Parsi—were able to voice their displeasure (i.e.

vote on existing communal custom), thereby anticipating the crystallization of Parsi matrimonial law in 1865. Shortly after the *Bombay Gazette*'s criticisms, the *Cābuk* decried the performance:

> In anticipation of joy and amusement, many persons disbursed their hard-earned money to see a certain play, however the majority were let down. Instead of being entertained they were saddened, in the place of *śokh* [merrymaking] they felt *śoṅg* [mourning] as these naïve performers depicted an entirely insincere and unequivocally deceitful portrait of our respectable community.

A 'nāṭakno ek kherkhāh' ('well-wisher of the theatre') responded forcefully: 'is the editor of the *Cābuk* blindfolded? When the theatre portrays evil customs that are evident for all to see in public, the writer [of the *Cābuk*] refuses to see so. What a disgrace such writers are!!'[29] Subsequently, the *Rāst* argued that the 'Parsi performers were providing *ḍāhāpaṇ* [wisdom] along with *gamat* [entertainment]. In doing so, they ... intended to reform people by rendering public and facilitating critique of our society's evil customs'. At work here were two divergent yet competing understandings of the function of the Parsi theatre. For the reformists, headed by the *Rāst*, the theatre was an extra-legal corrective apparatus for the scrutiny and denigration of prescriptive social customs in full view of Bombay's cosmopolitan public. In contrast, a growing group of traditionalists, headed by the now conservative *Cābuk*, resisted this normalizing mission, particularly in plays performed before non-Parsi audiences.[30] As in the conversion cases, 'publicity' gave the reformist theatre's juridical mechanisms official sanction; for a mounting faction of traditionalists, on the other hand, communal custom was 'private', and therefore the theatre was not licensed to vilify or attempt to transform existing communal practice.

Colonialism, as Sarkar notes, not only instigated the social reform movement but also galvanised other sources of hegemony that resisted the disciplinary programs of reformists with significant enthusiasm and success.[31] New, reformist forms of disciplinary control—from the denigration of child marriage to the appropriation of the English dinner table—introduced heterodoxy to the religious tradition,[32] prompting traditionalist and orthodox reaction to what was perceived as hasty, unthinking change. Orthodox Parsis, as Mitra Sharafi notes, desired strict adherence to preexisting Zoroastrian rituals, while reformists favoured practices that accommodated the circumstances of colonial modernity.[33] Consequently, these two factions sparred on a range of subjects: the reform of the Zoroastrian calendar, appropriate Parsi fashions, funerary and marriage customs, education, and not least the purpose of the new theatre. The *Rāst*'s reportage indicates that the first Parsi theatre troupe met considerable resistance from the traditionalist faction and was maligned for trying to make quick money at the expense of the community's reputation. Consequently, the *Rāst*'s articles reiterated time and again that 'the actors were not dependent on the theatre for their livelihood, plays were rehearsed during free time following work, and the Parsis failed to recognize the true value of these productions'.[34] Significantly, reformist attempts to buoy the position of the Parsi theatre in the vernacular public sphere prompted four, key, interrelated transformations in the conception of entertainment: (1) an internal, intellectual pursuit predicated on interior morality and a sign of colonial loyalty (2) a site for the ostensible modernization and emancipation of Indian women (3) a marker of prestige and self-representation (4) a locus for disciplining the communal body. As I will show, all four transformations rendered conspicuous the primary function of the theatrical public sphere: normative communal self-representation, self-discipline, and the organization of intra-communal power as public drama rather than rational-critical interlocution with the colonial state.

Rational Amusement and Shakespeare

On 11 January 1857, the *Rāst* published a front-page article entitled "Moj Śoḍhnār" (The Quest for Amusement), which proclaimed that it was impossible to procure entertainment from worldly things:

> Amusement is a peculiar thing, when you try to ensnare it, it flees. ... You may spend as much money and time as you will but it will always prance ahead and can never be grasped. ... My dear reader, you may indeed experience amusement but not from running after things external to you. All you need to do in order to procure it is to look within yourself.

Like religion, modern bourgeois recreation was conceived by the reformist press as a source of morality, promoting self-reflexivity and virtuous conduct. The disenchantment of religious ritual therefore paralleled the disenchantment of leisure, where a spiritual, essential moral core was distinguished and isolated from crude, myth-based bodily practice. An epistemic rupture thus reconfigured performative forms as precolonial economies of representation and play, from tantric mantras to the nautch, were superseded by forms of entertainment that epitomized the values of the ruling class.[35] In the interest of morality, science and progress, museums, zoos, gardens, vernacular literature, and especially the 'modern' theatre were allegedly of dire need in Bombay, even as alcohol, opium, *copaṭbājī* (traditional board games), *raṇḍībājī* (prostitution), and especially the nautch were relegated to the rank, squalid, and immoral.

Bombay's rapid development and the decline of princely states compelled performing women to seek their fortunes from wealthy *śeṭhs*, who hosted nautches to amuse professional acquaintances and government officials. By the mid-nineteenth century, however, Englishmen and reformists no longer distinguished between honourable performers and prostitutes.[36] On 14 November 1858, the *Rāst* published an article about the depravity of the older generation of *śeṭhs* who patronized *rāṇḍs* and *veśīās* (variably translated as women/dancers/prostitutes) at their *vāḍīs* at the outer limits of the city:

> To invite a woman who is publicly recognized as a prostitute into the inner sanctum of one's home is depraved and revolting. ... When reformed, knowledgeable men who have gained from the use of reason observe the wealthy inviting prostitutes into their homes, they truly comprehend what virtue and morality are amongst our people. ... If our *śeṭhs* want to entertain their guests there are many other alternatives.

Accordingly, when the sons of two of India's prominent mercantile families, Kharshedji Cama and Satyendranath Tagore, patronized 'alternative' entertainments such as exhibitions of coins and manuscripts in lieu of the nautch, the *Rāst* was euphoric.[37] 'Instead of doing *galagālī* (nonsense) in *vāḍīs*, it is much better to dine at home, spend a little, and visit the theatre', the newspaper proclaimed. Noteworthy here is the attempt to fortify the reputation of the Parsi theatre not only by juxtaposing precolonial, performance traditions and forms of social organization against modern plays but also by equating theatre with scientific entertainments such as exhibitions and the study of manuscripts. However, like museums, zoos, and public lectures, its accessibility made it a more powerful didactic tool than literature: 'Many people want to relax after work and so they become alcoholics. As they cannot read and use books, they need some entertainment and as they are unable to find entertainment elsewhere, they go to bars. At home there are more fights, more addictions and the public is affected...'.[38] The theatre, in the reformist purview, was therefore unambivalently pedagogical, inculcating virtue, morality, and obedience through 'the adoption of Christian sentiment if not of doctrine'.[39]

On 23 May 1857 the *Rāst* published notice of a performance of *The Taming of the Shrew* and the farce *ek "dhutārā" athvā "jādugar"* about superstitions, marking the crucial transition on the Parsi stage from Persian mythology to Gujarati translations of Shakespeare.[40] This transition was prompted by the English view that 'Iranian myths were not beneficial to the public at large' as they contained 'improbable stories of Iranian heroes which had better been allowed to drop into oblivion, as totally unsuited to the advanced spirit of the age'.[41] The repertoire of the Parsi theatre thus transmuted, from the more palpably coercive micro-penalties of *Dhanji Garak* to the subtler disciplinary apparatus of Shakespeare. No longer merely a microscope of conduct, Parsi adaptations of Shakespeare served to wean 'affections from the Persian muse' and 'inculcate a taste for the arts, the sciences and the literature of England'.[42] Translations and theatrical productions of Shakespeare, as Gauri Viswanathan and Jyotsna Singh have persuasively shown, reinforced the myth of English cultural authority and supremacy, a myth that was indispensable to colonial rule.[43] The Anglicists' triumph over the Orientalists through William Bentinck's English Education Act of 1835, which instituted English as the language of instruction in Indian education, was part of an elaborate design to create affordable, obedient clerks and civil servants for the lower levels of public administration. Through the promotion in 1855 of English literature as an important subject for the civil service examination, Shakespeare became the key for Indians' entry into public office, thereby politically legitimizing the agenda of the Anglicization of the subcontinent. The universality of the secular bard—whose works were both amenable to translation and appealing to the Indian public due to their repeated allusions to destiny, fortune, and mythical figures such as fairies—allowed for the estrangement between literature and religion while (initially) instilling 'morality'; that is, those qualities that were deemed necessary for an acquiescent, regimented colony.[44] Moreover, Shakespeare played an instrumental role in suppressing material relations. England's national literature designated English character as a moral and cultural benchmark, an ideal self, and an ideal rule distinct from the realities of invasion, monetary exploitation, and punitive action against locals.[45] Accordingly, Shakespeare functioned as a conciliating blueprint of social control clouding the material relationship between ruler and ruled, colonizer and colonized and assisting the consolidation of a moral civil society.

Gujarati adaptations of Shakespeare thus bore the ritual marks of aptitude and allegiance rather than discernible disciplinary submission. Conspicuously the turn to Shakespeare in the year of the Indian Rebellion coincided with other performative manifestations of loyalty such as the Junī Pārsī Nāṭak Maṇḍalī's (Old Parsi Theatrical Club) production, along with the *Comedy of Errors*, of a farce on unethical 'servants'.[46] Similarly, the Students Amateur Club performed *Pizarro* alongside a farce on the 'tyrannies and excesses of a Nabob over his subjects'; the Zoroastrian Nāṭak Maṇḍalī performed the play *Hīndu ane Fīraṅgī Rāj vace Tafāvat* (*The Battle between the Hindu and Foreign Raj*); and the Indian Theatrical Club performed *Nānā Sāhebno Natak* (*The Play of Nānā Sāheb*).[47] This last play included a song against the allegedly evil Nana Saheb of Peshwa that was immensely popular and often sung in Parsi neighbourhoods:

> Our child Nana has committed a bad deed,
> He has been utterly disloyal,
> Oh sinner, thief, criminal, oh murderer of the innocent
> Your evil deeds will bring you to a pitiable state.[48]

These demonstrations of loyalty on stage were accompanied by similar performances off stage. When the revolt broke out in the upper provinces of India, the Parsis immediately performed a *jaśan* (religious ceremony) for the safety of their rulers and 'embraced the first opportunity of presenting an address to the Governor, Lord Elphinstone, assuring him of their loyalty and attachment to the British Government…'.[49] Subsequently, the Parsi press went to great lengths to contradict the prevalent view that there existed 'no virtue but under a white skin',[50] to prove that the past administration of India was not 'one unvaried system of unworthy compromise and concession to Native prejudices and Native interests',[51] and to attest the Parsis' unwavering loyalty to the Company. This was achieved through articles written in English that, in the newspaper's view, would 'bring [natives] into ready communion with the civilization of their enlightened rulers, render the views and feelings of the governed and governing classes more intelligible to each other and prevent the machinations of the evil-disposed'.[52]

Shortly after the *Rāst's* commencement of its English section, in 1861 Parsi students and alumni of the Elphinstone College established the Elphinstone Theatrical Club that performed Shakespeare in English. Fealty to the company and the Crown was thus cultivated and expressed through both strategic performances of tyrannical nabobs and unruly servants as well as the more discrete testimony of English drama. Supported by *seṭhs* such as Sorabjee Jamsetjee Jeejeebhoy and Jagannath Shankarsheth, the Governor Bartle Frere, and English personnel of the Government's Education Department, the troupe was coached by the English actors Hamilton Jacob and Mr and Mrs Bennee.[53] This club was, according to the *Times of India*, 'the second instance of natives acting on the stage in the English language' after some Baboos of Calcutta who had played *Othello* a few years previously. Having rehearsed for two months, the troupe made its debut at the Grant Road Theatre on Monday 22 July 1861 with two comediettas entitled *Bengal Tiger* and *Love's Quarrels*.[54] In its first year it gave fourteen performances including Moliere's *Mock Doctor*, *Twelve Months' Honey-Moon*, and *The Taming of the Shrew*.[55] In 1862, 'at the request of some native gentlemen', it produced two plays in Gujarati: *Othello* and *The Case of the Fraud at Hyderabad by the Poona Thugs*.[56] Yet under the leadership of Kuvarjī Sorābjī Nājar (who would go on to become one of the Parsi theatre's leading figures despite a bitter end) (Fig. 3.2),[57] it continued to expose Bombay's public to a cornucopia of English plays such as *Our Wife: or The Rose of Amiens*, *Upstairs and Downstairs*, *The Merchant of Venice*, *Going to the Derby*, *A Lucky Hit*, *The Honeymoon*, *Living too Fast*, *Village Lawyer*, *Mock Doctor*, *Bombastes Furioso*, *Thumping Legacy*, *The Lying Valet*, *The Illustrious Stranger*, *Our Wife*, *Two Gentlemen of Verona*, *Sham Doctor Whitebait at Greenwich*, *Taming a Tiger*, and *Diamond Cut Diamond*.[58]

The Elphinstone, the professed 'nucleus of the [modern] Indian drama', performed plays in English 'with the view of strengthening their acquaintance with that language ... the main idea of the association being to improve themselves in English, to gratify their histrionic ambition or vanity, and to attempt to cultivate among their fellow countrymen a taste for a better class of entertainment than that to which they had for some time been accustomed'.[59] This English-language objective also facilitated the rise of many of the troupe's actors, 'the interpreters—the connecting links between the rulers and the ruled',[60] who went on to become

Fig. 3.2 Kuvarjī Sorābjī Nājar, member of the Elphinstone Theatrical Club (*Source* Paṭel, *PNTT*, 7. Courtesy: The Trustees, The K. R. Cama Oriental Institute, Mumbai)

prominent doctors, lawyers, teachers, and civil servants, thereby bringing to fruition the Anglicizing mission of Shakespeare. Dhanjīśāh Pārakh (Fig. 3.3) became a lieutenant colonel, Naśarvānjī Pārakh (Fig. 3.4) became a famous surgeon in Rangoon, Jamśedjī Dalāl became the head of Baroda's education department, and Jamśedjī Unvālā became a professor at Banāras College.[61]

The Elphinstone's enactments of Shakespeare on a college stage with ancient Greek scenery which smacked of 'classical reminiscences', entailed the dissemination of a relational power through an embodied knowledge of memorized verses, correct speech, sustained gesture, and costuming.[62] For instance, the onstage appropriation of European wigs (made by sticking goat hair to white caps that smelled of rotten fish), white-face, and pseudo Italian and Spanish costumes coincided with transformed Parsi tastes for clothing. During this time, while traditionalist Parsis continued to wear *angarkhās* (long cotton coats) and silk or cotton pyjamas (loose drawers supported at the waist by a cord) that were of Gujarati origin, reformist Parsis replaced the *pāghḍī* (Parsi turban) with a semi-English hat made by the Chinese from lighter material in keeping with the pseudo-scientific dictum of the need to keep one's head cool for the benefit of the brain.[63] Consequently, in addition to the perpetuation of the myth of English refinement through rational entertainment, a subtle coercion was brought to bear at the level of corporeal mechanisms—postures, language, discourse, emotions, mannerisms, and clothing. By the actors' passing as English through Shakespeare, the internal organization of the body was increasingly offered up to a normative structure of authority that transformed physical appearances and bearings both within and outside the proscenium.

Women

Yet Shakespeare served another more critical purpose. On the eve of the first Parsi performance of Shakespeare in 1857, the *Strī Bodh* (*Female Instructor*), a literary pamphlet founded for the moral and intellectual upliftment of Parsi women by the Parsi lawmaker Sohrabjee Shahpurjee Bengalee,[64] published a synopsis of *The Taming of the Shrew* for its female readers. Subsequently, in its description of the 1857 performance, the *Rāst* described the play as a depiction of the 'need to bring women to the right path through tenderness as opposed to physical beatings'.[65] A year later, an advertisement was published of the Junī Pārsī Nāṭak Maṇḍalī's

Fig. 3.3 Dhanjīśāh Navrojī Pārakh, member of the Elphinstone Theatrical Club (*Source* Paṭel, *PNTT*, 9. Courtesy: The Trustees, The K. R. Cama Oriental Institute, Mumbai)

Fig. 3.4 Naśarvānjī Navrojī Pārakh, member of the Elphinstone Theatrical Club (*Source* Paṭel, *PNTT*, 36. Courtesy: The Trustees, The K. R. Cama Oriental Institute, Mumbai)

'very praiseworthy effort' under the management of Kāvasjī Kohīdārū of the first performance of a Parsi play exclusively for Parsi women.[66] In the newspaper's words, *The Taming of the Shrew* in the Gujarati language with Italian costumes and the farce *ek "dhutārā" athvā "jādugar"* about local superstitions constituted a significant landmark in the movement for Parsi women's reform.[67]

As early as 11 March 1840, Jamsetji Jeejeebhoy had been praised for throwing a ball in honour of the Queen of England at which occasion his wife and daughters-in-law were present.[68] Jeejeebhoy's own daughters received a Western-style education in secrecy, even as, in 1842, a Meheribai Hormusjee Shroff publicly allowed her daughter Dosibai to attend an English private school, a social precedent that was severely opposed.[69] By 1855, the Student's Society's Girls School had 504 Parsi pupils as opposed to 65 Gujarati Hindu and 170 Marathi Hindu students.[70] A few years later, a Parsi girls' school that taught Gujarati literature, mathematics, ethics, and Parsi theology was established followed by the Alexandra School for Girls that was founded in 1863.[71] In the imagining of mothers as the carriers of modernity, it was professed that 'good mothers were needed for substantial reforms … [that the Parsis were] backward in domestic happiness, and [that the need existed] for moral and intelligent women, a Parsi Florence nightingale'.[72] Geraldine Forbes describes how loyal Indian wives were needed for loyal husbands. English-educated women, nurturing their children as accultured Anglophiles, would foil the mutinous schemes devised in unreachable zenanas.[73] Accordingly, an English education that included Shakespeare served to 'prevent the machinations of the evil-disposed' among not only men but also women. The underlying concern for female education, according to Forbes, was not with the individual development of women, but rather with the creation of companions who would facilitate opportunities for social and financial mobility for a new middle class.[74]

Feminist research on social reform in India has demonstrated how the private subjugation of women was masked by the conferral of public privileges. The reformist alignment of communal custom to bourgeois norms of domesticity resulted in a new form of patriarchy that did not interrogate but merely recast previous forms of subordination.[75] The nineteenth century was characterized by a paroxysm of discussion on the subject of Indian women, yet female voices were marginalized in these same discussions. Instead women functioned as the site on which traditionalists and reformists waged war for political and sociocultural authority through a variety of issues such as the necessity of English-language pedagogy, appropriate clothing, raising the Parsi age of consent, and abolishing child marriage that often denied women the right to an education.[76] However, few issues provoked as much consternation as Parsi women's entry into public spaces. In the mid-nineteenth century, Parsi women desisted from appearing in public as 'the native women met with in the streets belong[ed] to the lower orders'.[77] The juxtaposition of precolonial forms of entertainment such as the nautch, associated with sexual promiscuity, against modern, moral entertainments such as Shakespeare mirrored the definition of respectable Parsi women against other socio-economically marginalized women such as nautch girls who enjoyed self-sufficiency and access to the public areas of the boulevard and bazaar. The subtle disciplinary mechanism of Shakespeare thus went in tandem with new forms of policing female bodies. As Sumanta Banerjee has shown, a new form of seclusion was imposed on reformed women, whose character and behaviour, including modes of diversion, were expressed in contradistinction to that of 'the lower orders'.[78] Consequently, the reform of religious custom and tradition provided the backdrop for not only the reconfiguration of indigenous modes of entertainment on the basis of Victorian social norms but also the institution of a new public realm for moral women. In 1848, a Mr Hīlī of horse gymnastics fame performed exclusively for *deśī* (native) women, thereby introducing the practice of respectable plays for exclusively female benefit. Similarly, a Sinor Romānī performed several times in the first months of 1858 for women.[79] Subsequently, as mentioned above, the 'entertaining yet moral' *The Taming of the Shrew*—the first Parsi play performed solely for Parsi women—was performed on 28 April by the Junī Pārsī Nāṭak Maṇḍalī (Old Parsi Theatrical Company) under the management of Kāvasjī Naśarvānjī Kohīdārū.[80] The conception of rational, moral, pedagogic amusement thus not only facilitated the progressive acceptance of the Parsi theatre by the public but also sanctioned the entry of women into public spaces. At the numerous Parsi and non-Parsi theatrical performances produced exclusively for the benefit of 'native women' over the next decade, husbands waited for their wives in specially designated seating areas outside the theatre, an ordeal tempered by the presence of a band for their amusement,[81] and by 1860 Dave Carson of the San Francisco Minstrels was crooning:

> I've seen a deal of gaity, and lead a jolly life,
> My name is Ratai Madame, the Parsee Doctor's wife,

> The thing I most excel in, is dressing neat and tight,
> In silken suits and patent boots, the brightest of the bright.[82]

However, a veritable storm erupted in the vernacular press in September 1858 after the Parsi reformist and advocate of female education Manockjee Cursetjee hosted a mixed gathering of Parsi women and men.[83] Cursetjee, who had been at loggerheads with Jamsetjee Jeejeebhoy on the topic of women's education, was attacked by Āpakhatyār, the editor of the now traditionalist *Cābuk*, who in turn was reprimanded by the *Rāst* for his 'base, false and unfounded' attack.[84] The *Rāst* took pains to make *jāher* (public) the truth of what took place at this joint meeting through a three-part series. All of the women were allegedly accompanied by their husbands, men and women were seated separately, conversation was *nītī* (moral) and *nīrdoś* (innocent), and subsequently, all the guests returned home.[85] A few weeks later, the Zoroastrian Nāṭak Manḍalī rubbed salt in the wound when it performed the farce *Pārsī oratonā chuṭāpaṇā* (*The Liberty of Parsi Women*), which parodied the *khāṅgī* (private) affairs of Cursetjee's family, presumably the 'mixed gatherings' that he controversially hosted.[86] Although the troupe subsequently regretted the production, the *Rāst* demanded a public apology on behalf of Cursetjee's family and, in a curious turn of events, argued that theatre troupes that lampooned the private affairs of Parsi families should not be patronized by the *prajā* (public).

> We have been informed that the aforementioned Parsi troupe now regrets their inappropriate behaviour but the public cannot be convinced of the change in their outlook and behaviour if they repent in private. ... This is the beginning of the Parsi theatre and if, at its very commencement, a Parsi troupe behaves reprehensibly it affects the reputation of all the other groups.[87]

Even though the *Rāst* had publicly vilified the private behaviour of families a few years prior, the tables had swiftly turned when the newspaper reproached the Zoroastrian's public denigration of a 'respectable family'. At stake now was neither the search for 'truth' through publicity nor the emancipation of Parsi women but rather the deliberation between reformist and traditionalist understandings of public and private realms and, by analogy, of the self-definition of Parsi society. In October the traditionalist *Mumbai Samācār* and *Jāme Jamśed* posed seven questions to the Parsi public:

1. Are the Parsis imitating new social conventions to outdo each other? Are they examining their advantages and disadvantages before appropriating them?
2. Isn't it necessary for women to be completely cultivated, knowing full well the importance of conserving their chastity and morals before they mingle with men in public?
3. Have Parsi women been educated adequately?
4. Shouldn't the reformers discuss whether the reforms they intend to introduce are beneficial and if the community is equipped to take these up?
5. Shouldn't the reformists be more concerned with the overall welfare of the community than with their personal benefit?
6. If the imitation of certain reforms would cause mischief, shouldn't such reforms be avoided for the present?
7. Do Parsi men possess the courage required to defend their women against calumny? Do Parsis possess the values needed to speak to women with respect and decency?[88]

The rhetorical and hermeneutic shifts—between adequate education for Parsi women, the conservation of 'chastity and morals', colonial mimicry, Parsi values, and the overall welfare of the community—indicate the stakes of Parsi women's unrestricted movement. To open up women to the public was akin, I would argue, to exposing the community's innermost values to libel. Thus, when, in January 1868, the first Parsi 'family' performance of *Much Ado about Nothing* for both men and women took place at the Grant Road Theatre—a pyrrhic victory for reformists—reformists went to great lengths to ensure the respectability of the production, prohibiting 'servants', unaccompanied children, and children accompanied with single men from entering, proofreading the farce for objectionable terms, and electing a committee of 'high-ranking men' that thoroughly examined the play's rehearsals.[89] Nevertheless, critics rushed to point out after the production that many men ogled with *nīc nazar* (immoral gaze) through their opera glasses at 'innocent Parsi women' at the theatre.[90] Similarly, in 1869, a 'very bad' theatre company reserved an entire section of seats for single men who stared with *kharāb* (immoral) *nazar* at women.[91] 'We must be far more vigilant now as women have begun to attend the theatre', an unnamed writer proclaimed.[92]

Intriguingly, this ocular vocabulary echoes the terms first used to describe the deliberation of tradition in the public sphere. *Nazar*, previously coterminous with 'seeing one's faults before the *juddins* (nonbelievers) do' and 'being observed by other communities' in order 'to see' between pure and impure tradition, was here cited to critique the unavoidable visibility of women, the carriers of communal tradition. *Nazar* and its attendant visual frame served to deindividuate women, characterizing them as coterminous with a set of traditions that were perceived as alternately in need of reform or under attack. This discursive shift therefore designates how religious custom and its emblem—women—were subjected to a multiplicity of gazes that constituted part of the overall functioning of power. Visibility made it possible to know tradition, to alter tradition, and to exercise a subtly corporeal authority on tradition. Hence, we find the paradigmatic traditionalist scrutiny on women, as well as the gendering of the entire colonial project through the homology of sexual, economic, and political domination.[93] As Lata Mani has shown, women were neither subjects nor objects of the nineteenth century; the 'women's question' in indigenous movements for social reform was not about women. Rather, women functioned as the site for sociopolitical confrontation between the colonizer and colonized, modernists and traditionalists, through debates on what constituted authentic cultural tradition. Scripture rather than custom was viewed by missionaries, colonial officials, and the indigenous elite as the locus of this authenticity. Accordingly, women and scripture constituted 'interlocking grounds' for the social reformist reconfiguration of tradition.[94]

Law

As there existed no determinate set of Parsi scriptures, it was on the basis of orientalist literature on ancient Iran that Parsi reformists campaigned against child marriages, the *mā̃thū̃bā̃nū̃* (women's head scarf or the 'hideous band of calico'), and customs that denied menstruating women the freedom to socialize and labouring women medical facilities.[95] Simultaneously, the *Rā̃st* advocated for mixed gatherings by drawing on orientalist literature on ancient Iran through a series that described the ancient Zoroastrian practice delineated in the *Zend Avesta* of men and women socializing in public.[96] The newspaper reasoned that in Sassanian times (third to seventh century CE), Zoroastrian customs such as mixed social gatherings were 'neither corrupted nor adulterated', but after Parsis' exile to India, habits that were alien to authentic Zoroastrianism such as the *pardanaśīn* (the veil) were appropriated.[97] The reformists had thus begun to draw on oriental literature and history to justify social transformations that were viewed by traditionalists as mere mimicry of the English, thereby consummating the process of social transformation first initiated by Wilson. Noteworthy here is the incipient conception that an unwavering body of original, unadulterated customs had been despoiled during subsequent Hindu and/or Islamic interludes. Citing ethnographic accounts such as Ker Porter's *Travels* (1817–1820), which described women in the Persian Empire as 'neither shut up from public society, nor necessarily veiled in the presence of men', the reformists 'discovered' a utopian Persian past in order to reconfigure existing social practice. In the theatre, this process of 'discovery' would eventually take the form of a return to the Persian mythological play (see Chapter 4).[98]

Crucially, the specific formulary of scripture–women–authentic tradition had palpable fiscal, statutory, and corporeal repercussions. As religious affiliation had to be jurisdictional rather than merely sociocultural, government officials and English-educated reformists began advocating for systematized forms of communal administration or a set of personal laws. On 20 August 1855, a *jāher sabhā* (public meeting) of the entire community was organized to discuss the anomalous position of the Parsis, who, having no regular code, were subjected to the Islamic law in the mofussil and English law in Bombay.[99] A code of matrimony and inheritance would express the community's essential values by not only reconfiguring all Parsi customs (from polygamy to patriarchal privileges of inheritance) but also putting the community on a level playing field with Hindus and Muslims, who had possessed Anglo-Hindu and Anglo-Islamic law from the early years of colonial administration.[100] This first organized attempt to institute a special Parsi legal regime was eminently theatrical. Like the Parsi theatre, lawmaking was a medium for the articulation of group identity: spectators turned into actors and voted on the meetings, minutes, and resolutions that were eventually passed to the managing committee. The consolidation of Parsi law thus marked the culmination of the protracted process of the transformation of the most intimate aspects of Parsi communal life allegorized in plays such as *Dhanji Garak*, *Rustom Zabooli and Sohrab*, *Nādarśānā Lagan*, and

Pārsī oratonā chuṭāpaṇā where reformists and traditionalists fought for representative power. Chronotic markers of civilizational backwardness and progress guided the negotiation of Parsi law: 'Our friends should remember that progress is the law of humanity. To stick to immemorial customs when they conflict with the advancing civilization of the age, is to fall back on immemorial barbarism', the Law Commission argued.[101] After several subcommittee sessions and the distribution of three thousand copies of the drafted resolutions for obtaining Parsi public opinion, on 31 March 1860, a petition was sent to the Legislative Council of India to pass 'a Draft Code of Inheritance, Succession and other matters' into formal law.[102] While the draft code recognized the separate individuality of the wife as in the English law, allowing her the same rights and privileges to dispose of her property as her husband, women were only allowed a fourth of the share of the property of an intestate father, even as sons were allowed one share each. This significant disparity of distribution was not overlooked by the Legislative Council, even as traditionalists in the committee attributed the proposal to 'immemorial customs'.[103]

Parsi women were therefore the locus of contention within the drafting of Parsi law, propping up two entirely contradictory claims: the intrinsically tyrannical nature and civilizational backwardness of a religious tradition; and the timeless, spiritual superiority of indigenous custom. Naoroji Fardunji (one of the founders of the Parsi theatre) and Manockjee Cursetjee (the object of the Zoroastrian Nāṭak Maṇḍalī's satire on mixed gatherings) both played fundamental roles in shifting British opinion to the reformist perspective.[104] Drawing on their double experience in the courtrooms of the Parsi theatre and the colonial judiciary, Fardunji and Cursetjee 'manage[d] the earliest legislative project to codify matrimonial law in British India'.[105] Mitra Sharafi describes how they created a particular reformist vision of the Parsi home by reconfiguring a prescriptive image of the patriarch: while the new Parsi law of inheritance stipulated the spread of wealth among numerous family members, the new Parsi matrimonial law permitted a married man to select his children's partners and to corporeally punish his wife. Accordingly, the new Parsi law—created exclusively by elite, socially privileged male graduates of the Elphinstone College and erstwhile performers of Shakespeare—reconfigured patriarchal privilege even as Parsi women were held up as testimony of the community's civilizational advancement.

Moreover—as in the theatre, as Chapter 4 demonstrates—orientalist scholarship on ancient Persia cast a long shadow: traditionalist customs were attributed to Hindu influence and contrasted with those of the ancient Persians. For instance, Cursetjee and Fardunji consulted Martin Haug, who reiterated that it was not 'the spirit of old Zoroastrianism to exclude women from the right of Inheritance',[106] leading the commission to declare that 'three-fourths of ... [Parsi] social customs are borrowed from the Hindoos. So that if any innovations are being made in *these*, it is evident that the religion of the Parsees is not touched in the slightest degree'.[107] The creation of Parsi law therefore represented the desire to return to authentic Zoroastrian tenets, which were, according to the British commissioners and orientalists, superior to those of the Hindus.[108] The widespread epistemic rupture first prompted by Wilson had thus reached its apogee—oriental scholars functioned as 'legislative intellectuals' determining what constituted as authentic Parsi law by disenchanting Parsi ritual and emptying custom of history.

By attributing 'backward' traditions to Hindu influence, lawmaking therefore instigated the dangerous but long-standing idea that Parsis were more civilized than the Hindus. By analogy, the Panchayat, which implemented these ostensibly backward, inauthentic rules, increasingly came under fire.[109] Cursetjee, previously the object of traditionalist scorn, successfully lobbied for replacing the Parsi Panchayat with Parsi matrimonial courts to resolve marital disputes.[110] Additionally, the Panchayat's arbitrary dispensation of justice in Parsi domestic disputes (which often conflicted with English constitutional law) and the hereditary election of its members (a practice 'contrary' to the wishes of the Parsi public) strengthened the reformist view that it used old tools in governing a new people. The conflict between the old and the new, traditional authority and newly instituted self-governmental practices predicated on a modern, liberal education had prompted calls for a newly elected Parsi Panchayat organized through a *jāher mijlas* (public meeting) under the auspices of the Parsi lawmaking commission.[111]

The Parsi Panchayat

On 21 April 1860 the Zoroastrian Nāṭak Manḍalī performed a farce entitled *Pārśī Pancāet*, which depicted the corrupt workings of the Parsis' administrative body. This performance was, incontrovertibly, a direct consequence of the Parsi legal drama taking place on the larger stage of empire. As early as January 1855, the *Rāst*, the Panchayat's fiercest critic, not only rebuked its *kārobārī* (administration) due to the absence of written law, reports, elections, and *jāher sabhās* (public meetings),[112] but also described the Panchayat's anxiety that a play criticizing its workings would come to fruition.[113] When five years later it did, the *Rāst* condemned the 'hidden motives' behind the traditionalist faction's 'false and baseless criticism of the play'.[114] While the *Jāme Jamśed*, *Cābuk*, and *Āpakhatyār* rushed to condemn the performance, it was defended by the letter writer 'Ek Dost' ('A Friend') as a valuable contribution to the Parsi stage. 'The *Jāme* can't tell the difference between chalk and cheese!' 'Ek Dost' declared.[115] A few days later 'A Reporter' denounced 'Ek Dost' for his inaccurate portrayal and undue praise of the performance. The *Pārśī Pancāet* and a second play, *Sehtān te Faresto kem thāe* (*How a Devil Becomes an Angel*), were performed, according to 'A Reporter', 'solely to irritate a few newspapers'.[116] This was the tip of the iceberg of a long-standing dispute not only between the orthodox *Jāme* and *Cābuk* on the one hand and the reformist *Rāst* on the other, but also between several theatre groups, which were supported by warring factions. Parsi newspapers carried advertisements and reviews and even sold play tickets for their preferred theatre companies: the reformist *Rāst* supported the Old Parsi Theatrical Club,[117] the *Jāme* aligned with the Students Amateur Club, and *Āpakhatyār* supported the Pārsī Stage Players.[118] Each journal condemned the fabricated theatrical reviews of the others,[119] and each warned its readers that Parsis who patronized the other groups' plays were not 'true' Zoroastrians.[120] The Parsi theatrical public sphere was therefore grounded in a mutually imbricated relationship with the press, implying a harnessing of multiple channels in order to convey divisive ideologies through mediatized communication of different kinds.[121] Onstage enactments percolated offstage into the performance of power being played out in the Parsi legal world at large.

Eventually, the dispute left the Parsi public sphere, spilling over into the English press. In 1862 a 'Juliet' wrote in the *Bombay Gazette* of her supposed curiosity to see the Parsi drama, which led her to the theatre. 'But, Sir, I was sadly disappointed', she continued,

> The performance was a complete failure. ... The most beautiful tragedy of 'Lavinia' (which was very wretchedly rendered into Goozratee) was enacted in a slovenly manner, without the least sign of any life or feeling in the youthful actors, who each and all seemed merely to recite their respective parts, as if they were at school.[122]

After a similar critique by 'Togatus', a 'Romeo' replied:

> Juliet and Togatus are perhaps actuated by one and the same motive, viz:—to find an opportunity to vent their bile on a Company of Amateur Actors with whom some time past they are, (to use a vulgar phrase) at 'loggerheads'. ... I would strongly recommend [the actors] not to care for a class of native penny-a-liners and boy Editors fresh from school. ... But in future they ought to admit the Reporters of Goozeratee Journals like the *Rast Goftar &c.*, or at least those of the English dailies; even one of whom I scarcely noticed on the evening of their last performance. These gentlemen not being actuated by envy or rivalry, will pronounce their fair opinions, and thus shut the mouths of all detractors in the future. And now I bid *Juliet* and *Togatus* adieu. But not without hinting them, that Tybalt, or Pizarro, or Iago, would have been more appropriate names, instead of 'Juliet' and 'Togatus'.[123]

After a series of letters by a 'Togatus' and 'Pseudo-Togatus', the dispute here ended: '* * We cannot admit any more of this nonsense.—Ed. *B. G.*'[124]

This 'nonsense', I would argue, suggests several noteworthy characteristics of the new vernacular public sphere of British India. Patently, the new crop of Gujarati journals and the incipient Parsi theatre had little to do with bringing Indians into contact with the state for the exercise of political sovereignty through rational-critical discourse. Nor was this public sphere, at this stage, an inclusive arena where private citizens could deliberate topics without regard to creed, caste, or sex. The normatively masculine, vernacular public sphere, highly stratified by religion, language, and class, was not an interlocutory realm where the state could be meaningfully brought into contact with the needs of society. Instead, the minor courtroom of the press and theatre facilitated, first and foremost, self-inspection and self-policing within linguistic, ethnic, and religious communities, thereby excluding certain voices at the very outset. The genealogical account of rational-critical debate in the colonies, dating in the Parsi case back to Wilson's first theological attack, was embedded in the larger operation of a nocuous, normalizing power. Although in Europe belief had been situated outside the realm of public discussion, in the colonies rational-critical debate had rendered politics, religion, and the public inextricably intertwined by constituting communities as precisely legible and knowable. The parameters of debate had been defined at the outset: the 'domain of common concern' was spiritual rather than state based; politics dealt with the intimate sphere of domestic affairs rather than consequential critique of the colonial public administration. The colonial public was constituted through new hierarchies of knowledge, the redistribution of values, and the reconfiguration of the most intimate and cherished aspects of communal life through a constantly repeating ritual of power. Analogously, the Parsi theatre and the press were key arenas for thinking through the politics of religion in British India and functioned, at least initially, as a representational field where diverse factions fought for the authority to represent the community before the colonial administration. The petty, malicious bickering between Parsi reformist and traditionalist factions in the English press therefore suggests an elaborate performance of power within a self-representational rather than interlocutory realm, where a general visibility created a comprehensive, articulated, and internalized control. The question of 'Whose side will you take?' appeared to be the Parsi *cri de coeur* to an all-knowing, all-seeing arbitrator.

The Culture of Charity

The self-representational character of the public sphere was especially conspicuous through the growth of a civic culture of charity. The formulation of an imperial public culture predicated on 'patriotism' (that is, symbols of loyalty) first gained momentum in the aftermath of the Mutiny of 1857 but reached its height in the 1860s. On 12 April 1861 the Battle of Fort Sumter began, marking the beginning of the American Civil War and the discontinuation of the South's cotton supplies to Lancashire. As a result, Bombay's cotton exports soared from 87,323 bales in 1859–60 to 208,138 in 1864–1865, its value rising 150% from Rs 16 crores to Rs 40 crores.[125] The rising price of Indian cotton prompted scores of people, enticed by the prospect of amassing fortunes, to move to Bombay from the mofussil, and the city's population rose to 816,562 in 1864, a figure that would not be reached again until 1891.[126] With railway lines tapping the Deccan in one direction and Central India in the other—and with a geographic location that could control the trade of South Asia and East Africa, from Zanzibar to Karachi—Bombay was 'striving to gain a position inferior only to that of London, Liverpool, or New York'.[127] In those days of 'financial delirium' the *seṭhs* helped establish numerous banks, financial associations, and land reclamation companies, stimulating unbounded speculation.[128] Much of this speculation was carried out on the basis of the commonly held view that the benevolent *seṭhs* that founded these banks were 'respectable, trust-worthy and honourable', an image aided through the performance of philanthropy. With the sudden influx of wealth, Bombay's prosperous mercantile community began to allocate their riches to prominent, charitable schemes—from constructing public buildings to reclaiming large swathes of land from the eastern and western foreshores—for the lasting improvement of the city.[129] The University Library building and the Rajabai tower, the Jamsetji Jijibhoy School of Art, hospitals at Colaba and Byculla, the Victoria and Albert Museum, the Sassoon Mechanics Institute, and forty drinking fountains owe their existence to the largesse of the speculators of 1861–1865. Yet, Bombay was not the only beneficiary of these riches. In the year 1862 alone, Cowasjee Jehangir donated £60,000 and the Cama family subscribed nearly £10,000 towards London charities and educational endowments.

Against reformist advances in the press, schools, theatre, and law courts, the old class of Parsi *seṭhs* therefore sought to court recognition and acclaim within the Parsi community and the government through large, public projects. Philanthropy not only enabled the *seṭhs* to interact materially with British officials, but also symbolized shared values and loyalty. Accordingly, while reformists prepared farces of evil nabobs and Shakespeare as enactments of fidelity, the traditionalist elite who were typically against the amendment of customs such as child marriage, funded architectural embellishments and the construction of 'Frere Town', the central business district. As a form of soft power, charity facilitated for the largely traditionalist mercantile class political advancement and modes of publicity in municipal affairs. The British had long understood the importance of recognizing these performative gestures of steadfastness to the project of empire through public markers of social recognition from baronetcies to knighthoods. These stealthily sought-after imperial titles—the ultimate expression of British–Indian unity rather than of colonial hegemony—indicate, according to Jesse Palsetia, the considerable seductiveness of imperial ideology, especially for the Parsis.[130] The communal identity of the Parsis was heavily invested in this culture of colonial collaboration that was spectacular in every sense of the word—it was implicitly inscribed in countless edifices and infrastructural projects and explicitly celebrated through medals, press reportage, titles, and the sale of black and white and colour pictures of merchant leaders such as Jeejeebhoy for domestic worship.[131]

Charity was thus as much a cultural as an economic and political operation, consolidating ideological claims to intra- and inter-communal representation and crafting an early modern image of indigenous celebrity. Accordingly, the *seṭhs*' efforts to court recognition in Bombay had a noticeable impact on the theatre. On 12 December 1863 the Gentlemen Amateurs Club performed *Twelfth Night: or, What You Will*, singing songs in the interval 'under the patronage of Jamśedjī Jījībhāi'.[132] A few days later the Zoroastrian Nāṭak Manḍalī performed *The Moor Tragedy, or the Ingratitude of a Daughter* and *Early Marriages*, after which songs were sung in praise of 'the Hon'ble Rustomjee Jamsetjee'.[133] Other troupes followed suit, with the Pārsī Stage Players and the Elphinstone Theatrical Club singing the praises of 'The Hon'ble Jugonnathjee Sunkersett', and the Zoroastrian Nāṭak Manḍalī singing 'in memory of R. J. Jijibhai's wife' and subsequently in memory of 'Śeṭh Rūśtamjī J. Jījībhāi'.[134] Similarly, Naśarvānjī Forbes of the fittingly entitled Baronet Theatrical Club painted a drop scene depicting the bust of Sir Jamsetjee Jeejeebhoy, and the company's playwright Bandekhodā created a song in his memory:

> This colourful curtain edifies a man,
> Why achieve fame and glory;
> If you achieve fame you will never die.[135]

Forbes, unsurpringly, was reprimanded after the performance by the reformist press for 'base idol worship'.[136] Nevertheless, managers such as Āpakhatyār and Forbes were often requested to sing songs to 'advance the reputation of the mercantile community', in a practice that Dhanjībhāi Paṭel dubbed as 'Pārsī seṭhīāonī patronage levānu ceṭak' ('Parsi *seṭhs* mania for theatrical patronage')[137] and that the *Rāst* openly condemned: 'It is not enough that they give freely. That alone will never ennoble them. They must forbear to flourish their charities in the eyes of the public'.[138]

The Ruin of Reform

Although this patronage was the cornerstone for the expansion of the Parsi theatre, the newspaper had good reason to critique the liberal loosening of Parsi purse strings, a phenomenon that had begun to assume the character of a 'passion or an epidemic'.[139] By 1865, Bombay witnessed a mammoth rise in the number of joint-stock companies and banks, the latter amounting to twenty-eight, prompting the newspaper to warn that the ordinary man had been gripped by the 'disease' of the share mania.[140] In mid-March 1865 news began to percolate from England of the possibility of the termination of the American Civil War.[141] On 9 April 1865 (the same day that the war officially ended) share prices began to drop, and the price of Dhollera cotton in the Liverpool market, which had been 19½ pence at the beginning of the year, fell to 11 pence.[142] When news reached Bombay's vernacular press of the end of the Civil War, Bombay was stricken with terror.[143] 'Where are all the reclamation company advertisements? Where are all their so-called reputable owners? To where have the twenty-nine-crore premium of shares disappeared?' blasted the *Rāst*.[144] The Parsi *seṭh* Byramjee Hormusjee Cama suffered a loss of three crore (i.e. thirty million) rupees. Songs on the share mania such as 'Sher Bajārnū gīt' and 'śernā svapnānī garbīo' and farces such as *The Evil Effects of Gambling*, *Atī Lobh e Pāpnu Mul* (*Great Greed and the Price of Sin*), *King Commerce or Sink or Swim*, and *Śer ane Saṭāthī thatā Gerfāedā* (*The Detriments of Shares and Gambling*) articulated Bombay's distress while condemning the decline of the prodigious Indian mercantile class and by analogy Parsi communal prestige.[145] The latter was perceptibly felt at the theatre.

Shortly after the crash, Dave Carson, who had on previous occasions sung paeons to the 'Parsi girl of the period' as part of the San Francisco Minstrels, rudely attempted to unseat a Parsi spectator on behalf of Richard Barton, the chief magistrate of Bombay, who had bought the same seat at the theatre. In response, the *Rāst*, now headed by the formidable 'Father of the Parsi theatre' Kekhuśro Kābrājī, decried the occurrence[146]:

> Would any person with a particle of self-respect about himself submit to be moved out of his seat by a comedian in favour of one whom he looked upon as the greater personage of the two, but whom he had let no more right than the native. No law of civilization or society, no rule of morals or politics, and no maxims for the conduct of subject nations towards their superiors enjoins such a behaviour. If native gentlemen are after all to submit to a treatment similar to that of Dave's at the hands of those foreigners who have been handsomely paid for what they offer, what becomes of the boasted Christianity and the influence of a higher civilization which is so often flourished in our face? If we are after all to submit to insulting treatment at the hands of every white man where is the equality, and personal liberty for which Providence has placed India under Britain?

> … We are now reminded of our subjection, and then of our generosity, and our charity and our intelligence; we are now told that we inherit the earliest civilization in the world, and then that we are after all lady Pus; we are now congratulated on our enterprise and the adoption of European civilization, and then spoken of as an offensively presumptuous class to be humbled and improved by adversity; as occasion requires or interest dictates. When a European philanthropist has to amass subscriptions we are the subjects of the same sovereign and the creatures of the same God, but when an 'independent Britain' has to domineer over us we are after all a subject population, and held under control by the sword. As to the fact of India's subjection we are always aware of it, and should never endeavour to forget it were we not told that Christianity and a high civilization had changed the polity of nations mussled by their influence.[147]

If twenty years prior, the Parsis' clout had compelled Mrs Deacle into appeasing her Parsi patrons, Dave Carson's 'insulting treatment' in 1865 suggests how the economic, social, and cultural tides had turned against the community's favour. Carson's behaviour, according to the *Rāst*, epitomized the double standards incipient in English 'laws of civilization', which congratulated or humbled as 'occasion requires or interest dictates'. The effects of the share crash, refracted into this single, seemingly petty incident at the theatre, sensitized the Parsis (both reformists and traditionalists) to the hypocrisy of 'equality, and personal liberty' that formed the ideological basis of British colonial rule. However, English morals, contingent on belief in the inherent superiority of European civilization and epitomized by Shakespeare, had most radically been imbued by reformist Parsis. Parsi social reformists repeatedly legitimized the composite revolution in the community's domestic world on the grounds of civilization and progress, virtue and morality. 'Government has always naturally and properly shown a prominent respect to those rich natives who have shown a due appreciation of Western civilization and it hardly becomes now for it to counteract that course in however low a degree', the Parsi press argued a few months prior.[148] Consequently, although the mercantile class suffered irredeemable financial, material, and social loss in 1865, the real damage realized by the share crash was the ideological injury borne by the Parsi reformist movement, which 'had become weak', putting forth 'superficial rhetoric more than action'.[149] The drastic fall in trade resulted in the first thorough inquisition of English commercial morality, the irrevocable financial decline of the prodigious comprador

Indian *seṭh*, and especially the end of the dogma of Parsi reform, which could no longer assume an unequivocally aspirational character.[150]

> Men in the height of the speculating mania thought of nothing but filling their pockets. ... The dominant European bowed before a subject native, the strict official before a mushroom merchant, and the philosopher or the man of letters before humanized Laxmi. ... All went on merry as a marriage bell until the crash came. ... It was then that the public found out that the idol before whom they bent their knee, though golden, stank through fine concealed apertures. ... A class of our public writers have found in all this, as was expected, an opportunity of comparing Asiatic with European or at least English commercial morality. ... How many Englishmen have of late departed from Bombay secretly, leaving their creditors in the lurch? What is the proportion of European to native merchants? ... Englishmen have done all this with the advantage of a superior education, and a refined system of religion to which in their eyes nothing in the world can equal, we cannot help thinking that we have not much to envy in the results of 'centuries of Christianity and a higher civilization'.[151]

Here ends the ideological potency of those universal 'moral attributes of the human race [that] are ... essentially and substantially the same in London and Washington, Bombay and Calcutta', an ideology that had perpetuated the cause of civilization and progress through the reformation of the school, press, theatre, and communal law.[152] Here 'the public found out that the idol before whom they bent their knee, though golden, stank through fine concealed apertures', that there was nothing 'to envy in the results of "centuries of Christianity and a higher civilization"', that colonial power was a 'baseless fabric of a vision'. A new form of visibility—an awareness of a manipulation of authority that encompassed the entire social body—was brought to bear both within and outside the theatre, no longer to be 'kept in subordination to Morality and Virtue'. A different kind of truth, one that did not adhere to the dictates of European commerce, to Victorian social and moral norms, and to the linear evolutive time of colonial civilization and colonized savagery began to appear. Simultaneously, reformist rhetoric and by analogy the Parsi press metamorphosed.

Notes

1. Untitled, *RG*, 3 January 1858, 1–2. Also spelled 'Dādābhāi Navrojjī'; 'Jehangir Burjorji Vacha' and 'Jahāṅgīr Barjorjī Vāchā'; and 'Sorabjee Shapoorjee Bengallee', 'Sorābjī Śāpurjī Baṅgālī', 'Śorābjī Śāpurjī Baṅgālī', respectively.
2. 'Māhaśne Parmeśvar kem malec,' *RG*, 10 June 1855, 178–79; Untitled, *RG*, 13 May 1855, 149–50; Untitled, *RG*, 25 February 1855, 62; and Jāher Mat-Ek Mātbar Pārsī, 'Pārśīnī Pancāyat', *RG*, 31 January 1858, 53.
3. Tanika Sarkar, *Hindu Wife, Hindu Nation: Community, Religion, and Cultural Nationalism* (New Delhi: Permanent Black, 2017, first published 2001), 74–75.
4. 'Iṅglaṇḍno Mel', *RG*, 18 March 1855, 86–87.
5. The 'traditionalist' faction instituted the Rāhe Rāst Sabhā as a defence against these attacks; see 'The Lights and Shades of the East: By Framjee Bomonjee. Third Notice', *RG*, 1 November 1863, 561–62; 'Rāhānmāe Mājdīaśnānī śabhā', *RG*, 11 November 1855, 360–61; and 'Rāhānumāe ane Rāherāśt keṭlo fer', *RG*, 26 July 1857, 238.
6. Thus, the *Rāst* denounced the educated Rūstamjī, son of Vīkājī Meharjī who supposedly stained the community's reputation. Similarly, Jahāṅgīr Sorābjī Pāṭak and a Kharśedjī Jahāṅgīr Tārācand were vilified for behaving badly at a wedding.' See 'Śudhāro,' *RG*, 24 June 1855, 194–95. Untitled, *RG*, 8 July 1855, 212–13; 'Kharī Murkhāi', *RG*, 1 February 1857, 37–38; and Untitled, *RG*, 8 February 1857, 46.
7. For a description of the Parsi middle classes see 'Pārśīomā oratone teḍā karvānī rīt', *RG*, 6 December 1857, 390–91.
8. 'Parsi Theatre', *BG*, 25 October 1853, 1037; and Dhanjībhāi Na Paṭel, *PNTT* (Bombay: 'Kaysare-Hind' Paper Printing Press, 1931), 3. Also spelled 'Kharśedjī Naśarvānjī Kāmā', 'Khurśedjī Nośīrvānjī Kāmājī'; 'Ardeśar Farāmjī Muś', 'Ardeshir Moos', 'Ardesheer Moos', respectively.
9. 'Local', *BG*, 30 September 1853, 939; and 'Parsi Theatre', *BG*, 25 October 1853, 1039.
10. 'Local', *BG*, 13 November 1853, 1087.
11. Jahāṅgīr Pestanjī Khambātā, *Ek Jāṇītā Pārsī Ekṭarno Ardhī sadī Uparno Nāṭakī Anubhav* (Bombay, 1913), 6–7.
12. Khambātā, *NA*, 6–7.
13. Untitled, *BT*, 14 October 1854, 4448; 'Parsee Dramatic Corps', *BT*, 3 March 1855, 141; 'Bombay—Local', *BT*, 23 February 1857, 365; and 'Bombay—Local', *BT*, 30 May 1857, 1022.
14. 'Parsi Theatre', *BG*, 25 October 1853, 1039 and 'Local', *BG*, 30 September 1853, 939.
15. 'Hundred Years Ago', *TOI*, 6 October 1953, 6.

16. 'Local', *BG*, 13 November 1853, 1087.
17. Maneckjee Cursetjee, 'A Few Passing Ideas for the Benefit of India and the Indians', *Rāst Goftār*, 1 March 1863, 109–10.
18. Adam Smith, *Theory of Moral Sentiments*, 2nd ed. (London: A. Miller, 1761, first published 1759), 201.
19. Also spelled 'Pestanji Master'; 'Nānābhai Rustamjī Rā̃nīnā', 'Nāhnābhai Rustamjī Rānīnā', 'Nanabhai R. Ranina; Dadabhai Eliot'; 'Bhikhaji Moos'; 'Kāvasjī Kohīyārdārū', 'Kāvasjī Kohīyādārū', 'Kāvasjī Gurgīn', 'Kāvjī Bā', respectively. Rāṇīnā would become a famous journalist and the writer of the first comprehensive Gujarati-English dictionary. He would also write plays for the Elphinstone and subsequently the Alfred Theatrical Companies.
20. 'Parsi Theatre', *BG*, 25 October 1853, 1039.
21. 'Local', *BG*, 12 November 1853, 1083.
22. Tickets were to be sold at the offices of the *Bombay Gazette*, the Duftar Ashkar press (which printed the *Rāst Goftār*), and the newly opened Framjee Cowasjee Institute (Farāmjī Kāvasjī Institute/Framjee Cawasjee Institute), containing a library for learning.
23. Gauri Viswanathan, *Masks of Conquest: Literary Study and British Rule in India* (New York: Columbia University Press, 2014), 109.
24. 'Parsee Dramatic Corps', *BT*, 3 March 1855, 141; and 'Bombay-Local', *BT*, 30 May 1857, 1022.
25. 'Parsi Theatre', *BG*, 31 October 1853, 1039.
26. Untitled, *RG*, 25 February 1855, 61–62; and Untitled, *RG*, 1 March 1857, 69–70. Also spelled 'Naśarvānjī Dorābjī Apekhatīār', 'Nasarvānjī Dorābjī Āpakhtīyār', 'Kīkā Dāvar', 'Nassarwanjee Dorabjee Apakhtyar', 'Nusserwanjee Apakhtyar'.
27. Untitled, *BT*, 23 February 1857, 365.
28. Untitled, *BT*, 23 February 1857, 365.
29. Nāṭakno ek Kherkhāh, 'Pārśī Nāṭak-Cābuk', *RG*, 1 March 1857, 69–70.
30. This may have led to a steep decline in the theatre's receipts, resulting in threats that the theatre would be sold in 1855. The theatre was eventually sold for Rs 8,000, even though its debts amounted to 30,000. At the last moment, however, Shankarsheth stepped in and saved the day; see Untitled, *BT*, 27 June 1855, 311; and Untitled, *RG*, 2 September 1855, 277.
31. T. Sarkar, *Hindu Wife, Hindu Nation*, 194.
32. Jesse Palsetia, *The Parsis of India: Preservation of Identity in Bombay City* (Leiden: Brill, 2001), 171.
33. Mitra Sharafi, *Law and Identity in Colonial South Asia: Parsi Legal Culture, 1772–1947* (Cambridge: Cambridge University Press, 2014), 21.
34. Untitled, *RG*, 25 February 1855, 61–62.

35. The nautch, an anglicized version of *nāc* (dance) consisted of several traditional Indian dance forms performed by women in India during the late Mughal era.
36. See Richard David Williams, 'Songs Between Cities: Listening to Courtesans in Colonial North India', *Journal of the Royal Asiatic Society* 27, no. 4 (2017): 591–610; Davesh Soneji, *Unfinished Gestures: Devadasis, Memory, and Modernity in South India* (Chicago: Chicago University Press, 2012); and Rashna Darius Nicholson, '"A Christy Minstrel, a Harlequin, or an Ancient Persian"?: Opera, Hindustani Classical Music and the Origins of the Popular South Asian "Musical"', *Theatre Survey* 61, no. 3 (2020).
37. 'Mātbar deśīone', *RG*, 27 December 1863, 667; and 'Rāṇḍonā nāc - veśīānā pūjārīo', *RG*, 29 October 1865, 598.
38. Untitled, *RG*, 22 April 1855, 125; and Untitled, *RG*, 10 June 1855, 179.
39. Viswanathan, *Masks of Conquest*, 85.
40. 'Pārśī Nāṭak', *RG*, 17 May 1857, 158; and 'Pārśī Nāṭak', *RG*, 13 December 1857, 399.
41. 'The stately tread of the soldier was nothing but a ridiculous strut upon the stage, and the imitation of bloody combats between the heroes—not a bit more than ordinary cock-fighting!' From 'Parsee Theatre', *BT*, 23 February 1857, 365.
42. *The Oriental Herald and Journal of General Literature*, vol. V. (London: Sandford Arnot, 1825), 587.
43. Jyotsna Singh, 'Different Shakespeares: The Bard in Colonial/Postcolonial India', *Theatre Journal* 41, no. 4 (1989): 446 and Viswanathan, *Masks of Conquest*.
44. Thus, the first comprehensive Gujarati translation of Shakespeare's plays was undertaken by the Parsi reformist playwright Nāhānābhāi Rūstamjī Rāṇīnā in 1865 and was sold for Rs 2. 'Wherever the English flag flies high, there Shakespeare achieves renown' proclaimed the *Rāst*. See 'Śekspīr Nāṭak', *RG*, 24 December 1865, 827; 'Śekspīrnāṭak. Aṅk 1', *RG*, 24 December 1865, 832; and 'Śekspīarnā Nāṭak', *RG*, 31 December 1865, 839–40.
45. Viswanathan, *Masks of Conquest*, 20.
46. 'Pārśī Nāṭak', *RG*, 25 October 1857, 343. The change in moniker through the addition of Junī reveals the Pārśī Nāṭak Maṇḍalī's split into two rival playgroups.
47. 'Article 8—No Title', *BT*, 8 June 1859, 364.
48. Paṭel, *PNTT*, 191; and 'Pārsī Nāṭaknī Navī Ṭolī', *RG*, 25 April 1858, 211.
49. Untitled, *RG*, 25 October 1857, 341; and Karaka, *History of the Parsis*, 281–82.

50. 'The Anglo-Indian Press and Its Vernacular Contemporaries', *RG*, 24 January 1858, 43.
51. Untitled, *RG*, 3 January 1858, 5–6; 'The Conciliation Policy', *RG*, 10 January 1858, 17–18; 'The Feeling of the People', *RG*, 15 August 1858, 401; 'Vartamān Patranu Savtantrapaṇu', *RG*, 11 November 1860, 556–57; and 'The Joyous Frolics of Bombay Journalism', *RG*, 21 February 1858, 93–94.
52. 'Diffusion of the English Language in India', *RG*, 8 August 1858, 389.
53. 'Nāṭak', *RG*, 31 May 1863, 279; Untitled, *BG*, 3 August 1861; and Untitled, *BG*, 9 November 1861, cited in Kumud A. Mehta, 'Bombay's Theatre World 1860–1880', *Journal of the Asiatic Society of Bombay* 43–44 (1970): 251–78, 264.
54. Untitled, *TOI*, 15 July 1861, 3.
55. Mehta, 'Bombay's Theatre World', 264.
56. 'Grant Road Theatre', *BG*, 5 June 1862, 3.
57. Nājar was responsible for gathering together the troupe members Dhanjībhāi Masṭar (Palkhīvālā); Māṇekjī Surtī; K. H. Kāṅgā; the three brothers Mervānjī Naśarvānjī Vādīyā, Dhanjībhāi Naśarvānjī Vādīyā, and Pestanjī Naśarvānjī Vādīyā; Jamśedjī Unvālā; the brothers Dhanjīśāh Navrojī Pārakh and Naśarvānjī Navrojī Pārakh; and Khambātā's uncle Hīrjībhāi Aspandyārjī Khambātā. All of these individuals eventually became prominent members of the Parsi community.
58. Untitled, *BG*, 4 April 1864, 1; Untitled, *BG*, 8 February 1864, 2; Mehta, 'Bombay's Theatre World', 251–78, 264; and Khambātā, *NA*, 26. Also spelled 'Kūvarjī Sorābjī Nājhar', 'Kuvarjī Sohrābjī Nājar', 'Cooverji Sorabjee Nazer', 'Nazir'; 'Dādābhāi Śohorābjī Farāmjī Paṭel', 'Dadabhoy Sorabjee Patell', 'Dadabhoy Sorabji Framji Patel', 'Dādī Paṭel'; 'Wadia'; 'Dhanjīśāh Navrojī Pārekh'; 'Naśarvānjī Navrojjī Pārekh', 'Naśarvānjī Navroj Pārakh', respectively.
59. Joseph Delissa, 'The Vernacular Drama', *Baldwin's Monthly*, 1 September 1882, 5.
60. 'The Annual Commemoration of the Bombay and Calcutta Universities', *RG*, 19 April 1863, 197.
61. Khambātā, *NA*, 8, 12–13; and Paṭel, *PNTT*, 282.
62. Before the curtain rose, the principal of the college mentioned that the idea of these dramatic activities had 'originated solely with the young men themselves'. The college authorities had approved the activity as 'conducing to refinement and literary culture'. 'Dramatic Performance at Elphinstone College', *BG*, 8 February 1864, 2.
63. Henry George Briggs, *The Pársís: Or, Modern Zerdusthians: A Sketch* (Edinburgh: Oliver and Boyd, 1852), 15–16.
64. Nowrozjee Sorabji Bengallee, *The Life of Sorabjee Shapoorjee Bengallee* (Bombay: Times of India, 1920), 66–67.

65. 'Pārśī Nāṭak', *RG*, 17 May 1857, 158.
66. 'Pārśī Astrīone vāste nāṭak', *RG*, 18 April 1858, 198–99. Kāvasjī Naśarvānjī Kohīdārū, a renowned actor-manager and theatre treasurer would help establish and participate in other Parsi troupes such as the Gentlemans Amateur Club, the Victoria Nāṭak Maṇḍalī, and the Nāṭak Utejak Maṇḍaḷī. He acted in both Parsi and Hindu *sansārī* (social) productions as well as in Urdu language plays. Paṭel, *PNTT*, 97.
67. 'Pārśī Astrīone vāste nāṭak', *RG*, April 18, 1858, 198–99.
68. Untitled, *BT*, 11 March 1840, cited in Delphine Menant, *The Parsis in India* (Bombay: M. M. Murzban, 1917), 341.
69. Untitled, *Bombay Courier*, 23 August 1842, cited in Eckehard Kulke, *The Parsees in India, A Minority as Agent of Social Change* (Bombay: Vikas, 1974), 104.
70. Untitled, *RG*, 8 April 1855, 106–7.
71. '"Jartośtī Chokrīonī Nīśāl Maṇḍalī" aśthāpvā śārū tā 23 mī Mārc 1858 ne dāne bharāelī śabhānī ūpaj nīpajno eheval', *RG*, 28 March 1858, 160–63; 'Jarthostī chokrīonī nīśāl', *RG*, 18 March 1863, 144–46; and 'Āleksāṇḍrā insṭīṭīūśan', *RG*, 12 March 1865, 169–70.
72. 'Orat', *RG*, 8 February 1857, 42–44.
73. Geraldine Forbes, 'Education for Women', in *Women and Social Reform*, 73–74. Zenanas were dwellings reserved exclusively for women.
74. Forbes, 'Education for Women', 62–63.
75. See *Women and Social Reform*, 6.
76. 'Strī Kelavṇī - Tenī Hālnī Hālat', *RG*, 31 December 1865, 835–36; 'Strī Keḷavṇīne Ek Bījī Aḍcaṇ', *RG*, 22 April 1866, 252–53; 'Abhḍāelī Orato', *RG*, 29 January 1865, 65–66; 'Pārsī Strīonī Aḍkāvānī Rasam', *RG*, 5 February 1865, 83–84; 'Dastā̃nvālī Orat "nā̃pāk" kem?', *RG*, 24 December 1865, 827–28; 'Lying-in Customs of the Parsees', *RG*, 20 March 1887, 319; and 'Lagan - Bāḷ Lagan', *RG*, 14 July 1867, 471–72.
77. Julius Berncastle, *A Voyage to China: Including a Visit to the Bombay Presidency; the Mahratta Country; the Cave Temples of Western India, Singapore, the Straits of Malacca and Sunda, and the Cape of Good Hope* (London: W. Shoberl, 1850), 1:91.
78. Kumkum Sangari, and Sudesh Vaid, eds., *Recasting Women: Essays in Indian Colonial History* (New Brunswick, NJ: Rutgers University Press, 1990), 131.
79. 'Pārśī Astrīone vāste nāṭak', *RG*, 18 April 1858, 198–99.
80. 'Pārśī Astrīone vāste nāṭak', *RG*, 18 April 1858, 198–99.
81. See the advertisement for *As You Like It* by the Gentlemen Amateurs Club. Untitled, *RG*, 9 April 1865, 240.
82. 'Jarthostī chokrīonī nīśāl', *RG*, 18 March 1863, 144–46; 'Astrī gneān mālā', *RG*, 11 March 1860, 136; 'Āleksāṇḍrā insṭīṭīūśan', *RG*, 12 March

1865, 169–70; 'Mumbaimā̃ strī kelavṇī', *RG*, 5 April 1863, 169–70; and Mehta, 'Bombay's Theatre World', 263.

83. For a description of Cursetjee see Kaikhosro N. Kabraji, 'Reminiscences of Kaikhosro N. Kabraji (editor of *Rast Goftar*) Fifty Years Ago', *TOI*, 26 October 1901, 7.
84. 'Astrīone Mardonī Mījlasmā āmej karvānī bābatmā Mumbai cābukno vicar', *RG*, 5 September 1858, 437.
85. 'Ek e Kā̃mmā̃ śā̃melgīrī rākhnār', letter published in 'Astrīone Mardonī Mījlasmā̃ āmej karvānī bābatmā̃ mumbai cābukno vīcār', *RG*, 5 September 1858, 437; and 'Astrīone Mardonī Mījlasmā̃ āmej karvānī bābatmā̃ mumbai cābukno vīcār. Aṅk 3 jo', *RG*, 19 September 1858, 462–63.
86. 'Ek Pārsī Nāṭaknī māṭhī cāl', *RG*, 26 December 1858, 647.
87. 'Ek Pārsī Nāṭaknī māṭhī cāl', *RG*, 26 December 1858, 647.
88. 'Astrīone mardonī majlasmā̃ ā̃mej karvā̃ ...,' *RG*, 3 October 1858, 493–94; and 'Mumbai Samācārne Hamoe paḍtū̃ śū̃ karvā mukīo?,' *RG*, 3 October 1858, 489–90.
89. Untitled, *RG*, 22 November 1868, 753; Untitled, *RG*, 4 April 1869, 223; and Untitled, *RG*, 11 April 1869, 240.
90. 'Pārsīnā Chokrāone Lāgelū̃ Ceṭak', *RG*, 21 November 1869, 740–41. For further debates on mixed gatherings at the theatre see 'Deśī Strīone Māṭe Nāṭak—Strī Keḷavṇīno Ek ūpay', *RG*, 19 January 1868, 34–35; 'Ratai Maḍamno Kāgaj', *RG*, 19 January 1868, 41–42; and 'Pārsī Strīonī Āgalnī tathā hamṇānī Hālat vace mukāblo karvā sambandhī ek dastāvej', *RG*, 26 January 1868, 55.
91. 'Pārsī Strīonū̃ Chuṭāpaṇū̃', *RG*, 7 November 1869, 708–9.
92. 'Deśī Nāṭako vīśe thoḍāk agatnā̃ vīcāro', *RG*, 22 November 1868, 741–43.
93. See Ashis Nandy, *Intimate Enemy* (Oxford: Oxford University Press, 1989).
94. Lata Mani, *Contentious Traditions: The Debate on Sati in Colonial India* (Berkeley: University of California Press, 1998).
95. 'Pārsīonā̃ Dharamkhātā̃', *RG*, 13 December 1863, 636; 'Abhḍāelī Orato', *RG*, 29 January 1865, 65–66; 'Pārsī Strīonī Aḍkāvānī Rasam', *RG*, 5 February 1865, 83–84; 'Nā̃pāk Najar', *RG*, 26 February 1865, 132–33; 'Suvāvadnā Saṅkaṭ', *RG*, 27 January 1867, 56; 'Mā̃thūbānū̃', *RG*, 5 May 1867, 274–75; 'Mahlājo', *RG*, 12 May 1867, 289–90; and 'Mā̃thūbānū̃, Mahlājo ane dharam', *RG*, 26 May 1867, 3.
96. *Jagat Premī* of July 1852, cited in 'Astrīone mardonī Mījlasmā̃ āmej karvānā fāedānī bābatmā̃', *RG*, 5 September 1858, 437–39.
97. Similarly, one of the founding members of the Indian National Congress and the first Indian member of the British parliament, Dadabhai Naoroji published a series of articles on women's rights by presenting information

on the Assyrians, Babylonians, Greeks, Persians, Mongolians, Romans, Germans, and Ancient Hindus that supported the view that women were equal to men. 'Orat Jātnā̃ hak, darajā tathā hālat. 1', *RG*, 24 January 1869, 49–50.

98. 'Āglā tathā hālnā jamānānā jarthostīonī keṭlīek cāl calaṇno mukāblo', *RG*, 19 September 1858, 461–62. The *Rāst* also cited the works of a Mr Lane, which criticized the Islamic practice of imprisoning women, and a Farsi book that described the practice of mixed *gambārs* (feasts) in the time of Nośervān Adal. 'Āglā tathā hālnā jamānānā jarthostīonī keṭlīek cāl calaṇno mukāblo', *RG*, 26 September 1858, 476–78.
99. 'Jartośtī Komnā̃ Lokone vāśte dhārā bandhāvī maṅgāvvānī goṭhvaṇ karvā śārū bharelī jāher śabhānī ūpaj nīpajno eheval', *RG*, 26 August 1855, 268–71; and 'The Parsee Law Association', *RG*, 1 April 1860, 169.
100. Sharafi, *Law and Identity*, 7.
101. 'The Parsee Law Association', *RG*, 1 April 1860, 169.
102. Sorabjee Shapoorjee Bengalee, *The Parsee Marriage & Divorce Act 1865: Act No. XV of 1865*... (Bombay: Parsee Law Association, 1868), 161.
103. 'Pārsīone sārā̃ dhārā bandhāvī maṅgāvnārī sabhā', *RG*, 18 March 1860, 143–44; 'The Parsee Law Association', *RG*, 1 April 1860, 169; and 'Pārsīonī dhārā bandhnārī sabhā,' *RG*, 22 April 1860.
104. Sharafi, *Law and Identity*, x.
105. Sharafi, *Law and Identity*, 91.
106. Bengalee, *The Parsee Marriage*, 167, 211; 'Pārsīonī dhārā sabhāmā̃thī jatī arjī', *RG*, 29 January 1865, 66–67. See also Untitled, *RG*, 29 January 1865, 66–67.

    Described as having deep knowledge and respect for the Zoroastrian religion by the Parsi press, Martin Haug was subsequently both referred to for the reorganization of the Sir Jamśedjī Jījībhāi Zend ane Pehelavi madresā (Parsi religious school) as well as requested, after his professorial stint at the Poona College, to stay on in Bombay for the benefit of the Parsis' theological education. 'Jartostī dharam babe Ḍākṭar mārṭīn hāūge gejeṭmā̃ lakhelo patra', *RG*, 15 January 1865, 40; 'Sar Jamśedjī Jījībhāi zand ane pehelavi madresā', *RG*, 22 January 1865, 56; and 'Jartostīonā̃ hāthmā̃ ek sari tak', *RG*, 2 April 1865, 211–12.
107. 'Report (of the Parsi Law Commissioners) into the Usage Recognised as Laws by the Parsee Community of India, and into the Necessity of Special Legislative in Connection with Them', *RG*, 8 March 1863, 125–26, 125.
108. Sharafi, *Law and Identity*, 179.
109. Untitled, *RG*, 15 November 1863, 587–88, 587; 'Pancāet bīcārī śū kare!', *RG*, 4 July 1858, 323–24; 'Pārsīnī Pancāet', *RG*, 11 July 1858, 339–40; and 'Navī Pancāet', *RG*, 11 March 1860, 125.

110. The courts, according to Sharafi, allowed elite Parsi men who functioned as delegates a high degree of intra-group control, including the ability to punish wayward husbands, usually working class, by annulling their marriages. Sharafi, *Law and Identity*, 165.
111. 'Pancāet bīcārī śũ kare!', *RG*, 4 July 1858, 323–24. See also 'Pārsīnī Pancāet', *RG*, 11 July 1858, 339–40; 'Navī Pancāet', *RG*, 11 March 1860, 125; 'Pārsīnī Pancāet', *RG*, 4 March 1860, 110; and 'Agīār Pārsī Ghrastho Jāme Jamśednī mārfate potānī "satā" batlāveche', *RG*, 6 May 1860, 132–33, which criticize Jeejeebhoy's nomination of Panchayat members and describe the need for an elected Panchayat through *mat* (public opinion), thus facilitating the drafting of Parsi law. And yet, even at this stage class played a role in the *Rāst*'s notion of public opinion. Only intelligent men were expected to participate in the elections, not 'cooks etc.'.
112. Untitled, *RG*, 25 January 1855, 62; Untitled, *RG*, 25 May 1855, 161–62; *RG*, 17 June 1855, 188; and Untitled, *RG*, 7 February 1858, 71.
113. Untitled, *RG*, 21 January 1855, 18.
114. 'Rīporṭar' Ek, 'Jurovāsṭrīan Thīeṭrīkal Klab ane teno hīmātī', *RG*, 6 May 1860, 134.
115. 'Pārsī Nātko', *RG*, 29 April 1860, 122–23.
116. 'Jurovāsṭrīan Thīeṭrīkal Klab ane teno hīmātī', *RG*, 6 May 1860, 134.
117. The *Rāst* also supported the Gentlemen Amateurs Club. After having fallen out with the Pārśī Nāṭak Maṇḍalī, the share dealer Farāmjī Gustādjī Dalāl, popularly known as Falu Ghus, founded this club with other ex-members of the Pārśī Nāṭak Maṇḍalī such as Kāvasjī Kohīdārū, Naśarvānjī Behrāmjī Fārbs, Farāmroj Rūstamjī Jośī, the famous playwright Edaljī Jamśedjī Khorī, and Dhanjībhāi Kerāvālā. The club performed Gujarati renditions of *The Tragedy of the Fair Penitent*, *Twelfth Night or What you Will*, *As You Like It*, *The Honeymoon*, and *Othello*, along with songs played to fiddles, harmoniums, and concertinas. 'Parsee Theatre', *BG*, 19 November 1862, 1103; 'Grant Road Theatre', *BG*, 12 December 1863, 2; 'Grant Road Theatre', *BG*, 14 January 1864, 3; and Untitled, *RG*, 19 March 1865, 192.
118. The Pārsī Stage Players was the theatrical organ of the editor of the *Parsi Punch*, Naśarvānjī Dorābjī Āpakhatyār. Members included Māṇekjī Hormasjī Paṭel (Bārbhāyā), Fardunjī Kāvasjī Sanjāṇā, Fīrojh Bāṭlīvālā, and Fardunjī Karākā (the brother of the Parsi historian Dosabhai Framji Karaka). The troupe performed *The Seven Clerks or The Three Thieves and the Denouncer*, *A Queer Subject*, *A False Friend*, 'Playful Dances', 'Ethiopian' songs, and 'Ethiopian' farces in English, this last group presumably inspired by blackface minstrel shows of the Dave Carson variety. Untitled, *RG*, 16 April 1865, 256; and Untitled, *RG*, 24 September 1865, 626.

119. See the *Rāst*'s criticisms of Āpakhatyār for allegedly having attended the play blindfolded. 'Pārśī Nāṭak', *RG*, 25 October 1857, 343; and Untitled, *RG*, 19 April 1857, 25.
120. Untitled, *RG*, 25 February 1855, 61–62; and Nāṭakno ek kherkhāh, 'Pārsī Nāṭak—Cābuk', *RG*, 1 March 1857, 69–70.
121. Christopher B. Balme, *The Theatrical Public Sphere* (Cambridge: Cambridge University Press, 2014), 18.
122. 'The Parsee Drama', *BG*, 7 May 1862, 432. The performance was that of the Parsee Union Dramatic Corps that performed a piece by Lavinia Becket and Richard Brinsley Sheridan's *St. Patrick's Day or the Scheming Lieutenant* in Gujarati on 3 May 1862. Untitled, *BG*, 28 April 1862, 398.
123. Untitled, *BG*, May 10, 1862, 444. *Romeo Ane Juliet* was written by a 'Delta' in 1858 for the Student's Amateur Club and subsequently by Ḍosabhāi Raṇḍelīā for the Shakespeare Club in 1876. Khambātā, *NA*, 266.
124. Untitled, *BG*, May 10, 1862, 444.
125. *The Economist, Weekly Commercial Time* (London: Economist Office, 1865), 23:511; and Dinshaw Edulji Wacha, *A Financial Chapter in the History of Bombay City*, 2nd ed. (Bombay: A. J. Combridge, 1910), 15.
126. Stephen Meredyth Edwardes, *The Gazetteer of Bombay City and Island* (Bombay: Times Press, 1909), 1:163; and 'A Nuisance', *RG*, 20 December 1863, 649–50.
127. 'Bombay Pier and Reclamation Scheme', *RG*, 28 October 1860, 533.
128. Stephen Meredyth Edwardes, *The Gazetteer of Bombay City and Island* (Bombay: Times Press, 1909), 2:171; and Dinshaw Edulji Wacha, *Premchund Roychund: His Early Life and Career* (Bombay: Times Press, 1913), 40.
129. Edwardes, *The Gazetteer of Bombay*, 2:171.
130. Palsetia, *Jamsetjee Jejeebhoy*, 161.
131. 'Marhum Sar Jamśedjī Jījībhāinī tasvīr', *RG*, 28 October 1860, 539.
132. Untitled, *RG*, 29 November 1863, 618.
133. 'Grant Road Theatre', *RG*, 4 December 1863, 3.
134. Untitled, *RG*, 24 September 1865, 626; and Untitled, *RG*, 24 May 1868, 337. In a similar vein, the *Bombay Gazette* noted that Sorabjee Jamsetjee Jeejeebhoy, 'with his usual liberality, gave a treat to the Parsee pupils of the Sir Jamsetjee Parsee Benevolent Institution and the Elphinstone Institution' by engaging the Christy Minstrels to perform a concert at the town hall for their benefit; see Untitled, *BG*, 30 November 1863, 2. Additionally, Cowasjee Jehangir not only allegedly paid the expenses of the performances of the Elphinstone Theatrical Club but also built 'the ample quarters' to admit such performances at the college; see Untitled, *BG*, 8 February 1864, 2.

135. Paṭel, *PNTT*, 195.
136. Khambātā, *NA*, 8–9.
137. Paṭel, *PNTT*, 202.
138. 'The Decencies of Charity', *RG*, 23 April 1865, 263.
139. 'Charities in Bombay', *RG*, 18 October 1863, 531.
140. 'Gaeū varas', *RG*, 1 January 1865, 1–5.
141. *The Economist, Weekly Commercial Time*, 23:511; and 'Amerīkānī Laḍāi māṇḍī valāvānī goṭhvaṇo hevāl', *Rāst Goftār*, 19 March 1865, 185–86.
142. 'Saṭāe Mārelo Paṭo', *RG*, 9 April 1865, 228–29; and Edwardes, *The Gazetteer of Bombay*, 2:167.
143. 'Amerīkānī agatnā samācār svatantrapaṇānī fateh', *RG*, 7 May 1865, 296; 'Serono Saṭā', *RG*, 7 May 1865, 299–330; and 'Mumbaino Bargaste dāhāḍo—Have karvū śū?', *RG*, 4 June 1865, 355–56.
144. A crore, according to the Indian numeral system, amounts to ten million. 'Saṭāe Mārelo Paṭo', *RG*, 9 April 1865, 228–29.
145. 'Mumbainī Moṭī sāhebo, sac svarg samān, Dīlgīrī vālī dekhāyche, jevū moṭū maśāṇ' ('Mumbai's big men, who appeared honest and great, Now appear disheartened as if at a big funeral'). From 'Śernā svapnānī garbīo. Set to 8 different tunes by Dalpatrām Ḍaheābhāi', *RG*, 1 October 1865, 640; and 'Śer Bajārnū Gīt', *RG*, 16 July 1865, 459.
146. Also spelled 'Kekhaśrū Navrojī Kābrājī', 'Kekhaśrū Navrojjī Kābrājī', 'Kaikhosro Kabraji'. Kābrājī joined the *Rāst Goftār* in 1862 as sub-editor under Karsandas Mulji and in the following year became the editor of the paper. Apart from his role in the standardization of South Asian music, Kābrājī was instrumental in the establishment of both the Victoria Nāṭak Maṇḍalī and the Nāṭak Utejak Maṇḍalī (Society for the Amelioration of the Drama). Additionally, he was honorary secretary of the Dnyān Prasārak Maṇḍalī (Society for the Diffusion of Knowledge), a reformist organization that would organize lectures and exhibitions for many decades. He wrote numerous plays of great acclaim, took an interest in the dissemination of physical education, and was a member of the managing committee of the Rahnoomai Mazdiasni Sabha (Rāhnumai Mājdīaśnī Sabhā/Parsi Religious Reform Association). 'The Police Courts', *TOI*, 21 March 1882, 3; and 'The Police Courts. The charge of Defamation against a Parsee Editor', *TOI*, 28 March 1882, 3.
147. 'The Last Scene in the Theatre', *RG*, 21 May 1865, 327.
148. 'An Unprogressive Step', *RG*, 12 February 1865, 105.
149. 'Hīnduonā Sudhārāno ek ūpāy', *RG*, 5 April 1863, 171; 'Sudhāro kem thāe?', *RG*, 17 May 1863, 245–46; 'Sudhāro ane Sudhārā vālāo', *RG*, 12 July 1863, 343–44; and 'Iaṅg Bombe', *RG*, 8 January 1865, 18–19.
150. 'Paisā', *RG*, 16 July 1865, 451–52; 'Dolatno kharekharo arth', *RG*, 30 July 1865, 485–86; and 'The Late Hon'ble Mr. Jagannath Sunkerset', *RG*, 6 August 1865, 507.

151. 'The Morality of the Bazaar', *RG*, 16 July 1865, 455–56.
152. 'The World Is Veering to the Right. Problem of the Future Government of India', *RG*, 9 May 1858, 231.

CHAPTER 4

Corporeal Discipline

By the mid-1860s, the reformists found themselves confronted with abrupt and overwhelming Parsi poverty, accusations of native and particularly Parsi dishonesty and depravity,[1] warnings of the impending annihilation of the Parsi community,[2] and criticisms that Young Bombay, educated in liberty and justice, had little courage to stand up against English atrocities and was incapable of advancing native public opinion, instead squandering its energies on the latest fashions, tableware, clubs, and the indiscriminate pursuit of wealth.[3] In response to these pressures, the reformists directed their energies inwards, focusing on the perils of superficial *nakal* (mimicry):

> There is the class of go-ahead young men who have imitated and adopted to *perfection* the *externals* of civilization of their English rulers, whose wants are multiplied, tastes varied, and habits artificialized, … [having] shaken off the restraining salutary checks of orthodox conservatism.[4]

Or, as another article lamented, referencing three great reformists of the preceding decade: 'Gone are the days of the Dadabhai Naorojis, Naoroji Fardunjis, and Ardeshir Framjis'.[5] Even if greater numbers of Parsi youth were acquiring higher education—something that was still perceived as

R. D. Nicholson, *The Colonial Public and the Parsi Stage*, Transnational Theatre Histories,
https://doi.org/10.1007/978-3-030-65836-6_4

attractive due to the ever-increasing demand for bookkeepers and secretaries—they were perceived as lacking in the 'inner courage, independent thought, and patriotism' of their forefathers.[6]

At the heart of this moral dilemma was the burgeoning debate on Indian self-governance. Dadabhai Naoroji's drain theory—which stressed that large amounts of India's wealth were being funnelled away to England—was met with great fanfare by the Parsi press after it was delivered before the newly established East India Association in 1867. Coming on the heels of the 1865 share crash, this 'first major reassessment of the moral and economic relationship between Britain and India since the beginnings of the colonial economy', undercut colonial attempts to thwart native civil service recruitment through aspersions of Indians' inherent indolence, weakness, and corruption.[7] The beginnings of consequential interlocution with the colonial state, thus began to take shape. Parsi hopes were raised when on 21 August 1867, the East India Association applied to Sir Stafford Northcote, the Secretary of State for India, requesting that the examination for a quota of the appointments to the Indian Civil Service be held in India so that more Indians could take up administrative positions. At the time, British India was obliged to pay Rs 200,000,000 annually for European recruits of the Indian Civil Service, even as Indian universities were churning out numerous 'BAs and MAs' for mere clerical work.[8]

The *Rāst Goftār* used the discussions on the lack of Indian administrative officers not only to promote Indian civil rights but also to recast its critical eye on the striking question as to whether the next generation, which focused all its energies on *mannī kelavṇī* (mental education), possessed the required '*tannī kelavnī* [physical education] or Moral Courage' necessary to be civil servants. 'They may be intelligent but [they] are feeble, cowardly, and spine-less. ... How would they make good collectors, magistrates, and judges without these necessary qualities? How will they bear sundry weather, difficult terrain, and arduous journeys through distant kingdoms and jungles?'[9] These questions stemmed from the developing view that Parsi boys were *mīnnā̃ putlā̃* (statues) who were forced to read all day without play, who were fattened on *ghī* (clarified butter), soaked *khicḍī* (rice), and chicken legs, and who hid at the sight of a sailor.[10] Much like Friedrich Jahn's early nineteenth-century 'patriotic gymnastics', which was perceived as a necessary counterbalance to Germany's cerebral curriculum, harking back to the myth of the Teutonic warrior, a significant portion of the Parsi public now equated 'moral courage' with *tannī kelavṇī* (bodily exercise)—and financial weakness with physical weakness—through an increased emphasis on the ideas of *Keānī Lohī* (Kyani blood) and the *Irānī Pehelvān* (ancient Iranian warrior).[11] Therefore, while orientalist scholarship had originally been used to support the reconfiguration of Parsi law, the same literature would now be used to inscribe corporeal reform in the Parsi communal body. Drawing on orientalist scholarship, the Parsis would attempt to reconceive themselves in the latter half of the 1860s: from blind mimics of the English to an '*aslī, bāhādur, laḍāiak*' (ancient, brave, warrior-like) community that had forgotten that it ruled a vast empire.[12] True *nītī* (morality) would accordingly transition from following the English example to a return to roots.

The Persian Warrior Performed

As orientalist discoveries of the glories of ancient Persia replaced Anglican doctrine on the social and intellectual benefits of European civilization, Iranian corporeality superseded Victorian morality and a new hyper-masculine art of the body came into being. The disciplinary apparatus of the school and university, the minor tribunal of the public sphere, and the major tribunal of law gradually transitioned into a technology of bodily power even as the site of reform was regendered from female laws of inheritance to male virility. The violence of the body of law therefore prompted the development of a law of the body, a new repository of communal values and ideals. Against the background of a perceived communal emasculation after the share crash and a renewed awareness of the dialectic between colonial masculinity and colonized femininity, physical education rather than reason's power of knowledge was deemed necessary to secure the community's sociopolitical authority and corporeal invulnerability. Truth therefore would no longer be inscribed in text but rather inscribed in the body, the new site of reform.

Significantly, the theatre became the key site for the conception and exposition of communal, corporeal ideals, manifesting the process described by Walter Benjamin of the aestheticization of politics and the politicization of aesthetics.[13] In January 1860, the Pārsīonī kaśrat ane Gujrātī Gāeṇ Maṇḍalī (Parsi Gymnasium and Music Company) was founded on the premises of the Parsi school at Dhobitalao by Naśarvānjī Āpakhatyār, the editor of the *Parsi Punch* and manager of the Parsi Stage Players, as 'a remedy for the terrible physical condition of Parsi youth and consequent fears for the community's future'.[14] Strabo, Herodotus, and Xenophon—who had described Persian instruction in the bow and the javelin, public hunting, and *kaśrat* (gymnastics)—were not only translated in the press but also directly contrasted with the Parsi Gymnasium's activities.[15] Through the invocation of Greek history, the Parsi Gymnasium attempted to establish itself as a school for a new class of virile Persians. Its first public performance, on 4 February 1860, comprised songs that criticized the Parsi Panchayat, rope dances, awe-inspiring *kaśrat* (which had never before been witnessed in Bombay), and *ḍhong* (skits).[16] The combination of gymnastics and music is striking. Shortly after the company's founding, the *Rāst* ran two articles entitled 'Pārsīomā̃ Gāeṇ' (Music among the Parsis), which described references in the tenth-century *Shahnama* and the thirteenth-century *Sikandarnama* to songs sung by Persian men and women to musical instruments such as the sitar (Hindustani stringed instrument), *ḍaf* (Persian drum), and *caṅg* (Persian harp). Additionally, it described European travellers' paintings that portrayed an instrument known as the *vīn* (harp) in Sassanian Iran, and it urged Parsi men and women to take up this ancient, respected Iranian pastime.[17] Like the German *Turnlied* (gymnastic song), which inculcated patriotism and a sense of belonging or *volk*, an 'authentic' Parsi music in combination with athletics came to be perceived as more beneficial in the cultivation of 'moral courage' than were classroom readings of John Stuart Mill. Music in combination with athletics was constituted as incontrovertibly didactic, standardizing the counterpoint of movements, regulating the use of time, and facilitating a group identity contingent on militarized control. Moreover, music and gymnastics stood synecdochally for an ancient, superior martial civilization that had fallen from grace and that needed to be revived. Consequently, intrinsic to the Gymnasium's activities was a degenerationist theory of Eastern society, with the Parsis seeking to return to a utopian past culture that had not (yet) been contaminated by centuries of Hindu and Muslim influence.

The theatricality of gymnastics was an idea that would catch on among other communities through the establishment of a Hindu Gymnasium in June of the same year at Bhuleshwar, and subsequently, the Gymnastic Stars of Bombay and the Cūlvāḍī Hīndu Nāṭak Kaśrat Company (Chulvadi Hindu Gymnastics Company). Touring gymnasts from Europe were also popular, among them the French Professor Busvān, the Cirque de Paris (which performed with fire and horses), the American Pāhāḍī Kaśrat (Mountain Gymnastics), Mr Stevens who jumped forty feet, Japanese acrobats, and Professor Abraham's Company, which featured tightrope walking and gymnastics by 'boneless boys'.[18] Nevertheless, the Parsi Gymnasium was accused by the Parsi press of conducting unvarying exercises; poorly instructing a mere 160 lazy, fat, and unhealthy boys in cricket, drill, boxing, and riding; imitating the costumes of the European gymnasts that performed in the tent on the esplanade; and failing to secure its finances.[19] Consequently, with the magistrate Dosabhai Framji Karaka as chair, the Gymnasium held a meeting to find a solution to these problems, resulting in the establishment of a fund for its benefit.[20]

The Origins of the First Professional Parsi Theatre Troupe: The Victoria Nāṭak Maṇḍalī (Victoria Theatrical Company)

On 3 November 1867, news was published that some of the Parsi theatre's best actors, both retired and active, had been selected from a number of diverse, competing troupes to perform together for the benefit of the Gymnasium.[21] On 21 December 1867, the Gujarati *Bhul Cuknī Hasāhas* (*Comedy of Errors*; in Italian costume) and a local farce entitled *Lalu Mehetānī Nīśāḷ* (*Master Lalu's School*) were performed to great acclaim, featuring the actors Pestanjī Dhanjībhāi Māsṭar, Kāvasjī Naśarvānjī Kohīdārū, Dārā(b)śāh Ratanjī Cijgar, Dādābhāi Ratanjī Ṭhuṭhī (Fig. 4.1),[22] Farāmjī Gustādjī Dalāl (Fig. 4.2), Hormasjī Dhanjībhāi Modī, Pestanjī Naśarvānjī Vāḍīyā, Kharśedjī Mancerjī Jośi, Barjorjī Farāmjī Mejar, Hormasjī Mancerjī Cicgar, and Farāmroj Rūstamjī Jośī (Fig. 4.3).[23] Two further performances, for 'families', took place on 4 January and 11 January 1868; the audiences primarily comprised Parsi women.[24] As the *Comedy of Errors* had been translated in its entirety in the women's reform magazine *Strī Bodh* for the moral education of Indian women, the performances were viewed as instructive in 'marital duty and the difficulties often faced by a loyal wife'.[25] The *Rāst* showered praise on the play, contrasted it with the purportedly childish productions that the Parsi theatre had become known for, praised its receipts (which exceeded the princely sum of Rs 1000), and reiterated the important edifying role of 'family' performances for women.[26] Some letter writers guaranteed generous donations on the condition that the troupe continue its work under the supervision of an able, educated director.[27] However,

Fig. 4.1 Dādābhāi Ṭhuṭhī (*Source* Paṭel, *PNTT*, 158. Courtesy: The Trustees, The K. R. Cama Oriental Institute, Mumbai)

Fig. 4.2 Farāmjī Dalāl (*Source* Paṭel, *PNTT*, 285. Courtesy: The Trustees, The K. R. Cama Oriental Institute, Mumbai)

the performances were not universally lauded. Much like the condemnations of blind mimicry of English habit in the aftermath of the share crash, letter writers panned the Portuguese band (which played European instruments instead of the Hindustani sitar or sarangi) and the choice to perform Shakespeare rather than one of the great Hindustani plays.

Fig. 4.3 Farāmroj Jośī (*Source* Paṭel, *PNTT*, 38. Courtesy: The Trustees, The K. R. Cama Oriental Institute, Mumbai)

The *Rāst*'s extensive coverage of the unnamed troupe indicates that its editor, Kekhuśro Kābrājī (Fig. 4.4), had a vested interest in these benefit performances. Kābrājī, one of the most prolific playwrights of the Parsi stage, had assumed a leadership role within the provisional company, a move that embittered the founder of the Gymnasium, the rival editor

Fig. 4.4 Kekhuśro Kābrājī (*Source* Tārāporvāḷā, Pe. Kha. *Kābrājī-Smruti*. Bombay: 'Sāñj Vartamān' Press, 1905, n.p. Courtesy: The J. N. Petit Institute, Mumbai)

Naśarvānjī Āpakhatyār. On the insistence of the actor Farāmjī Dalāl, who needed a source of income due to the breakup of his Gentlemen Amateurs Club, Kābrājī persuaded the actors who had performed in the *Comedy of Errors* to create a company, marshalled together four owners (Kāvasjī Kohīdārū, Dādābhāi Ṭhuṭhī, Farāmjī Dalāl, and Hormasjī Modī), and became the secretary of what is considered to be the first professional company of the Parsi stage. The Victoria Nāṭak Maṇḍalī (Victoria Theatrical Company) was named after no less than the queen herself, setting a benchmark for the colonial designations used by numerous Parsi theatre troupes and their South and Southeast Asian impersonators.[28] News of the Victoria's establishment was published as early as 23 February 1868 along with an announcement seeking salaried actors.[29] A nine-member managing committee of luminaries such as Jagannath Shankarsheth (president), Kharshedji Nusserwanji Cama, Dr Bhau Daji, Sohrabjee Shahpurjee Bengalee, Kharshedji Rustomji Cama, Dosabhai Framji Karaka, Ardeshir Framji Moos, Jehangir Merwanji Pleader, and Kekhuśro Kābrājī, along with the salaried director Pestanjī Dhanjībhāi Māsṭar, chose the plays and oversaw the rehearsals, which took place at the Parsi High School in Dhobitalao on weekday evenings and Saturdays due to the actors' professional commitments.[30] According to Khambātā, the Victoria's plays were rigorously examined for quality: an initial grand rehearsal took place in Shankarsheth's bungalow, followed by a second grand rehearsal at the Grant Road Theatre for the committee. After receiving the committee's approval, the play could be performed before the public. The company had an identity-defining function for reformist Parsis and Bombay's new indigenous middle classes, which, as mentioned in Chapter 3, sought respectable public spaces for themselves and their women.

The Parsi Theatre's First Playwrights

Finally on 3 May 1868, the *Rāst* announced the performance of *Khaṇvo Ḍungar ane Kāhāḍvo Undar* (*Much Ado about Nothing* in the Gujarati language and with Italian costumes) along with *Nav Naval Neāedhīśo*, a burlesque on lawmakers.[31] The advertisement carried news of the sale of return tickets at cheap prices for special omnibuses hired to transport residents of the Fort and Bāhārkoṭ (Native Town) to the then-distant Grant Road Theatre.[32] The company also announced the important shift from songs sung to English musical instruments to 'pure, high-class, well constructed native songs' performed by 'a first class singer'.[33] However the troupe was to court polemic even before its first performance. In March 1868, two years after the establishment of the East India Association and the ensuing campaign for Indian rights, a letter writer, 'Na. Ja. Bī', asked whether the new troupe intended to persist with translations of Shakespeare or, instead, to support a nascent group of young, educated, Gujarati playwrights of the 'native modern drama'.[34] Subsequently, the *Rāst* insisted that the troupe perform a 'Ṭrejeḍī' (Tragedy), learn reformed *ākṭīṅg* (acting), and forego Shakespeare for plays that were 'relevant to native life'. Significantly, it alluded to the possibility of a public competition for Gujarati plays that would be judged by the Victoria's committee.[35] The next week, 'Na. Ja. Bī' wrote again, praising the *Rāst* for heeding his remarks while insisting that the troupe select a play that was simple and easy to memorize, was written in plain language or verse, possessed a 'plot' devised by the owners or the playwright, and was written in a style of the playwright's choosing.[36] On 5 July, an advertisement was published announcing three prizes of Rs 100 each for Gujarati plays. Adaptations and translations were permissible (if not universally welcomed), so long as they referenced their sources.[37]

Of the thirteen entries examined, Edaljī Jamśedjī Khorī's *Karṇī tevī pār ūtarnī, ane pāk dāmānnī fatehe*, an adaptation of Sir Walter Scott's *Ivanhoe*, was chosen as the first play to be performed. It premiered on 21 November 1868 in English costume with English *ḍhapchap* (mannerisms), along with the farce *Horājī ane Andhīārūjī athvā lagan talākno ek navo dhāro* (*Horaji and Andhiaruji or New Laws on Marriage and Divorce*).[38] Two months later, the second award-winning play, *Vīktorāinā* or *Bandīkhanethī Bāpne Chodāvnār ek Beṭī* (*A Daughter Releasing Her Imprisoned Father*), which portrayed 'a daughter's abiding affection for her father and pure feminine love', was performed by the Victoria, along with a 'local farce' entitled *Keuek Dākṭaro* (*Quack Doctors*).[39] However, the three prize-winning plays and the ten other contributions came under fire for their 'unoriginality'.

> The public does not like to see foreign subjects. ... Iranian chronicles from the *Śāhānāmā̃*, Hindustani history, classic texts, and folk tales would be wonderful sources for plays and would find favour with our audiences. ... All the three prize-winning plays are adaptations from European sources. The award-winning *Ivanhoe* was well written, but a similar tale can be found in Marathi history. As *Ivanhoe*'s "Robinhood" corresponds with

> the Marathi Rādhojī Bāṅgrīā it is unacceptable that the young talented graduate that wrote the play did not draw inspiration from a native source.[40]

However, the Parsi theatre was on the cusp of great change. On 7 March 1869, the *Rāst* published a two-page article entitled 'Ek Pehelvā̃nī Nāṭak—Aslī Irā̃ṇīono Thoḍok jā̃ṇvājog hevāl' (A *Pehelvā̃nī* [Warrior] Play—A Noteworthy Narrative of the Ancient Iranians):

> With the advent of the English Rāj in this country our people have begun to wear vests, trousers, and boots; roam in horse-drawn carriages, use tables, chairs, desks, and numerous fashionable objects. … Our public has differing opinions with regard to reforms. Some believe the ancient Persians had little to do with these new customs and that these are mere *nakal* [mimicry] of the English. They find fault in those who wear vests and trousers, etc., on the grounds that these new trends are *jaṅglā* [savage] and have nothing to do with the tradition of our ancestors. This matter has been taken up as the subject of serious study in certain quarters, and we are obliged to inform our readers of the results of this investigation. It is evident from the advertisements of the famous Victoria Nāṭak Maṇḍalī that the company has foregone its prize-winning plays for a *pehelvā̃nī* production. In order to produce an exact portrayal of ancient Iran, much research has been conducted on the costumes, etc. … Our *pehelvā̃nī* plays were performed in the past, however the decision has now been made to present a meticulous reproduction of ancient Iranian clothes and manners. The company's managing committee set up a subcommittee of three individuals that went to great lengths to study scientific works on Iran to craft the plot.[41]

The turn from Shakespeare to Persian subjects is critical. While orientalist scholarship had previously been employed to consolidate an authentic Parsi *law*, from 1863 the same research was used to discover an authentic Parsi *body*. The Victoria's managing committee based its new play on the works of Henry Rawlinson and on miscellaneous academic descriptions on Behistun, Persepolis, Taq-e Bostan, and Naqsh-e Rostam.[42] While describing current representations of Iranian attire as historically inaccurate— as a copy of current Chinese and Turkish costume—it asserted that true Sassanian clothes, with the exception of the 'Median robe', looked remarkably similar to contemporary fashions such as boots, gloves, and crinoline. Likewise, current tastes for perfume, attar, liquor, tables, chairs, and tableware could be traced back to ancient Persian times. Additionally, readers were repeatedly promised that the Victoria intended to portray an exact representation of Iranian mannerisms and thought through its gestures and props.[43] As with communal law, which was conceived as the recovery of the lost truths of tradition rather than the blind imitation of European custom, 'vests and trousers' were taken as evidence of the Parsis' culturally superior past. The Parsi theatre, by meticulously reproducing 'ancient Iranian clothes and manners' that curiously resembled those of the 'modern' English Rāj, was to be the guardian of a hitherto neglected yet superior indigenous physical culture unmediated by European sway. Exterior clothing was expressive to the extent that it presented an interior, non-visual understanding of oriental essence. By denoting visual icons of modernity as authentically Persian, Parsis refuted the perception of their enfeeblement and feminization and emphasized the male body as the commemorative site of moral courage. Consequently, a performed bodily politic began to replace its penned legal equivalent for the conservation of social order and discipline.

At long last, on 20 March 1869, this first allegedly historically accurate theatrical representation of the Iranian kingdom, *Bejān ane Manījehnū Dāstā̃n* (translated directly from Firdausi's Farsi *Shahnama*) was performed, along with the Hindustani farce *Premkuvarnā̃ Premno Peālo athvā Navāi Jevā̃ Janā̃var* (*Premkuvar's Love Goblet or A New Type of Animal*), by approximately twenty-five Parsi actors at the Grant Road Theatre.[44] Austen Henry Layard's lithograph of the 'Assyrian Palace', which was the closest available depiction of how King Kekhuśro's court may have appeared, was used by an Italian painter 'Ceroni' as the basis for the drop scene (Fig. 4.5).[45] 'Scientific' accuracy in Kayanian dress and custom thus coincided with its equivalent in setting. The Victoria's drop scenes, painted on the basis of a lithograph that emphasized optical convergence (linear perspective), rendered the Persian court unlike anything that had hitherto been seen in the subcontinent's indigenous theatres, marking the beginning of South Asian theatrical verisimilitude and a composite blurring of scholarly and nonscholarly literature.

Layard's Assyrian lithographs had a long history on the British stage, first featuring in Edward Fitzball's *Azaël the Prodigal* (1851) and Charles Kean's *Sardanapulus* (1853).[46] Edward Ziter notes how this new phenomenology of the stage space offered new forms of knowing to the public. The surfeit of detail in the lithograph was evidence that the mysterious East could be comprehensively mapped and known, an indication of Britain's technological superiority. Through visual references to

Fig. 4.5 Austen Henry Layard, 'Hall in Assyrian Palace, Restored', 1849. From General Research Division, The New York Public Library, New York Public Library Digital Collections. Accessed July 15, 2020, http://digitalcollections.nypl.org/items/510d47dc-46e4-a3d9-e040-e00a18064a99

archaelogical and ethnographic research, British plays according to Ziter, performed an authenticity that marked a dialectic between (on the one hand) oriental religious despotism, sexual promiscuity, and social primitivism and (on the other) European modernity, science, and progress. Conversely, by appropriating the British mastery of foreign topography implied in the lithograph, the Parsi stage muddled European flights of fancy embedded in a larger project of unequal knowing. In contrast with theatrical depictions in the capitals of Europe, which emphasized the realism of an antimodern orient through the lithograph, here the combination of Layard's picture with modern costumes and implements such as boots, vests, gloves, and chairs collapsed the past and present, inscribing the orient within a project of modernity. Unlike Fitzball's despotic East, Kābrājī's *Bejan ane Manījeh*, the first to muddle illusion and reality, was unambivalently pedagogical, a lesson in the community's ancient and advanced theology, history, and geography. Layard's image stood in synecdochal relation to 'modern' costumes, legitimizing the play as an authentic cultural document of the ancient Persians and a key to understanding the civilization in its totality as progressive and utopian.

According to Dhanjībhāi Paṭel, 'the public was wild about this Iranian play'; audiences adored its songs and its portrayal of the strength of *Irāṇī Lohī* (Iranian Blood).[47] The actors Dhanjībhāi Kerā̃vālā (who played Bejan) (Fig. 4.6), Jamśedjī Kāvasjī Dājī (who played Manījeh), and Kāvasjī Naśarvānjī Kohīdārū (who played Gurgīn) (Fig. 4.7) became known for posterity as Dhanju Bejan, Jamsu Manījeh, and Kāvasjī Gurgīn, respectively. *Bejan ane Manījeh* was performed approximately fifty times, and the Victoria's owners became wealthy overnight. This success prompted the construction of Bombay's second theatre, the Victoria Theatre, even as the Grant Road Theatre was undergoing a facelift.[48] The Bombay Theatre Company, a joint-stock company with capital of Rs 200,000, was established and announced its intention to sell two hundred shares of Rs 1000 each.[49] In the interim, the Victoria's owners used their newfound wealth to set up a temporary playhouse with a thirty-foot-wide and forty-eight-foot-long stage and a capacity of approximately 1200 spectators in a rented plot opposite the existing Grant Road Theatre.[50] Built of iron and lit with gas lights, it was described as 'tastefully got up … well lighted, though … badly ventilated'.[51]

Due to the success of *Bejan ane Manījeh*, the Victoria announced a second competition, awarding two prizes of Rs 300 each for plays based on ancient Persian history—that is, those set in the 'Peśdādīan, Keā̃nīan, Eśkānīan, Hakhā̃mīnīan, or Śāsānīan' empires.[52] These 'historical' plays were to be selected by a managing committee that comprised intellectuals and religious scholars such as Ardeshir Moos, Mehervā̃njī Mā̃ṇekjī Seṭhnā̃, Berā̃mjī Fardunjī Marajbā̃n, Bamanjī Pestanjī Māsṭar, and most significantly Dādābhāi Sorābjī Farāmjī Paṭel (Fig. 4.8).[53] It was at this juncture, then, that Kābrājī resigned from his position as secretary. Dādābhāi Paṭel, whose supposedly domineering ways would lead to the breakup of the Victoria's prestigious managing committee, filled the esteemed editor's shoes.[54] Dādī Paṭel, as he was often referred to, had initially been praised by the *Rāst's* venerable editor for securing an MA at the newly instated Bombay University, unlike other traditionalist *seṭhīā* scions, who boycotted higher education.[55] Paṭel, the descendant of one of the first Parsis to have settled in Bombay, Dorabji Nanabhai, subsequently joined his family's flourishing business empire while pursuing a theatrical career as an amateur. He made his first entry into the Parsi theatre as a

Fig. 4.6 Dhanjībhāi Rūstamjī Kerā̃vālā (*Source* Paṭel, *PNTT*, 330. Courtesy: The Trustees, The K. R. Cama Oriental Institute, Mumbai)

member of the Pārsīonī kaśrat ane Gujrātī Gāeṇ Maṇḍalī, while continuing his professional commitments as a government employee and private trader. However, he was soon in the eye of a journalistic storm when he was imbricated in a scandal with an Italian prostitute.[56] During the controversy, Paṭel was supported by the traditionalist organ of the Parsi

Fig. 4.7 Kāvasjī Naśarvānjī Kohīdārū (*Source* Paṭel, *PNTT*, 286. Courtesy: The Trustees, The K. R. Cama Oriental Institute, Mumbai)

Fig. 4.8 Dādābhāi Sorābjī Paṭel (*Source* Paṭel, *PNTT*, 95. Courtesy: The Trustees, The K. R. Cama Oriental Institute, Mumbai)

community, the *Jāme Jamśed*, and he was therefore at the epicentre of Parsi communal factionalism throughout his short-lived existence.

On 21 November 1869, the *Rāst* declared that of eight plays received, the committee had chosen *Rūśtam ane Sohorāb* (*Rustom and Sohrab*) by the winner of the first playwriting competition, the barrister Edaljī Jamśedjī Khorī.[57] After weeks of anticipation, the play—which was adapted from the *Shahnama* and accompanied by songs written especially for the troupe by the scholar-poet Dalpatrām Dāhāyābhāi—was performed on 12 February 1870.[58] Subsequently, the play was patronized by the Nawab of Junagadh on the occasion of Prince Alfred's visit to Bombay, thus making it the first Parsi theatrical production performed before royalty. A 'Civis', writing in the *Bombay Gazette*, described the performance in a manner markedly similar to how the first Parsi play, *Rustom Zabooli and Sohrab*, was described seventeen years earlier (see Chapter 3). A Persian noble, seen in the midst of a wild forest, complains 'in a droll manner of the ill-luck that induced him to a hunt with the indefatigable Rustom'. Subsequently, the hero appears bearing a bow and battleaxe and wearing white kid gloves. He then cooks up a dish of kebabs. While the noble and Rustom take a nap after the meal, a group of soldiers abscond with Rustom's horse, Raksh. On waking and discovering his loss, Rustom proceeds to Teheran, where the king's daughter declares her love for Rustom. 'The dresses of the Princess and her attendants give one a very good idea of how Persian ladies got themselves up, as they are very faithfully represented', the reviewer stated, noting that though tedious, the play was 'assuredly instructive,—to the Parsees at least, for whom it is expressly written'.[59]

If the 1853 production of *Rustom Zabooli and Sohrab* attempted to de-allegorize Persian myth to demonstrate the Parsis' intellectual maturity, the 1870 production was a step towards the discovery of ostensibly forgotten Persian corporeal values of heroism, beauty, and virility based on orientalist scholarship. Although the *Rāst* subsequently panned the long-winded scenes, tiresome plot, and unnatural acting, the production, with its white kid gloves and authentic dresses that referenced the scholarship of William Jones and Henry Rawlinson, was evidently part of a more diffuse web of discovering a utopian Persian corporeal past in order to look forward to a modern utopian Parsi future.[60] Khorī regendered ancient Persia as a hyper-masculine culture by appropriating visual icons of colonial power which, through a metonymic logic, marked martial enactments of the ancient Persian's historical, social, and military superiority as truth. By drawing on ancient Persia rather than modern Europe to defend the use of gloves, wine, and chairs, the Parsi theatre rendered the politics of time as spectacle, complicating the narrative of the lawful domination of the technically superior West over the East and translating the problematic of the dialectic of tradition and modernity into visual metaphor. *Bejan ane Manījeh* and *Rūśtam ane Sohorāb* indicate how, as the political anatomy of discipline passed from the realm of social custom to bodily norm, representations of historical time grew in complexity: from the linear, deterministic, and irreversible temporality of modernity to a romantic, emancipatory, kairotic time that complicated the traditional opposition between the technically superior, progressive West and the unchanging, backward East.

Aryanism

At this same moment in time, strong forces were at work in the world of Zoroastrian scholarship. The belief in a global family of Asian and European languages known variously as the Indo-European, Indo-Germanic, or Aryan family began to take root, and Avestan, the professed primordial language of Zoroastrianism, would be at the heart of this conception. In 1871, the Society for the Diffusion of Knowledge was revived, and Kharshedji Rustomji Cama began delivering his influential lectures on the *aslī erīan loko* (original Aryan peoples), the origins of language, and Irānvej or Erīanvej, a place in Central Asia where the ancestors of the Parsis, Hindus, and Europeans lived together in harmony before migrating across the globe.[61] He also described the three linguistic branches—Aryan, Semitic, and Turanian—with Avestan purportedly being the sister of Sanskrit and Greek.[62] Cama was essentially expounding on theories of monogenesis or the single origin of language and race posited by comparative philologists and orientalists such as Eugene Burnouf, Franz Bopp, Arthur de Gobineau, and especially Max Müller, and which culminated in modern race theory epitomized by social Darwinism and eventually fascism and Nazism. The conception of the Aryan race, as Romila Thapar has shown, became endemic to the remodelling of South Asian history, providing indigenous communities with social standing as they were ostensibly linguistically and racially of the same origin as their colonial rulers.[63] Moreover, implicit in Müller's racial migration theory was the distinction between the Aryans or the fair-skinned Indo-European speakers (e.g. Hindu 'upper castes') and the dark-complexioned Turanians of Scythian origin (e.g. 'lower castes'). This taxonomy of the world's peoples became the underlying blueprint for a developing vision of Parsi society, and Parsi popular works—literary and theatrical—began to reflect a half historical, half mythical antagonism between Aryan Iran and Turan.[64] Accordingly, at the Zoroastrian Nāṭak Maṇḍalī's performance of Dādābhāi Edaljī Pockhānāvālā's *Khuśru Śīrīn* on 27 November 1869, Parsi spectators bellowed with pride when the Iranian army at war with the Turanians raised the Kayanian flag.[65] Similarly, the Alfred Nāṭak Maṇḍalī, so named to commemorate the Duke of Edinburgh's impending visit to Bombay, produced as its first play Farāmjī Bamanjī Writer's *Śāhājādā Sīāvakhś*, based on the mythical combat between the Iranians and the Turanians.[66] The play recounted the trials of the Iranian king Sīāvakhś, from his early days to his untimely death at the hands of the Turanian king Afrāsīāb.[67] Afrāsīāb, performed by the comedian Naśarvānjī Jīvājī Dāvar, was portrayed as a naïve man who was hoodwinked by his courtier Garsīvej into killing his son, while Bhīkhājī N. Kalyānīvālā (King Sīāvakhś) 'looked every part the true Iranian'.[68] The theatre thus became the primary space for the invention and dissemination of a popular version of the Aryan theory and a racialized geographic imagination emerging in disciplines such as ethnology and archaelogy, both acquainting audiences with these regions and espousing an incipient ideology of higher and lower peoples through the exploration of racial essence. The Parsi theatre thereby influenced the course of history, instructing contemporaries about the religious, physical, and ethnic identity of themselves and others, imagined enactments that were subsequently passed down through generations as truth.

Significantly, *Śāhājādā Sīāvakhś* comprised several Kalgīr Torānā songs, which were sung on the Zoroastrian holy days of *muktād* in order to recount the courageous deeds of the *niyāgāho* (ancients).[69] According to Jahāṅgīr Khambātā, 'when the Iranian army sang on the battlefield, Parsi chests brimmed with pride':

> Preserve Farīdun's example, oh honest people of Irān,
> Preserve his honest name and hold it on your tongues
> Hold your weapons warriors—hold courage,
> Brave Irānīs become one.
> You are vital for the war,—fight a majestic war,
> Destroy the kingdom—let their realm fall to dust.[70]

Through the blend of gymnastics and music, a trend that was in keeping with the original principles of the Parsi Gymnasium, the marching war song played an instrumental role in not only eliciting Persian patriotism for an imagined community but also disciplining the body through rhythmic time. Duration was seriated, as beats regulated the counterpoint of gestures and the minutiae of movements performed. It was 'a body manipulated by authority', as Michel Foucault explains. Discipline increased 'the forces of the body (in economic terms of utility) and dimishe[d] these same forces (in political terms of obedience)'.[71] Accordingly, in the theatre, a martial culture was brought to bear that, through patriotic exercize, conceived the male body as an emblem of self-sacrifice: simultaneously subservient to command and superordinate because it had a loftier social objective, the attainment of communal power. The ritual combination of chants and music, Aryan ideology, gymnastics, and the performance of war worked to rebut claims of the feminization or weakening of the Parsi community, offering instead representational icons of social authority and feelings of security and belonging.

The exaltation of the virile ancient Persian body through music in the Parsi theatre would reach its climax when the controversial *Jamśed*, Kābrājī's final Iranian epic drawn from the Peśdadian period of Persian history, was performed on 31 December 1870 at the renovated New Victoria Theatre.[72] Although the costumes were not as lavish as those of the Parsi theatre's later years, they were 'specially prepared to correspond to the times of Jamshed'. Furthermore, the drop scene of Jamshed's palace 'combine[d] European art of a high order with the Oriental splendour ... supposed to have existed in ancient Persia'.[73] On the first night of the performance a large crowd gathered on the street facing the theatre, thus blocking the road, and, according to Khambātā, hundreds returned home as they were unable to find seats.[74] At nine o'clock, the curtain lifted to a scene of a bejewelled tent on a field, the Iranian army marching to the beat of a drum and chanting:

> Ka Ra Ka Ra Ka Ra Ka Ra Ka Ra Ga
> Dha Ra Dha Ra Sa Ra Pa Ra Pa Ra Va Ra—Kar.
> Da Ra Da Ra Da Ra Da Ra Da Ra Da
> Ga Ra Va Ra Kha Ra Kha Ra Na Ra Dha Ra—Kar.[75]

Jamśed's marching songs received multiple encores each night and garnered such public popularity that they were allegedly sung in every house, in every quarter of Bombay.[76] The lyrics, with their repetition of monosyllabic sounds, created a new 'experience of simultaneity', constituting well after this production a community-strengthening exercise for the Parsis of Bombay, who knew the sounds by heart, singing them as they went around their daily business.[77] The aural quality (of 'sweet songs, various instruments, the community singing in unison') of Kābrājī's play was a key component of a new cult of the martial male body, restoring forgotten cultural, historical, and racial insights. Music would, in the Parsi press's words, elicit Parsi patriotism for the motherland, thereby serving as a symbol of communal brawn and an instrument of political ambition.[78]

Controversy, however, was quick to brew after the play's first performance. The *Times of India* described the plot of the play as follows:

> According to Persian tradition, Jamshed claimed divine rights, and power to cure all human ailments, such as loss of sight or speech, lameness and deformity, &c.; but his pride and indiscretion so overpowered his otherwise good sense, that considerable disaffection prevailed among his courtiers, his subjects, and his army, which eventuated in his overthrow and ultimate death in misery. ... [The] play is almost entirely original, very little of Firdousi's thoughts or language being laid under contribution.[79]

The newspaper's description of the plot contains an incongruity: the narrative was written in keeping with 'Persian tradition', but the play was 'entirely original, very little of Firdousi's thoughts or language being laid under contribution'.[80] This inconsistency, one that is further reflected in Khambātā's description of the plot, can be traced back to the playbook's introduction:

> Firdausi's description of Jamśed comprises merely a single event, and if Jamśed had not fallen in love then it would well be considered the dullest story in Firdausi's *Shahnama*. ... As a result I have had to invent most of the action ... to show how his courtiers fanned the flames of his pride despite the entreaties of far-sighted well-wishers. ... The love story sweetens the plot even if this feature is not only inessential but also deemed by many scholars as historically inaccurate. ... Most of the characters are imaginary, however Firdausi hints of the presence of two sisters in his narrative. They could not have been hidden away, as Rawlinson tells us that in the Median age women were immensely respected. ... I am grateful to the

> friends that informed me of the faults in *Bejan Manījeh* but I can differentiate between them and those who merely wish to break my spirit. … Thus I maintain that only those who truly understand the drama have the right to make their opinion known to the public.[81]

This last line is thought provoking. Kābrājī was aware that his portrayal of King Jamśed as a proud tyrant who thought himself a god—and of ancient Persian women as not 'hidden away'—would ignite the ire of both the traditionalist faction of the community (which was campaigning against the presence of women in public spaces) and the rival newspaper bearing the king's name: the *Jāme Jamśed*. Shortly after the play's first performance, the editor of the *Jāme* published a scathing critique of the Victoria's production, with particular regard to '1. the portrayal of Jamśed as an evil, proud tyrant without a single allusion to his great character and deeds … and 2. the fact that Jamśed never referred to himself as a god'. In response Kābrājī anonymously published a two-and-a-half page defense of his less than flattering portrayal of the principal character by citing Firdausi, Arthur de Gobineau, and Parsi scholars such as Dastur Fardunjī and Mancerjī Lāṅgḍā.[82] The controversy, however, showed no sign of abating. Over the course of seven weeks, the *Rāst* published 'proofs' of Jamśed's arrogance and stupidity, and the *Mumbai Sāmācār* joined the fray in support of the *Rāst* by providing additional 'scientific proofs' of Jamśed's pride.[83] Although the play's prologue plainly specified that the characters and events depicted were largely the fruit of the playwright's imagination, orientalist scholarship on ancient Persia was called on to vindicate the purportedly accurate historical portrayal of an Iranian emperor. Thus following the new, realist logic of the Persian mythological play, Kābrājī amalgamated the real and the represented, 'fable' and 'fact', scientific principle and political ideology in the presentation of historical truth, as is further evinced by the playbook itself, which reads as a scholarly treatise with references to the *Vendidad*, the *Avesta*, and the scholarly works of James Atkinson, Martin Haug, and John Malcolm.[84] While orientalist scholarship had previously undermined the authority of the traditionalist *seṭhs* and the Parsi priesthood, it now—when viewed against the growing field of Aryanism—set a precedent for legitimizing through citation a new influential form of performative history-making, where fabricated events, characters, and customs transformed into historical truth through enactments. Science, as epitomized by lithography and orientalist literature, constituted unassailable truths resistant to manipulation and therefore granted playwrights such as Khorī, Rānīnā, and Kābrājī the power to play with the historical record. The theatre—more than the schools (Mullā̃ Fīroj [Mulā Fīroj] and Jamśedjī Jījībhāi Zend ane Pehelavi Madressas [Jamsetjee Jeejeebhoy Zend and Pahlavi Schools]), the library (Mullā̃ Fīroj Ketābkhā̃nū), the public religious lectures by the Religious Reform Association, the growing body of scholarly books on Zoroastrianism, or the study of Persian at the Bombay University—created history, establishing a transregional historical-fictive identity of the Parsis as erstwhile rulers of a vast, militant, masculine empire.[85]

Pan-Zoroastrianism

This transregional Persian identity was significantly strengthened by an auxiliary factor: an increased communal anxiety with regard to the condition of Zoroastrians in Iran, abetted by travellers' accounts of their supposed persecution under the 'Muslims'.[86] As early as 1834, Barjorjī Farā̃mjī Pāṇḍe had set up a fund for the benefit of Iranian Zoroastrians that had raised Rs 30,000 by 1847.[87] The year 1853 witnessed both the building of a *dharamśālā* (religious accommodation) at Chowpatty for their benefit and the establishment of the Society for the Amelioration of the Condition of the Zoroastrians in Persia, which lobbied for the lifting of the *jazieh* (non-Muslim) tax on Iranian Zoroastrians. A year later, the 'Zoroastrian missionary' Manekji Limji Hataria was sent to Iran as a representative of the Society to 'report upon the social, political, and intellectual condition of the Zoroastrians in Persia' only to describe on his return the abysmal state of the Parsis' co-religionists.[88] By 1855 scores of Zoroastrian refugees had reached Bombay's shores, and criticisms began to be levelled against the lack of efforts to provide them with adequate means of employment.[89] In 1863 the refugees in the *dharamśālā* were 'stuffed like goats', and lacked clothes and adequate food.[90] A few years later the *Pioneer* declaimed, 'The Proverb "As rare as a Parsee beggar" has unfortunately no longer any point. Parsees from Persia may now be seen begging for alms in the streets of Bombay'.[91] Drought in Iran between 1869 and 1871 aggravated the plight of the Iranian Zoroastrians. Hataria's descriptions of skyrocketing food prices, unemployment, and a fast-declining population in Iran resulted in the creation of a second fund on 3 June 1871; this one was directed towards transporting the Parsis' Iranian brethren to Bombay, the new home of the followers of the Zoroastrian religion.[92] Parsi reformist newspapers justified the Iranian Zoroastrians' much-needed exodus on the grounds that their physically stronger co-religionists could be employed in professions for which Bombay's Parsis were too weak, such as the police force. Furthermore, echoing the martial Aryan rhetoric of the genre of the Persian play, the press used terms such as *deśhītkārīpaṇũ* (patriotism) and *deś* (country) in reference to Iran, stressing the common origins of the refugees and the Parsis in the Kayanian empire and the necessity of fighting for the survival of the religion:

> Get up! Parsis! Get up, awaken and bear the colossal responsibility that is before you! Patriotism and duty are calling you and oh! Descendants of the Kayanians! The time has come to rise with joy and enthusiasm to fulfil all your obligations—towards humanity, towards your country, and towards your god. In the name of our ancient land, in the name of our co-religionists, in the name of our religious precepts, in the name of the fervour in our souls, in short in the name of all that you hold pure and true in the world, oh Parsis! We beg you to rise up! ... Those times are past that you fought to win great kingdoms but you are strong enough and ready to fight for your religion ... so get up! Parsis get up![93]

A pan-Zoroastrian identity, first historicized through orientalist scholarship on Aryanism, was thus reinforced through relief efforts for the Iranian Zoroastrian refugees, crystallizing, as Simin Patel says, a 'new sense of community consciousness among the Parsis'.[94] Parsi philanthropy for the Iranian refugees by scattered groups across South Asia, channelled through the epicentre of Bombay, had a narratological function, generating an imaginary geography of a surrogate empire. The performative function of charity thus also transformed during this period: from signifying financial and sociopolitical clout of the traditionalist *seṭhs*, to mapping a transregional ethno-religious landscape. The Parsi theatre played no small part in not only creating and diffusing a pan-Zoroastrian geographic imagination, but also rallying financial support for the Iranians. On 3 June 1871, the usually reticent Kābrājī consented to perform as Bejan in his *Bejan ane Manījeh* at the New Victoria Theatre, thus raising Rs 425 for the Persian Famine Fund.[95] As Kābrājī's participation was 'pretty well-known before, the house was crammed with spectators'.[96] At the same time, the Alfred Nāṭak Maṇḍalī performed *Jehānbakhś ane Gulrūkhśār*, raising Rs 1200, even as the Zoroastrian Nāṭak Maṇḍalī donated the proceeds of its *Khodābakś* for the fund.

Subsequently, the Victoria produced a series of performances of *Gule Bakāvalī*, half of the profits going towards 'the benefit of the poor Iranis'.[97]

Simultaneously, even as veneration for the motherland reached new heights through the publication of Farsi books alongside pamphlets of theatre songs,[98] the institution of Anglo-Persian classes,[99] the popularization of travelogues on Iran—'the land of our forefathers',[100] the creation of a Pahlavi grammar,[101] and even calls for a Pārsī Rāj with its own president, congress, and senate,[102] the theatre played an influential role in assimilating the Parsis' co-religionists to their new home in India. Although European royalty had been showcased in Parsi theatre company names of the 1850s and 1860s, the year 1870 witnessed a short-lived change in appellation. Under the leadership of Dādābhāi Paṭel several Iranian refugees were assembled to form the Irānī Nāṭak Maṇḍalī (Persian Theatrical Club).[103]

On 10 December 1870 the troupe performed 'the well known drama of *Roostum and Burjor* [*Rūstam ane Barjor*] ... in Persian character and language'.[104] A reviewer in the *Bombay Gazette* noted that the number of actors was 'unusually large', observing further that their physical proportions were also quite large, like that of true Persian warriors. Other notable characteristics of the play included the appearance on horseback of the two principal combatants, the 'extremely fine' scenery prepared by Messrs. Sykes and Dwyer, and the excellent quality of the silk and satin costumes that had been brought from Persia by the actor who played Barjor. Crucially, the reviewer emphasized that though the three-hour-long play was performed in Persian, 'no one seemed to feel weary of it': every part was first explained by Paṭel in Gujarati verse.[105] Evidently, from these early days, Paṭel—the mastermind behind the popularization of Parsi theatre across the subcontinent—understood the greater importance of theatrical action over dialogue. It mattered little that the Parsis of Bombay could not understand the meaning of the Farsi sentences. Instead, as both Khambātā and the company's advertisements make clear, it was the rising sun, battles on horses, grassy fields (made with wooden boxes filled with real grass), 'views', and costumes that drew audiences by droves.[106] As Khambātā notes:

> They didn't act but quite literally screamed and jumped on the stage like lunatics as if they were truly in the Iranian and Turanian battlefields. They would pummel and injure each other, and made their entries on real horses.

> … Scores of Parsis went to see the play, first because it was performed by Iranians and second because the play was in Farsi. People enjoyed the novelty and the actors' eccentricity. I was surprised that the actors didn't kill each other, yet even for a juvenile like me the actors were very successful in fostering many memories of our land.[107]

Through the combination of pride for the motherland Iran, 'singing, athletic sport, and cycloramic views', and magic lantern shows and dissolving views, *Rūśtam ane Barjor* exemplified a critical transition in the South Asian modern theatre: from a moral and corporeal disciplinary apparatus to a place of sensual pleasure and spectacle.[108] The inclusion of real horses exemplified the Parsi theatre's use at this stage of an abundance of visual detail to support the authenticity of the performance, leading in turn, to a fetishization of spectacle. Despite Kabraji's preliminary pedagogical intentions for the Persian mythological play, the incorporation of ethnographic detail by Paṭel appears to have been motivated by the growing demand for visual wonders rather than an interest in exploring the authentic customs of the ancients. Paṭel's Iranians were essentially bridging an increasingly wide gap between didactic verisimilitude and spectacular entertainment, the visual here having taken on a new function in the production of meaning. An agenda of physical instruction and self-discipline was increasingly giving way to a desire for ocular amusement, marking the commencement of the secularization of the Parsi stage.

Perhaps for this reason, the success of the Irānī Nāṭak Maṇḍalī was short lived. On 17 December 1870 an accident occurred while Rūśtam and Barjor were combatting on horseback onstage. In the middle of the stage was a tightly screwed and well-secured trapdoor, big enough, when open, to let a horse fall through to the ground floor of the theatre. An unknown individual had loosened the screws, making the trapdoor unstable. When one of the horses trod on the door, it collapsed, and the animal fell into a deep hole that normally contained the sweepings of the stage. On that day, the hole was deeper than usual and contained fresh water, yet the horse was extricated without harm, while the rider suffered only a bruise to his shin. According to the *Bombay Gazette*, the great success of the Persians had prompted an 'evil-disposed person connected with another theatrical company to attempt a diabolical act to thwart them'.[109] The perpetrator was never found. Matters worsened when Pestanjī Farāmjī Velātī, who played the part of Gurgīn, absconded to found the Persian Zoroastrian Nāṭak Maṇḍalī. More significantly, Dādābhāi Paṭel, who was now knee deep in his theatrical pursuits, left the Irānī Nāṭak Maṇḍalī and his lucrative day job in his family's thriving business for a position as director of the Victoria, marking not only the end of the disciplinary role of the drama and the Parsi community's affirmative association with the mainstream Parsi theatre, but also the beginning of the Parsi theatre's now well-known and enormously influential diffusion across the subcontinent and beyond. A transregional pan-Zoroastrian identity thus prompted the development of a soon-to-be pan-Asian performance form whose primary mode of communicative exchange was visual rather than verbal.

Notes

1. See the long-drawn dispute between the Parsi press and the *Native Opinion* (a Bombay newspaper aimed at the English-speaking public), which cast aspersions on the Parsi community's character, ranking Parsis lower in morality than Hindus or Muslims. 'Pārsīonī Nītī', *RG*, 26 September 1869, 613–14; 'Pārsīonī Nītī, *RG*, 26 September 1869, 613–14; 'Pārsīonī Hālat. Aṅk 1 lo', *RG*, 3 October 1869, 627–28; and 'Pārsīo ane "Neṭīv Opīnīan"', *RG*, 21 November 1869, 739–40.
2. 'Pārsīonī Hālat. Aṅk 3 jo', *RG*, 17 October 1869, 660–61.
3. Dīndār, 'Carcā Patra', *RG*, 6 January 1867, 10; and 'Pārsī Klabo', *RG*, 1 September 1867, 545–46.
4. Untitled, *RG*, 4 October 1867, 630–32. See also 'Sudhāro kahī Batāvīe ke karī batāvīe', *RG*, 2 February 1868; and 'Bolo nā—karī dekhāḍo', *RG*, 5 April 1868, 215–16.
5. 'Iaṅg Bombe', *RG*, 8 January 1865, 18–19. The *Rāst* was here referring to the reformist Ardeshir Framji Moos.
6. 'Iaṅg Bombe', *RG*, 18–19.
7. Jesse S. Palsetia, *The Parsis of India: Preservation of Identity in Bombay City* (New Delhi: Manohar, 2008), 294. See also 'Be Pārsī grahasthone malelā moṭā hothā', *RG*, 3 May 1868, 278.
8. "Hīndustān", *RG*, 9 June 1867, 353–534; "Profesar Dādābhāinū Bhāśāṇ - Keḷvāylā deśīo ūpar ek tohomat.", *RG*, 16 June 1867, 373–74 and "Mumbai Āsosīeśannā Pehelū Kām", *RG*, 5 January 1868, n.p.
9. 'Sīvīlsarvīsmā̃ koṇ jaśe? Āpṇā̃ kelvāelā juvānīā̃ ke?', *RG*, 28 February 1869, 130–31. See also 'Gāmṭhī Kānśteblo', *RG*, 21 June 1857, 199–200; 'Pārśī Rījmīṭ', *RG*, 19 July 1857, 228–29; 'Pārśīone Śucnā', *RG*, 31 May 1857, 171–72; 'Mīlīśīā-Pārsīone sari tak', *RG*, 31 May 1857, 172–73 for similar arguments that were made as early as 1857 in the

aftermath of the Indian Rebellion, when Parsi boys were deemed to have obtained an education that, in prioritizing the mental over the physical, 'was fit merely for women'.

10. 'Āpṇā̃ mīnnā̃ putlā', *RG*, 29 July 1866, 467–68; 'Pārsīonū śū thaśe?', *RG*, 3 February 1867, 65–66. This conception of the weak Parsi body prompted publications such as the magazine *Tandarostī* (*Health*) and lectures on the 'science of the body' 'Tandarostī', *RG*, 3 February 1867, 79; 'Śarīr Vīdīā', *RG*, 17 December 1871, 820; 'Dnyān Prasārak Maṇḍaḷī', *RG*, 14 January 1872, 24–25.
11. 'Pārsīo', *RG*, 18 November 1866, 723–25; Robert Crego, *Sports and Games of the 18th and 19th Centuries* (Westport, C.T.: Greenwood Press, 2003), 147.
12. 'Pārsī Vālanṭīaro', *RG*, 25 August 1867, 533; 'Pārsīonū śū thaśe?', *RG*, 3 February 1867, 65–66.
13. Walter Benjamin, 'The Work of Art in the Age of Mechanical Reproduction', *Illuminations*, tr. Harry Zohn (New York: Schocken Books, 1969), 241–42.
14. 'Jāher Khabar', *RG*, 29 January 1860, 60; 'Jāher Khabar', *RG*, 26 February 1860, 108; and Dhanjībhāi Na Paṭel, *PNTT* (Bombay: 'Kaysare-Hind' Paper Printing Press, 1931), 55.
15. 'Pārsī Vālanṭīaro-Irā̃nī Kavāed', *RG*, 8 September 1867, 562–63; 'Kasratśāḷāmā̃ Norojno Akhāḍo', *RG*, 19 September 1869, 600.
16. 'Jāher Khabar', *RG*, 29 January 1860, 60; 'Jāher Khabar', *RG*, 26 February 1860, 108; Paṭel, *PNTT*, 55; and 'Kasratśālā sthāpak maṇḍalī', *RG*, 21 March 1869, 184.
17. 'Pārsīomā̃ Gāeṇ', *RG*, 29 January 1860, 40–41.
18. 'Hīndu Kasrat Śālā', *RG*, 3 June 1860, 183; untitled, *RG*, 8 May 1870, 310; 'Profesar Baśvanāno chelo khel', *RG*, 3 June 1860, 183; untitled, *RG*, 17 March 1867, 174; 'Ajāeb jevā Jepānīs Khelāḍīo', *RG*, 4, February 1872, 74; and untitled, *RG*, 14 November 1869, 737.
19. 'Kasratśāḷā-Cahaḍtī Kaśrato', *RG*, 31 March 1867, 194–95; 'Kasratśālāno navo rīporṭ', *RG*, 25 June 1865, 408; and 'Āpṇā̃ mīnnā̃ putlā', *RG*, 29 July 1866, 467–68.
20. 'Kaśrat Śāḷā', *RG*, 10 November 1867, 713.
21. 'Nāṭak', *RG*, 3 November 1867, 701.
22. According to Dinshaw Edulji Wacha, Dadi Christ was so known because 'at one time he had avowed Christianity as his religion till brought back to the old path of his Zoroastrian ancestors'. Dinshaw Edulji Wacha, *Shells from the Sands of Bombay; Being My Recollections and Reminiscences, 1860–1875* (Bombay: K.T. Anklesaria, 1920), 355.
23. Paṭel, *PNTT*, 81. Also spelled Dādābhāi Ṭhūṭhī, Dadī Christ, Moṭābāvā; Horamjī Dādābhāi Modī, Kākāvāl, respectively.

24. These performances were the first to be attended by both men and women. Paṭel, *PNTT*, 81; and 'Pārsī Strīonī Āgalnī tathā Hamṇānī Hālat vace mukāblo karvā sambandhī ek dastāvej', *RG*, 26 January 1868, 55.
25. 'Deśī Strīone Māṭe Nāṭak—Strī Keḷavṇīno ek ūpay', *RG*, 19 January 1868, 34–35.
26. 'Pārsīomā̃ nāṭak', *RG*, 29 December 1867, 819.
27. 'Pārsī Nāṭako Viśe Sucnā̃', *RG*, 29 December 1867, 821.
28. Paṭel, *PNTT*, 81–82; and Jahāṅgīr Pestanjī Khambātā, *NA* (Bombay, 1913), 11–12.
29. 'Navo Nāṭak', *RG*, 23 February 1868, 121.
30. Paṭel, *PNTT*, 329; Khambātā, *NA*, 11–12; and untitled, *Rāst Goftār*, 3 May 1868, 289.
31. 'Vīkṭoriā Naṭak Maṇḍaḷī', *RG*, 3 May 1868, 284.
32. 'Vīkṭoriā Naṭak Maṇḍaḷī', *RG*, 284. The town's refuse was deposited on either side of Grant Road making the district uninhabitable and unhealthy. In its early years, the Grant Road Theatre was the only building among these flats, standing, according to Kābrājī, as an oasis in the desert. Consequently, its location was not only initially insalubrious but also dangerous. Kaikhosro N. Kabraji, 'Reminiscences of Kaikhosro N. Kabraji (editor of *Rast Goftar*) Fifty Years Ago', *TOI*, 26 October 1901, 7.
33. Untitled, *RG*, 24 May 1868, 336.
34. Na. Ja. Bī., 'Navo Nāṭak', *RG*, 8 March 1868, 155.
35. 'Navo Nāṭak', *RG*, 24 May 1868, 330.
36. Na. Ja. Bī., 'Vīkṭorīyā Nāṭak Maṇḍaḷīne Ek Sucnā', *RG*, 31 May 1868, n.p.
37. 'Vīkṭorīyā Nā̃ṭak Maṇḍaḷī. Ināmnā̃ nā̃ṭako lakhāvā babe jāher khabar', *RG*, 5 July 1868, 433. A letter by 'Nāṭak' decried the Victoria's acceptance of translations, accusing it of not supporting Indian playwriting. 'Without rice, fire and water it is not possible to make a meal despite adding ghee and spices (..) The plot is what matters', he decried. Nāṭak, '"Vīkṭoriā Nāṭak Maṇḍalī" ne śucnā', *RG*, 18 October 1868, 666.
38. 'Vīkṭorīyā Nāṭak Maṇḍaḷī', *RG*, 4 October 1868, 634.
39. 'Vīkṭoriā Nāṭak', *Rāst Goftār*, 3 January 1869, 8; 'Vīkṭoriā Nāṭak', *RG*, 10 January 1869, 24; untitled, *Rāst Goftār*, 10 January 1869, 30; untitled, *RG*, 17 January 1869, 46; and untitled, *RG*, 24 January 1869, 63.
40. 'Deśī Nāṭako Viśe Thoḍī agatnā̃ vicāro', *RG*, 22 November 1868, 741–43. Moreover, those familiar with the English *Ivanhoe* found the adaptation to be lacking, and in a manner reminiscent of the Parsi theatre's earliest controversies, letter writers criticized the farce for its negative portrayal of the Parsi community. 'Vīkṭorīyā Nāṭak Maṇḍalī', *RG*, 29 November 1868, 762.

41. 'Ek Pehelvā̃nī Nāṭak—Aslī Irā̃ṇīono Thoḍok jā̃ṇvājog hevāl', *RG*, 7 March 1869, 149–50.
42. These studies purportedly described King Kekhuśro's Bactrian Kingdom (which was ostensibly older than Prophet Zarathustra himself by three thousand years), the ensuing Assyrian and Median kingdoms, and Iranian clothes and customs such as men and women dining together and respect for women. 'Ek Pehelvā̃nī Nāṭak—Aslī Irā̃ṇīono Thoḍok jā̃ṇvājog hevāl', *RG*, 7 March 1869, 149–50.
43. 'Ek Pehelvā̃nī Nāṭak—Aslī Irā̃ṇīono Thoḍok jā̃ṇvājog hevāl', *RG*, 7 March 1869, 149–50; and 'Aslī Irā̃ṇīono Thoḍok Jā̃ṇvājog Hevāl', *RG*, 28 March 1869, 199–200.
44. Untitled, *RG*, 14 March 1869, 174; and Paṭel, *PNTT*, 90.
45. Khambātā, *NA*, 13–14; and 'Vīkṭorīyā Nāṭak Maṇḍaḷī', *RG*, 21 March 1869, 184.
46. Edward Ziter, *The Orient on the Victorian Stage* (Cambridge: Cambridge University Press, 2003), 78, 150–51.
47. Paṭel, *PNTT*, 329–33; and 'Vīkṭorīyā Nāṭak Maṇḍaḷī', *RG*, 11 April 1869, 233.
48. Paṭel, *PNTT*, 97–99; and 'Nāṭakśālā', *RG*, 30 May 1869, 344.
49. 'Navī Nā̃ṭakśāḷā', *RG*, 14 November 1869, 731.
50. 'Navī Nā̃ṭakśāḷā', *RG*, 5 December 1869, 778; Khambātā, *NA*, 13–14; and 'The Victoria Theatre', *BG*, 10 February 1870, 2.
51. 'The Victoria Theatre', *BG*, 17 February 1870, 3.
52. 'Vīkṭorīā Nāṭak Maṇḍalī', *RG*, 20 June 1869, 399; and Paṭel, *PNTT*, 99.
53. 'Vīkṭorīā Nāṭak Maṇḍaḷī', *RG*, 26 September 1869, 618.
54. Paṭel, *PNTT*, 93–94, 99–100.
55. 'Mumbai Iūnīvarsīṭī', *RG*, 15 April 1866, 229–30.
56. 'Pārsīomā̃ Gāeṇ', *RG*, 22 January 1860, 38–39; 'Pārsīonī kasrat ane Gujrātī Gāeṇ Maṇḍalī', *RG*, 12 February 1860, 75–76; and Dādābhāi Śorābjī, 'Pārsīonī kaśrat ane Gāeṇ Maṇḍalīno ek adhīkārī', *RG*, 26 February 1860, 106.
57. 'Vīkṭorīā Nāṭak Maṇḍalī', *RG*, 21 November 1869, 746.
58. Paṭel, *PNTT*, 92; Khambātā, *NA*, 13–14; and 'Rūstam ane Śohorāb', *RG*, 6 February 1870, 85–86.
59. Civis, 'The Victoria Theatre', *BG*, 17 February 1870, 3.
60. 'Navo Nāṭak', *RG*, 20 February 1870, 117–18.
61. 'Dnyān Prasārak Maṇḍaḷī', *RG*, 26 November 1871, 771–72.
62. 'Dnyān Prasārak Maṇḍaḷī', *RG*, 4 February 1872, 71–72; and 'Dnyān Prasārak Maṇḍaḷī', *RG*, 16 June 1872, 378–79.
63. Romila Thapar, 'The Theory of Aryan Race and India: History and Politics', *Social Scientist* 24, no. 1/3 (1996): 3–29.
64. See 'Barjo Nāmū', *RG*, 6 September 1868, 577.

65. Paṭel, *PNTT*, 240–42. However, the *Rāst* criticized the playwright for having 'no idea how to write, spoiling beautiful Farsi words with long-winding sentences'; the schoolboy actors, for standing like statues and reciting their dialogues in singsong intonation; and the entire production, for being a cheat, sham, and child's play. Tellingly, tickets were sold at the *Jāme Jamśed* and *Cābuk* presses, which explains much of the *Rāst*'s vitriol. 'Khuśro ane Śīrīn', *RG*, 17 April 1870, 250.
66. 'The Alfred Dramatic Club', *BG*, 22 April 1870, 2. The new Alfred Nāṭak Maṇḍalī had four owners: Māṇekjī Jīvanjī Māsṭar, Rūstamjī Bāṭlā, Bhīkhājī Kalyānīvālā, and Kharśedjī Bāpāsolā, as well as an honorary director, Hīrjī Aspandyārjī Khambātā. Khambātā, *NA*, 13–14.
67. Untitled, *BG*, 17 April 1870, 257.
68. The Alfred rehearsed the play for approximately eight months and, in keeping with the tradition instituted by the Victoria, performed before a number of esteemed members of Bombay society at a grand rehearsal. In the play, the minor part of a singing Rāhmeśgar was played by Jamshedji Framji Madan, marking the cinema baron's first appearance on the Parsi stage. 'Ālfreḍ Nāṭak Maṇḍaḷī', *RG*, 24 March 1870, 266; and Khambātā, *NA*, 13–14. Also spelled Bhīkhājī Kalīyāṇīvāḷā.
69. The *muktād* or Farvardegan takes place ten days before the Parsi New Year and is a period where Parsis pray for the souls of the departed.
70. Khambātā, *NA*, 15.
71. Michel Foucault, *Discipline and Punish*, 155, 138.
72. Khambātā, *NA*, 25.
73. The scene was prepared by the enterprising Ceroni according to Kābrājī's rigorous demands for Rs 150. 'The Victoria Theatrical Company', *TOI*, 6 January 1871, 3.
74. According to the *Times of India*, the audience was 'present in such numbers as to "crowd out" many who came anxious to see the new play "Jamshed"'. 'The Victoria Theatrical Company', *TOI*, 6 January 1871, 3.
75. Kekhuśro Navrojjī Kābrājī, *Jamśed* (Bombay: Daftar Āśkārā Press, 1870), 1.
76. Khambātā, *NA*, 25–27.
77. Benedict Anderson, *Imagined Communities: Reflections on the Origin and Spread of Nationalism*, London: Verso, 2006, 145.
78. 'Bandagīmā Gāeṇno Ūpyog', *RG*, 26 February 1871, 131–32.
79. 'The Victoria Theatrical Company', *TOI*, 6 January 1871, 3.
80. 'The Victoria Theatrical Company', *TOI*, 6 January 1871, 3. See also 'The Persian Drama', *TOI*, 21 January 1871, 3.
81. Kekhuśro Navrojjī Kābrājī, *Jamśed* (Bombay: Daftar Āśkārā Press, 1870), dībāco (prologue).
82. '"Jamśed" no nāṭak', *RG*, 8 January 1871, n.p.

83. '"Jamśed" ane Jāme Jamśed', *RG*, 15 January 1871, n.p.; 'Ek Vadhu Purāvo', *RG*, 22 January 1871, n.p.; 'Jā̃me Jamśed', *RG*, 5 February 1871, 88; and 'Gujarātī Nāṭakonī Tapās', *RG*, 22 October 1871, 688–89.
84. *Jamśed* would remain a bulwark amidst the many changes witnessed by the Parsi theatre, subsisting well into the twentieth century under the new title *Ājamśāh*. It would, however, eventually lose its role as a historical chronicle of an ancient Persian past. Khambātā, *NA*, 22–23.
85. 'Mullā̃ Fīroj Ketābkhā̃nũ', *RG*, 1 January 1865, 13; 'Jartostī Dharam Pustakono Abhīās', *RG*, 11 January 1863, 13–14; 'Sar Jamśedjī Jījībhāivālī Jand ane Pehelvī Madresā', *RG*, 22 January 1865, 56; 'Jartośtī Dharamnī Fīlsufī', *RG*, 3 January 1869, 6–7; 'Jartostīonā̃ Hāthmā̃ ek sari tak', *RG*, 2 April 1865, 211–12; 'Jartośtnāmũ', *RG*, 8 May 1870, 294–95; 'Irā̃nnī Musāfrī', *RG*, 16 January 1870, 33–34; 'Jartośtī Dīnnī Khol karnārī maṇḍaḷī ane tenā̃ sambandhmā̃ bhāśā̃ṇ', *RG*, 23 May 1869, 327–28; and 'Jartostī Dharamne Lagtī Bābado upar bhāśaṇo', *RG*, 6 February 1870, 87.
86. See Ek Pārsī Vīdīārthī, 'Irā̃n Deśnā̃ Jartośtīo, temnā̃ dharam ane temnī hālat babe ek frenc musāfre āpelo hevāl', *RG*, 4 April 1868, 217–18.
87. 'Pārsīonā Dharamkhātā̃', *RG*, 20 September 1863, 479–80.
88. Dosabhai Framji Karaka, *History of the Parsis, Including Their Manners, Customs, Religion, and Present Position* (London, 1884), 72; 'Irānnā Jartośtīonī hālat sudhārnārā̃ dharamkhātā̃nā kārobārīonī ek faraj', *RG*, 18 June 1871, 394–95.
89. 'Irā̃nīonũ Faṇḍ', *RG*, 6 May 1855, 137–38.
90. 'Pārsīonā Dharamkhātā̃', *RG*, 20 September 1863, 479–80; 'Irā̃nthī Nāhāsī āvelā jartośtīomā̃ kevī ūcī tokhamnā māṇasoche?', *RG*, 11 February 1872, 86–87; and 'Irā̃nīone bhulī jaiśũ ke?', *RG*, 17 March 1872, 166–67.
91. Untitled, *RG*, 28 April 1872, 263–64.
92. 'Gai Kāle…', *RG*, 4 June 1871, 364.
93. 'Pārsīo Ūṭho!', *RG*, 14 January 1872, 19–20.
94. Simin Patel, 'The Great Persian Famine of 1871, Parsi Refugees and the Making of Irani Identity in Bombay', in *Bombay Before Mumbai: Essays in Honour of Jim Masselos*, eds. Prashant Kidambi, Manjiri Kamat and Rachel Dwyer (Oxford: Oxford University Press, 2019), 57.
95. Untitled, *TOI*, 2 June 1871, 1; Untitled, *BG*, 2 June 1871, 1; and 'Fund for the Persian Parsees', *BG*, 16 June 1871, 2.
96. 'The Victoria Theatrical Company', *BG*, 2 June 1871, 2.
97. Untitled, *RG*, 3 March 1872, 147.
98. Untitled, *RG*, 4 June 1871, 370.
99. Untitled, *RG*, 5 May 1872, 291.
100. 'Irā̃nnī Musāfrī', *RG*, 16 January 1870, 33–34.

101. 'Pehlavī Bhashānū Vyākraṇ', *RG*, 3 March 1872, 138.
102. 'Pārsī Rāj!', *RG*, 18 December 1870, 815–16.
103. 'Parsee Theatricals in the Persian Language', *BG*, 10 December 1870, 2.
104. 'The Persian Theatrical Club', *BG*, 12 December 1870, 3.
105. 'The Persian Theatrical Club', *BG*, 12 December 1870, 3. Similar praise was showered by the *Rāst* in its columns. 'Fārsī Nāṭak', *RG*, 4 December 1870, 789.
106. 'Barjor Rūśtamno vakhnāelo Khel', *RG*, 22 January 1871, 65.
107. Khambātā, *NA*, 4.
108. 'The Persian Theatrical Club', *BG*, 25 January 1871, 2.
109. 'The Persian Theatrical Club: Singular Accident at the Theatre', *BG*, 19 December 1870, 3.

PART II

Re-Enchantment

The Parsi theatre is most well-known for its spectacular stage effects and sumptuous fittings of elaborately painted drop scenes and exquisitely constructed costumes, a 'display of splendor, a lavishness that dazzles the eye', unlike anything that had been seen in the theatres of South and Southeast Asia before.[1] Fairies fluttered down from the vaults of heaven, ogres and evil spirits emerged from the sulphurous depths of the netherworld, ships plunged into the briny deep, and trains dropped off bridges into unfathomable ravines. Part II of this book attempts to answer a seemingly modest question first posed by Edward Ziter in a dissimilar context: why all this stuff?[2] To be more specific, what and how were audiences observing and perceiving? What structure of power shaped this new ontology of the visual? What deeper purpose over and above skittish diversion and ocular pleasure did spectacle fulfil? Chapters 5 and 6 analyse how the theatre's magic profoundly shaped colonial society and culture. They demonstrate how the seemingly trivial fairy floss of the Parsi stage was, in fact, powerful and insidious, allowing the drama to not only transgress linguistic, ethnic, and cultural boundaries but also convey nostalgia for lost innocence, a mild form of social rebellion. Through a seemingly innocent alteration in a spiritual economy of representation—from reformist disenchantment to secular re-enchantment—the theatre's commercial aesthetic of outwardly incoherent attractions inadvertently generated fault lines in colonialism's monumental project of knowing and its agenda of emancipatory progress.

Part I of this book, covering the period of social reform, describes how 'disenchantment' (*Entzauberung*) marked an epistemic rupture in the self-definition of Indian society. According to Max Weber, disenchantment—or uninterrupted contact with reality through the discrimination of myth or magic from religion—was the primary feature of capitalist modernity.[3] Nature was conceptualized as determinate, manipulable, uniform, and 'subject to mechanical laws', while the rest—illogical incidents and fictional creatures, devil worship and idolatry—were demarcated as imaginary trappings of the actual world.[1] The individual becomes the deliverer of his own salvation, wealth, and success, capitalist reason supplants mysticism; science breaches magical covenants; knowledge deposes of superstition; and technology controls nature.[4] The world, according to this new ontology, was comprehensively knowable. Myth—representing false science, barbarity, and otherness (an heirloom of Protestant liberalism)—legitimized colonial expansion and intervention in the beliefs and behaviours of the world's 'primitive' peoples.

Recent scholarship, however, has shown that disenchantment was accompanied by parallel processes of re-enchantment, *Bezauberung* (mystification).[5] The desacralization of rituals, objects, language, and individuals coincided with the sacralization of other fields and ideas: civil rights, property, risk-taking, commodity exchange, and science. Old fetishes and totems conceded to new ones—a cornucopia of saints and demons and a cosmology of transubstantiation and fate gave way in a modernizing Europe to sacred, inviolable, transcendental beliefs in money spirits and the metaphysical uncertainty of the market. Similarly, as much as reformists such as Kekhuśro Kābrājī formulated the role of the Parsi theatre as didactic, disciplinary, moral entertainment through the de-allegorization of the ancient Persian past, directors such as Dādābhāi Paṭel emphasized spectacle that collapsed the distance between science and magic, a technologically advanced modern Europe and the despotic oriental past, and the underlying political motivations that undergirded these distinctions. If religion was rationalized in the 1850s and 1860s, science was concurrently spiritualized, provoking questions on materiality and materialism, reality and illusion, seeing and believing, the inner mind and outward appearance, and the nature of truth. In Paṭel's and his followers' hands, there was no phenomenological disjuncture in the

[1] Asad, *Formations of the Secular*, 27.

move from Mughal minarets and ancient Hindu temples to modern panoramas and dioramas, magic lanterns, and electric wonders. By mediating between self- and reverse orientalism, the Parsi theatre confused the conception of the orient as belonging to a space outside of modernity while suggesting that truth could not be found through perceptual experience, that which is seen and demonstrable. A widespread epistemological ambiguity as to the relationship between the physical senses and knowledge coincided with the theatre's inversion of the panoptical logic of the museum, exhibition, law-making association, and public sphere, places where observers gazed at timeless custom to discover the essence of the East. The exceptional heterogeneity of plots and inchoate themes in the no longer reformist Parsi theatre from the mid-1860s may therefore be attributed less to diversity of style, multiphonal cultural syncretism, and eccentricity than to an exploration of phenomenological and ideological issues. A new hermeneutics of perceptibility and visual literacy through the appropriation of the imperial perspective was the ultimate contribution of the Parsi theatre, whose excess facilitated the development of a common cultural foundation legible across South and Southeast Asia that increasingly generated disquiet as it provided room for the development of alternative networks of power. Chapter 5 demonstrates how the theatre developed a 'secular mythology', a common visual vocabulary or set of symbols and meanings that instated a cultural homogeneity, which was the groundwork for underlying narratives of the progressive historical development of unified political units. Chapter 6 then gives an account of the theatre's expansion across South and Southeast Asia. By resolving the presumed contradiction between modern technology and the indigenous, ancient past, Parsi drama not only provided a form of escapism from the oppressive doctrinal project of colonial reason but also discovered an independent domain of imaginative sovereignty that combined the material and the spiritual—a viable ideological basis for distinctive, uniform cultural identities.

Notes

1. Sisir Kumar Das, *History of Indian Literature: 1911–1956, Struggle for Freedom: Triumph and Tragedy* (New Delhi: Sahitya Akademi, 2005), 175; Kathryn Hansen, 'The Birth of Hindi Drama in Banaras, 1868–1885', in

Culture and Power in Banaras: Community, Performance, and Environment, 1800–1980, ed. Sandria B. Freitag (Berkeley: University of California Press, 1992), 77.

2. Edward Ziter, *The Orient on the Victorian Stage* (Cambridge: Cambridge University Press, 2003), 9.
3. Max Weber, *The Sociology of Religion*, trans. Talcott Parsons (London: Methuen, 1971), 270; Talal Asad, *Formations of the Secular: Christianity, Islam, Modernity* (Redwood City, CA: Stanford University Press, 2003), 13.
4. See Saurabh Dube, *Enchantments of Modernity: Empire, Nation, Globalization* (London: Routledge, 2012), 1.
5. Peter van der Veer, *The Modern Spirit of Asia: The Spiritual and the Secular in China and India* (Princeton, NJ: Princeton University Press, 2014), 131.

CHAPTER 5

Science, Secular Mythology, and the Professionalization of the Parsi Theatre

Technology

> The time in which we live seems to bridge two vast eras, and we stand midway between the old and the new. We have witnessed the end of one era, and are now the spectators of another, the era of steamers, railways and telegraphs, and have seen what no generation has seen before, nor will ever see again.
>
> —James Douglas, *A Book of Bombay* (1883)

On 16 April 1853, shortly before the commencement of the Parsi theatre, South Asia's first twenty-one miles of rail between Bombay and Thane were opened to the public. The day was declared a public holiday, and the commander-in-chief deployed the garrison band for the firing of salutes. Although much has been written of the administrative and financial history of India's railway, little mention has been made of the popular response to the 'Great Iron Road'. Kekhuśro Kābrājī reminisced of the locals' 'awe, wonder and eager curiosity' when the railways first opened:

> Most of them would not believe at first, that this strange locomotive called the steam engine could be a product of human skill and science. They saw that no horses or bullocks were employed to draw the train and were convinced that the wonderful white man who could work other miracles

R. D. Nicholson, *The Colonial Public and the Parsi Stage*, Transnational Theatre Histories,
https://doi.org/10.1007/978-3-030-65836-6_5

> had employed some demons or other invisible powers to draw so swiftly and easily the enormous load of wagons and carriages. There was no other way to account for this wonder and so they brought propitiatory offerings of coconuts to the unearthly power and were ready to worship it.[1]

The term *wonder* repeatedly punctuates Kābrājī's description of the train. The expression similarly recurs in descriptions of Bombay's first hot air balloon ride. For the thunderstruck Parsi historian Dinshaw Edulji Wacha, the 'transcendent scene enacted at Byculla' of a flying Mr. Kyte surpassed that of the first railway. After an aborted attempt, the 'sky-chariot' along with its rider ascended into the air.[2]

> What may be that fairylike ball which could enable one to soar empyrean height, cleave the liquid air till in a few minutes' time it sped upward and upward on its ethereal course ...! ... It was the wonder of wonders and the talk of every unit for many a day.[3]

Although the balloon eventually plunged into the sea,[4] Kyte came to be known for posterity as 'the modern "Pavan Pavri," that is, he who in the legendary lore of the Aryans was known to achieve miracles by flying from the heavens to the earth in the twinkling of an eye'.[5] Similar references to Hindu and Persian mythology were made in relation to the telegraph, the first wires being laid between Bombay, Calcutta, and Madras in 1854–1855.[6] 'Gone are the days that news took more than a year to arrive. ... It is *camatkār* [magic] ... our natives will be astonished beyond belief'.[7] In the aftermath of the Indian Rebellion of 1857, public faith in the telegraph amplified as its magical powers had ostensibly rewon the empire for the English. The subcontinent's three thousand miles of telegraphic wire were soon extended to eight thousand, and by 1861, 'news could be received from England within two days, a feat that no one could ever have dreamt of'.[8] The annihilation of time and space—further engendered through advances in steam navigation, an organized postal service, and the construction of the Suez Canal—consolidated colonial authority, despite Hindu metaphysical fears of the shortening of their life span.[9] Newspapers publicized the first attempts to install gaslights in Bombay on Queen Victoria's birthday in 1860 by describing gas and coal as 'God's wonderful creations', even as announcements were made of the discovery of the brighter, cheaper, and more convenient white magnesium lights in 'reformed' countries.[10] By 1865, with the opening of the Red Sea route, the Suez Canal, and the Bhore Ghaut railway, the Empire's centre of gravity imperceptibly shifted and Bombay established itself as the Gateway to India and the ideal colonial metropolis, the 'Brightest Jewel of [the] British dependencies'.[11]

These subtle yet pervasive changes ushered in a curious dialectic. On the one hand, reformists, missionaries, historians, and colonial officials disenchanted religion through moral reason or the scholarly instruction of Bacon, Hobbes, and Mill; the orientalist study of scripture; and eventually the manufacturing of indigenous religious law. On the other, however, 'science' was enchanted in popular discourse through allusions to Hindu and Persian mythology, occult rituals, and spectacle. To put it more simply, while religion was made scientific, science propelled by industrialization was accommodated in the realm of the spiritual. According to Peter van der Veer, a significant outcome of the interactional history between colonizers and colonized is the distinction between magic and religion, one that defines the secular age. Myth was a failed science to be substituted by original, authentic moral repositories of beliefs—religions whose truths could be compositely known.[12] Simultaneously, however, magical taxonomies became fundamental to understandings of technology and science. The understanding of science as enchantment derived from a fundamental epistemological uncertainty as to the relationship between seeing and believing, knowledge and perceptual experience. By severing vision from the plane of the human observer, mechanical and optical devices nullified prior understandings of representation and observation and put into question the relationship between outer reality and the inner mind—that which is viewed and demonstrable and that which is known. Jonathan Crary describes how this state of de-rangement or sensorial dislocation, encountered in numerous ways, affected the way that reality was understood in the nineteenth century. Technology evoked a new awareness of the incapacity, undependability, and arbitrariness of the perceptual field. Consequently, in 1850s Bombay, science was comprehended through pre-modern or 'indigenous sociologies of knowledge'.[13] Just as British rites drew from erstwhile imperial ritual to reinforce the legitimacy of colonial rule, science was understood through precolonial forms of social regulation. Through indigenous narrative building strategies that harked to Indo-Persian myth, the physical was rendered commensurate with the metaphysical, thus foregrounding a modernity of alterity marked by a contradictory, counter-hegemonic heterotemporality that confused linear understandings of civilization and progress.

A Pedagogy of Wonder

According to Iwan Morus, pedagogical intent was the primary difference between nineteenth-century technological illusions and their 'natural magical predecessors' such as the displays of witchdoctors or exorcists. Magic lantern shows, scientific exhibitions, and panoramas ostensibly had a didactic purpose: they performed magical feats that conjurors of yore alleged to accomplish, but they also addressed the mechanisms that rendered the illusions possible.[14] As mentioned in Part I, edification was crucial in legitimizing modern entertainments as honourable against precolonial forms of amusement such as the nautch. Accordingly, even as the *Rāst* was advertising the moral lessons of the new reformist Parsi theatre in 1858, it published news of the 'sacred' Crystal Palace.[15] The series 'Ek śīlīṅgmā keṭlū joso?' (How Much Can You See in One Shilling?) described the Royal Colosseum in London as a place where visitors could observe dissolving views, 'Chinese natives', 'klerovāenś' (clairvoyance), sinking ships, simulations of nature such as thunder and lightning, and a device called the panorama that 'no man would believe was a picture ... because of the use of "perspective"'.[16] A few months after this series was published, Bombay's government and merchant elite proposed the construction of the Victoria Museum, a 'second Crystal Palace of all nations', 'a diamond palace of industry surrounded with gardens that [would] outshine the dazzling visions of the Arabian Nights and the Hindoo Drama'.[17] Additionally, that same year, news was published of the establishment of the Framjee Cowasjee Institute in Bombay, which comprised a vast library, a large hall for public meetings, an exhibition of natural artefacts, and a 'laboratory'.[18] Conveniently located for the inhabitants of the 'Native Town' at the erstwhile site of the Alma Hotel, this institute was to be the new home to the Society for the Diffusion of Knowledge, which gradually conceded its public lectures on moral themes to scientific demonstrations.[19] A decade later, in 1868, the institute would host Bombay's first art exhibition, where paintings and photographs, a 'window to the world', ushered a new 'perspective'.[20]

These descriptions purposefully coincided with the vernacular press's coverage, beginning in 1857, of the burgeoning spectacular element in the European theatre. On 13 December 1857, Bombay's Gujarati readers were acquainted with Charles Kean's works at the Princess Theatre in England that portrayed thunder and lightning, turbulent seas and storms, magicians, fairies, and transformation scenes with the aid of 140 stage-hands. 'The audience was *heratmand* [awestruck] and *acratī* [full of wonder]. What you read in storybooks was actually happening before your very eyes', the *Rāst* proclaimed.[21] Such advances seemed far beyond the Bombay mainstays of McCollum's circus and the melodramatic and minstrel performances of Emma Grattan, Dave Carson, and Mr and Mrs Bennee. Bombay's residents, however, did not have to wait long to witness England's 'wonder-inducing' spectacles for themselves. A cultural revolution was just around the corner.

Mesmerism

After a whirlwind tour of Europe, Japan, Australia, New Zealand, and America, the electro-biologist Professor Bushell reached Bombay in April 1866, yet his reputation in 'elucidating the study of Mesmerism and its collateral phenomena of clairvoyance and electro-biology' preceded him.[22] By the mid-nineteenth century, mesmerism, popularized by the German Franz Anton Mesmer, pervaded Victorian society and beyond, taking hold of the European imagination by infiltrating presses, hospitals, universities, chapels, private residences, and the theatre. Just as the railway and the telegraph yoked the technological and the occult despite being tools of progress intended 'to defeat superstition in primitive lands',[23] mesmerism tapped into a widespread Victorian spiritual episteme. On 15 April 1866, the *Rāst*, in an article entitled 'Camatkārīk Tamāso—Vījlīnī Asar' (Magical Theatre—The Effects of Electricity), urged its readers to witness Professor Bushell's 'magic show, staged with the help of science':

> These feats are so inexplicable that they will take your breath away; that mankind can perform such feats is hard to believe. ... Professor Bushell has divided his performance into two parts. In the first part, he will explain the mechanism of electricity and provide several demonstrations of its utility and power. ... In this same section he will demonstrate the *khel* [play] of spirit-rapping or *parīā̃nā̃ avāj* [the sounds of fairies]. For many years, a section of European society has believed that fairies enter our world and their souls occupy inanimate objects that consequently make particular sounds. This rumour has gained such credence in Europe that many esteemed intellectuals believe the same. Professor Bushell intends to prove that this is all an act, that there are no real fairies. ... However, the second part of this *khelāḍī*'s [performer's] *khel* [play] is far more entertaining and magical. The reader must have heard of 'mesmerīsam', a science that

> allows a person to destroy people's volition, making them follow his every command. ... Professor Bushell will show this. He believes this to be the effect of electricity and its forces.[24]

Implicit in this description is the professedly pedagogical function of Bushell's demonstrations; cynics were to be convinced of the hypnotic potential of electricity, and fools believing in fairies would see the error of their ways. Yet, the theatrical frame of these scientific shows shaped a special poetics of representation where the natural and authentic merged with the spiritual and supernatural. Mesmerism as science overturned the basic premise of 'moral reform': instead of dissipating superstitions, it amplified belief in the astral, extra-mundane, and imponderable.

Central to the paradoxical amalgamation of the logical and heretical in nineteenth-century sensational science was the performative role of the travelling showman. According to Morus, technological inventors were in a quandary when they presented their devices. 'Show too much, and their hopes of gaining a patent were dashed. Show too little, and their spectators were left skeptical and unconvinced'.[25] Accordingly, and in the interest of profit, although artists highlighted the scientific logic behind these spectacles, they deployed language that was inherently sensational, pseudo-spiritual, performative, and embedded in existing doctrines of divination, occultism, and witchcraft, enabling not so much the erosion of wonder as its absolute converse, the seizing of popular imagination. Dramaturgical protocols of rising anticipation, climactic revelation, and spectacular references to cabbalistic ritual, alchemy, and fairy worlds were at the heart of the business of disseminating popular science in the nineteenth century, drawing large crowds and enthralling them with wonders even as these performances were described as unorchestrated, realistic events.[26] Consequently, the boundaries were unequivocally blurred between scientific lecture and theatrical entertainment, polytechnic and playhouse, scholarly posturing and superstitious belief, and reality and illusion.

Professor Bushell's impending arrival stirred hitherto unseen excitement in Bombay. Numerous articles described and attempted to verify mesmerism's application in medicine, *prāṇīonū lohocumbak* (animal magnetism), and *Ilekṭro Bāyālājī* (electro-biology), as well as the ability of electricity to bring the dead back to life.[27] However, even as spirit reaping, table turning, and the mesmeric mania gripped Bombay's public, controversy began to brew. On 22 April 1866, one of the most important playwrights of the Parsi theatre, the reformist Nāhānābhāi Rūstamjī Rāṇīnā (Fig. 5.1), published a letter in the *Rāst*, questioning the legitimacy of Bushell's performances at the Grant Road Theatre. Rāṇīnā offered Bushell Rs 300 on the condition that the latter would successfully mesmerize him and his trusted acquaintances at a private gathering.[28] In a response published in the *Rāst*, Bushell rebuked Rāṇīnā for his impudence, accepted the challenge (albeit at the public premises of the theatre), and promised to pay back the cost of every ticket in full if the mesmerism was unsuccessful. While Rāṇīnā did not accept these conditions, a number of 'elderly, respectable men' subsequently attested to the validity of Bushell's performances, piquing Bombay's interest in mesmeric phenomena.[29] The conflict between Rāṇīnā and Bushell exemplifies the battle that would be waged in Bombay's public sphere in the 1860s and 1870s between pedagogy and marvel, the search for authentic truths through orientalist scholarship and archaeological study, and the deliberate confusion of reality and imagination through spectacle. Here, the hegemonic textuality of the movement of colonial social reform—which assumed documentary proofs, historical accuracy, and the unwavering fixity of tenet for the creation of law-abiding rational subjects—clashed with a spiritual economy of representation where magic commingled with knowledge. For the first time in the theatre, the project of knowing met one of profound unknowing, a new antidisciplinary, syncretic, and heterotemporal realm that troubled post-Enlightenment conceptions of civilization and progress, morality and virtue. Despite Bushell's professed censure of beliefs in fairies, audiences thronged the theatre to witness his demonstrations of magical chairs, rains of fire, and the dead coming to life, seemingly viewing these displays as communications with an alternative universe that was spiritual, ahistorical, and intimate. In India, sensational performance thus began in the theatres, which exploited the dominant language of didactic illustration and thereby acclimatized Bombay's public to a new bridging of the spiritual and profane, the conscious and subconscious, the real and unreal, and—as a corollary—the stage and auditorium.[30]

Bushell soon left the shores of Western India. His place was quickly filled by the fire and horse gymnastics of the Cirque de Paris, the Great World Circus, the Rocky Mountain Wonders with French and American gymnasts, the Chinese magician Chong Wang (who like Bushell

Fig. 5.1 Nāhānābhāi Rūstamjī Rāṇīnā (*Source The Calcutta Parsi Amateur Dramatic Club Golden Jubilee Souvenir Volume. 1907–1947*, Calcutta, 1957. Courtesy: The Calcutta Parsi Amateur Dramatic Club)

claimed to cut a man's throat and bring him back to life), and Professors Stevens, Abraham, and Wales, who performed 'electro-biology' and 'psychology'.[31] At the same time the Elphinstone and Victoria Nāṭak Maṇḍalī were performing Persian mythological plays and topical farces that combined the authentic and the represented through the presentation of archaeology, orientalist scholarship, and real-life events in a dramatic frame. However, a cultural upheaval was simmering beneath these Iranian trappings.[32] On 22 May 1870, the *Rāst* announced the production by the Victoria Nāṭak Maṇḍalī of *Dāde Darīāv athvā Khuśrono Khāvand Khudā*, an Iranian adaptation of Shakespeare's *Pericles, Prince of Tyre* (Fig. 5.2). Set in the times of 'Alexander and Ardesar Bābegān [Ardeshir Babakan], when *juddin* [non-Zoroastrian] customs had mixed with the authentic Iranian religion', the play was the first in the Parsi theatre to feature spectacular effects such as stormy seas, ships, mountains, thunder, and lightning—that is, all that was 'true to nature'.[33]

The *Talesmātī Khel* (Spectacular Play)

According to Khambātā, after the success of the Alfred Nāṭak Maṇḍalī's first play, *Śāhājādā Sīāvakhś* (1870), the Victoria's monopoly was considerably undermined.[34] The production of *Dāde Darīāv* was an attempt to restore the company's leading position in the Parsi theatre, and it succeeded in part due to its new director, Dādābhāi Paṭel, and the charisma of its actors Dādābhāi Ṭhuṭhī (who played Khuśro) and Pestanjī Farāmjī Mādan (who played Āvān, Shakespeare's Marina).[35] However, the primary reason for the company's success was the play's portrayal of a boisterous sea that rose up and down due to the efforts of many leaping stagehands. As the *Times of India* noted, 'several marine views, which were represented to give natural effect, and which were worked by machinery, formed the chief attraction of the play. The scenes, nearly all, were brilliant and beautiful'.[36]

The Victoria's change in repertoire—from Persian history to spectacle—was, nevertheless, not unanimously praised.

> Ever since the production of *Bejan ane Manījeh*, our public has developed an inexplicable passion for the theatre. Plays were never repeated a dozen times before, spectators were never sent back due to a lack of seats, encores did not exist, gifts were never showered upon the actors. ... That the professions of dancing girls and prostitutes will be destroyed with these

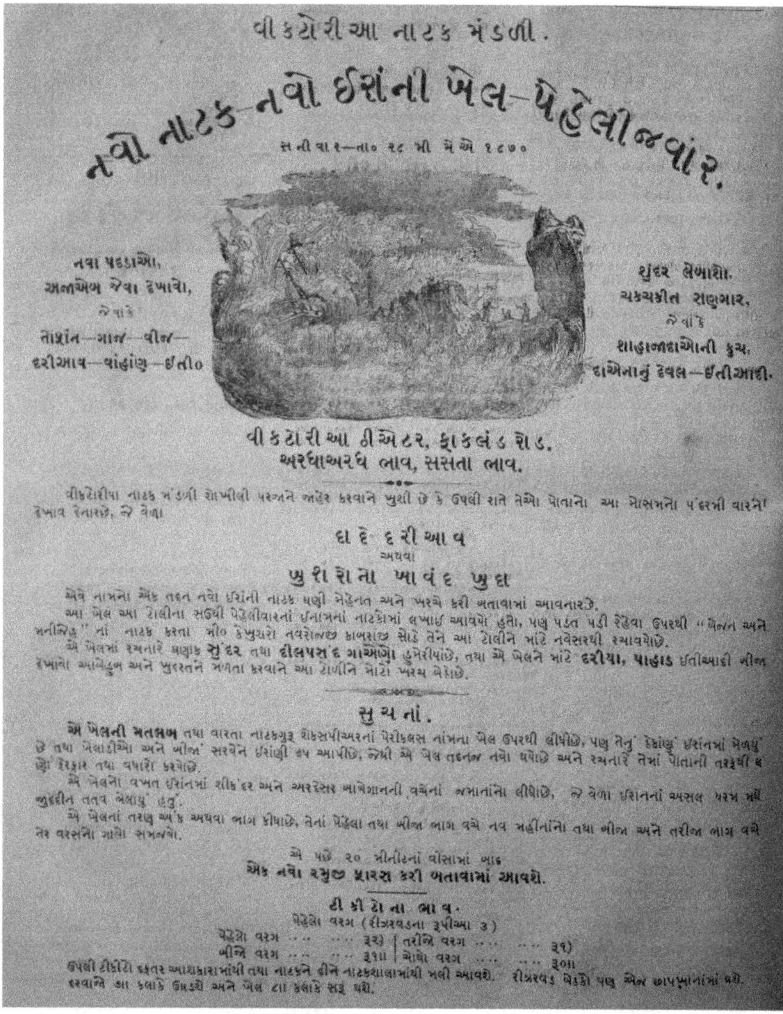
વીકટોરીઆ નાટક મંડળી.

નવો નાટક નવો ઈરાંની ખેલ-પેહેલીજવાર.

સનીવાર—તા० ૨૮ મી મે એ ૧૮૭૦

વીકટોરીઆ ઠીએટર, ફ્રાકલંડ રોડ.

અરધાઅરધ ભાવ, સસતા ભાવ.

દાદે દરીઆવ

અથવા

ખુશરોના ખાવંદ ખુદા

સુચનાં.

ટીકીટોના ભાવ.

Fig. 5.2 Advertisement for *Dāde Darīāv* by the Victoria Nāṭak Maṇḍalī. This advertisement was the first in the Parsi theatre's history to include a picture (*Source RG*, 22 May 1870, 342. Courtesy: The J. N. Petit Institute, Mumbai)

> successes is praiseworthy. ... However, the audience must learn to distinguish between good and bad performances. ... We publicly admit that the Victoria's performances last season gave us much cause for concern. ... Their *Rūśtam ane Sohorāb* was a failure. Nonetheless, all that we can say with regard to their *Dāde Darīāv* is this, that if the Victoria continues to produce such plays it would be better that the troupe were disbanded. ... Last season the public adored their plays as they spent a great deal on scenes, curtains, and costumes. However we must reiterate that the Victoria should not attempt to appease *sādhāraṇ loko* [laymen] at the expense of the scholar and critic.[37]

The shift from 'moral' and patriotic ancient Iranian themes to spectacle—and with it hitherto unseen profits and a new demographic of spectator—thus generated a singular disquiet among the reformist founders of the Parsi theatre. The public sphere, once an observatory where citizens could see and be seen within a complex architecture of power, here transmuted into a new, intimate arena for play that overturned the disciplinary regime of the Parsi theatre. In this move from 'honourable amusement' for the social and corporeal reform of Bombay's Parsi community to commercial entertainment for the masses, the Parsi theatre threw off its traditional function as minor tribunal that provided intellectual elites closely associated with the state a powerful form of intra-group authority. The theatre—and, as a corollary, the vernacular public sphere—here became an inclusive arena untethered from self-inspection and self-policing within religious, ethnic, and linguistic groups.

Shortly after *Dāde Darīāv*, on 25 February 1871, the Zoroastrian Nāṭak Maṇḍalī performed *Khodābakś* at the Grant Road Theatre before an audience of 'Pārsī and Khojā ladies and gentlemen', marking the first mention in the press of the attendance of non-Parsi communities at the Parsi theatre.[38] At this pivotal juncture, then, the Parsi theatre ceased to exist exclusively for the benefit of the Parsi community. Described as a '"lungs-cracking" comedy' in Turkish dress or 'ek turkī hasmukho khel' (a Turkish comic play), this play successfully amalgamated the Iranian epic with the spectacular play of fairies, genii, and demons.[39] Written and directed by Edaljī Jamśedjī Khorī, the production—with its rising moons, frightening jungles, storm, thunder, lightning, beautiful gardens, and fountains—was so esteemed that the High Court pleader Shantaram Narayen gifted the troupe's secretary, Dhunjeebhoy Rustomjee Ranina (brother of the playwright Nāhānābhāi Rāṇīnā), Rs 50 for 'the preparation of a dress for the gentleman who acts the character of "Khodabux"', despite the play's purportedly lewd language.[40] The new fantasy world of the vernacular theatre, no longer an arena where orthodox and reformist Parsis fought for representative power, thus began to enjoy an extraordinary reach across religion, caste, class, and even language. Thereafter, the troupe performed before the Nawab of Sachin and left for Poona in August 1871, marking the first Parsi theatre performance outside of Bombay.[41]

Simultaneously, the Alfred staged a landmark production of the Parsi stage, *Jehānbakhś ane Gulrūkhśār*, in order to compete with the Victoria's *Dāde Darīāv*, prompting a meteoric rise in the theatre's spectators.[42] According to Khambātā, Bombay's Gujarati readers 'rubbed their eyes in disbelief' when they turned to the Alfred's advertisements in their Sunday newspapers:

> Everyone considered the advertisements that described the flying monster, quaking mountain, collapsing earth, icy rain, and blazing jungle [to be] mere gimmicks. … These advertisements raised the ire of the late Kekhaśru Kābrājī, who attempted to destroy the play with his weapons [the *Rāst Goftār*], but his efforts were in vain. A crowd gathered as early as 3 p.m. outside the Grant Road Theatre … while the Victoria Theatre was completely deserted, barring a solitary barking dog. At 9 p.m. the curtains rose. Jehānbakhś and Gulrūkhśār were speaking of love when suddenly a mighty monster came flying in from one of the wings, gripped Gulrūkhśār, and took off like lighting. Neither ropes, nor wires, nor chains were used. It was magic. People screamed in awe, and there was such chaos that when Jahānbakś entered for the next scene, the audience would not allow him to perform. They kept shouting 'once more, once more, once more'. … This was the first mechanical scene in Bombay … and was proclaimed one of the wonders of the world.[43]

The English press showered its praises on this 'sensational hit of the season', 'universally spoken of as being the best scenic display ever attempted by a native theatrical company' thus ranking the troupe 'among the foremost vernacular dramatic companies now performing in Bombay'.[44] Houses were 'crowded to excess', and the scenic effects of the play 'surpass[ed] anything that [had] ever been attempted by a native dramatic company in Bombay'.[45] Although the acting was 'of a high order', it was the mechanical scenery by the enterprising Dady Ruttonjee and 'Bhau' that drew audiences to the Grant Road Theatre like moths to a flame.[46]

A closer analysis of the plot, however, indicates that there was more to the play than meets the eye. Jehanbux, the grandson of Rustom, is in love with Goolrookhsar, the daughter of a wealthy merchant. The play commences with a love scene between the two, but all at once, the sky darkens, and a monster descends and absconds with Goolrookhsar. Jehanbux sets off on a quest to find his beloved, as does—separately—Prince Jehansooj, who has also heard of her plight and decided to save and then marry her. A spirit discerns the men's shared task and directs them through two dissimilar paths, the first by the Huptekhans (seven stages), famed in Persian myths as the dwelling of the *devs* (demons), and the second an easier but longer route. In the interim, the genie Malekool hands Goolrookhsar to his eight-handed 'Bubbur-e-bulla', who in turn dispatches her with his wand to a murky cave in a forest. One day, while hunting, the fairy Jurrookhsar (sister of the genie Malekool) overhears the distraught Goolrookhsar and attempts to raise her spirits. Meanwhile, Jehanbux advances through treacherous lands until he reaches the last Huptekhan, a colossal iron wall beyond which there is no passing. At the entrance, he loses consciousness. Jadoobaj, a revolting sorceress and the wife of Bubbur-e-bulla, sees him and falls instantly in love. Filled with desire, she wakes Jehanbux and showers him with affections, which he pretends to reciprocate. She entrusts him with a phial of coloured liquid that is the key to her life, but he breaks this phial, killing her and Bubbur-e-bulla, freeing Goolrookhsar, and causing the magic wall to collapse. In its place is a beautiful garden where flying fairies welcome them. But all is not yet resolved: Malekool seeks revenge, and a series of fights commence, which result in Malekool's death at the hands of Goolrookhsar and—after Jehansooj finally arrives and joins in the fight—the eradication of all the monsters. At this juncture Jehansooj meets Jurrookhsar and, believing her to be Goolrookhsar, falls in love with her. Only after they pledge their love for each other does he discover his error, but Jehansooj willingly weds the fairy, leaving Goolrookhsar to marry Jehanbux. The play ends with a double wedding and jubilation.[47]

While the combination of the authentic and fictional in topical farces and Persian mythological plays served the clear objective of communal social and corporeal discipline, the purpose behind this amalgamation of the mundane and magical, ancient Iranian warriors and oriental ghouls and demons that unmistakeably falls afoul of the corrective agenda of reform, is not as easily discernible. Tracy C. Davis suggests that depictions of fairyland on Victorian and Edwardian stages constituted insights into a modernity affected by tradition, nostalgia, and mild rebellion.[48] Fairies were metonyms of belief in magic as they obliged individuals to consider that a lack of demonstrable proof was not proof of non-existence.[49] That which seemed impulsive, haphazard, or incredible onstage was the outcome of highly codified practices. By embodying domestic values, Victorian fairies reminded audiences to appreciate worldly comforts and simple values, ensuring that the world of Britons was kept in order.[50] What, however, were the oriental fairies of the Parsi theatre for? Why the change in repertoire from the Iranian mythological to the *talesmātī khel* (theatre of talismans)? Why were non-Parsis increasingly drawn to the Parsi theatre, which, as specified earlier, was initially an intrinsically self-representational, disciplinary, communal realm?

Herat, *talesam*, *camatkār*, and *ajāeb*, four terms loosely connotating 'wonder', that had consistently been used to describe local responses to technology feature in nearly all of the Parsi theatre's advertisements dating from 1870. If the contents of England's Polytechnical Institute were described by Parsis as scenes from the *Arabian Nights*, if railways and hot air balloons were denoted as 'demons', 'fairy-like thing[s]', and 'wonders of the world' by spectators who had 'seen what no generation has seen before, nor will ever see again',[51] then the fairies, demons, and *ajāeb* (strange), *heratmand dekhāvo* (wonder-inducing scenes) viewed by comparably awestruck audiences within the four walls of the theatre demonstrated a strong cross-referential velocity between scientific and theatrical enchantments. The Parsi secular mythological drama deliberately tapped into the pedagogical design of performative science, which played on the epistemological incertitude between the seen and unseen, the known and unknown. No longer was truth—characterized by evidence gathering, intellectual inquiry, and historical proofs—unequivocally understood. The world, self, and other, according to the disorienting spectacle of the Parsi theatre, were no longer objective and analysable bodies of knowledge, subject to controlled administration and the exercise of an empirical power. *Dāde Darīāv*, *Jehānbakhś ane Gulrūkhśār*, and scores of spectacular Parsi plays produced over the course of a century sought to grasp a new ontology of the undependability of the visual field, mystifying spectators and thus instilling in them an appreciation of hitherto disparaged indigenous sociologies of knowledge in antievolutive, ahistorical time.

Crucially, however, in Western India—in contrast with Europe—science constituted the most obvious emblem of empire. Technology functioned as synecdoche for the colonial mastery of space and time—that is, nature—vindicating claims to European moral, intellectual, and racial superiority and power. Were Parsi secular mythological plays then celebrations of the sciences that rendered empire possible or pedagogic exercises in technology (the Indian equivalent of Bushell's demonstrations)? Or was the eclectic hodgepodge of Hindu and Persian tales, *Arabian Nights*, Shakespeare, magicians, eight-handed creatures, and depictions of trains, ships, and bridges mere jocund distraction? What was the convoluted yet highly influential play-world of the Parsi theatre doing?

Significantly, *Jehānbakhś ane Gulrūkhśār* ends not with the reestablishment of boundaries between the real and ethereal worlds—as in European dramatizations of fairies—but rather its converse, a marriage between the two. This trope, a regular feature of the Parsi 'talismanic play', complicates the historiography of the spectacular Parsi theatre as simple performative flights of fancy from the oppressive present. Order does not reign in the end. Fairies destabilize the domain of humans, irreversibly meddling, through marriage, in the internal social and racial harmony of humankind. Unlike their English counterparts, Indian fairies had little interest in propagating domesticity and setting the world right through a renewed awareness of mundane comforts and inherent goodness. The unification of two seemingly distinct races (humanoid and fairy), and the associated joining of two ostensibly disconnected worlds, overturned the dramaturgical logic of the reestablishment of order. The Indian theatre thus articulated for the first time a distinct and highly mutinous set of answers to the questions conjured by European fairies: '(1) Does the irrational have a place in national identity; (2) what, or who, suffers in the wake of progress; and (3) is it too late to turn back?'[52] The merging of the real and fairy realms functioned in allegorical relation to the two conceptual worlds of empire: the timeless orient and the presentist occident, the orient's culturally superior hoary past and a technologically superior modern Europe, self and other. The world, according to the ontology of *Jehānbakhś ane Gulrūkhśār*, was no longer clearly divided between the timeless East and contemporary West, tradition and modernity. In the guise of skittish diversion, the amalgamation of mythic oriental characters and icons and cutting-edge mechanical scenery (which indirectly epitomized the scientific might of empire and the possibility of its appropriation) reflected a new way of conceiving knowledge. This ontology confused what had been the dominant imagery in the press, colonial exhibition, and schoolroom: the progress of the occident and the immutable stasis of the orient.

Consequently, the 'mild rebellion' of fairyland in Indian hands constituted an imaginative sphere of sovereignty—a new private sphere—where, in the name of playful diversion, the superiority of a foreign culture was simultaneously acknowledged and refuted. The absence of despotic immoral crowds, romantic landscapes, and stagnant temporal frames that characterized Victorian theatre and archaeological truths, historically accurate costume, and righteous sermon that distinguished the reformist Iranian mythological play, reflected the new Parsi theatre's obfuscation of established truths. Religious, moral, cultural, and racial conceptualizations of self-identity, hitherto firmly demarcated as either superior or barbaric, were revealed as mysterious, impenetrable, and unessentializable. This new profound ambivalence in the theatre towards the authority of rational, colonial knowledge was metonymically evoked through a scepticism towards the authority of vision, which was now splintered into a plurality of perspectives that annulled socially established conceptions of the observer and observed. Industrial technology, optical devices, and the proscenium itself rendered sight as fractured, beyond the individual's power: Who sees what or whom? Through what prism? Is perception truth? Advertisements of the Elphinstone Theatrical Company's *Ālādīn*, referring to disorienting optical devices and mechanical effects such as flying, declared, 'Svapnānū Svarūp! Khyālī Vicār ke Kharo Citār?' (Like a Dream! Is it illusion or reality?).[53] Likewise, in the play *Barjo ane Mehersīmīn Ojār*, performed on 4 November 1871 by the Persian Zoroastrian Nāṭak Maṇḍalī, references to *caśmā* (spectacle) and *nazar* (vision) abound. For example, Śeroe, hearing from Gurgīn that Barjo is lost in a jungle in Jābulistān with tigers and cheetahs, asks, 'Gurgīn, did you see him yourself with your own eyes or are you narrating a dream?'[54] If, in the Persian epics of the 1860s, *nazar* was articulated in relation to the idea of *jāher mat* (public opinion), a realm where Parsi religion and culture was 'open' to critique, the term's connotation had here transformed, signifying the impossibility of distinguishing between the occult and the real, illusion and reality, fact and falsehood. If visibility made it possible to know, modify, and exert a corporeal power on tradition, then the confusion of visibility compromised and endangered the complex colonial disciplinary regime that was part of the overall functioning of power. The new, highly ambiguous, symbolic universe of the Parsi secular mythological play thus proposed the revolutionary idea that the locus of truth (ahistorical, invariable, and preternatural) was elsewhere, unrelated to the post-Enlightenment Victorian morals promulgated in colonial history, science textbooks, and compendiums of law.

A third example, *Śirīn Farhādno Gāyanrūpī operā*, an adaptation of *Romeo and Juliet* by an unnamed 'Mahmadīyan Munśī', makes *caśmā* (spectacle) and *nazar* (vision) sought-after objects.[55] The Emperor of China, King Kaikhasrū, falls in love with Śīrīn when a merchant tells the king of her beauty. She in turn falls in love with the Emperor after seeing his picture and they are married. Subsequently, the King sets off on an errand and Śīrīn, consumed with fear as she is not able to see her husband due to a mountain that lies between them, asks for the mountain to be broken. Accordingly, Farhād is sent by the court to restore *caśmā* to Queen Śīrīn and they fall in love. They are discovered by the king, who orders Farhād to break the entire mountain (presumably an impossible task) for Śīrīn's hand in marriage. After Farhād nearly completes his mission, the king commands a wicked old woman to kill Farhād. She goes to the young man and informs him that Śīrīn is about to give birth to another man's child. Consumed with sadness, Farhād kills himself. The old woman then informs Śīrīn of his death, and the play ends with the dead Farhād singing to Śīrīn from his coffin. *Śīrīn Farhād* exemplifies a highly ambivalent model of theatre-making, both derivative of and antagonistic to the aesthetic form that it mimics. Even as theatre productions imitated colonial spectacular effects, narratives with evil kings who destroyed honourable subjects attempting to locate an inaccessible 'vision' exemplify allegorical assertions of an independent cultural identity, the theatre concurrently acknowledging and repudiating the epistemic power of a despotic evil ruler. The Parsi theatre thus began to craft a different moral economy, one that was illegible to colonial administrators and reformist elites. This self-determined, antidisciplinary, autonomous fantasy world was a realm where myths, no longer signs of barbarity and backwardness, promulgated subversive values, epistemic frames, and conceptions of nonteleological time. Moreover, most Parsi spectacular plays, such as *Barjo ane Mehersīmīn Ojār*, were set between Turkey and China, the extremities of the imperial oriental imagination. By abandoning the geographic specificity of ancient Iran, the Parsi theatre began to produce an alternative, counter-hegemonic, nonoccidental imaginary space and, by analogy, an imagined community somewhere in between.

Competition and Class

Despite the success of *Jehānbakś ane Gulrūkhsār*, the Alfred in its original avatar would come to an untimely end. Kuvarjī Nājar, the rival manager of the Elphinstone Theatrical Club, who had set his sights on altering his company's repertoire—from sophisticated amateur English plays to the now more profitable professional Gujarati productions—began a three-year lease of the Grant Road Theatre in July 1871. Nājar sublet the theatre to Hīrjībhāi Khambātā of the Alfred, who, in order to prevent rival companies from stealing stage secrets, permitted only a few members of his troupe to roam behind the curtains, in the wings, and beneath the trapdoor. On the first day of rehearsals for *Jehānbakś ane Gulrūkhsār*, Nājar instructed his carpenter to spy on the mechanical devices backstage. This activity stoked the indignation of the members of the Alfred, who hurled the carpenter off stage. Not one to throw in the towel, Nājar went to a room located above the stage to better observe the Alfred's effects, allegedly paying no heed to cries to get out as the company was late in setting up their secret contraptions. The 'Alfredwallas', left with no alternative, locked Nājar within his room at 8 p.m., unlocking the door only after the play had come to an end. As there existed merely two theatres in Bombay at the time, the Alfred soon found itself, perhaps unfairly, without a much-needed place to perform.[56]

The epoch of the popular, commercial, secular mythological play—an era characterized by cycloramas and magic lanterns, pilfered stage secrets, actors lured by rival troupes for better salaries, and theatre companies that were as prolific as 'breeding mosquitos'—had thus begun.[57] Critically, even as the Parsi theatre confused conventional dichotomies of civilizational progress and backwardness onstage, it interrogated colonial standards of character and conduct offstage. As early as April 1859, two Parsis and two Bohras were prosecuted for publicizing a counterfeit performance at the Grant Road Theatre and absconding from the building after collecting the entrance money.[58] A few years later, on 15 October 1865, the *Rāst* declared,

> It is very upsetting that naïve children are throwing their education aside for the theatre. It is unfortunate that on the pretext of providing innocent entertainment to the public, they cheat and steal money from people. ... These children create a huge ruckus onstage and off. ... They have made the word theatre impure.[59]

The boundaries between amateur and professional theatre, and between reform and profit, thus began to consolidate, and class became a fundamental concern of the erstwhile reformist founders of the Parsi theatre. The rebellious, mildly seditious visual motifs of the spectacular Parsi theatre found concomitant expression in the subversive behaviour of spectators, relational antidisciplinary mechanisms that overturned the reformist enforcement of Victorian morality and virtue.

The shift in the function of the Parsi theatre—from light-hearted moral pedagogy to commercial, spectacular, playfully inflammatory amusement—therefore generated a special anxiety among the reformists, who almost immediately found a scapegoat in schoolteachers who engaged in the drama as dilettantes. Accordingly, when scores of children packed the theatre to witness the onstage 'ruckus' of their teachers Fardunjī Kāvasjī Śanjāṇā from the Dhobitalao public school and a Dārābsā from the Jījībhāi Dādābhāi school in Parel, the *Rāst* was swift to call on government education inspector Jāhāṅgīr Hormajjī to take legal action against the schoolmasters.[60] Subsequently, letters to the editor averred that one of the teachers had resigned and that the other had pledged never to perform in the playhouse again. Teachers—the purported purveyors of discipline, both moral and corporeal—were thus officially and unofficially penalized for partaking in commercial shows: 'no person holding a position in public office should participate in such disrespectful and base forms of entertainment that have no claims to reform', Hormajjī declared.[61] Similarly a letter writer named 'Dhāḍī' argued that the Parsi theatre should desist from becoming a profitable enterprise:

> In reformed countries theatre artists are neither naïve children nor teachers and public men, they are professionals. ... The days that editors praised Parsi thespians have passed. ... The city of Bombay will no longer allow silly boys to shout and cause a nuisance on the stage. The public has showered its disgust on them, and the *seṭhs* will no longer let their hallowed feet touch the grounds of the theatre.[62]

Increasingly, English newspapers published letters from anonymous writers that complained of juvenile Parsis spending 'a major portion of their time attending the club and preparing their parts of the performance, instead of allotting their time towards the preparation of their school lessons'.[63] Simultaneously, news pervaded the press of adolescent men who behaved like inebriated sailors, volleying rotten eggs, slippers, mud, and cow dung onstage during performances.[64] For example, on 29 April 1865, the *Bombay Gazette* published news of a Manockjee Dadabhoy employed in a Gujarati newspaper office, who had been taken into custody for throwing sugarcane on the stage of the Grant Road Theatre during a performance.[65] Likewise, on 4 August 1873, a squabble broke out at the Grant Road Theatre when several boys swore at the Parsi 'blackface' actors who had falsely advertised themselves as the Mī. Jo. Has Company intending to perform a Christy Minstrels' play. The children hissed choice phrases at the actors such as 'Are jā bhāi suijā' (go to sleep), 'kāle āvje' (come back tomorrow), 'jarā khāṇḍ khāi ghā̃ṭu sāf karī āv' (wash your face), and 'are mohḍu dhoi āv nahīto tārī mābī tũne olakhśe nahī' (wash your face or even your mother will not recognize you), the last one prompting a physical altercation.[66] Subsequently, a Hindu schoolboy was indicted by his father for stealing the family jewels in order to join the theatre as an actor.[67] Unmistakeably, children were especially prone to the 'dramatic mania', thronging theatres to witness the mechanical effects, make mischief, squabble with their peers, and even act in companies that increasingly and controversially began to hire child actors.[68]

However, children were not the only irksome spectators of the increasingly profit-driven Parsi theatre. As theatre companies catered more frequently to the demands of *sādhāraṇ loko* (laymen) by staging spectacular plays, the class of the theatre's patrons changed along with the trappings and plots onstage.[69] 'It is entirely contrary to every dramatic law that spectators express their "filing" [feeling] out loud. Our audiences need to learn discretion as to when to clap. Our spectators have taken it on themselves to *aplās* [applaud] every time actors embrace', the *Rāst* blasted.[70] Similarly, 'A Colonial' in the *Times of India* described a gentleman who sat in the stalls and 'acted as a sort of order-keeper', intermittently requesting the audience 'to keep "order," "silence," and "hold your tongue"'. Aggravated by this person's behaviour, a European constable and his assistant were summoned to escort the delinquent outside.

> But presto! He was back again in the twinkling of an eye and took his seat amidst the plaudits of his coadjutors, and distending his cheeks in a most unParseeanical manner, he looked towards the peelers and—well he made a noise. An attempt, made by one constable and four or five 'yellow-heads'

> [constables] to dislodge him from his hold on the railings, proved abortive, so he was let alone.[71]

More tellingly, on 22 March 1871, the owner of the Alfred, Māṇekjī Jīvaṇjī Māśtar, published a letter in the *Rāst*, criticizing Kekāus Tātā, a spectator who had attempted to force entry into a performance that was exclusively for 'families'. When Tātā was refused entry at the door at 11 p.m., he allegedly proclaimed, 'Femīlī nathī te śū bhāḍenī lāu?' (If I don't have a family should I rent one?), and he returned with a supposedly 'sārā khāndānnī orat' (respectable woman) who, according to one witness, was a man dressed in female attire. A new public thus began to ride roughshod over the strict disciplinary protocols implemented by the reformists to police the admission of women into the public space of the theatre. Although the press consistently reiterated that 'family performances' were *khāṅgī* (private), intended strictly for women accompanied by their male relations, and that *jāher* (public) performances were for single men, spectators such as Tātā progressively put into question the gendered character of private and public realms.[72]

The Parsi theatre, no longer a propagandistic tool for disseminating Victorian values of companionate marriage, domestic virtue, and the importance of moral and physical education, therefore began to have a remarkably broad, downward reach, permanently altering the edificatory role of the vernacular public sphere. An antidisciplinary society, a new form of surveillance over the state, was thus born through the commercial theatre. The volleying of sugarcane and the concomitant deprecation of reformist dictum offstage were essentially commensurate with the Parsi drama's cheerfully subversive spectacle, which interrogated the premises of truth and conceptualizations of self and other. The 'lower', illiterate classes, previously subjected to a multiplicity of gazes in the minor tribunal of the public sphere in the 1850s, had now (in the 1870s) become subjects impairing the panoptical principle of the theatre. Proceedings both within and beyond the proscenium gave spectators what they sought in contrast to what the local elite of Bombay thought that they needed, provoking considerable class-based apprehensions and antagonisms.

As a consequence, plays began to offer highly ambiguous depictions of traditionally fixed hierarchical relations such as masters and slaves and husbands and wives, as well as increasingly sexualized women. This development is exemplified in the Victoria's *Hajambād ane Ṭhaganāj*, written by Khorī, directed by Dādābhai Paṭel, and performed for the first time on 13 May 1871. Comprising 'cycloramic views, specially ordered out from England, representing the principal incidents in the late Franco-Prussian war',[73] and scenes from *The Honeymoon*, *The Mock Doctor*, *The Two Gentlemen of Verona*, *The Merry Wives of Windsor*, and *The Twelfth Night*, the comedy consisted of four parts that were ostensibly 'well and cleverly arranged, ... represented by the amateurs in a lively spirit'.[74] While the *Times of India* published a glowing review of the performance, extolling its 'racy style' and 'humour well adapted to the Guzerati vernacular of the language',[75] the *Rāst* had a different take.[76] After initially attempting to support the play,[77] the newspaper published a scathing review of this 'high-class ruckus' that had 'no real meaning' and only served 'to make people laugh'. Much of this denunciation was directed towards the use of curse words such as *satyānāś* and *khānekharāb* and Hindu terms such as *dīvālī*, which purportedly had no place in an Iranian play.[78] 'If a servant such as Hajambād spoke such words to his master in real life, he would have been beaten black and blue and thrown out, but in the play Śehrīār caresses him and embraces him as his family!' However, the *Rāst* saved most of its vitriol for the many double entendres that peppered the performance and that were unfit for 'families':

> Parīceher—Sisters how sweet this sherbet is—drink—drink and enjoy it. [All drink]
> Dīlnavāj—Ha? Such are the world's ways that we drink sherbet, and men drink our sherbet.
> Meherbānu—What do you mean, sister Dīlnavāj?
> Parīceher—Dear Dīlnavāj, I don't understand what you mean.
> Dīlnavāj—Indeed, how would you understand? You both are like flower buds; when the thirsty bees suck the flowers' honeydew when they bloom, you will understand.
> Meherbānu—So were you too at one time a flowerbud? And what was your bee like?
> Dīlnavāj—My bee is my rightful husband, Hormajd.[79]

'If the purpose of the theatre is to inculcate its spectators in morality, this play did just the opposite', the *Rāst* thundered.[80] The switch from a utopian ideal of Persian womanhood to a conscious eroticism spelled not only the commencement of a fundamental disconnect between the Parsi theatre and the reformists but also the popular representational failure of the project of social reform. No longer rooted in a communal corrective optic, the theatre now eluded the control of its reformist founding fathers, providing a reassuring vision of social regress in the midst of purported progress.

The First Hindustani Play of the Parsi Stage

By putting into question the new middle-class conception of Indian womanhood mediated through European categories, the theatre also troubled the so-called women's question in the agenda of Indian social reform, which, as mentioned in Chapter 3, was not so much about women as it was about the encounter between colonialism and the tradition of the colonized. Nowhere is this disturbing of the women's question more apparent than in the first Hindustani play of the Parsi stage, *Sonānā Mulnī Khorśed* (*Soneke Mulkī Khorśed/Khorshed, Worth her Weight in Gold*), a watershed play in the history of Asian drama. On 24 September 1871, shortly after Bombay's press articulated the need for a single language in Hindustan in order to unify the country (following the example of *Hochdeutsch*),[81] the *Rāst* published the first advertisement for *Sonānā Mulnī Khorśed*, the earliest Parsi full-length play in Hindustani. The play was written by Edaljī Jamśedjī Khorī in Gujarati and then translated into Hindustani by Behrāmjī Fardunjī Marajhbān (Beherāmjī Fardunjī Marajhbān). The Victoria's production, according to the advertisement, portrayed the *dabdabo* (might) of a Hindustani Muslim kingdom, *hīndī* and *sīndhī* costume, and monuments such as the Taj Mahal that dated to the times of Islamic power and prestige.[82] According to Khambātā, this thematic change was in keeping with the director's initial objective, which was, controversially, to attract a new Muslim demographic to the theatre.[83] However, according to the translator's preface, the play's use of Hindustani was tempered by the omission of a number of Persian and Arabic words so as not to alienate the theatre's Hindu and Parsi spectators.[84] Consequently, the Victoria began developing its own brand of Hindustani that would have a profound impact on the subcontinent, especially when Hindu nationalist politics began to play out in the 1880s.

According to Paṭel, Parsi readers scoffed in disbelief when they read of the Victoria's new enterprise as it was inconceivable that Parsi actors could perform in a language that was, to a considerable degree, alien to them.[85] After weeks of rigorous preparation, on 7 October 1871, the play, loosely adapted from the Hindu tale *Kāmāvatī* and Shakespeare's

Cymbeline, was staged for the first time at the Victoria Theatre.[86] The production was a thunderous success, and Khojas, Bohras, and Memons allegedly thronged the theatre. The principal actors Khurśedjī Mervānjī Bālīvālā (Fig. 5.3) and Pestanjī Farāmjī Mādan, who played Khorśed and

Fig. 5.3 Khurśedjī Mervānjī Bālīvālā (*Source* Gulfām, *Bhamto-Bhut*, Bombay: Fort Printing Press. Courtesy: The PARZOR Foundation, New Delhi)

Fīrojśāh, respectively, enjoyed an almost instantaneous rise to stardom due to their singing talent. They were garlanded after each performance and showered with presents, and Khoja and Parsi businessmen vied to roam with the actors publicly in their horse-drawn carriages.[87]

This first Hindustani performance of the Parsi theatre was nevertheless not commended by the reformist press. Although the *Rāst* praised the play's pure and beautiful language, it reiterated that the Victoria's *ākṭīṅg* (acting) catered merely to *sādhāraṇ loko* (laymen). 'They cannot even follow the simple theatrical rule of advancing to the front of the stage before speaking'.[88] Additionally, Kābrājī—a pedant for historical accuracy—condemned the presence of an English sofa in a Hindustani court, the location of the Taj Mahal in the kingdom of Sindh, incorrect costumes, and even the escape ladder, which extended an improbably long distance across a river. Scrupulous historical study and archaeological faithfulness were manifestly no longer relevant to the success of Parsi performances, which, on the contrary, very nearly parodied the repertoire of their erudite reformist precursors. The *Rāst* also rebuked the company for its inability to control a number of *cībāvlā* (mischievous) spectators who brawled on the night of the performance.[89] The play, however, had set larger wheels in motion. Other troupes began to follow the precedent set by the Victoria of 'hīndī lebāś, hīndī dekhāv and hīndī ḍhapchap' ('hīndī costume, hīndī setting and hīndī gestures') and, notably, a female-centric plot.[90]

The Inception of Cultural Nationalism

> The drama's laws the dramas patrons give,
> For we that live to please, must please to live.

These famous lines—penned by Samuel Johnson and first spoken by David Garrick in 1747—open the preface of the 1871 play *Sonānā Mulnī Khorśed*, which traces the travails of a beautiful, chaste woman named Khorśed, wife of the tyrannical Fatehśāh, king of Delhi. Due to the machinations of a Kotwal (magistrate) who is besotted with Khorśed, she is secretly auctioned off to the noble Fīrojśāh, the disguised prince of Faizabad, for an incalculable sum. Nevertheless, she is subsequently kidnapped and brought to the court of her previous husband to be remarried. Thereafter, she is rekidnapped by a 'lowly' thief; then she becomes the centre of a dispute between two enamoured princes, Jā̃hā̃gīr and Jahāmbakhś; and finally, she is the object of affection of a woman, Gulceher, who kisses Khorśed when she is disguised as a man. Curiously, the play concludes with Khorśed's return to her 'rightful', second husband—Fīrojśāh. The play's Gujarati and Hindustani titles—*Sonānā Mulnī Khorśed* and *Soneke Mulkī Khorśed*, respectively—correspond to the English *Khorshed, Worth her Weight in Gold*, indicating the transferable value of Khorśed as an entity who is passed from hand to hand but who maintains fidelity to her 'lawful' second husband, the man who truly holds her in esteem. As with the permanently inverted master–slave relations in *Hajambād ane Ṭhaganāj*, the play's dubious ending and title yielded no easy answers to troubling questions of marital fidelity and chastity, gender identity, subaltern agency, and legitimacy of proprietorship and rule.

The inimitable strangeness of *Sonānā Mulnī Khorśed* marks the beginning, in my view, of not only the delineation of an autonomous modern subjectivity in the theatre but also a revivalist nationalism whose conceptual core was a spiritual conjugality. As noted earlier, the status of women at the heart of the project of social reform indicated not so much colonialism's preoccupation with the uplift of the fairer sex as its need to reconfigure previous forms of social organization and governance as despotic and barbaric. The tyrannized woman was a metaphor for the tyrannical nature of indigenous religion and social practice, sanctioning the civilizing mission of the transformation of indigenous custom, ritual, and law through the discourse of reason. Similarly, Khorśed, the first central female character on the Parsi stage, does not make known the words of a modern Indian female subjectivity, otherwise unseen and unheard. Rather, the figure of 'woman as gold' engenders an indigenous subject position at the key moment when the bourgeois-rationalist conception of knowledge was coming to be questioned. To put it more simply, Khorśed is a sign for a subjected tradition, one that numerous men have unsuccessfully attempted to capture, violate, and call their own. Through Khorśed, whose chastity remains untainted though she is married and remarried, chased and kidnapped, the play reverses the theme of the rescue of oriental women popular in the British theatre, implying that although the colonial state had conquered a people, it had failed to invade the special, private, spiritual, sovereign domain of its subjects. Missionary proselytism, colonial education, and indigenous social reform had not succeeded in violating a superior, undominated inner self. According to Partha Chatterjee, the formula of the inner and outer, the material and spiritual was a fundamental feature of anticolonial nationalisms in Asia and Africa:

> The material is the domain of the 'outside,' of the economy and of statecraft, of science and technology, a domain where the West had proved its superiority and the East had succumbed. ... The spiritual, on the other hand, is an 'inner' domain bearing the 'essential' marks of cultural identity.[91]

In contrast with the period of social reform, in which women were positioned as sites on which traditionalists, priests, missionaries, colonial officials, and reformists waged war for sociopolitical power, *Sonānā Mulnī Khorśed* conceptualizes the inner domain of the spiritual (gender coded as feminine) as immune to colonial intervention, becoming the sacred fountainhead of a nation to be born. 'Eastern' nationalism, Chatterjee says, arises from the fundamental awareness that the dominant standards of civilization and progress are alien to indigenous culture.[92] Cultural regeneration rather than imitation was necessary for the conceptual articulation of the future nation. Similarly, Tanika Sarkar notes the growing belief that household and conjugality were the last independent spaces left to Indians, becoming a new repository of power for the colonized.[93] Chaste Khorśed, the first dramatization of Indian womanhood as a loyal, pure, and nurturing figure who seeks her own husband and destiny, manifested intuitive knowledge of the innate superiority of ancestral life—and was therefore at the core of the consolidation of a new private sphere for the protonationalist rediscovery of tradition. To be more specific, Khorśed in years to come would transmute into the future motherland or *Bharatmātā*, who generates the special genius—spiritual devotion, revolutionary messianism, cultural homogeneity—for ideologically equipping the future nation. Paṭel's production offered a distinctive view of the gendered imperial encounter, metonymically upturning the conception of the orient as historically passive, intellectually stagnant, and susceptible to military domination, commercial interventionism, and ideological abuse. The play therefore marks the beginning of both the knotty project of the dislocation of the empire's ideological theatre and the period of popular nationalism, long before anticolonialism surfaced in the realm of politics.

The Commercialization of the Parsi Theatre

Sonānā Mulnī Khorśed was shadowed by the Elphinstone's unusually similar *Pākdāman Gulnār* or *Goolnar the Chaste*, written by Nāhānābhāi Rāṇīnā based on a plot by Khurśedjī Bahmanjī Farāmroj.[94] Like Khorśed, the heroine *Gulnār* attracts the attention of the monarch of the country where she is resident. Captivated by her beauty, the besotted king tries to take 'forcible possession of her', but she escapes with her husband to the jungle, where they encounter numerous creatures. Subsequently, the wife is separated from her husband and meets the dejected monarch, who uses the opportunity to press his suit. In the encounter, *Gulnār* stabs the king in the heart, and he dies. His followers discover his remains and bear him away with great sorrow. After innumerable adventures, husband and wife are reunified, and the curtain falls on the overjoyed couple to the tune of 'God Save the Queen'.[95] The juxtaposition of the murder of the monarch and the play's conclusion set to 'God Save the Queen' was eminently legible as deliciously insurgent to Bombay's now heterogenous theatre public. Implicit in plays such as *Sonānā Mulnī Khorśed* and *Pākdāman Gulnār*—with their titular female characters that escaped or slaughtered evil monarchs—was not just the burgeoning logic that the Indian spirit as woman was already sovereign despite being subject to the menace of an evil imperial power but also an elaborate ideological reappropriation of representative power. By reclaiming the role of tradition through woman and retrieving the authority of a previously undermined set of beliefs, the secular mythological plays of the 1870s, in contrast with the reformist plays of the 1860s, provided a universe of insurrectionist motifs to the multitudes, thus preparing the foundation for a cultural congruity that eventually converged into political doctrine.

Although *Pākdāman Gulnār* met with success among local publics, the English press's review of the performance was less than stellar:

> The husband and wife while conversing with some shepherds one day in the jungle were startled by the cry that 'a tiger was comin'. … A visible tremor announces the approach of the King of the Forest. First his head peeps round the corner of the stage to see if all's clear; then he cautiously advances the rest of his body, and proceeds to take stock of things in a most untigerlike manner. Laboriously he turns his head from side to side, his tail hangs limp, and altogether he looks a very sick tiger indeed—perhaps he had the jungle fever. … He proceeds past the tree, not even stopping to look at it, and, as if awfully disgusted with everything, and jungle-life

in particular—goes to his lair. ... Imagine, gentle reader, and you cannot stretch your imagination too much, a hairy triple-headed monster... An unfortunate young man, fascinated by the monster's appearance, is drawn towards him—nearer and more near; while this was proceeding, the sound of a pin falling might have been heard—the audience leaning forward in breathless excitement until—horrible to relate—the weak-minded youth is taken into the cavern and slowly swallowed, the last thing visible of him being the heels of his boots, striving to make themselves invisible. This accomplished, a terrific explosion takes place, followed by the disappearance of the monster and the appearance of a number of fairies ... Fairies, every one will admit, are sweet little creatures, but as represented here, they have a fault. Some may think it is a great one. Their lower extremities are thin—distressingly so, and they appear to neglect to garter up their stockings properly—but perhaps—who knows, like the tiger, they may have been indisposed.[96]

Evidently the letter writer—listed as 'Colonial', a fittingly titled representative of Bombay's English and Indian reformist public—found the new repertoire of the Parsi theatre with its scrawny-legged fairies, triple-headed monsters, and feverish tigers unpalatable. After *Gulnār*, the Elphinstone produced *Ālādīn* with Chinese costumes and spectacular scenes such as djinns flying on black clouds, the disappearance of a magician's cave, and the sudden appearance of a genie from a lamp, magical wands, rings, and earthquakes.[97] The play, despite its popular appeal, was similarly rebuked by the *Times of India*:

Two heavenly beings or giants, or whatever you call them, descend unsupported, from the sky, and after uttering a few words, again disappear. But, while reascending, they seem as if they could not bear their own weight, rising a bit at a time, while the pulleys creak horribly. ... The conjurer's table, full of various viands, comes out smartly enough, but on its disappearance some booby beneath the stage, most probably a cooly, closes the plank with a cool indifference, almost ridiculous. The waves of the sea are good enough, but the whole expanse of the deep stands still every five or ten minutes, very likely with the benevolent intention of giving some rest to the arms of the person who brings forth the storm.[98]

At play in these criticisms of the commercial Parsi theatre was a special apprehensiveness with regard to middle-class self-identity and interracial difference. Spectacular plays—which animated intuitive awareness, made new claims to representative authority through mimetic convention, and catered to the layman—elicited a class-based anxiety tied to the emergence of a large, steadily growing, and increasingly influential popular public sphere. As discursive interaction was now no longer at the level of communal reform, the theatrical public sphere metamorphosed from intra- to inter-communal engagement. The Parsi theatre thus provided the space for the first time in colonial history for members of diverse religious, linguistic, caste, and ethnic groups to assemble and engage in unmediated, vernacular, subtly heretical dialogue.

However, key differences in repertoire, membership, and patronage still existed between theatre troupes. As the Elphinstone still counted a number of 'respectable' artists as members of its company, its increased attention to mechanical scenery escaped much of the virulent criticism that was beginning to be directed towards the Victoria.[99] The Victoria's production of the Hindustani *Gule Bakāvalī*, the first production under Dādābhāi Paṭel's sole proprietorship, immediately came under fire from both the English and the reformist Gujarati press:

> Brilliant scenes are no doubt enchanting to the admiring eyes of the illiterate mass, and are sure to bring to Mr. Dadabhoy Sorabjee Patell a large profit, but the advantages of good composition and good acting are more solid and substantial. … This very play of *Gule Bakavlee* is a very dull and tedious affair, with all its wonders of scenery. It has little of real wit in it, and it is poor in language, in thought, and in sentiment. The acting in it is also miserable. Plays written with care and acted with ability will alone restore to the 'Victoria' its reputation of a first class dramatic Company.[100]

Ten days later, the *Rāst* published the following cutting review:

> The Victoria was founded with great care under the watchful eye of a committee. However, the troupe has now stooped so low as to use words such as *eśk* and *mohobat* [love] in their farces. … Ever since the troupe did away with its committee it has gone to dust. … Recently the Victoria's ownership has changed to that of Dādābhāi Sohrābjī Paṭel, who is now its sole proprietor. One would think that a well-educated man from such a respected background would have a positive effect on our theatrical profession, but this is not so. … It is necessary to publicly declare to Mr. Paṭel that our spectators need instructional plays written according to certain theatrical rules. The *Hindu Reformer* rightly complains of the immoral double meaning of the dialogues delivered by actors playing female roles.[101]

Through gendered metaphors, double entendres, and brilliant scenes for the 'admiring eyes of the illiterate mass', the Victoria disturbed and even caricatured reformist and colonial conceptions of morality and virtue and, correspondingly, the original edifying function of the Parsi theatre. The Victoria's cheaper ticket prices, its creation of variety 'progrāms' as opposed to proper productions, and its establishment of a 'fifth class' at the price of a mere four annas were additional signs of the ostensible decline in the 'reputation of a first-class dramatic company',[102] prompting 'scholar[s] and critic[s]' such as Kābrājī to habitually attack the Victoria and its imitators.[103] Gone were the Parsi theatre's reformist days, predicated on the pursuit of civilization and progress. The Parsi theatre had changed from 'a tool of *sudhārā* [reform] to [one of] *kudhārā* [deterioration]'.[104] Bombay's children wished to become a 'Jehānbakś and Manījeh rather than a Dadabhai Naoroji and Naoroji Fardunji'.[105] According to the Parsi press, the Parsi public was unable to distinguish between good and bad plays, Parsi 'public opinion' having still not reached its full maturity.[106]

Subsequently, the theatre became the object of inter-communal censure, as reports emerged of 'mushroom troupes' that threatened to lampoon 'respectable citizens' if they were not bribed with hush money.[107] While the city's Protestant Bishop H. A. Bombe prohibited Christians from pursuing the theatre professionally, the Bohra Mulla announced a fatwa prohibiting the Bohra community's patronage of the theatre as it purportedly prevented them from being good citizens, businessmen, and husbands.[108] Simultaneously, the Parsi community was pressed by reformist journals into boycotting Bombay's playhouses, and calls were issued for the institution of a 'censor' on European lines.[109] Within the Parsi community, intra-group politics reached a breaking point when the *Jāme Jamśed*, whose editor had begun to write plays for the Victoria, accused Kābrājī of jealousy and of the use of the *Rāst* as an organ for private vindication.[110] Unmistakably, Paṭel, who was the highly educated scion of one of the Parsis' wealthiest and most respected merchant families but who now 'had curtain painters for company', lay at the heart of the class conflict raging in the decreasingly 'Parsi' public sphere. However, even as some of his co-religionists would blame him for causing the downfall of their beloved theatre, others would memorialize him for spreading mass theatrical entertainment across the subcontinent and beyond.

Parsi–Muslim Animosity

On 2 February 1873, news was published in the Gujarati press that Sir Mir Turab Ali Khan, Salar Jung I, intended to build Hyderabad's first proscenium theatre for the Victoria's use, indicating that the company had left the year before for its first tour outside the Bombay Presidency.[111] While half the company, known as the 'night club', performed Dārāśāh Śohrābjī's *Kekāuś ane Rūstam* (*Kekāuś and Rūstam*) in Bombay, the other half—the 'day club'—comprising full-time, professional actors took off in 1872 for Hyderabad. No railway line existed between Bombay and Hyderabad, and the journey was both lengthy and perilous, due to wild animals, dacoits, and bandits. The day club's expedition lasted approximately twelve days, beginning with a railway journey between Bombay and Gulbarga. From Gulbarga, bullock carts sluggishly transported the actors and their wares to Hyderabad. The arduous and extended expedition was, nevertheless, worth the effort. Several plays including the Hindustani-language *Rūstam ane Sohrāb* were performed to acclaim for the courtiers, businessmen, and zenana over the course of several weeks, and no less than the Nizam himself commended the troupe.[112] After the company's return to Bombay, Paṭel produced the first Urdu 'opera' of the South Asian stage, *Benajhīr ane Badremunīr* (*Benajhīr and Badremunīr*), written by Naśarvānjī Mervānjī Khānsāheb.[113] The opera, however, spurred a deep fissure in the troupe when Dādābhāi Ṭhuṭhī absconded due to professional and personal differences to set up a rival company along with many of the Victoria's erstwhile amateur actors. His Hīndī Nāṭak Maṇḍalī, which would, according to Khambātā, 'reform' the now depraved Parsi theatre (see Chapter 6), was contrasted with the Victoria's 'kacrā jevā nāṭak' (garbage plays), which derived meagre profits of Rs 50–75 per night from 'low-class Muslims'.[114]

The term 'low-class Muslims' menacingly resonates with the *Rāst*'s long-winded vitriolic outbursts. Parsi–Muslim animosity that had a long-drawn history had here seeped into the rhetoric of class and the moral decline of the theatre even as managers explicitly catered to this new demographic. On 20 October 1872, an 'A' condemned the attendance of 'single Muslims' at the Victoria's family performances, warning Parsi families of attending such potentially dishonourable plays. Trouble began when 'A' spotted the 'single Muslims' entering the Victoria Theatre although numerous 'respectable Parsi men and women' had already seated themselves. He reproached the doorkeeper for permitting them entrance, but the doorkeeper allegedly retorted that the men were seated at a distance. After several bystanders joined the fray and matters threatened to get out of hand, the troupe's owner asked the Muslims to leave. However, once the play was underway and the spectators were engrossed in its proceedings, the Muslims returned.[115] Similar tensions surfaced two months later when Parsi men assaulted a man for 'staring improperly' at a 'respectable Parsi woman', evincing an increased patrolling of Parsi female virtue and by analogy a rising apprehension about Parsi middle-class dignity and prestige.[116]

Nevertheless, these controversies paled before the hitherto unseen outpouring of collective wrath that irrevocably changed the relationship between the Parsi community, its press, and the theatre after Paṭel announced the production of the play *Indra Sabhā* at the New Victoria Theatre. Described as 'a revolution in the theatre business, a novelty never before undertaken by any other theatre troupe', the performance of the play on 11 October 1873 featured 'respectable native women'. According to the Victoria's advertisements, after immense training and great expense, four 'respectable Begams' from Hyderabad graced the stage as fairies,[117] an act that provoked both the resignation of such stalwarts as Kāvasjī Kohīdārū, Hormasjī Modī, Farāmjī Dalāl, and Dhanjībhāi Rūstamjī Kerā̃vālā from the Victoria as well as proclamations by the Parsi community of the 'downfall' of 'their' beloved theatre and Parsi domestic well-being.[118] On the day of the first performance, the Victoria Theatre was crammed beyond capacity. Although special arrangements had been made with the police, when Paṭel graced the stage with one of the actresses at the end of the performance, Farāmjī Dāvar of the wealthy Dāvar clan (popularly known by the name Falu Gāṇdo, Falu the Madman) stood up from his seat in the first row of the orchestra and roared 'are andar jā tāhrā bāpdādānā̃ nāmne eb lagāḍec!' (Go back where you came from, you are a disgrace to your forefathers' names!).[119] According to Khambātā, numerous short-lived theatre companies swiftly followed Paṭel's precedent of hiring women and 'low-class Muslims', ticket prices declined to the impossibly low figures of one and two annas for the pit, respectable audiences ceased to patronize the theatre, and *nāṭak* (theatre) became a term of abuse.[120]

Paṭel, as I have argued elsewhere, was essentially preserving Mughal practices of sociability, establishing new forms of nonconjugal publicity for women, and opening up new worlds of performative meaning that destabilized reformist-mediated, middle-class visions of modernity.[121]

However, to Bombay's middle classes, pirouetting women dressed in fairy costumes upturned reformist conceptions of submissive, home-bound, asexual Victorian femininity. Along with other ostensibly nonrespectable—that is, nonlegitimate—performers, actresses wholly undermined the reformist conception of the Parsi theatre as an honourable pursuit due to the equivocacy of female self-sufficiency and sexual danger, performance and prostitution. Paṭel's daring endeavour, which completely overturned the Parsi reformist distinction between the honourable Parsi theatre and nautch entertainments, had possibly come too soon, prompting a significant decline in the Victoria's earnings and eventually the auctioning of the Victoria Theatre and its properties. Press reportage indicates that the theatre was 'saved in the nick of time' by a 'private businessman'—the rival manager of the Elphinstone Nāṭak Maṇḍalī, Kuvarjī Nājar.[122]

The Parsi–Muslim Riots of 1874

The inter-communal tensions in the Parsi theatre were signs of a more sinister drama brewing offstage. Shortly after the implementation of the census of 1872 and the prediction by the respected orientalist Max Müller of the 'Last Century of Parseeism'—that is, the community's 'extinction' as Parsis were so few that they were at risk of 'flying away with the wind' if 'a sudden blow were to strike'[123]—the Parsi–Muslim riots of 1874, the severest the city had hitherto seen, rocked Bombay.[124] The riots, which broke out on 13 February, were in response to the 1873 publication of a book entitled *Prasiddha Pegambaro ane Kāmo* (*The Renowned Prophets and Nations*) by Rūstamjī Hormajjī Jālbhāi.[125] Allegedly, one week before the riots broke out, the book reached 'the educated class of Mahomedans at their nautch parties', where it raised ire for the claim 'Mahomed nee rakhaillee rand Mareea nae paite Ebrahim namno beto peda thio hutto' (From Mareea, the kept *rand* of Mahomet, a son named Ebrahim was born), the Gujarati term *rand* or *rāṇḍ* meaning both *woman* and *prostitute*. The Muslim community formed a deputation under the leadership of Cazee Abdul Lutiff to approach police commissioner Frank Souter, arguing that the author had insulted their religion and that unless he 'was punished in some way they could not answer for the conduct of the Mahomedans towards Parsees'. Although Jālbhāi claimed that Washington Irving, the writer whom he had relied on for his description of the

Prophet, referred to 'Ibrahim, Mahomet's son, by his favourite concubine Mariyah' in his work, Jālbhāi was held responsible by Souter, who instantly withdrew all copies of the book. Yet this action, according to certain sections of the government, only added fuel to the fire, strengthening the view that the Prophet had in fact been denigrated by a Parsi.[126] Accordingly on that pivotal Friday, a group of armed Muslims began attacking Parsi property in Bhendi Bazar, parts of Dhobitalao, and especially Khetwadi and Baharkot.[127] The crowd, consisting primarily of Arabs, Sidis, and Pathans, outnumbered the Parsis on this first day, and according to eyewitness accounts, the police arrived on the scene as late as two hours after the riots began. Consequently, numerous Parsis were injured and scores of homes and shops were ransacked. The next day the protestors moved from Abdul Rehman Street, the Bhendy Bazar, and Null Bazar to Khetwaddy, where many Parsis resided. In the meantime, a mob of Parsis began arming themselves with bludgeons. On Sunday 15 February, six people died when Parsis and Muslims attacked each other in Sonapur. The military was summoned the same day, although its presence was only felt on Monday, at which point there was less violence and peace was, to a degree, reinstated. On the same night, amid insinuations of Nero and the destruction of Rome, Government House Ball occurred at Parel, highlighting the termination of the Parsi–Muslim riots of 1874.

During and after the violence, vernacular and English newspapers in India and abroad primarily focused on the breakdown of law and order. As an English regional newspaper, the *Northern Echo*, argued,

> It is impossible not to regard the rioting at Bombay with considerable alarm. If poor innocent WASHINGTON IRVING'S 'Mohammed' set Bombay in flames, what will be the case when our controversial literature is transplanted to Hindostan? Even our poetry will kindle a rebellion. ... Whatever course our representatives may adopt, they must remember that the conditions upon which they govern are, first of all, to maintain order; and then to preserve unimpaired the freedom of the press.[128]

This emphasis on public order was reiterated by the secretary of state, Lord Salisbury, in a despatch of July 1874. Most of England's newspapers supported the tone of the dispatch, replacing 'the suppression of the liberty of the *press*' with 'the suppression of the liberty of the *Parsi community*'; the disagreement thus becoming one of inter-religious conflict.[129] This lexical shift had a profound impact on the subsequent development of the Parsi theatre, highlighting not so much 'the death of a birthright' (as suggested by the Parsis) as the elementary differences between the Westphalian rational-critical and South Asian religio-political public spheres.[130] Although, in Westphalian Europe, print made possible 'homogeneous, empty time' and the conception of a unified social imaginary, in colonial South Asia existing convictions in the power of religious icons and texts assumed new intensities, 'messianic time' here being the modal time for modernity.[131] Religion, as demonstrated in Chapter 2, generated the colonial public, functioning as a channel for the transformation of ephemeral, figurative, and allegorical custom into disenchanted detail. This reformist project of disenchantment was, as the Parsi theatre of the 1870s so evocatively shows, not successful. The affronted political actors in the Parsi–Muslim riots clearly did not partake in the Westphalian-reformist vision of the world as novel with its concomitant self-reflexive mode of subjectivity. The epistemological injury prompted by the insult of the Prophet Muhammad, and the necessary retribution for this injury, is evidence of the modern formulation of sociopolitical imaginaries in which ostensibly mundane objects (trains and hot air balloons), communitarian dialogue, and claims to justice were formulated and comprehended on the basis of pre-Saussurean conceptions of language.[132] For the dissenters, the actual contents of Jalbhoy's book mattered little, as the sign of the Prophet was invested with the divine. Despite the thoroughness of the disciplinary project of social reform—in which virtue, morality, and obedience were inculcated through 'the adoption of Christian sentiment if not of doctrine'[133]—enchantment inhered for the majority of Indians in every aspect of daily (and extra-daily) activity. Consequently, the violation of the sacral sign of the Prophet provided a popular base for political mobilization, the development of new group solidarities, and performative enactments that challenged the moral economy of colonial reason.[134]

The riots thus also highlight the broadening of and the fundamental shift in the character of the vernacular public sphere: from intra- to inter-communal self-representation. From the time of the census of 1872 and the related burgeoning of a national consciousness (*nation* here being commensurate with a religious, ethnic, or linguistic community), the violence of representational politics—who can represent whom—permeated inter-religious dialogue. For instance, shortly after the riots, despite an edict issued by Souter banning public events on the occasion of Eid, the Victoria staged a variety performance in the hotbed of Grant Road. The *Jāme Jamśed* described how 'Muslims' attacked the Victoria's Parsi actors onstage while other performers armed themselves with weapons behind the curtains, even as the police brought the fracas to a speedy halt and arrested the troublemakers. 'How can Parsis patronize such a theatre?' cried a 'halkā nāṭakone dhīkārnār paṇ sārā nāṭakone pasand karnār' (hater of low plays but lover of good ones) in a letter entitled 'Nāṭakśālā ke bhaṅgarkhānā?' (Theatre or scrapyard?).[135] The next week, the Victoria issued a proclamation in its advertisement declaring that 'troublemakers' would be thrown out, indicating the indistinct boundaries between class and religious affiliation. The theatre had therefore become a metatheatrical site where religious communities symbolically and physically battled for sociopolitical legitimacy and the recognition of disparate moral frames.

These dissensions would persist and even grow in strength, as when the Zoroastrian Theatrical Club in 1881 declared in its advertisements for *Keikaus and Sodabeh* that 'PARSEES ARE ONLY ALLOWED'.[136] A few years later, the owners of the Victoria personally appealed to Souter to post senior detectives as well as plain-clothes and uniformed police officers throughout the premises of their theatre due to rabble rousers in the pit, all of whom were curiously Muslim.[137] Thus 'Abdoola Mosajee, Samsoodin Latif, and Jaffer Cooverjee, three Mahomedan servants' were charged with creating disturbances at the Victoria's performance of *Fasānaye Ajāyab*.[138] The theatre, critically, was therefore neither dispassionate in nor independent of the inter-communal 'divide and rule' politics that began at the end of the nineteenth century. On the contrary, it was an active participant in the deepening sectarian violence, even as it transgressed long-standing ethnic, religious, and linguistic divides in its peddling of optical enchantments and technological delights. Cosmopolitanism and communalism thus merged in the theatrical public sphere. While particular visual attractions such as the secular mythological play assumed homogenous indigenous frames of comprehension and appeal, so too were the politics of religion (a fundamental feature of the South Asian public sphere) contested across rather than within communities through a multiplicity of discordant scripts that profoundly disturbed the normative premises of classical liberalism. Thus, although Parsi performances enjoyed remarkable cross-cultural appeal, engaging peoples of all religious, class, and ethnic denomination, a brisk cross-citational velocity between the religious icons depicted in the Parsi theatre and those deployed for political protest begins with the riots, marking the commencement of not only the period of high nationalism but also the theatre's imbrication in the forging of new social imaginaries, the development of popular forms of political rebellion, and the rise of long-standing inter-communal conflicts that exist to this day (see Chapter 7).

Notes

1. Kaikhosro N. Kabraji, 'Reminiscences of Kaikhosro N. Kabraji (editor of *Rast Goftar*) Fifty Years Ago', *TOI*, 26 October 1901, 7.
2. Extract from the *Dnyanodaya*, cited in Govinda Nārāyaṇa Māḍagāvakara, *Govind Narayan's Mumbai: An Urban Biography from 1863*, trans. Murali Ranganathan (New Delhi: Anthem Press, 2008), 257–58.
3. Dinshaw Edulji Wacha, *Shells from the Sands of Bombay; Being My Recollections and Reminiscences, 1860–1875* (Bombay: K.T. Anklesaria, 1920), 431–33.
4. *Allen's Indian Mail, and Register of Intelligence for British and Foreign India, China, and All Parts of the East*, vol. 12, January–December 1854 (London: Wm. H. Allen, 1854), 35.
5. Wacha, *Shells from the Sands of Bombay*, 555–56.
6. Wacha, *Shells from the Sands of Bombay*, 555–56.
7. Untitled, *RG*, 29 July 1855, 234.
8. 'Dīlīnī Fateh', *RG*, 4 October 1857, 317. See also 'Hīnduśthānmā̃ vijlīno tār', *RG*, 24 January 1858, 39–40; Untitled, *RG*, 7 February 1858, 74; and 'Iṅglaṇḍ ane Hīndusthānnī vace vījlīno tār', *RG*, 11 July 1858, 340–41.
9. Aguiar cites Calcutta journals that describe travellers' anxieties of train travel as the annihilation of time and space was perceived as curtailing the length of life. Marian Aguiar, *Tracking Modernity: India's Railway and the Culture of Mobility* (Minneapolis: University of Minnesota Press, 2011), 48.
10. 'Geās Lāiṭ', *RG*, 9 December 1860, 603–4.
11. Daniel R. Headrick, *The Tools of Empire: Technology and European Imperialism in the Nineteenth Century* (New York: Oxford University Press, 1981), 134; Mrs. Postans, 'The Brightest Jewels of Our Dependencies,' in *The Charm of Bombay, an Anthology of Writings in Praise of the First City in India*, ed. R. P. Karkaria (Bombay: D. B. Taraporevala, 1915), 191–94.
12. Veer, *The Modern Spirit of Asia*, 117.
13. Sandria B. Freitag, 'The Realm of the Visual: Agency and Modern Civil Society', *Contributions to Indian Sociology* 36, no. 1–2 (2002): 366.
14. Iwan Rhys Morus, 'Seeing and Believing Science', *Isis* 97, no. 1 (2006): 103–4.
15. 'Ek śīlīṅgmā keṭlū joso?', *RG*, 18 July 1858, 349–50.

16. 'Ek śīlīṅgmā keṭlū joso?', *RG*, 18 July 1858, 349–50.
17. 'The Proposed Victoria Museum', *RG*, 21 November 1858, 580.
18. 'Farā̃mjī Kāvaśjī Inśṭīṭuṭ', *RG*, 13 December 1857, 396–97.
19. 'Farāmjī Kāvaśjī Inśṭīṭuṭ', *RG*, 28 February 1858, 110; 'Science Associations', *RG*, 4 July 1875, 453. See Khoshru Navrosji Banaji, *Memoirs of the Late Framji Cowasji Banaji* (Bombay: Bombay Gazette Steam Printing Works, 1892).
20. 'Farāmjī Kāvasjī Insṭīṭīūṭ', *RG*, 23 February 1868, 120.
21. Untitled, *RG*, 13 December 1857, 397.
22. 'Seances Mesmeriques', *Golden Era*, 23 June 1861, 4.
23. Roger Luckhurst, 'W.T. Stead's Occult Economies', in *Culture and Science in the Nineteenth-Century Media*, ed. Louise Henson et al. (Aldershot: Ashgate, 2004), 132.
24. 'Camatkārīk Tamāso—Vījlīnī Asar', *RG*, 15 April 1866, 233–34.
25. Morus, 'Seeing and Believing Science', 105.
26. See Morus, 'Seeing and Believing Science', 104–5.
27. 'Is it science, performance, or all a cheat?' the *Rāst* proclaimed in 'Mesmerīsm', *RG*, 22 April 1866, 249–50.
28. 'Mī. Nāhānābhāi Rūstamjī Rā̃ṇīnā ane Profesar Buśal', *RG*, 22 April 1866, 251–52.
29. 'Mī. Nāhānābhāi Rūstamjī Rā̃ṇīnā', *RG*, 29 April 1866, 266–67; Untitled, *RG*, 13 May 1866, 305.
30. Joe Kember, John Plunkett, and Jill A. Sullivan, eds., *Popular Exhibitions, Science and Showmanship, 1840–1910* (London: Pickering and Chatto, 2012), 5.
31. Untitled, *RG*, 25 November 1866, 753; 'Sarkas', *RG*, 2 December 1866, 766; Untitled, *RG*, 20 January 1867, 47; 'Navā Sarkas', *RG*, 10 February 1867, 93; Untitled, *RG*, 23 December 1866, 816; Untitled, *RG*, 14 November 1869, 737; Untitled, *RG*, 3 March 1867; Untitled, *RG*, 17 March 1867, 174; Untitled, *RG*, 28 April 1867, 271; and Untitled, *RG*, 3 February 1867, 79.
32. 'Iṅglaṇḍnī nāṭak śālāo', *RG*, 20 January 1867, 41.
33. Untitled, *RG*, 22 May 1870, 342; 'Vīkṭorīyā Nāṭak Maṇḍaḷī', 29 May 1870, 352.
34. Jahāṅgīr Pestanjī Khambātā, *NA* (Bombay, 1913), 15–17. The Alfred's success under Mā̃ṇekjī Jīvaṇjī Master prompted a slew of announcements in newspapers for plays and professional actors: 'Ālfreḍ Nāṭak Maṇḍali', *RG*, 10 July 1870, 454; and 'Ālfreḍ Nāṭak Maṇḍali', *RG*, 10 July 1870, 455.
35. Mādan's sweet voice was one of the chief attractions of the play. He would subsequently retire to Calcutta where he would open a photography studio and help his wealthy brother Jamśedjī Farāmjī Mādan with his theatre and film businesses.

36. 'Victoria Theatrical Company', *TOI*, 9 December 1871, 3.
37. 'Gai Mosamnā̃ Nāṭako', *RG*, 17 July 1870, 459–60.
38. 'The Zoroastrian Theatrical Club', *RG*, 8 March 1871, 2; Khambātā, *NA*, 31–32. See also 'Jorāsṭrīan Nāṭak Maṇḍaḷī', *RG*, 22 February 1871, 140. See also Khambātā, *NA*, 10–11; and Untitled, *RG*, 14 February 1869, 110 for a description of how in 1869 the Zoroastrian Nāṭak Maṇḍalī broke up into two theatres: the Zoroastrian Nāṭak Maṇḍalī and the Original Zoroastrian Nāṭak Maṇḍalī.
39. Untitled, *RG*, 19 February 1871, 129; 'The Zoroastrian Theatrical Club', *TOI*, 4 March 1871, 3; untitled, *TOI*, 12 April 1871, 1; and Untitled, *TOI*, 11 March 1871, 1. Khodābakś was performed by Pestanjī Pāvrī, Nādir by Farāmjī Kāvasjī Mehtā (Framjee Cowasji Mehta; the soon-to-be editor of the *Kaiser-i-Hind*, the Parsi organ of the Indian National Congress), and Nūrdin by the soon-to-be renowned actor-manager Farāmjī Apu. Dhanjībhāi Na Paṭel, *PNTT* (Bombay: 'Kaysare-Hind' Paper Printing Press, 1931), 194. The songs of the play were written by Dalpatrām Dāhāyābhāi. 'Gujrātī Nāṭakonī Tapāś', *RG*, 31 March 1872, 200–201.
40. 'The Play of "Khodabux"', *BG*, 1 April 1871, 3.
41. 'Bombay Zoroastrian Theatrical Club', *TOI*, 23 August 1871, 2. See also the patronage of a performance by a Parsee gentleman of Poona. 'The Zoroastrian Theatrical Company', *TOI*, 15 March 1871, 3.
42. 'Nāṭaknī Mośam', *RG*, 9 July 1871, 440. The Alfred was owned by Hīrjībhāi Khambātā and subsequently co-owned by Kharśedjī Bāpāsolā, Rūstamjī Bāṭlā, Māṇekjī Jīvanjī Māsṭar, and Bhīkhājī N. Kalyāṇīvālā.
43. Khambātā, *NA*, 19–20.
44. 'Alfred Dramatic Club', *TOI*, 3 June 1871, 3.
45. 'He has for the first time introduced the splendid scenes now witnessed...The attractions and novel scenes are too many individually to mention'. 'The Alfred Dramatic Club', *TOI*, 12 May 1871, 3.
46. 'The Alfred Dramatic Club', *TOI*, 24 June 1871, 3.
47. 'Jehanbux and Goolrookhsar', *TOI*, 17 May 1871, 3. See also untitled, *TOI*, 26 April 1871, 1; Untitled, *TOI*, 28 April 1871, 1; Untitled, *TOI*, 16 September 1871, 1; and 'Alfred Dramatic Club', *TOI*, 20 September 1871, 3.
48. Tracy C. Davis, 'What Are Fairies For?', in *The Performing Century*, eds. Tracy C. Davis and Peter Holland, (London: Palgrave Macmillan, 2007), 53.
49. Davis, 'What Are Fairies For?', 33.
50. Davis, 'What Are Fairies For?', 54.
51. James Douglas, *A Book of Bombay* (Bombay: Bombay Gazette Steam Press, 1883), xii–xiii; Kaikhosro N. Kabraji, 'Reminiscences of Kaikhosro

N. Kabraji (editor of *Rast Goftar*) Fifty Years Ago', *TOI*, 26 October 1901, 7; and Wacha, *Shells from the Sands of Bombay*, 431–33.
52. Davis, 'What Are Fairies For?', 34.
53. 'Alādīn', *RG*, 7 January 1872, 6; Untitled, *RG*, 7 January 1872, 16.
54. Bandekhodā, *Barjo ane Mehersīmīnojār* (Bombay: Reporter's Press, 1871), 50.
55. Ek Mahmadīyan Munśī, *Śīrīn Farhādno Gāyanrūpī operā* (Bombay: Oriental Press, 1882), 15–16.
56. Khambātā, *NA*, 19–20.
57. 'Jorāsṭrīan Nāṭak Maṇḍaḷī', *RG*, 22 February 1871, 140. Whereas four theatre troupes existed in 1858, this number had increased to twenty in three short years: Paṭel, *PNTT*, 2–3.
58. 'The Drama under Difficulties', *BT*, 12 February 1859, 100.
59. 'Nāṭak ane Nāṭaksālā', *RG*, 15 October 1865, 666–67.
60. 'Nāṭak ane Nāṭaksālā', *RG*, 15 October 1865, 666–67.
61. Jā̃hāṅgīr Hormajjī, 'Nāṭak karnā̃rā chokrāo tathā temnā̃ śīkhsako', *RG*, 29 October 1865, 700–1.
62. Dhāḍī, 'Pārsī Nāṭko', *RG*, 5 October 1865, 716.
63. J. D. S., *TOI*, 7 May 1864, cited in Kumudini Mehta, *English Drama on the Bombay Stage*, 261.
64. Jā̃hāṅgīr Hormajjī, 'Nāṭak karnā̃rā chokrāo tathā temnā̃ śīkhsako', *RG*, 29 October 1865, 700–1; Nāṭaknu Ceṭak', *RG*, 26 November 1871, 770.
65. 'Mazagon Police Office', *BG*, 29 April 1864, 3.
66. 'Grāṇtroḍ Nāṭakśāḷāmā thaylū hulaḍ', *RG*, 10 August 1873, 527.
67. 'Nāṭaknu Ceṭak', *RG*, 26 November 1871, 770; Untitled, *RG*, 1 June 1873, 356; and 'Pārsī Nāṭako', *RG*, 8 June 1873, 360.
68. Khambātā, *NA*, 11.
69. Following Edward W. Said, I use the term *secular* to mean worldly rather than antireligious. See Said, *The World, the Text, and the Critic* (Cambridge, MA: Harvard University Press, 1983).
70. 'Nāṭaknī Mośam', *RG*, 9 July 1981, 440–41.
71. Colonial, 'The Parsee Elphinstone Dramatic Club', *TOI*, 10 April 1872, 3.
72. 'Femlīonā Nāṭakne lagto kāydo', *RG*, 12 March 1871, 171–72.
73. 'Victoria Theatrical Company', *TOI*, 10 June 1871, 3.
74. 'There is a large fund of wit and humour in it, which kept the audience in a pleasant mood throughout the performance. The singing of the young men, as usual, was much liked'. 'The Victoria Dramatic Company', *BG*, 16 May 1871, 2. See also 'The Victoria Dramatical Club', *BG*, 13 May 1871, 3; untitled, *TOI*, 25 March 1871, 3; and 'The Alfred Dramatic Club', *TOI*, 20 May 1871, 3.
75. 'The Alfred Dramatic Club', *TOI*, 20 May 1871, 3.

76. The play's production deepened the antagonism between the Victoria's director and the editor of the *Rāst* when the former (Paṭel) ignored the latter's (Kābrājī's) recommendation to assign the title role of Hajambād to Dhanjībhāi Vīmādalāl. Instead, the director decided to perform the part himself, a move that he would regret in due course. See Paṭel, *PNTT*, 354.
77. On 28 May 1871, the *Rāst* published an article praising the actors and disclosing that the play had been *sudhroḍ* (reformed) of coarse language. 'Vīkṭorīyā Nāṭak Maṇḍalīno …', *RG*, 28 May 1871, 348.
78. 'Gujrātī Nāṭakonī Tapāś', *RG*, 31 March 1872, 200–1.
79. 'Gujrātī Nāṭakonī Tapāś', *RG*, 31 March 1872, 200–1.
80. 'Gujrātī Nāṭakonī Tapāś', *RG*, 31 March 1872, 200–1.
81. 'ā̃khā̃ Hīndustānne Māṭe ek bhāśā', *RG*, 11 June 1871, 375.
82. Untitled, *RG*, 24 September 1871, 632; Untitled, *RG*, 1 October 1871, 648; Untitled, *RG*, 8 October 1871, 664; and Untitled, *RG*, 15 October 1871, 680. See also Untitled, *RG*, 24 December 1871, 844, describing the sale of the playbook.
83. Paṭel, *PNTT*, 33–34.
84. Edaljī Jamśedjī Khorī, *Sonānā Mulnī Khorśed* (Bombay: Daftar Āśkārā Press, 1871), 5.
85. Paṭel, *PNTT*, 104.
86. Untitled, *RG*, 24 September 1871, 632.
87. Paṭel, *PNTT*, 105; and Khambātā, *NA*, 33–35: According to Khambātā, it is here that Bālīvālā's success began. Bālīvālā played the important part of Fīrojśāh as he had a sweet singing voice, a trait that would become a requirement in the Parsi theatre. Delhi's King Fatehśāh was performed by Hormasjī Modī, and the King of Sindh Malekśāh was performed by Dārāśāh Tārāporvālā. Jāfar Khān was performed by Dhanjībhāi Kerāvālā, Gājī Khān was played by Dhanjībhāi Vīmādalāl, and the King of Faizabad Jā̃hā̃dārśāh was played by Kāvasjī Kohīdārū.
88. 'Navo Hīndustānī Nāṭak', *RG*, 15 October 1871, 670–71. Parsi standards of acting were based on those of English actors such as Mr and Mrs Gīl, members of Dave Carson's entourage. Parsi actors were often urged by the press to learn directly from these performers. See 'Nāṭako', *RG*, 11 June 1871, 378.
89. 'Navo Hīndustānī Nāṭak', *RG*, 15 October 1871, 670–71.
90. 'Nāṭak', *RG*, 1 October 1871, 642; and Paṭel, *PNTT*, 388–89.
91. Partha Chatterjee, *The Nation and Its Fragments: Colonial and Postcolonial Histories* (Princeton, NJ: Princeton University Press, 1993), 6.
92. Partha Chatterjee, *Nationalist Thought and the Colonial World: A Derivative Discourse?* (London: Zed Books, 1993, first published 1986), 2.

93. Tanika Sarkar, *Hindu Wife, Hindu Nation: Community, Religion, and Cultural Nationalism* (New Delhi: Permanent Black, 2017, first published 2001), 198.
94. 'Nhānābhāi Rūstamjī Rāṇīnā, Pāk Dāmānnī Gulnār', *RG*, 31 March 1872, 209.
95. Colonial, 'The Parsee Elphinstone Dramatic Club', *TOI*, 10 April 1872, 3.
96. Colonial, 'The Parsee Elphinstone Dramatic Club', *TOI*, 10 April 1872, 3.
97. 'Alādīn', *RG*, 7 January 1872, 6.
98. 'Aladdin; or, The Wonderful Lamp', *TOI*, 12 January 1872, 3.
99. Alādīn was performed by Dr Naśarvānjī Navrojī Pārakh, Abnejar by the public school master Dhanjībhāi, Abnejar's dumb servant by Naśarvānjī Edaljī Vāchā, and the princess of China, Badrul Badar, by Jamśedjī Farāmjī Mādan. 'Elfinsṭak Nāṭak Ṭolī', *RG*, 23 June 1872, 396; and Paṭel, *PNTT*, 34–35.
100. H. C., 'The Victoria Theatrical Company', *TOI*, 8 February 1872, 2.
101. 'Pārsī Nāṭako—Dhastī Bharelī Hālat', *RG*, 18 February 1872, 104.
102. Ticket prices were as follows: 'First Class: 2, Second Class: 1, Third Class: 0 III, Fourth Class: 0 II, Fifth Class: 4 annas !!!'. See untitled, *RG*, 1 June 1873, 355. In Gujarati, the language of commerce in Bombay, 'I' denoted a quarter-rupee, '-' an anna and '૧' a pie. Stephen Meredyth Edwardes, *The Gazetteer of Bombay City and Island* (Bombay: Times Press, 1909), 1:329.
103. 'Vīkṭorīyā Nāṭak Manḍaḷī', *RG*, 9 June 1872, 364; and 'Gai Mosamnā̃ Nāṭako', *RG*, 17 July 1870, 459–60.
104. 'Nāṭaknū Ceṭak', *RG*, 22 December 1872, 816–17; 'Pārsī Nāṭako—Dhāstī Bharelī Hālat', *RG*, 18 February 1872, 104–5.
105. Dhāḍī, 'Pārsī Nāṭko', *RG*, 5 October 1865, 716.
106. 'Nāṭaknū Ceṭak', *RG*, 22 December 1872, 816–17; and 'Pārsī Nāṭako—Dhāstī Bharelī Hālat', *RG*, 18 February 1872, 104–5.
107. 'Disreputable Theatricals', *RG*, 19 September 1875, 630. For a description of the phenomenon of 'mushroom companies' see Paṭel, *PNTT*, 2–3.
108. "Nāṭak Karvāne Khrīstīonā Bīśapnī Manāi", *RG*, 22 December 1872, 824–25 and "Gujrātī Nāṭako bābe Horāonā Mulā̃no Fatvo.", *RG*, 21 June 1874, 424.
109. 'Nāṭaknū Ceṭak', *RG*, 22 December 1872, 816–17. The policing of the theatrical public sphere also took on other forms, as when Rāṇīnā filed a landmark copyright case against Nājar in the small causes court for using his *Pākdāman Gulnār* for an extended period without his express permission. See 'Deśī Nāṭak Lakhnārāonī ek muśkel—dhārānī ek khā̃mī', *RG*, 30 March 1873, 200–1.

110. 'Vīkṭorīyā Nāṭak Maṇḍaḷī', *RG*, 7 July 1872, 427–28.
111. 'Hedrābādmā Nāṭakśāḷā', *RG*, 2 February 1873, 72.
112. Paṭel, *PNTT*, 112–14.
113. Untitled, *RG*, 20 April 1873, 259; and Paṭel, *PNTT*, 110.
114. Khambātā, *NA*, 39–40; and Bombe, 'Ḍrāmāṭīk Sosāiṭī', *RG*, 23 June 1872, 391–92.
115. 'Femīlīonā Nāṭakmā Ekhlā muśalmān dākhal thai śakeche', *RG*, 20 October 1872, 680.
116. 'Pārsī Ṭolānī', *RG*, 22 December 1872, 821.
117. Untitled, *RG*, 5 October 1873, 658.
118. Paṭel, *PNTT*, 180, 284.
119. Khambātā, *NA*, 31.
120. Khambātā, *NA*, 31.
121. Rashna Darius Nicholson, '"A Christy Minstrel, a Harlequin, or an Ancient Persian"?: Opera, Hindustani Classical Music, and the Origins of the Popular South Asian "Musical"', *Theatre Survey* 61, no. 3 (2020), 344–45.
122. 'The Stage in Its Last Stage in Bombay', *RG*, 1 February 1874, 66–67.
123. 'Extinction of Parseeism Anticipated by Max Muller', *RG*, 4 January 1874, 7; 'The Last Century of Parseeism', *RG*, 18 January 1874, 38–39.
124. 'Usefulness of a Free Native Press', *RG*, 11 January 1874, 21; 'The Outrage on the Parsees of Bombay', *TOI*, 15 February 1874, cited in *The Bombay Riots of February 1874. Re-printed from the Times of India* (Bombay: Times of India Printing Works, 1874), 17. For a description of the riots, Parsi–Muslim relations and the development of a transnational public sphere see Rashna Darius Nicholson, 'The Picture, the Parable, the Performance and the Sword: Secularism's Demographic Imperatives', *Ethnic and Racial Studies* 41, no. 12 (2018): 2197–214.
125. Untitled, *RG*, 15 June 1873, 390.
126. *The Bombay Riots of February 1874. Re-Printed from the Times of India*, 9.
127. 'An Account of the Mahomedan Riot', *RG*, 15 February 1874, 102.
128. 'An Incident of Empire', *Northern Echo*, 16 March 1874, 2.
129. '...before the outbreak of the riots the Commissioner sent for the author of the book, obtained possession of the unsold copies, and collected from the subscribers as many of those that had been sold as he could discover. If the danger of a popular outbreak was imminent, this extreme measure of restraint upon the liberty of the Parsee community might be justified by considerations of public order...' 'The Riots at Bombay', *Pall Mall Gazette*, 7 August 1874, 7.
130. *The Bombay Riots of 1874* (Bombay: Bombay Gazette Steam Press, 1874), 39; 'The Death of a Birthright', *RG*, 5 April 1874, 223–24.

131. See Christopher Pinney, *'Photos of the Gods': The Printed Image and Political Struggle in India* (London: Reaktion Books, 2004), 11–12.
132. See Christopher Pinney, 'The Nation (Un)Pictured? Chromolithography and "Popular" Politics in India, 1878–1995', *Critical Inquiry* 23, no. 4 (1997): 834–67.
133. See Gauri Viswanathan, *Masks of Conquest: Literary Study and British Rule in India* (New York: Columbia University Press, 2014), 85.
134. Nicholson, 'The Picture, the Parable'.
135. Halkā nāṭakone dhīkārnār paṇ sārā 'nāṭakone pasand karnār, 'Nāṭakśālā ke bhaṅgarkhānā?', *RG*, 29 October 1876, 732.
136. Untitled, *TOI*, 18 April 1881, 1; Untitled, *RG*, 3 April 1881, 236; Untitled, *RG*, 17 April 1881, 271; Untitled, *RG*, 24 April 1881, 288; Untitled, *RG*, 15 May 1881, 337; and Untitled, *RG*, 22 May 1881, 355.
137. 'Wit in the Pit', *RG*, 27 February 1887, 235; 'Nāṭakśāḷāmā̃ ghoṅgāṭ karnārāo. 1', *RG*, 6 March 1887, 271; and Tamāśbīn, 'Nāṭakśāḷāmā̃ ghoṅgāṭ karnārāo. 2', *RG*, 6 March 1887, 271.
138. 'A Fight in the Theatre', *TOI*, 29 April 1887, 3.

CHAPTER 6

The Expansion of the Parsi Theatre

Fall Out

Shortly after the Elphinstone performed its first Hindu-themed play *Karaṇ Ghelo,* the Parsi–Muslim riots broke out and Grant Road's Parsi owned theatres abruptly bolted their doors. The Parsi theatre resumed its activities on 11 April 1874 with the Elphinstone's *Lālā Rūkh* and *Kharī Mohbat iāne Falkaśur ane Śalīm* (*True Love or Falkaśur and Śalīm*), written by Naśarvānjī Pārakh and performed at the Grant Road Theatre.[1] The next week a landmark in the history of the Parsi theatre was made known to Bombay's Gujarati-reading public: the Victoria and the Elphinstone, once cutthroat rivals, began to publish their advertisements in unison.[2] Kuvarjī Nājar, the owner of the Elphinstone and lessee of the Grant Road Theatre, had finally fulfilled his ambition of monopolizing the largest troupes and playhouses of the Parsi theatre by becoming joint owner of the Victoria, alongside Dādābhāi Paṭel. However, such a union of strong-minded individuals was doomed to fail. Nājar implemented increasingly laborious rules compelling the actors to work at both spaces: the Victoria's actors, finishing a performance of *Jehaṅgīrśāh ane Gohar* (*Jehaṅgīrśāh and Gohar*) or *Gule Bakāvalī* at 10 p.m. at the Victoria Theatre, would need to rush to the Grant Road Theatre to perform at 11 p.m. in the Elphinstone's *Gulbā Sanobar Cekard*, and vice versa. These policies impelled Paṭel to take the Victoria

R. D. Nicholson, *The Colonial Public and the Parsi Stage*, Transnational Theatre Histories,
https://doi.org/10.1007/978-3-030-65836-6_6

on tour, first to Poona and then to Gujarat (Surat, Bharuch, Ahmedabad, and Rajkot), where the company successfully performed before Sir Philip Wodehouse (Governor of Bombay), the collectors of Surat, and the judges of Ahmedabad. After returning to Bombay from Gujarat in February 1875, Paṭel, infuriated with Nājar's dictatorial ways, stormed out of the Victoria to set up the Original Victoria Nāṭak Maṇḍalī.[3] The decision irrevocably fractured the Victoria, as many of Paṭel's faithful actors followed the esteemed director, despite the stringent termination clauses of their contracts. Hence, Naśarvānjī Khānsāheb, Naśarvānjī Farāmjī Mādan (Naslu Tehmīna),[4] Kāvasjī Naśarvānjī Dārūvālā (Kāu-Rodābe),[5] Sorābjī Farāmjī Ogrā,[6] Bhīkhājī Kalyānīvālā (Bhīkhu Śyavakṣ), Jamśedjī Kāvasjī Dājī (Jamsu Manījeh),[7] and especially the famous actor Pestanjī Farāmjī Mādan absconded from the Victoria to commence a lengthy series of tours across South Asia under the leadership of their venerated director.

Paṭel was not the only director to abscond and establish his own theatre company. As mentioned in Chapter 5, Dādābhāi Ṭhuṭhī split from Paṭel's Victoria Nāṭak Maṇḍalī between 1872 and 1873 during rehearsals for *Benajhīr ane Badremunīr* to set up his own Hīndī Nāṭak Maṇḍalī, where the famous actor-manager Kāvasjī Pālanjī Khaṭāu began his theatrical career.[8] Ṭhuṭhī allegedly considered the Victoria's mechanical scene (created by Dādābhāi Ratanjī Dalāl) of the besotted fairy Māhrūkh lifting Benajhīr's bed into the air to be 'childish' (that is, not up to par), prompting Paṭel to retort, 'if you want to show a better way of lifting Benajhīr's bed, do it in your own club!' Consequently, the Hīndī Nāṭak Maṇḍalī's first play was *Benajhīr ane Badremunīr*, performed in a new playhouse christened the Hīndī Theatre (later known as the Royal Theatre) that Ṭhuṭhī built following the 'American' model.[9] The theatre, erected opposite Bombay's Muslim cemetery (Bada Qabrastan) in present-day Marine Lines, had a capacity of a thousand spectators, with the third and fourth classes seated below and the first and second seated upstairs, and it cost Rs 12,000 to build. Significantly, although the stage was forty-eight feet long and thirty-nine feet wide, the visible area in front of the curtains was only twenty feet wide, an indication of the increasing importance of mechanical scenery in the Parsi theatre.[10]

For *Benajhīr ane Badremunīr*, Ṭhuṭhī, aided by the entrepreneurial Bhāu, who had left the Victoria, prepared the mechanisms for many new, expensive spectacular scenes such as that of the Kālo Dev (Black Monster) who lifted Benajhīr fifty feet into the air while the court was rendered smaller in size and replaced with a terrifying jungle.[11] Despite these attractive visual effects and the notable feature of 'pure' Hindi dialogue, the play bombed at the box office.[12] As the company was in a financially precarious position due to the failure of the play and the inordinate expenses that Ṭhuṭhī had incurred in setting up his new theatre, Kābrājī gifted the company his third and last Iranian play, *Faredun* (*Faredoon*), for the Hīndī Nāṭak Maṇḍalī to perform in May 1874. Kābrājī personally supervised the company's rehearsals of this sequel to *Jamśed* that portrayed the tyranny of the Emperor Zohak.[13] Zohak, then considered by Parsis to be a demon with snakes for hair, was portrayed by Kābrājī as a mere mortal who eventually became 'the usurper and tyrant of ancient Iran'. Kābrājī, in keeping with his reformist credentials, thus demythologized the eponymous figure. However, he had little say in the production's portrayal of, for example, 'the subterraneous fire at Azer Bizan', which appears when the mountain opens and gives way to 'the scene of the guardian angel of the natural fire'.[14] A surfeit of 'talismanic charms' were highlighted even in the Parsi reformist's last Iranian opus, proof that spectacular effects had become the *sine qua non* of the commercial theatre.[15]

Touring

Notwithstanding the rigorous rehearsals and lavish scenery and costumes, due to the wane in public demand for Persian epics in the (no longer Parsi) Parsi theatre, *Faredun* too incurred substantial losses. Following the advice of a few trusted associates, Ṭhuṭhī left Bombay with his company for Bhavnagar to perform at the wedding of Maharaja Raol Sir Takhtsinhji Jaswantsinhji, while subletting his Hīndī Theatre to the Zoroastrian Nāṭak Maṇḍalī for its *Sosan Rā̃mesgar*.[16] As with Paṭel's trip to Hyderabad, the journey was arduous due to the absence of train tracks to Bhavnagar. The troupe initially travelled on the mail train from Bombay to Surat, where, despite much counsel to the contrary, the company did not perform as no 'proper' theatre existed there at the time. Mechanical devices had by this time, therefore, become a requisite of Parsi theatrical success. After a hasty meal, the actors left by steamer for an overnight expedition to the kingdom.[17] These efforts were not in vain. The troupe received a princely sum of between Rs 10,000 and Rs 15,000, jewelry, lavish garments, and numerous other gifts for eight performances comprising the Urdu

Benajhīr ane Badremunīr, the Gujarati *Faredun*, and the farce *Jāfar ane Keśar* (*Jāfar and Keśar*).[18]

The Parsi theatre's tours to Hyderabad and Bhavnagar constitute a milestone in South Asia's cultural history for several reasons. After the companies' travels, several 'imitation' Parsi theatre forms developed in these territories, adopting Parsi techniques of stagecraft and management. Simultaneously, Parsi managers hired poets and writers such as Raunak Banārasī, Husainī Miyā̃ Zarīf Lakhnavī, Vināyak Prasād Tālib, and Hāfiz Abdullā, as well as local musicians and artists trained in indigenous performance traditions such as the Svang, Dastan, and Nautanki.[19] The excursions outside Bombay thus mark the beginning of an intense period of cross-cultural exchange between the spectacular trappings of the Parsi theatre and the plots, music, dialogue, and acting styles of long-standing local theatrical forms. The Parsis, historical compradors of the colonial opium and cotton trade and translators and middlemen for Hindustan's many native kingdoms, were here sociopolitically ambiguous cultural mediators—that is, cultural compradors—facilitating a multidirectional overflow of aesthetic resources that tapped into globalist cosmopolitan desires. By creolizing local and foreign artistic forms—translating sonically and visually between Victorian theatrical codes and precolonial aesthetic practices—the Parsi theatre forged subtle associations between seemingly distinctive worlds.

Concurrently, while functioning as a crucible for articulating the complex, uneven cultural displacement between Mughal and colonial aesthetic forms, the theatre capitalized on European associations of refinement, contemporary vogueishness, and cultural power through names such as Victoria, Elphinstone, and Alfred; European costumes and musical instruments; a repertoire of melodrama, comedy, opera, and pantomime; and, not least, the use of white-face. These European associations thus constituted for the Parsi theatre's many patrons an identity-building process through consumption. The Parsis were trading in a modish European cosmopolitanism that, as I have demonstrated elsewhere, was articulated through a performative cross-referencing between the theatre's up-to-date technological devices, proscenium stage, Indo-European plays, and especially the actor's painted body.[20] The itinerant Victoria and Hīndī Nāṭak Maṇḍalīs were therefore not only artistic brokers in an incipient global consumer culture where the symbolic value of merchandise assumed greater import than the physical fulfilment of necessity; they were also middlemen bartering a reverse orientalism that subverted the racial taxonomies traditionally expressed socially, historically, economically, and corporeally in European theatres, exhibitions, and museums. By muddling the boundaries between Europeanness and non-Europeanness through their performances of whiteness, the Parsi theatre facilitated first, the detachment of cosmopolitan citizenship from material circumstances, geographic origin, and race and thereafter, enabled audiences to consume otherness in a manner that upturned established hierarchies of power. This democratization of the privilege of newness, of the symbolic, non-corporeal excess of Europeanness through cosmopolitanism, indicates why the theatre's first excursions to Indian princely states were made on the basis of personal invitations. The Parsis were patronized by Indian and subsequently East Asian royal audiences because their particular capital within a matrix of globalist desires was indubitably symbolic. A new generation of royals increasingly felt the necessity to interact with and articulate a 'Europeanness' or worldliness in order to demonstrate sociocultural authority. From the commencement of the Parsi theatre's transregional tours, 'Parsi' and 'Bombay' therefore became signifiers outside Bombay of cutting-edge, high-class entertainment, stimulating not only new sociologies of visual comprehension but also, and as a consequence, new spatial configurations of theatre publics.

In contrast, Bombay's public, spoiled for choice due to a cornucopia of mushrooming theatre companies, dismissed the Hīndī Nāṭak Maṇḍalī after its successful tour to Bhavnagar. After several box office failures, Ṭhuṭhī was obliged to give up his beloved Hīndī Theatre as he was unable to pay the mortgage, which he owed to a Parsi priest. However, while his leading actor, Jamśedjī Dājī, began a precarious existence, touring the subcontinent with other troupes,[21] Ṭhuṭhī soon found himself a place as director of the Victoria due to the fall out between Nājar and Paṭel.[22] Under Ṭhuṭhī's leadership, the theatre's first *Cavcavno Murabo*—a show in the model of the Christmas pantomime, comprising a selection of popular scenes and songs from plays—took place in honour of Queen Victoria's birthday.[23] Purportedly Khurśedjī Bālīvālā's idea, the *Cavcav*, which did not need elaborate scenes or costumes, was regarded as an easy method to make quick money in Bombay when troupes had packed their wares to go on tour. The development of performance forms that required limited playwriting indicates that the Victoria had replaced its star journalist-playwrights such as Kābrājī and Rāṇīnā with poorly paid (initially) unidentifiable Hindu and Muslim *munśīs* (writers). These new scriptwriters, often denoted in such bylines as 'Ek Mahmadīyan Munśī' (A

Mohammedan Writer), elaborated on the predetermined plots dictated by Parsi managers, a practice that propelled the wane of orientalist and historical scholarship in the mainstream theatre and a corresponding rise in music, visual effects, and 'action'.[24] The collaborative system of writing in the early heyday of touring (songs by an anonymous lyricist, dialogues by an anonymous playwright, all under the command of a celebrated Parsi manager) led not only to the exploitation of countless underpaid Hindustani dramatists but also to subsequent communal conflicts on questions of cultural property. Initially, Parsi managers such as Jahāṅgīr Khambātā employed *munśīs* to 'translate' existing plays into 'changed' verse spurring established companies such as the Victoria to publish copyright notices, albeit with little long-term success:

NOTICE.

WHEREAS the VICTORIA THEATRICAL COMPANY are the PROPRIETORS and ABSOLUTE OWNERS of the undermentioned PLAYS and of the Copyright thereof, respectively, and the same Plays are duly registered under Arts XX. Of 1847 and XXV. of 1867, according to law, NOTICE IS THEREFORE HEREBY GIVEN, that if any Theatrical Company, or any Company, person or persons shall publish, perform, or represent any of the undermentioned, Plays or Operas, either wholly or in part, or any piracy or imitation thereof, the Proprietors of the said Victoria Theatrical Company will forthwith institute proceeding against such Theatrical or other Company or person or persons to obtain an injunction against them or him, and also to recover damages which may be sustained by reason of any such wrongful publication, performance, or representation.

TITLES OF PLAY ABOVE REFERRED TO.

Sitame Haman or Farete Azuzil
Anjan e Ullat, or Humayun Nasir.
Hir Banza.
Benzir Budremunir, &c
Puran Bhagat.
Saifus Suleman.

Dated at Bombay this 16th day of October 1880.

KHURSHEDJI MEHERWANJI BALIWALLA,
DHUNJIBHOY CURSHEDJI GADIALI,
DOSABHOY FURDOONJI MOGUL,
Proprietors of the Victoria Theatrical Company.[25]

Subsequently, historians would contest the ownership of plays, as when the Parsi Dhanjībhāi Paṭel reproached Śekh Mohammad Ahmad, posthumously known as Raunak Banārasī, for having claimed more than eleven of the Parsi Naśarvānjī Khānsāheb's Hindustani plays as his own.[26] Conversely, despite being fully cognizant of the substantial contribution of Hindu and Muslim *munśīs*, the Parsi press rarely if ever acknowledged them prior to 1890. Instead, managers such as Dādābhāi Paṭel, Kuvarjī Nājar, and Khurśedjī Bālīvālā, with the support of a flourishing vernacular and English public sphere, progressively became household names across South Asia and beyond.

North India

The mid-1870s thus marks a series of Parsi whirlwind tours across the Indian subcontinent, beginning with Nājar's travels with his sixteen-member Victoria to North and East India, including Delhi, Calcutta, Lucknow, Benares, and Allahabad.[27] Parsi chroniclers have recorded the minutiae of the trials and tribulations that the Parsi actors faced in their first journeys to this new, tremendously lucrative market. One of the Victoria's star actors, Edaljī Dādābhāi (Edu Colleger), absconded by 'missing' the train (Fig. 6.1). As Dādābhāi played female parts for which actors had to be both naturally talented (possessing high-pitched voices and slender bodies) and specially trained, the entire program was turned on its head, putting the Victoria's enterprise at risk from the beginning.[28] Providentially, Nājar's accomplices accosted Dādābhāi in Bombay and forcibly escorted him to Delhi.

The Victoria's problems did not end there. The troupe's carpenter had poorly driven several iron nails into the company's makeshift wooden stage. Inopportunely, during one of the performances, Khurśedjī Bālīvālā stepped on a nail and was left incapacitated for a protracted period.[29] Similarly, during an impassioned sword fight in the performance of *Sonānā Mulnī Khorśed*, a sliver of Ḍosābhāi Fardunjī Mogal's (Fig. 6.2) sword found its way into the eye of a howling Nājar, who was seated in the first row with four European acquaintances.[30]

Fig. 6.1 Edaljī Dādābhāi (*Source* Paṭel, *PNTT*, 274. Courtesy: The Trustees, The K. R. Cama Oriental Institute, Mumbai)

Fig. 6.2 Ḍosābhāi Fardunjī Mogal (*Source* Paṭel, *PNTT*, 159. Courtesy: The Trustees, The K. R. Cama Oriental Institute, Mumbai)

The troupe subsequently set off for Lucknow, a trip notable not only for amorous dalliances, lethal illnesses (cholera), and near-death experiences but also for a historic milestone in spectatorship: according to Delissa Joseph, 'Mohammedan women ... [came] to the theatre dressed in male attire, in order that they might be able to be present at performances which they would not have been allowed, in the ordinary course, to attend in company with a male audience'.[31] The company had thus begun to radically alter the nature of public culture and public space outside the confines of their hometown. After Lucknow, the company journeyed to Calcutta, where, as I have demonstrated elsewhere, it performed *Indra Sabhā* to much acclaim.[32] The Victoria then left for Benares and thereafter made a short halt in the Bombay Presidency, only to resume its subcontinental touring after a mere two performances in Poona.[33]

The Prince of Wales in India

Even as Bombay's Parsi theatre troupes fanned out across the subcontinent, they would find, in the year 1875, the subcontinent at their doorstep. In October, the eldest son of Queen Victoria, Albert Edward Prince of Wales, began his tour of India. Bombay, the prince's first stop, therefore witnessed what was termed a 'deluge of native princes' accompanied with trains full of treasures and horses.[34] The vernacular press carried news of the arrival of the Rajas of Dhrangadhra, Gaekwad, Kolhapur, Kutch, Idar, and Lunavada; the Dewan of Pahlanpur; the Maharana of Rajpipla; the Nawabs of Junagadh, Balasinor, and Radhanpur; the Jam of Nawanagar; the Thakurs of Dhrol, Bhavnagar, Rajkot, Limbdi, and Palitana; the Desai of Sawantwadi; Sir Salar Jung of Hyderabad; and the Viceroy Lord Northbrooke.[35] The tour was an opportunity not only for Britain to forge close political ties with Indian royal families but also for Indian statesmen to perform a self-conscious cosmopolitanism through the patronage of Bombay's modern entertainments. Against the backdrop of the prince's visit, the Parsi theatre was a desirable marker of internationalism, bound up with the globalization of material desires and consumer modernity linked to self-identification through market symbols. The Parsi theatre's 'thoroughly comprehensive' repertoire, ranging from '"Mother Goose" ... to plays founded upon Mohammedan religious histories and upon stories in the 'Arabian Nights', historical plays such as 'Darius' and 'Alexander the Great', original plays bearing upon modern life in India, and translations of English plays',[36] allowed Indian royals to interpolate themselves into a larger geography of the cosmopolitan imagination. As with the tours to Hyderabad and Bhavnagar, royal families thronged Bombay's Parsi theatres to culturally invest in newness—that is, in the relational logic of worldliness, progress, high civilization, and state-of-the-art technology in a familiar idiom.

Consequently, although the Parsi theatre was not patronized by the prince in Bombay, it experienced breakneck expansion during these dizzying months. Each royal family bore both economic and symbolic capital for Parsi theatre companies, which highlighted the names of their patrons in their advertisements. The Victoria and Elphinstone under Nājar's ownership went out of their way to cater to these royal guests: while the Victoria announced a special daily program for the express benefit of Indian royal families, the Elphinstone publicized its production of *Sulemānī Śamśeher yāne Nīrdoś Nurānī* as having been patronized by Baroda's Dewan T. Madhava Rao, Sayajirao Gaekwad III, Maharani Jamnabai, and the Nawab of Radhanpur.[37] According to Khambātā, the actors worked night and day, scampering from one theatre to the other between acts.[38]

During this time (October 1875), the Zoroastrian, which had hitherto performed Persian epics, advertised its production of Edaljī Khorī's *Jālem Jor ane Jālam bet khuvār*. The play portrayed the war between the Hīndīs (Indians) and Turkīs (Turks) for the benefit of the royal families residing in Bombay. Although Khorī purportedly wrote the play in Gujarati, the text reveals a marked emphasis on the Urdu songs written by Bandekhodā (the pen name of Dādābhāi Edaljī Pockhānāvālā), as well as a profusion of Hindustani words, presumably due to the new, esteemed guests to whom the Zoroastrian was catering its repertoire. The play begins with a declamation by Mohobatejān, the Indian mistress of the Turkish Jālem Jor, who 'lost her parents, her country, her virtue, and a peaceful existence' for the sake of profane lust.[39] The importance of female characters in Khorī's melodrama is further emphasized by Gīraftār, sister of Jālem Jor, who, disguised as a courtier, eschews gender norms by fighting at battle and saving both her brother and her lover, the Indian Bāhādharjaṅg. Through the characters of Mohobatejān and Gīraftār, who had ostensibly defected from their respective countries for love, the play questioned the meaning of 'true' loyalty between husbands and wives, masters and slaves, and not least rulers and subjects.[40] Take, for example, the following exchange between Kamarceher, a Turkish renegade, and his lover, the Indian princess Rūpvantī:

Kamarceher: The Turks and Indians have begun fighting. Consider [Rūpvantī], what a Turk truly is. Isn't Turkey my motherland? Haven't I readied myself to fight against my own land and my own people?
Rūpvantī: You too should remember that your people, on the pretext of reforming us, attempted to destroy us.[41]

The Turkish 'other' in *Jālem Jor* was, to the many Indian kings and princes witnessing the Zoroastrian's performance, recognizably not an evil Ottoman. By referring to those people who 'on the pretext of reforming us attempted to destroy us', the plot surreptitiously articulated a deep-seated discontent with colonial reform. Furthermore, along with the themes of loyalty, legitimacy of rule, and destiny, the play enunciated the term *svadeś* for the first time in the Parsi theatre's history, an expression that would, over the coming decades, assume the loaded signification of 'home-rule'.[42] Many of the subversive ideas articulated in Khorī's play resonated in the press, which condemned the skewed portrayal of the fairer side of empire during the prince's visit.[43] However, in these early days, when the concept of sedition had scarcely been thrown into relief in the theatre, Khorī's oeuvre, which gave new meaning to the phrase *tradu-torre traditore* (translator traitor), was overlooked, possibly due to the numerous other entertainments that spawned in the wake of the prince's arrival.

Having begun his visit in the Gateway of India, the prince left for Poona, Baroda, and Madras. The Original Victoria under Paṭel's leadership was quicker than other Parsi companies to respond to the symbolic opportunities presented by way of the prince's visit to India: Paṭel secured the chance to stage a scene from his *Śakuntala* for the prince in Madras, a landmark event in the annals of colonial theatre history.[44] However, the prince, a representative of the British Empire, was subsequently lambasted by the Scottish missionary Alexander Duff for attending Paṭel's performance, which prominently featured nautch girls, and for forgetting that 'the eye of England was closely watching him'.[45] Paṭel's staging of *Śakuntala* and Bombay's reformist crusade against women on the Parsi stage thus became the subject of international debate, especially when the *Globe* rebuked Duff's attack by comparing the nautch girls' 'discrete' costumes with the tiny clothes worn by European dancers. The *Rāst* controversially supported Duff, arguing that the question was not one of dress but one of morality, as European dancers did not work as prostitutes—a statement that indicates the strong cross-referentiality between Indian reformists and Victorians, who were profoundly sceptical of the sexual *naïveté* of actresses.[46] Performing women, who were fleeing India's princely states due to the paramountcy of the British Crown and who increasingly looked to the Parsi drama for occupational recourse, were therefore at the eye of the moral storm that raged regionally (Western India) and globally around the delineation of honourable and dishonourable theatrical entertainment, a process of demarcation that was outside of the women's control.[47] As demonstrated in Chapter 3, the precolonial nautch, associated with stigmatized sexual promiscuity, and the modern Parsi theatre were differentiated along lines that mirrored the divide between courtesans and middle-class women. Paṭel's productions confused these painstakingly delineated distinctions between the moral, salutary, and sanitized and the immoral, adulterous, and unfaithful, thereby indicating class-based fault lines in the development and reception of the colonial Indian stage.

Although the controversy was swiftly forgotten, dame fortune would only smile for a little while on the scion of the Paṭel family. After performing for the prince, the company set off on 19 December 1875 for Bangalore, where Paṭel fell mortally ill. He was hastily sent back to Bombay to the care of numerous physicians employed by his wealthy family, only to succumb on 17 March 1876 after an operation of the stomach, at the ripe age of thirty-two.[48]

Thus, wretchedly ended the life of the founder of the modern Hindustani drama.

The Growth of the Victoria Nāṭak Maṇḍalī

Due to the Prince of Wales' visit and the 'flood of princes' in Bombay, Nājar, the joint owner of the Victoria and Elphinstone, had accumulated a princely sum. His companies now counted among their patrons such dignitaries as the Gaekwad of Baroda, the Nawab of Radhanpur, the Raja of Kolhapur, the Rao of Kutch, the Raja of Dharampur, the Jam of Nawanagar, Mir Ali Murad Khan of Khairpur, the Raja of Rajpipla, the Maharana of Lunawars, the Thakur Sahib of Morbi, the Raja of Sonth, the Thakur Sahib of Rajkot, the Raja of Baria, the Thakur Sahib of Wadwan, the Raj Sahib of Dhrangadhra, and the Chiefs of Southern Maratha.[49] Worn down by the liability of running two large theatre troupes and cognizant of the low-risk yet lucrative business of subletting theatres, Nājar convened a private meeting with his best and most trusted actors, announcing his intention of giving up his position as owner of the Victoria and Elphinstone Nāṭak Maṇḍalīs while retaining his ownership of the Victoria and Grant Road Theatres.[50] Nājar, now more businessman than advocate of the arts, stipulated that the new owners would be able to lease the theatres for Rs 250 per month for a period of ten years. After a protracted period of negotiation, the contracts were signed, and the Elphinstone gained three new owners: Naśarvānjī Navrojī Pārakh, Farāmjī Saklātvāḷā, and the future mogul of Indian cinema, Jamśedjī Farāmjī Mādan (Fig. 6.3), who would in time become the company's sole owner.[51] On 6 January 1876, the troupe advertized its *Khuśkamar yāne Khvābe Khalāsī* at the Elphinstone Theatre, the previous site of the New Victoria Theatre, now under changed ownership.

Like the Elphinstone, the Victoria speedily changed hands, from Nājar to Dādābhāi Ratanjī Ṭhuṭhī, Khurśedjī Bālīvālā, Farāmjī Dādābhāi Apu (Fig. 6.4), Dhanjībhāi Kharśedjī Ghaḍīāḷī, and Ḍosābhāi Mogal. The Victoria thus commenced the fourth phase of its existence. In January 1876, its advertisements for *Chelbatāū ane Mohenā Rāṇī* specified that tickets were to be collected from 'Mr Kharśedjī Mehrvā̃njī Bālīvārā's shop', indicating the troupe's change in proprietorship.[52]

Soon after, the Victoria set off for Madras on the Great Indian Peninsular Railway. Ghaḍīālī had made prior arrangements for the company to stay at a mansion near Popham's Broadway and perform in a tent made of coconut leaves in the Esplanade in front of the China Bazaar, the present location of the High Court. The Victoria, however, was not alone. According to Khambātā, 'the army of the Original Victoria' had set up its more extravagant and beautiful tent next to that of the Victoria.

After Paṭel's death, the Original Victoria was taken over in the first week of April 1876 by twelve new owners including Naśarvānjī Mādan, Kāvasjī Dārūvālā, Bhīkhājī Kalyānīvālā, Pestanjī Farāmjī Mādan, and Dhanjībhāi Fardunjī Dumasīā. The company performed its *Padmāvat*, *Layelī Majnu*, *Gule Bakāvalī*, and *Indra Sabhā* in Bombay, before setting off on tour.[53] The Original Victoria, capitalizing on Dādābhāi Paṭel's controversial yet renowned performance for the Prince of Wales in Madras, highlighted the late manager's name in its advertisements to attract more patrons. Concurrently, its owners contracted one of the actors, Ratanśāh Jīvājī Dāvar, to sell tickets door to door, on the condition that he was to receive 10% of the proceeds. Khambātā, who was then a member of the Victoria, claims in his autobiography that these were cheap peddling tactics to which the ostensibly respectable Victoria did

Fig. 6.3 Jamśedjī Farāmjī Mādan (*Source The Calcutta Parsi Amateur Dramatic Club Golden Jubilee Souvenir Volume. 1907–1947*, Calcutta, 1957. Courtesy: The Calcutta Parsi Amateur Dramatic Club)

not stoop. The rivalry further affected both companies' programs: only morning rehearsals were conducted, and the day's performances began as early as 2 p.m.[54] Profit margins therefore configured the organizational

Fig. 6.4 Farāmjī Dādābhāi Apu (*Source* Paṭel, *PNTT*, 160. Courtesy: The Trustees, The K. R. Cama Oriental Institute, Mumbai)

forms, repertoire, and quality of Parsi theatre companies, which increasingly focused on advertising, variety, and audience numbers at the expense of adequate rehearsal.

It is significant to note the volatility of theatrical touring at a time when theatrical infrastructure and subcontinental transport and communication left much to be desired. The Victoria's tour of Madras of 1876 was punctuated by a storm that shattered its tent and drenched all its props. As a result, the Victoria was compelled to spend approximately twelve days restoring its scenery and costumes. The company's tribulations did not stop there. Although Bombay was becoming a 'central terminus of a series of arterial railways, radiating in various directions across the continent of India',[55] there were, as yet, no direct train tracks between Madras and Bombay. The wagon carrying the company's properties had mistakenly not been attached to the train in Madras, an error that Ṭhuṭhī, who was in charge of the props, only apprehended when the company had to transfer between trains in Raichur. As advertisements had already been published in Bombay for *Farrokh Sabhā*, to be performed on 9 September 1876, Ṭhuṭhī ordered Khambātā to remain behind to ensure that the properties were transported to Bombay before the performance. Although the wagon reached Raichur the next day, it did not possess a 'footboard' and consequently could not be attached to the mail train. With the assistance of a Parsi priest, Khambātā speedily arranged to have only those properties needed for *Farrokh Sabhā* moved to a new wagon, thus ensuring that the troupe's wares reached Bombay in time for the production.[56] The Parsi theatre's early, risky tours thus paralleled the rise of Bombay as the aptly named Gateway of India, the increased integration of South and Southeast Asia in the global economy, and the development of modern transportation and communication. As high economic stakes rested on the as yet precarious web of railways and telegraphs, Parsi transregional itinerant performance could only succeed with the help of local aides. Parsi theatre managers therefore inadvertently followed the well-trodden paths of Parsi commerce and shipping, touring an established circuit where local knowledge, financial equity, and contextual cultural awareness were supplied by community acquaintances. Long-standing Parsi comprador networks facilitated the movement of the theatre; the Parsis' legacy of hotels, shopkeeping, and opium inadvertently provided the necessary logistics for the erection, maintenance, and relocation of theatrical infrastructure (Fig. 6.5).

Delhi and Jaipur

In addition to revealing the hazards faced by the first Parsi travelling companies, Khambātā's autobiography provides invaluable nuggets of information on intergroup competition, daily itineraries on tour, and the early audience reception of the Parsi theatre. On 19 November 1876, the new owners of the Victoria announced their intention to leave on a

Fig. 6.5 The Pandal under construction in Mysore of the Parsee Victoria Theatrical Company of Bombay, 1st July 1902 (Courtesy: Shirin Vakil)

grand tour of North India on the occasion of the Delhi Durbar, when Queen Victoria would be proclaimed as Kaiser-i-Hind.[57] New curtains were painted, costumes embroidered, and mechanical scenes crafted, and Dhanjībhāi Ghaḍīāḷī soon left Bombay to construct the troupe's tent near the Jumma Musjid. Subsequently, the actors set off from Bombay's Victoria Terminus on the Jubbulpore Mail for Delhi, and after a nondescript journey, they settled in a mansion near Delhi's Chandni Chowk. Once again however, the Victoria was not alone. The *Pioneer*, describing entertainments at the Delhi Darbar, wrote,

> Parsee dramatists are in strength at Delhi. Two Parsee theatres have been opened there, one near the Jumma Musjid, and one outside the Lahore

> Gate of the city. The performances will be in Hindustani and English. One of the troupes will produce several of Shakespeare's plays. Would that Irving could be there to see.[58]

This second Parsi theatre troupe was the rival Elphinstone, which had set up its tent at the more strategic Lahore Gate, where many Indian royals stayed.[59] According to Khambātā, the Elphinstone attracted more royal patrons than the Victoria even as it subsequently followed the same route as the Victoria, making stops in Amritsar and Jaipur.[60] Parsi theatrical touring had thus become a relatively predictable complex in which multiple troupes were drawn to the same cultural contact zones in a burgeoning network of minor kingdoms, military cantonments, and colonial *entrepôts*.

The Victoria's troubles did not end with the Elphinstone's departure. Khambātā offers intimate insight into the daily workings of the Victoria, whose rules played a significant role in his flight from the company. According to Khambātā, in the morning every actor had to finish bathing by 8:30 a.m. and subsequently eat their breakfast in isolation. Rehearsals lasted from 9 a.m. to 12 p.m., and thereafter the company would sit for lunch. At 3:00 p.m., tea was served, and between 4:00 and 7:00 p.m. the actors could leave the premises if they obtained permission from one of the five owners. After dinner at 7:00 p.m., the actors left for the theatre, where they would perform until past 2 a.m. One day, Khambātā overslept and was admonished by Ṭhuṭhi, who denied him his breakfast. Khambātā then skipped rehearsal, leaving the premises to buy tins of jam and sardines and bread, further enraging Ṭhuṭhī. The next day the actors 'wrapped Khambātā in additional blankets causing him to oversleep once again'.[61] An infuriated Ṭhuṭhī denied him breakfast and water for a bath. A comparably incensed Khambātā called a water carrier from the streets, doused himself in ice cold water, and submitted his notice despite the counsel of the prudent Ḍosābhāi Mogal.

The rapidity of the actor's resignation may be explained through conjecture. Khambātā had been in correspondence with a Lālā Lāl Siṅgh *before* leaving the Victoria. The Delhi businessman offered him the necessary capital for the institution of a joint-stock company in order to found a new company, the Empress Nāṭak Maṇḍalī. The loss of qualified actors due to the lure of quick profit and the rise of mushroom companies that dotted the subcontinent had become signs of the dynamic volatility of the commercial theatrical trade, and Khambātā, fleeing from his erstwhile tutors and best friend Bālīvālā, epitomized this development. Khambātā swiftly left Delhi for Bombay in search of 'histrionic talent',[62] and hired Kāvasjī Mīstrī (Kāu Hāṇḍo),[63] Dorābjī Navrojī Sacīnvālā, Dhanjībhāi Foṭogrāfar (Dhanju Lāmbā), Edaljī Berāmjī Cīcgar (Bhaglā Hajām), Naśarvānjī Ratanjī Sarkārī,[64] and most importantly Kāvasjī Pālanjī Khaṭāu (who would become known as 'Hindustan's Henry Irving').[65] The newly formed Empress then travelled from Bombay to Delhi on the Jubbulpore Mail, and on 19 May 1877 the company made its first appearance with the ever popular *Indra Sabhā*, in which Khaṭāu performed as Gulfām, Sarkārī as sabz parī (green fairy), and Mistrī as King Indra. Khambātā also hired the Victoria's painter, Pestanjī Kharśedjī Mādan, to make scenes for his plays, which were staged at a temporary theatre near Chandni Chowk. After Delhi, the company toured Meerut and Lahore before returning to Bombay. This, according to Paṭel, was the age of 'stealing thespians', and incensed company owners such as the Victoria's Farāmjī Apu increasingly filed for damages in Bombay's small causes courts against employees who broke their stringent contracts.[66]

Despite his tempestuous resignation, Khambātā (Fig. 6.6) fondly recounts the public excitement that greeted the Victoria's actors. 'Delhi's habitants did not know what *nāṭaks* [plays] were, and so they went wild for the performances'.[67] Penurious spectators sold their *maśks* (traditional water-carrying bags) and animals in order to buy theatre tickets, famous actors were showered with gifts during 'special appointments' with the well-to-do, and crowds followed the Parsi performers with their strange hats around the city, playing guessing games as to whether the actors played Gulfām, Lāl Parī, or Lāl Dev.[68] Delhi's audiences thronged the theatre, not so much to acquaint themselves with Persian mythology, English melodrama, pantomime, and Shakespeare as to engage in a hitherto unknown form of cosmopolitan consumerism. Through these peripatetic tours of the subcontinent, the Parsi performance world crafted the earliest form of indigenous audience development in proscenium theatre, familiarizing Indians, who hitherto had little access to the European drama, with scenic divisions and proscenium stages, modern scenery, costumes, and properties, and peculiarities of class divides, celebrity culture, and especially paid tickets—the ultimate sign of investment in the aesthetic economy of the modern world.

On the behest of Maharaja Sawai Ram Singh II, the Victoria left Delhi for Jaipur. The Victoria's spectacular fare of flying fairies, sparkling water fountains, and perspectival scenery flummoxed Raja Ram Singh, who

Fig. 6.6 Grandpa Jehangir (Courtesy: Shirin Vakil)

requested that Edaljī Dādābhāi, Pestanjī Jījībhāi Baṭlīvaḷa (Pesu Pokhrāj), Ardeśar Pīrośāh Tabelāvālā (Ado), Rūstamjī N. Rūstam Frāmnā,[69] and the director Dādābhāi Ṭhuṭhī remain to perform for his private benefit.[70] Ṭhuṭhī remained in Jaipur until the king's death—that is, for approximately three years—before returning to Bombay.[71] The Victoria's five owners thus decreased to three.[72] In Jaipur, Ṭhuṭhī was given a handsome salary of seven hundred rupees, a magnificent bungalow, carriages, food and drink, and two bodyguards.[73] In 1878, the Maharaja ordered the erection of Jaipur's first proscenium playhouse, the Ramprakash Theatre, for Ṭhuṭhī's express use. The theatre, built of Burma teak, was an important marker of modernity for the Raja, along with other infrastructural developments such as the Mayo Hospital and Ramniwas Gardens, which comprised a museum, public library, schools, and colleges. The Victoria, through its travels and the construction of the Ramprakash Theatre, not only transplanted European techniques of performance and stage management to the kingdom but also set a precedent for other proscenium-based theatres erected through royal benefaction across northern India.[74] The Parsi theatre's realm of influence through its redistributory function of modern drama thus exponentially increased with the Victoria's, Original Victoria's, and Elphinstone's long, circuitous journeys across the landmass of South Asia. The Parsi vocabulary of up-to-date technology and Indo-Persian myths that transgressed the traditionally reified borders of colonies and princely states incited the development of a complex web of cultural parallelisms, spurring a new form of reflexivity across class, religious, and ethnic barriers. Audiences in the North—in Jaipur, Jodhpur, Faizabad, and Allahabad—could intermittently laugh, cry, cheer, and boo at the same *Indra Sabhās*, *Benajhīr Badremunīrs*, and *Alādīns* as pedantic spectators in Bombay, Calcutta, and Madras, the theatre thus creating an experience of simultaneity that was critically not contingent on literacy. The Parsi theatre therefore worked simultaneously as a symbol of cultural imperialism and as an archive for colonial subversion, a point of contact for far-flung port cities, minor kingdoms, urban centres, and rural settlements that incubated and relayed an expanding body of visual information on the East by the East. By enabling heterogenous audiences to consume newness, organizing and interpreting technology in a familiar indigenous frame, and conveying visual and aural forms of subtly seditious reverse orientalism, the Parsis—shifting from economic and administrative to cultural go-betweens—limned the boundaries of what could and could not be said, influencing long-term interactions between numerous, hitherto unconnected publics.

Regulations

However, all was not milk and honey in the business of Parsi theatrical touring. As minor 'mushroom companies' with modest talent and paltry experience increasingly spawned outside the Bombay Presidency, audiences from small towns and cantonments flocked to makeshift tents to consume topical declamatory plots, glittering costumes, composite Indo-Persian-European music, and not least the marvels of modern technology. This mushrooming brought in its train numerous institutional, interpersonal, and moral dilemmas. For example, fire was a grave hazard, as theatre managers and colonial officials were coming to realize, because of the hodgepodge of old weather-worn playhouses, transient tents, and semipermanent school and university auditoriums that Parsis resorted to using to stage their performances. Although the Original Victoria had surpassed the rival Victoria Nāṭak Maṇḍalī in Madras due to the sturdier make of its tent, on 11 May 1878 while the Original Victoria was performing *Situmgar* at Ahmednagar, its pavilion accidentally caught fire. While a private telegram received in Bombay indicated that the performers escaped unharmed, forty-nine people were burnt alive, and many more were severely injured.[75]

> On Saturday night, the 11th ult., the house was unusually crowded. The play was over by ten o'clock, and the audience were laughing over the humours of an amusing farce, when suddenly a bustling, crackling noise, which increased to a roar as it neared them was heard from the lower end of the temporary theatre. Then arose a cry of 'fire,' which deepened into a terrible shriek when it was seen that the ceiling was already in a blaze. ... The whole fire did not occupy more than five minutes; but as the scorched and wounded people were pulled out from near the entrance and passed into the open air it seemed an eternity before the flames died down sufficiently to enable the rescuing party to drag the dead out of the centre of the auditorium. ... The Victoria Company, more fortunate than their audience, escaped without any loss of life, but all their accessories and costumes were consumed. The total of deaths, according to the latest accounts amounts to between 47 and 49.[76]

The calamity brought to light the unregulated building of temporary playhouses, which were often poorly erected, with merely one exit for a thousand spectators.[77]

The lack of fire exits in temporary playhouses was not the only hazard at this time. Cigarette smoking inside theatre premises had also become a serious liability, prompting managers to announce in their advertisements that 'those who smoked *bīḍīs* [cigarettes] within the theatre [would] be handed over to the police'.[78] On 6 January 1876, for instance, the Elphinstone advertized its *Khuśkamar yāne Khvābe Khalāsī* at the Elphinstone Theatre, the previous site of the New Victoria Theatre, publicizing the improved upholstery, new drop scenes and the introduction of fans, while forbidding the smoking of *bīḍīs* in the theatre.[79] Concurrently, hazardous gas lights concealed in wooden cylinders gradually came to be recognized as particularly dangerous. In 1883, the prestigious Gaiety Theatre, built by Kuvarjī Nājar in 1879 opposite the Victoria Terminus, replaced its gas lamps with electricity. This change was prompted by a gas leak that occurred due to a break in one of the taps during the Victoria's performance on 5 September 1883, resulting in a hasty evacuation.[80] With the management's procurement of 160 electric boxes, the equivalent (according to the press) of 3,200 gas lamps, the Gaiety became the first theatre in Western India to enjoy electric lighting.[81] However, such efforts to improve the safety of playhouses were the exception to the rule. Newspapers often reported benches holding dozens of spectators that collapsed during performances, and in one case, a rooftop fatally fell through during a Parsi production in Madras.[82] In 1887 Calcutta's deputy commissioner made the first move in the subcontinent towards instituting safety regulations in theatres, a precedent that was quickly followed in Bombay.[83]

There was, therefore, a dark side to the twinkling lights and fairy dust of the Parsi theatre. In addition to the hazardous playhouse conditions, as well as the conflicts that played out over class and religion, newspapers described other adversities and misfortunes such as the death of the Original Victoria's Jamśedjī Ādarjī Tā̃trā, a thirty-year-old actor who committed suicide in Alīghar in the early hours of 4 May 1880 by jumping in a well. The *Rāst* used the event to criticize mofussil Parsis for their patronage of fickle companies comprising young impressionable boys who were barely able to eke a living from the theatre.[84] Another tragedy was the death of the esteemed editor, playwright, and manager Naśarvānjī Āpakhatyār on 20 June 1878 in far-flung Jhansi, while his troupe, the Zoroastrian, was on tour.[85] In its pursuit of profitability and commercial success, the Parsi theatre exposed its many young travelling actors, writers, and musicians—champions of the dramatic cause—to life-threatening diseases such as cholera and dysentery, familial and communal estrangement, and heavy financial liabilities resulting in destitution and abandonment.

Yet, despite these considerable physical, economic, and, according to the press, moral calamities, this bleak, often terrifying side of the Parsi theatre did not negatively affect the growing economy of theatrical touring. Within four short years of the Victoria's first tour outside the Bombay Presidency, Parsi troupes dotted the subcontinent and were praised by newspapers such as the newly established *Kaysare Hinda* for their extensive travels: 'those stories that would have fallen to dust because of English rule have now been revived in far-flung places through their example'.[86] As compradors, the proverbial connecting links between the rulers and the ruled, the Parsis redistributed new ways of seeing and thinking, the beating heart of the imperial project containing the seeds of its discontent, along the time-worn route mapped by their ancestors. It was, therefore, only a matter of time before they crossed the subcontinental landmass for Singapore, Batavia, and Burma, sites where the community thrived as commercial middlemen.

Parsi Theatre in Southeast Asia

On 9 October 1881, the managing proprietor of the Victoria, Dhanjībhāi Ghaḍīālī, issued an announcement from Mandalay to quell rumours that the company members had drowned on their long journey from Singapore to Rangoon. 'Whosoever catches the scandal-monger that spread these false rumours shall be awarded Rs 500', he cried.[87] The announcement indicates not just the cutthroat rivalry between Parsi troupes in Bombay (who often lied about the misfortunes of their peers) but also, and more importantly, the advent of Parsi theatre in Southeast Asia.[88] Between mid-March and 20 June 1881, the Victoria had been engaged by a syndicate (under contractor Faizally Faizool Hoosain) for thirty performances in Singapore at $200 per night, for a total payment of $6,000.[89] One of its first performances, *Aladdin, or the Wonderful Lamp*, was immediately a hit with Singapore's audiences due to the belief that the story was 'so well known as to require no explanation, and the plot could be easily followed by those who do not understand Hindostani'. The farce that followed, *Bholey Mia, or Half a Face for 50 Rupees*, was allegedly irresistibly funny, and 'though also in Hindostani, was readily comprehended owing to the explanation given in the printed bills'.[90] Similarly, the *Straits Times Overland Journal* commended its *Furrokh Sabha*: 'the fairies and genies ... [were] especially admired,—the two fairies continually floating about the air adding greatly to the effect of the tableau'.[91] Similar praise was showered on *The Quack Doctor*, a comic pantomime in Chinese costume:

> The costumes were purchased from a Chinese theatrical company, and the get-up, especially of the old doctor (Mr. Mogul) and of one of his patients (Mr. Balliwalla), as well as the three ladies, was inimitable, and the acting was a capital imitation of a Chinese burlesque, affording intense merriment.[92]

Consequently, despite the Victoria's rivalry with Italian opera troupes, the Parsi theatre's nightly performances of such plays as *Indra Sabhā*, *Gule Bakāvalī*, *A Trip to Fairy Land*, *Situmgar*, and *Puram Bhagat* were given to 'overcrowded houses' at the Victoria Theatre, erected at the erstwhile location of the Clarendon Hotel, Beach Road.[93] As in Delhi, Calcutta, Lahore, Amritsar, and Madras, audiences crowded the Victoria Theatre to partake in a democratized cosmopolitanism that upheld industrialization, science, and technological novelty. Concurrently, the haunting of Europeanness through Shakespeare, English scenery and costume, and white-face facilitated a quietly insubordinate lampooning of colonial ideology and rule. Crucially, the 'immense superiority of the Parsee Company, whether in language, acting, or scenery' propelled Singapore's newspapers to encourage 'local amateurs and professionals [to] follow their example', a development that would swiftly come to fruition.[94] The Parsis thus began to stimulate tectonic shifts in forms of cultural production and consumption in Southeast Asia,[95] creating, as in the subcontinent, a repertory of iconographic references that were brought into the service of sociopolitical revolution.

After a series of impressive successes, as indicated by gross receipts of $14,000, the Victoria announced the end of its Singapore engagement on 24 June 1881.[96] Singapore's audiences were thrilled with the Parsi theatre's composite repertoire of the *Arabian Nights*, Shakespeare, and tales of Indo-Persian royalty, and news of the troupe's spectacular repertoire spread far and wide, reaching both Batavia and Burma.[97]

According to an anonymous member of the troupe writing an anecdotal account of his journey in the *Rāst*, the company intended to set off for Penang (and subsequently Hong Kong and Japan) and had already reserved a theatre there for Rs 1,200. Accordingly, when it received an invitation to perform in Mandalay for Thibaw Min, the last king of Burma's Konbaung Dynasty, who had heard of their performances while travelling within Rangoon, the company was not overtly enthusiastic.[98] This mood was also dampened by rumours of the king's tyrannical ways and the costs (totalling Rs 5,000 per month) of maintaining both the forty-member troupe and a Parsi translator, Kāvasjī Mancerjī Gandhī. However, King Thibaw's offer was too good to refuse. The company sold its theatre in Singapore by auction for a pittance at $320 to Hoosain and left for Rangoon on 27 July 1881 on the steamer Chupra. Its engagement was for twenty-five performances for the royal family, for an advance payment of Rs 25,000 or Rs 1,000 per night.[99] The first inkling of the Victoria's reception in Burma was disclosed on 22 February 1885, when the *Rāst* dismissed the false account published in one of Calcutta's newspapers that three members of the Victoria had been put to death by the King of Mandalay as some of the palace's women had fallen in love with them. The Victoria's managers, writing in the *Rangoon Gazette*, not only asked for sandalwood to be placed in Bombay's Atash Behram (principal fire temple) on their behalf but also briefly stated that the king had bestowed them with many gifts.[100] This was an understatement.

The Victoria Theatrical Company in Burma

Prior to setting off for Mandalay, the company, wary of being duped, stipulated with the king's agent that it was to receive half of its payment in Rangoon. On 4 August the Victoria reached Rangoon, received the promised money, and left for Mandalay by steamer on the Irrawaddy River. The company disembarked on 2 September after receiving the remaining payment, and the actors readied themselves to perform before the king.[101] According to an unnamed member of the Victoria writing in the *Rāst*, every play had to be translated into Burmese for the royal family's reading pleasure before the performances took place. Furthermore, the actors hastily memorized Burmese songs for the king and queen's amusement. As with its performance of *The Quack Doctor* in Singapore, the Victoria adapted its repertoire according to the royal family's tastes.

Yet, although the company enjoyed every creature comfort in Mandalay, the lack of a modern playhouse proved to be a difficulty. The existing theatre in Mandalay, used for traditional Burmese performances, possessed only a single curtain that was only ten feet in length. On the king's instruction, a new theatre, suiting the Parsis' tastes, was built at a cost of Rs 4,000. The troupe members then readied themselves to perform for the royal family on 21 September, but at the last minute, the day was deemed inauspicious. Consequently, the Victoria performed for the benefit of Mandalay's courtiers, who assessed whether the play was suitable for the king and queen.[102] At long last, on 23 September at 7 p.m., the royal couple attended their first Parsi performance—*Saef-us-śulemān*—and, according to the anonymous writer, were 'amazed and dumbfounded'. The court was so taken by the verisimilitude of the performances that the king immediately ordered a second, larger theatre to be built for the troupe at a cost of Rs 8,000, even though Rs 4,000 had already been spent on the first. The company subsequently performed *Hariścandra* and *Rām Sītā*, for which a drop scene of the palace of Mandalay was especially painted by Mādan. Soon after, Burmese actors were sent to study the Parsis' mechanical contraptions for use in their own plays.[103]

The company members were treated handsomely during their visit. According to the anonymous chronicler, the royal family's 'blind generosity', the 'equivalent of English blind justice', knew no bounds, and the actors were gifted gold and silver ornaments, silks, diamonds hidden in oranges, diamond and ruby rings, sacks of rupees, trays filled with jewels, and pearl necklaces.[104] Subsequently, the company was invited by the queen to play a game called *luṭ* (loot). The Victoria's owners and subsequently the other actors were called on to seize as many currency notes as they could grab from a platform, one foot tall and seven feet wide, that was filled with rupees. As Khurśedjī Bālīvālā had small hands, the allegedly gracious queen assisted him in the game. On another occasion, the actors were asked to select silver coconuts filled with diamonds, emerald rings, and gold leaves from a golden tray for as long as the queen deemed appropriate.[105] In addition, the Victoria's owners were handsomely rewarded with several thousand rupees over and above their promised payments. 'These were truly scenes out of the *Arabian Nights*', the writer recounting the saga animatedly cried.[106] In between its many performances in Mandalay, the Victoria performed in Singapore at a new theatre in Middle Road, built a short distance away from its former playhouse.[107] Subsequently, the company performed in Batavia, where it had an enormous impact on local audiences and artists, who developed their own brand of Parsi theatre, Komedie Stamboel. After a series of lengthy, circuitous tours spanning several years, twenty-three members of the Victoria returned on the SS Kohinoor from Southeast Asia on 9 May 1885 and began performing their *Farebe Fītnā* and *Karṇī tevī pār ūtarṇī* at the Gaiety on 13 May, to the great praise of the vernacular press.[108]

The Victoria's precedent was followed by the Original Victoria, which left Calcutta for Singapore on 26 July 1882.[109] However, the Original Victoria did not enjoy as much success as its rival in Southeast Asia. Three months after the company returned to Bombay, the *Times of India* noted,[110]

> The petitions of the following persons have been presented to the Court for … Relief of Insolvents:— … Pestonji Framji Madon and Cursetji Framji Madon, proprietors of the Parsee Original Victoria Dramatic Company in joint partnership with Kawasji Nusserwanji Daruvala, Nusserwanji Framji Madon, and Anandrao Sabaji Naik, also the first-named insolvent is an actor, and the second a manager of the said Dramatic Company.[111]

The increasing number of bankruptcies had, nonetheless, little long-term influence on the business of pan-Asian theatrical touring. The Victoria and Original Victoria were soon followed by the Elphinstone, and thereafter, in July 1885, a Prince Edward Parsi Theatrical Company reached Hong Kong, the first Parsi theatre company to do so according to written record.[112] By 1890 Parsi companies enjoyed an established presence in theatres in most major East and Southeast Asian port cities. Although most spectators did not understand the dialogues in Hindustani, the Parsi theatre's visual spectacle, which combined European stagecraft with Indo-Persian themes, offered an immediate experience with a different, distinctly modern 'orient'. The Parsi theatre was so eminently successful in its eastward journeys as it complicated established European visual and aural signs and meanings and rescaled, transformed, and redistributed a vision of the East that upset the colonial social and racial pecking order. However, these eastward journeys diminished in symbolic value and prestige when the Victoria announced its intention to perform before London's eagle-eyed audiences.

The Victoria Theatrical Company in England

In 1885, due to the Anglo-Burmese War, King Thibaw's patronage of the Victoria came to a standstill, prompting the Victoria to look to other untapped markets. In August 1885, Bombay's journals published news that the Victoria intended to travel to London to perform in the context of the Colonial and Indian Exhibition. The endeavour was symbolically significant for the Parsis; if the Victoria was successful in London, Parsi theatre companies would be lauded as true emissaries of global, cutting-edge, cosmopolitan entertainments. On 4 November 1885, forty Indians including twenty-five members of the Victoria took off via second-class passage in the Clan Ogilvie (at a cost of Rs 8,000) for England, marking, according to the Parsi press, an important endeavour in the subcontinent's theatre history even though the press simultaneously noted that many were doubtful of the troupe's success.[113] As the *Times of India* proclaimed,

> The pieces selected for representation are those which illustrate modern native manners and customs, and selections will be made from the classic Indian dramas, which, however, it is thought may be too dull from the spectators' point of view to command approval in England.[114]

'India in London', designated by the *New York Times* as an Indian village inhabited by forty-five natives, and comprising a troupe of 'Parsee actors and musicians, several Nautch girls and a little army of artisans', opened at Portland Hall in January 1886.[115] In a series of letters written to the *Rāst*, a second anonymous writer recounted the company's visits to London's theatres, the aquarium, Westminster Abbey, the Crystal Palace, and the London Tower. Perhaps most significantly, the writer also noted English lords' taste for Parsi food.[116] For example, the *Rāst* described how on 20 January at 1:30 p.m., Lord Hariss, Sir George Birdwood, Mr W. G. Pedder, Mr J. S. V. Fitzgerald, W. T. Maitland, and many others dined as guests of the Victoria and enjoyed such Parsi delights as palāv, fish pudding, capātī, and sweet samosās.[117] The company made little mention of its earnings from performances, noting instead its many wealthy patrons.[118] In May, the unknown writer's account divulged a decline in the Victoria's revenue and the company's intention to depart for Bombay. A few days later, the *Times of India* briefly noted the Victoria's arrival to Bombay, the English daily's terse welcome possibly echoing the less than half-hearted reception that the Victoria received in England.[119] As a writer of the *Era* proclaimed:

> What with the evidently modern scenery, the strange language, the droning of the orchestral music, and the rendering in slow time of such old friends as 'The Camptown Races' and 'The King of the Cannibal Islands,' the performance, as a whole, resembled nothing so much as a fantastic nightmare produced by a study of Hindu literature, a visit to a pantomime, and a heavy supper. ... The whole thing was partly an ethnological study and partly a stupendous joke.[120]

Similarly, the *Devon and Exeter Daily Gazette*, in an article titled 'A Dramatic Absurdity', noted that the makeup 'with powder, rouge, and like auxiliaries, ... "to look like ourselves" [was] hardly complimentary to the English actor', and the pantomime was 'condescendingly announced to be played in English'.[121] 'English flesh and blood can stand no more of it', the *Standard* bemoaned, noting 'ominous sounds of derision, quite distinct from good-natured laughter', and thereafter 'a stampede' for the exit.[122] Reviewers paid far more interest to another element of the exhibition: 'a number of exact models of Hindu shops, where many ... beautiful curiosities in carved ivory, gold embroidery, &c., which, excite European admiration' were made.[123] As I have demonstrated elsewhere, against the 'real' customs of India—'the ancient, timeless practices of the village'—the Parsis' mechanical scenery, Indo-European costume and music, 'white-face' (fashioned 'to look like ourselves'), and composite repertoire of ancient Hindu myth, minstrel songs, *Arabian Nights* spectacle, and local farce troubled Victorian audiences and the established distinction between the civilized and barbarous, appearing not only as a caricature of British culture but also as evidence of the redefinition of India's relationship to itself.[124] Parsi spectacle, which overturned the primitivizing logic of the exhibition (freezing an eastern civilization in time outside of modernity), was consequently here penalized. The only aspect of the Parsis' offerings that fulfilled existing European fantasies of the sensual authentic East was the food. Therefore, although the Victoria's performances were ridiculed, its tiffin of 'fish à la doobash, mutton potatomised, ducks onionised, [and] fowl sweetenised', 'along with "Country Captain" *Pulav* and curry *Byramji Rustomji Oodwaria*', was esteemed by 'the Anglo-Indians who [brought] their sisters, aunts and cousins' for this genuine Hindustani fare.[125] Parsi cuisine was the sole marker of the documentary verisimilitude of the Parsis' performances, enabling Europeans to consume purportedly bona fide cultural totems of the unchanging orient. Although Parsi delicacies tempered the company's pecuniary damages, the Victoria's six-month stay, while earning Rs 5,000, cost the troupe Rs 7,500 to travel to London and Rs 11,000 to return to Bombay. Additionally, Rs 17,000 had been spent on rent for Portland Hall, Rs 8,000 on advertisements, and Rs 60,000 on maintaining the troupe for six months in England.[126] The company therefore incurred the unheard-of loss of Rs 95,500, squandering all the riches that it had earned in Mandalay in one fell swoop. These financial losses and the public derision that the Parsis experienced in England prompted the breakup of the company's ownership and, more broadly, established an unspoken understanding that the Parsi theatre could not tour Europe, Australia, or the Americas, although it continued to flourish for the next half century.[127]

Consequently, in its heyday, the Parsi theatre transplanted modern techniques of stagecraft and performance, a complex multiphonal Indo-European repertoire, and a proscenium theatre to places as far apart as present-day Indonesia, Malaysia, Singapore, and Sri Lanka, while also prompting the emergence of such theatrical phenomena as Bangsawan, Komedie Stamboel, Konkani tiatr, and Nurti. And yet, the theatre's unmistakeable failure in England constitutes evidence of profound inequities in cultural flows, border crossings, and the possibilities of cosmopolitan citizenship during this crucial first phase of globalization.[128] Although the London catastrophe was eventually erased from both South Asian history and the Parsis' public memory, this discrepancy in theatrical circuitry was a compelling prediction not only of the imbalances in cultural globalization but also and relatedly of the political disquiet that was just around the corner, thus bringing us, indubitably, to Part III.

Notes

1. Untitled, *RG*, 5 April 1874, 240.
2. Untitled, *RG*, 26 April 1874, n.p. *Ābe Ebḷīs* (*Aube Eblis*) was praised by the *Rāst* as a model for the Parsi theatre despite the inclusion of words such as *āśak* and *iār* [lover] and the actors' poor delivery. 'Ābe Ebḷīs', *RG*, 24 May 1874, 357.
3. Dhanjībhāi Na Paṭel, *PNTT* (Bombay: 'Kaysare-Hind' Paper Printing Press, 1931), 133.
4. One of the illustrious Mādan brothers, Mādan was famous for playing female roles due to his good looks, despite allegedly having a bad voice.

However, after performing the part of the fairy Mārūkh in Dādābhāi Paṭel's *Indra Sabhā*, he became a singing actor.

5. Dārūvālā started his theatrical career at the Irānī Nāṭak Maṇḍalī, where he became famous as Rodābe. He subsequently joined the Victoria before absconding to the Original Victoria.
6. Ogrā worked variously at the Empress and Original Victoria, before joining the Alfred Nāṭak Maṇḍalī. He was renowned not only as a good comedian with an impeccable Hindustani accent, having trained at a college in Kanpur, but also as the mastermind behind the portrayal of such scenes as a moving train. Additionally, he became known in Parsi circles for refusing to recruit actresses for his productions.
7. Dājī left school at nine to work in a factory in Colaba before setting off for a life in the theatre through the Victoria. However, due to a spat with Ṭhuṭhī, he would subsequently play minor roles such as that of a female helper. Eventually he joined the Hīndī Nāṭak Maṇḍalī.
8. Jahāṅgīr Pestanjī Khambātā, *NA* (Bombay, 1913), 39–40; and Paṭel, *PNTT*, 276–79. The actors who joined him included Dādābhāi Aspandīyārjī Mīstrī (Dādābhāi Asfandīārjī Mīstrī), Ardeśar Śrāf (Shroff), Jahāṅgīr Khambātā, Kāvasjī Klīṅgar (Clinger), Navrojī Bāṭlā, Navrojī Edaljī Tambolī, Kāvasjī Pālanjī Khaṭāu, Farāmjī Dalāl, Jamśedjī Dājī, Jehāṅgīr Navrojī Mīnvālā (Jehāṅgīr Nāllo), Ḍosābhāi Farāmjī Kāṅgā, Māṇekjī Mīstrī, and Barjorjī Kutār; see Paṭel, *PNTT*, 278. Kāvasjī Pālanjī Khaṭāu is also spelled as Cowasji Khatao and Cowasjee Khatow.
9. Paṭel, *PNTT*, 276–78.
10. A gallery was also built for private boxes; see 'Mumbaimā̃ Trījī Nāṭakśāḷā', *RG*, 25 May 1873, 334–35. The Hīndī Theatre subsequently burned down.
11. Untitled, *RG*, 18 May 1873, 322; untitled, *RG*, 25 May 1873, 341; untitled, *RG*, 1 June 1873, 357; untitled, *RG*, 15 June 1873, 391; and Paṭel, *PNTT*, 279–81.
12. Paṭel, *PNTT*, 281. The Hīndī Nāṭak Maṇḍalī attempted to uphaul its theatrical fare; see untitled, *RG*, 19 October 1873, 690; untitled, *RG*, 2 November 1873, 722; and untitled, *RG*, 30 November 1873, 790.
13. The actors included Farāmjī Dalāl, Jamśedjī Dājī, and Ḍosābhāi Kāṅgā; see Paṭel, *PNTT*, 281–82; and Khambātā, *NA*, 40–41.
14. *The Nátuck Uttejak Mandali* (Bombay: Education Society's Press, 1879), 24.
15. *The Nátuck Uttejak Mandali*, 24.
16. Khambātā, *NA*, 40–41; Paṭel, *PNTT*, 282; and untitled, *RG*, 14 June 1874, 410.
17. Khambātā, *NA*, 40–41; and Paṭel, *PNTT*, 282–83.
18. Khambātā, *NA*, 40–41; and Paṭel, *PNTT*, 282–83.

19. Abul Faiz Usmānī, 'Urdū Ḍrāmā aur pārsī thiyeṭar', in *Pārsī Thiyaṭar Sampādak*, ed. Raṇbīr Sinha (Jodhpur: Rajasthan Sangeet Natak Akademi, 1990), 24–26.
20. Rashna Darius Nicholson, 'Troubling Englishness: The Eastward Success and Westward Failure of the Parsi Theatre', *Nineteenth Century Theatre and Film* 44, no. 1 (2017): 79.
21. According to Paṭel, Dājī did not know how to sing, a setback in the theatrical business in those days. As the Victoria was the only company with some standing, he was forced to join a small-time touring troupe that travelled from Surat to Rander and Olpad. Dājī was unable to survive in this business for long and subsequently began to recite Shakespeare's monologues at private gatherings: Paṭel, *PNTT*, 334–35.
22. Khambātā, *NA*, 40–41; and Paṭel, *PNTT*, 283. Nājar's anxiety to retain and recruit theatrical talent, of which there was a great dearth in Bombay, is evinced through both his raising of star actors' salaries and his public announcements in search of substitutes who could both sing and enact female roles; see untitled, *TOI*, 30 January 1875, 1.
23. Untitled, *RG*, 17 May 1874, 347. Similarly, the Victoria began to advertise a change in its program every night, performing on all nights except Sunday; see untitled, *TOI*, 14 October 1874, 3.
24. The play *Indra Sabhā*, performed on 2 October 1875, was thus advertised as written by a specially employed *munśī*; see untitled, *RG*, 26 September 1875, 657. See also Ek Mahmadīyan Munśī, *Śīrīn Farhādno Gāyanrūpiī Operā* (Bombay: Oriental Press, 1882); and Joseph Delissa, 'The Vernacular Drama in India', *Baldwin's Monthly*, 1 September 1882, 5.
25. Victoria Theatrical Company Copyright Notice, *TOI*, 13 November 1880, 4.
26. Also spelled as Raunak/Raunaq. Paṭel, *PNTT*, 131; and Usmānī, 'Urdū Ḍrāmā', 18–26, 24. For a description of the communalization of knowledge on the Parsi theatre see Kathryn Hansen, 'Parsi Theater, Urdu Drama, and the Communalization of Knowledge: A Bibliographic Essay', *Annual of Urdu Studies* 16 (2001).
27. Untitled, *TOI*, 27 February 1875, 1. The troupe included Ḍosābhāi Mogal, Khurśedjī Bālīvālā, Farāmjī Apu, Kāvasjī Māṇekjī Kantrāktar, Pestanjī Rūstamjī Lālī, Naśarvānjī Lālī, Edaljī Dādābhāi, Ardeśar Pīrośāh Tabelāvālā, Sorābjī Bādśāh, Pestanjī Farāmjī Mādan, Ardeśar Cīnāī, the German painter Kraus, Bamanjī Kāvasjī Gardā, and the all-important Parsi cook; see Paṭel, *PNTT*, 138.
28. Paṭel, *PNTT*, 146.
29. Paṭel, *PNTT*, 148.

30. Paṭel, *PNTT*, 149. Also spelled Ḍośābhāi Fardunjī Magol and Dosabhoy Furdoonjee Mogul. Mogal would die a premature death in 1889 in Delhi.
31. Joseph Delissa, 'The Vernacular Drama in India', *Baldwin's Monthly*, 1 September 1882, 5.
32. Rashna Darius Nicholson, 'Italian impresarios, American Minstrels and Parsi Theatre: Sonic Networks and the Negotiation of Opera in Colonial South and Southeast Asia', *Italian Opera in Global and Transnational Perspective: Reimagining ITALIANITÀ in the Long Nineteenth Century*, eds., Axel Körner; Paulo M. Kühl (Cambridge: Cambridge University Press, forthcoming).
33. Paṭel, *PNTT*, 150–56; untitled, *RG*, 14 February 1875, 115; and untitled, *RG*, 13 June 1875, 417.
34. 'The Deluge of Native Princes in Bombay', *RG*, 31 October 1875, 732–34.
35. 'Rājvāśīonī Padhrāmṇī', *RG*, 24 October 1875, 718; and 'Mumbai āvelā rājāonī hīlcālnī khabaro', *RG*, 7 November 1875, 755–56.
36. Joseph Delissa, 'The Vernacular Drama in India', *Baldwin's Monthly*, 1 September 1882, 5.
37. Untitled, *RG*, 17 October 1875, 707; and untitled, *RG*, 7 November 1875, 759.
38. Khambātā, *NA*, 44–45.
39. Edaljī Jamśedjī Khorī, *Jālem Jor* (Bombay: Mumbai Vartamān Press, 1876), 2.
40. Because Jālem Jor desires a second wife (the Indian Rūpvantī), his lover, Mohobatejān, plots his death. Additionally, the farce within the play pertains to two servants, the Turkish Topankhān and the Indian Ṭhokankhān, who fight to prove whose master is more powerful.
41. Khorī, *Jālem Jor*, 29.
42. Khorī, *Jālem Jor*, 60.
43. 'The Other Side of the Picture', *RG*, 14 November 1875, 764; and 'Another Discourtesy', *RG*, 14 November 1875, 765–66.
44. Paṭel was rewarded Rs 5000 for the scene, which lasted for fifteen minutes; see Khambātā, *NA*, 44–45.
45. 'Immorality of Indian "Nautching"', *RG*, 6 February 1876, 86; and untitled, *New Zealand Herald*, 29 March 1876, 2.
46. 'Prostitutes *versus* Professional Dancers', *RG*, 27 February 1876, 139; and Tracy C. Davis, *Actresses as Working Women: Their Social Identity in Victorian Culture* (London and New York: Routledge, 2002), 1.
47. Nicholson, '"A Christy Minstrel, a Harlequin', 14.
48. Paṭel, *PNTT*, 184; and untitled, *TOI*, 29 December 1876, 3.
49. Untitled, *TOI*, 27 November 1875, 1.
50. Paṭel, *PNTT*, 156; and Khambātā, *NA*, 44–45.

51. Khambātā, *NA*, 58–61.
52. Untitled, *RG*, 2 January 1876, 14. See also untitled, *RG*, 9 January 1876, 31.
53. Untitled, *RG*, 9 April 1876, 256; untitled, *RG*, 16 April 1876, 273; untitled, *RG*, 23 April 1876, 291; untitled, *RG*, 23 April 1876, 292; untitled, *RG*, 7 May 1876, 328; untitled, *RG*, 21 May 1876, 361; untitled, *RG*, 28 May 1876, 377; and untitled, *RG*, 4 June 1876, 395. It returned to Bombay in December 1876 to perform only for a short period; see untitled, *RG*, 24 December 1876, 882; untitled, *RG*, 31 December 1876, 902; and untitled, 22 May 1881, 354.
54. Khambātā, *NA*, 58–61.
55. Stephen Meredyth Edwardes, *The Gazetteer of Bombay City and Island* (Bombay: Times Press, 1909), 2:182.
56. Khambātā, *NA*, 58–61; and untitled, *RG*, 3 September 1876, 604.
57. Untitled, *RG*, 19 November 1876, 795.
58. Untitled, *TOI*, December 115, 876, 3.
59. Khambātā, *NA*, 61–62.
60. Khambātā, *NA*, 73–74.
61. Khambātā, *NA*, 65–66.
62. Khambātā, *NA*, 65–66.
63. Mistrī would subsequently leave the Empress to join the Hīndī Nāṭak Maṇḍalī and, later, the Pārsī Nāṭak Maṇḍalī.
64. Sarkārī had been stolen from the Victoria by Khambātā. He would eventually become the leading star of J. F. Madan's Elphinstone.
65. Khambātā, *NA*, 65–66.
66. Paṭel, *PNTT*, 383–84.
67. Khambātā, *NA*, 62–63.
68. Khambātā, *NA*, 62–63.
69. Also known as Rūstam Moṭā Farām and Rūstam Kārīcāval.
70. The Victoria returned to Bombay in October 1878; see untitled, *RG*, 27 October 1878, 734.
71. Khambātā, *NA*, 73–74. The comic actor Rūstamjī N. Rūstam Frāmnā stayed behind to build a guest house and subsequently a billiard saloon in Jaipur. Defying all odds, the initially poverty-stricken man eventually erected the Savoy Hotel in Agra and thus lived out his life surrounded by great wealth (one of the few exceptions to the rule of impoverished actors). This wealth was used to build a fire temple at Bombay's Dadar Parsi Colony that still exists in his name; see Paṭel, *PNTT*, 327–29.
72. Farāmjī Apu, who had been having skirmishes with the other owners for some time, also left the Victoria along with Ṭhuṭhī at this juncture; see Paṭel, *PNTT*, 162.
73. Paṭel, *PNTT*, 166, 354–55. This figure is contradicted by the Jaipur state council report of 1880, which states that Ṭhuṭhī received a wage

of Rs 979 and a rail allowance of Rs 100, a Barjorjī Rs 60 and Rs 50, Rūstamjī (presumably Rūstam Frāmnā) Rs 75 and Rs 50, and a Kāvasjī Rs 29.8 and Rs 50; see Aśok Kumār Dās, 'Jaypur mẽ Pārsī Thiyeṭar', in *Pārsī Thiyeṭar Sampādak*, ed. Raṇbīr Sinha (Jodhpur: Sangeet Natak Akademi, 1990), 135–51, 138.

74. Similarly, the Maharaja of Patiala built a theatre for the Victoria in 1891.
75. A Correspondent, 'Latest Telegraphic Intelligence. Dreadful Fire at Ahmednuggur Loss of Forty Lives', *TOI*, 13 May 1878, 3; and 'Ek Nāṭakśāḷāmā̃ bhayankar āg', *RG*, 19 May 1878, 332.
76. Untitled, *Dundee Courier and Argus*, 12 June 1878. The troupe went on to perform in Nagpur in 1879.
77. 'Ek Nāṭakśāḷāmā̃ bhayankar āg', *RG*, 19 May 1878, 332. Thus, for instance the Society for the Amelioration of the Drama announced that those who smoked *bīrīs* (beedis) within the theatre would be handed over to the police; see untitled, *RG*, 4 September 1881, 629; untitled, *RG*, 11 September 1881, 650; and untitled, *RG*, 18 September 1881, 669. For the report of a fire at a theatre in Tīnāvlī that killed seventy people, see 'Nāṭakśāḷāmā̃ āg; 70 jānnī khuhārī', *RG*, 1 August 1886, 838.
78. Untitled, *RG*, 4 September 1881, 629; and untitled, *RG*, 18 September 1881, 669.
79. The Elphinstone's advertisement alludes not only to the hazards of fire but also to the class consciousness that increasingly pervaded Parsi theatrical management: untitled, *RG*, 6 February 1876, 100. *Bīḍī* (local cigarette) smoking became a key way for *uncā vargnī maṇḍalīo* (high-class companies) to distinguish themselves from *nīclā vargnī maṇḍalīo* (low-class companies); see 'Our Native Theatrical Companies', *KIH*, 28 January 1883, 63–64.
80. 'A Scare at the Gaiety Theatre', *TOI*, 7 September 1883, 3. The Gaiety Theatre, Bombay's finest theatre at the time, was designed by John Campbell, erected by Kuvarjī Nājar and opened on 6 December 1879.
81. 'Geiṭī Thīyeṭarmā̃ thaylo ghabhrāt', *KIH*, 9 September 1883, 710; 'Geṭī Thīeṭarmā̃thī', *KIH*, 7 October 1883, 796; and 'Nāṭakśālāmā̃ gabhrāṭ', *RG*, 9 September 1883, 730. The Gaiety was also the first theatre to buy a telephone; see untitled, 21 January 1883, 56.
82. See also the case of a woman dying due to the collapse of a temporary theatre's roof in Madras. 'Nāṭakśāḷānũ Chāprũ paḍvāno akasmāt', *RG*, 19 October 1884, 1032.
83. 'Nāṭakśāḷāomā̃ āg lāgvānā bhaythī', *RG*, 30 October 1887, 1232.
84. 'The Dramatic Folly of Parsi Boys', *RG*, 13 June 1880, 388–89.
85. Mī. Nasarvānjī Dorābjī Āpekhatīyārnũ maraṇ', *RG*, 30 June 1878, 435.
86. 'Our Native Theatrical Companies', *KIH*, 28 January 1883, 63–64. The *Kaysare Hinda* under Framjee Cowasji Mehta (Farāmjī Kāvasjī Mehtā),

erstwhile member of the Zoroastrian Nāṭak Maṇḍalī, rapidly enjoyed popularity not only due to the superior quality of its printing and its inclusion of beautiful images, but also and more crucially because it was the first Parsi newspaper to inaugurate a special telegraphic service for itself from England; see 'The Kaiser-I-Hind', *KIH*, 15 January 1882, 48; and Stephen Meredyth Edwardes, *The Gazetteer of Bombay City and Island* (Bombay: Times Press, 1910), 3:151.

87. Untitled, *RG*, 9 October 1881, 723.
88. A few days later, the troupe published an advertisement in Bombay soliciting men under the age of eighteen who could perform women's roles and sing: untitled, *RG*, 23 October 1881, 759.
89. Untitled, *STOJ*, 19 May 1881, 10; untitled, *STOJ*, 24 June 1881, 6; and untitled, *STOJ*, 28 July 1881, 6.
90. 'The Parsee Victoria Theatrical Co.', *STOJ*, 2 June 1881, 5.
91. Untitled, *STOJ*, 30 June 1881, 7.
92. Untitled, *STOJ*, 21 July 1881, 7.
93. 'Summary of the Week', *STOJ*, 9 June 1881, 1; untitled, *STOJ*, 24 June 1881, 6; 'News of the Week', *STOJ*, 14 July 1881, 6; untitled, *STOJ*, 21 July 1881, 7; and untitled, *STOJ*, 30 June 1881, 7. The cost of erecting the theatre was paid by the Victoria, along with maintenance, gas, ground rents, and so forth; see untitled, *STOJ*, 19 May 1881, 10; untitled, *STOJ*, 24 June 1881, 6; and untitled, *STOJ*, 28 July 1881, 6. See also, 'Troubling Englishness', 81.
94. 'News of the Week', *STOJ*, 14 July 1881, 6.
95. See also Jan van der Putten, 'Bangsawan', *Indonesia and the Malay World* 42, no. 123 (2014).
96. 'Monday, 20th June', *STOJ*, 24 June 1881, 6.
97. See 'Berichten uit de laatste Straits Times', *Bataviaasch handelsblad*, 31 May 1881.
98. 'Rājā Thībāūnā Mulakmā̃ Pārsīnī Musāfarī', *RG*, 7 June 1885, 597–99.
99. The cost of erecting the theatre was $1,500; see untitled, 'Wednesday, 27th July', *STOJ*, 28 July 1881, 6; untitled, *STOJ*, 21 July 1881, 7; and 'Monday, 20th June', *STOJ*, 24 June 1881, 6.
100. 'Māṇḍle khāte nāṭak karvā gaylā pārsī nāṭkīo', *RG*, 22 February 1885, 161. Two weeks later, the troupe sent a telegram to the *Rāst* that was published on the newspaper's front page, confirming that the troupe had received Rs 22,000 in addition to Rs 10,000 worth of gifts: 'Māṇḍle Khātenī Pārsī Nāṭak Ṭoḷī', *RG*, 8 March 1885, 243.
101. 'Rājā Thībāūnā Mulakmā̃ Pārsīnī Musāfarī,' *RG*, 7 June 1885, 597–99.
102. 'Rājā Thībāūnā Mulakmā̃ Pārsīnī Musāfarī,' *RG*, 7 June 1885, 597–99; and Rājā Thībāū vīshe pārsī anubhav', *RG*, 21 June 1885, 648–50.
103. For further information on the Victoria's tour of Burma, see Nicholson, 'Troubling Englishness', 82.

104. 'Rājā Thībāūe Pārsīone āpvā māgelī "luṭ"', *RG*, 12 July 1885, 728–30; 'Rājā Thībāūe Pārsīone āpvā māgelī "luṭ"', *RG*, 19 July 1885, 757–59; and 'Rājā Thībāūnī Pārsīo Taraf Prasannatā', *RG*, 28 June 1885, 674–75.
105. 'Rājā Thībāūe Pārsīone āpvā māgelī "luṭ"', *RG*, 19 July 1885, 757–59.
106. 'Rājā Thībāūe Pārsīone batāvelū dravya', *RG*, 26 July 1885.
107. Hence, on 7 May 1884 the company left from Singapore for Mandalay; see untitled, *Straits Times*, 17 March 1884, 2; untitled, *Straits Times*, 8 April 1884, 2; untitled, *Straits Times*, 26 April 1884, 2; and untitled, *Straits Times*, 3 May 1884, 2.
108. Untitled, *TOI*, 11 May 1885, 3; and untitled, *RG*, 10 May 1885, 504. See also 'Progress of the Native Drama', *RG*, 31 May 1885, 570; and 'Vīkṭorīyā Nāṭak Manḍaḷī', *RG*, 19 July 1885, 765.
109. 'Pārsī ...,' *KIH*, 23 July 1882, 521.
110. 'Grānṭroḍ khāte', *KIH*, 5 October 1884, 915.
111. 'Insolvency Court', *TOI*, 27 December 1884, 3.
112. 'Pārsī Nāṭkīo chek cīn sudhī', *RG*, 2 August 1885, 821.
113. 'A Native Dramatic Company *en route* to England', *RG*, 1 November 1885, 1171–72.
114. 'The Parsee Theatrical Troupe for England', *TOI*, 31 August 1885, 4.
115. 'India in London', *New York Times*, 24 April 1886, 3. For an analysis of the Victoria's controversial participation in the Colonial and Indian exhibition and the reasons for their failure see Nicholson, 'Troubling Englishness', 74–88.
116. 'Inglanḍmā̃ Pārsī Nāṭkīo', *RG*, 21 February 1886, 201–2; 'Inglanḍmā̃ Pārsī Nāṭkīo', *RG*, 28 February 1886, 229; and 'Lanḍannā ek nāṭak ūpar pārsī nāṭakkāronī heratmandī', *RG*, 14 March 1886, 282. See also 'Pārsī Nāṭakkārono Lanḍanmā̃ anubhav', *RG*, 21 March 1886, 309–10; 'Ūlīcnū Ṭopkhānū—Lanḍannā navā nāṭako', *RG*, 4 April 1886, 359–60; and 'Lanḍannā̃ Thoḍā̃k Jovā Lāyak Sthaḷo', *RG*, 18 April 1886, 414–15.
117. 'Lanḍanmā̃ Pārsī Nāṭkīo', *RG*, 14 February 1886, 174–75.
118. 'Lanḍanmā̃ Kasrat ane Nāṭak', *RG*, 28 March 1886, 333–34.
119. Untitled, *TOI*, 21 June 1886, 5.
120. 'Parsee Actors at the Gaiety', *Era*, 20 December 1885, 8.
121. 'A Dramatic Absurdity', *Devon and Exeter Daily Gazette*, 23 December 1885, 3.
122. 'Parsee Actors at the Gaiety', *Standard*, 12 December 1885, 2.
123. 'The Prince and the Potter', *South Australian Register*, 1 February 1886, 6.
124. Nicholson, 'Troubling Englishness', 86; and Saloni Mathur, *India by Design: Colonial History and Cultural Display* (Berkeley: University of California Press, 2007), 63–66.

125. Untitled, *TOI*, 3 March 1886, 5; and 'India in London', *TOI*, 14 January 1886, 8.
126. 'Parsee Theatricals in England', *RG*, 27 June 1886, 689.
127. 'Parsee Theatricals in England', *RG*, 27 June 1886, 689.
128. 'Gaiety Theatre', *Morning Post*, 21 December 1885, 2.

PART III

Revolution

Part III covers the period from 1874 to 1893, the halfway point in the Parsi theatre's eighty-year history. It traces the beginnings of a political revolution incubated in the complex interplay between the familiar and unfamiliar, chance and intention, fantasy and partial truths in the now pan-Asian Parsi performance world. From the 1870s onwards, the Parsi theatre was the most significant arena for the conceptualization of the politics of religion in colonial India, profoundly affecting the course of history through its detailed imaginative renderings of a singular, culturally homogeneous past. Illegible to some but eminently legible to most others, Parsi plays—which depicted Hindu visual iconography, popular myths, and social themes such as the evils of modernity—propagated the twofold historical process noted by Sumit Sarkar, blurring differences internal to 'Hinduism' and sharpening boundaries between 'Hindus' and other religious groups.[1] As has often been noted, the symbolic correlation between Indian and Hindu nationalism (or Hindutva) and the parallel formulation of 'foreign' Islamic, Christian, and Parsi minoritarian identities are relatively recent, fundamentally modern colonial inheritances.[2] The drama played an instrumental role in not only the agglomeration of hitherto unheard voices within a more 'inclusive' public domain, but also, paradoxically, the hardening of intergroup boundaries and the rise of nationalist and sectarian sentiment. The sequential, derivative grammar of 'our' history, 'our' bloodlines, 'our' futures—the most influential legacy of the nineteenth century—was ultimately the hermeneutic work of the cultural imagination, involving the downward percolation and subsequent internalization of racial theory in popular form, the horizontal dissemination of a reconstituted historical consciousness, and the phenomenological shift from reverse-orientalist imaginings to revealed mythopoetic truths. Chapters 7 and 8 delineate this evolution of racialized group identities, the discursive formation of Hindutva, and the shared cultural vision within which nationalist thought first appeared on the stages of empire, a process that troubles Benedict Anderson's canonical formulation of the newspaper's enabling of nationhood. While print capitalism allowed literate bourgeois publics to conceive of themselves as members of a nation in empty, homogenous time, the wider circulation and more persuasive visual renderings of religion, ethnicity, and kinship through 'performative capitalism' provided a popular base in South Asia where subaltern subjects wholly disconnected from the state apparatus visualized themselves as interconnected in kairotic, messianic time.

Scholars such as Partha Chatterjee and Tanika Sarkar have shown how the origins of South Asian nationalism lay not in the 'outer' political sphere but in ideas of conjugality within the 'inner' home.[3] As demonstrated in Part I, the reformist elite—who interiorized colonial theories of the barbarity of contemporary Indian customs due to their irreparable decline from a pure, ancient golden age—attempted to reconfigure all the fundamental elements of Indian legal, social, and political life. This reconfiguring was achieved through the women's question, the most important site for the cultural encounter between colonizer and colonized and a crucial tool in colonialism's assertion of its moral superiority. Beginning in the 1870s, however, a surfeit of gendered imagery that would eventually be associated with communalism, Hindu militancy, and Gandhian pacifist nationalism pervaded the vernacular public sphere—of goddesses who were devoted, selfless, and who willingly suffering monumental adversity for the wellbeing of their husbands, families, and all mankind. These visual representations, which melded female sacrifice and submissiveness with martyrdom and victorious power, lay at the heart of the self-introspection, religious revivalism, and totalitarian conservatism that characterized the beginnings of a radicalized nationalism in the late nineteenth century. If, previously, colonial officials and reformists posited women as symptoms of the deterioration of Indian civilization, they were now signs of the ultimate sanctity, durability, and virtue of a pre-existing culture, the last bastion of freedom for the colonized.

Significantly, this symbol of the inviolate, unreformed woman untainted by the prison house of reason—a representative of a hoary

Indian utopia—was gestated primarily in Indian playhouses, the most popular and accessible public realm for the development of mass literacy in a standardized visual grammar. These female icons eventually escaped from the theatre into the wider public arena of politics, embodying the antidote to and critique of an extrinsic, forcibly imposed moral order. As early as the 1870s and 1880s, the Parsi theatre—which performed a homogenous repertoire of high-brow and low-brow mythological plays, melodramas, pulp farces, and topical satire for a composite public of clerks, millworkers, soldiers, landowners, and housewives across the subcontinent and beyond—began to celebrate the pure, devoted, ritual-observing indigenous woman through narratives of romantic, 'traditional', precolonial pastoral life, forms of congregational devotion, and a new ideology of sacred domesticity. For example, in the new genre of the social play, the chaste, faithful, spiritual wife—the germ cell of the future nation—was juxtaposed against the self-indulgent, degenerate, evil, bourgeois man or woman who preferred entertainment over familial duty, this latter figure being symbolic of the ideological influence of market values as disseminated through foreign rule.[4]

The Parsi drama thus assumed the influential, transformative, epistemological purpose of disputing the overriding narrative of native barbarity and despotism through elaborate dramatizations of feminine difference, a manifestation of the irreconcilably differentiated colonized self. Fundamental to this mission were popular, cyclical, and implicitly critical conceptions of history and time. Kalyug, the most dissolute of the four Hindu ages marked by the inversion of gender and caste hierarchies, replaced linear, chronotic time in histrionic expositions of 'truth'. Myth, history, and the present were indistinguishable in the new theatre, merging into a common dystopic temporal frame in plays that portrayed real knowledge as a return to an intuitive wisdom distinct from colonial law and moral doctrine. Women as passive signs of spectacle were thus demarcated as sites where an authentic, non-textual understanding of reality that penetrated the illusions of the modern world was revealed in messianic time. Every gesture, movement, and phrase in the Parsi theatre thus steadily and cautiously composed conceptions of the past that were subsequently accepted as revealed truths, providing an aesthetic currency for the future legitimization of indigenous leadership and putting disparate communities across the subcontinent into contact with the cultural tradition of the putative burgeoning nation.

Plays offered Indian audiences a hitherto unknown, unmediated interconnectivity, making Parsi theatre an equivocal yet formidable site for the broadcasting of anticolonial nativist thought, and shaping an impression of 'India' that, though illusory, generated and primed the future nationalist public. Consequently, despite never directly referring to colonialism, Parsi plays were implicitly anticolonial, gradually but deliberately seeing the nation into being.

While this new nativist revivalism that was disseminated through the transcontinental powerhouse of the Parsi theatre steadily eroded colonial power, tensions grew between the ethnic and religious communities that lived in uneasy propinquity in Bombay. Racial thinking, which spilled into the playhouse to legitimize forms of ethnonationalism, worked concurrently as a crucible for growing hostilities among Hindus, Muslims, and Parsis. This section shows how the colonial public was progressively fissured not merely along linguistic lines but also according to religion, caste, and ethnicity, due to the expressive economy, myths, and ethnonational moral universe that the Parsi theatre propagated. Parsi plays functioned as a living archive generated by innumerable authors, determining what occurred when and where and accordingly what had salience in the organization of collective discourse. By methodically compiling, curating, and circulating an authoritative ethnic, religious, and historical narrative of the future nation, the Parsi theatre simultaneously generated and further segmented the South Asian public. The following pages seek to portray this indistinct complex of the parallel development of South Asian proto-nationalism and -fascism, requiring the reader to intermittently gaze from afar and look up close.

Notes

1. Sumit Sarkar, '"Kaliyuga", "Chakri" and "Bhakti": Ramakrishna and His Times,' *Economic and Political Weekly* 27, no. 29 (1992): 1553.
2. Partha Chatterjee, 'History and the Nationalization of Hinduism', in *Representing Hinduism: The Construction of Religious Traditions and National Identity*, eds. Veena Dalmia and Heinrich Von Stietencron (New Delhi: Sage, 1995), 126.
3. Partha Chatterjee, *The Nation and Its Fragments: Colonial and Postcolonial Histories* (Princeton, NJ: Princeton University Press, 1993), 6; and Tanika Sarkar, *Hindu Wife, Hindu Nation: Community, Religion, and Cultural Nationalism* Reprint (New Delhi: Permanent Black, 2017, first published 2001), 37, 191.

4. Sumit Sarkar, 'Renaissance and Kaliyuga: Time, Myth, and History in Colonial Bengal', in *Between History and Histories: The Making of Silences and Commemorations*, eds. Gerald M. Sider and Gavin A. Smith (Toronto: University of Toronto Press, 1997), 113.

CHAPTER 7

The Reformers in Need of Reforming

A collective communal depression began to fester among Bombay's Parsis in the aftermath of the 1874 riots. The *Rāst*, in an article entitled 'Distress among Parsees', described a substantial increase in communal poverty.[1] Other religious and ethnic groups had allegedly caught up with them in education, trade, and commerce; 'the *śeṭhs* [were] gone in all but name', having given way to clerks and public servants[2]; scores of families had moved from the affluent Fort to the insalubrious quarters of Dhobitalao[3]; and there was a marked rise in Parsi suicides due to unemployment.[4] This dwindling of communal economic power was attributed to a decline in morality: theirs was 'the age of science ... young Parsis worshipped at the altar of technology, not religion'.[5] The Parsis, according to the Gujarati press, had developed expensive tastes for European goods such as hair brushes, lavender incense, pomade, corsets, crème de rose, boots, and imported cloth that could not be maintained by the paltry incomes of university graduates.[6] As a consequence, the reformers—who had kindled the 'mania' for Western boots, stockings, polkas, butlers, and the Parsi theatre, where women mingled freely with *kacrā loko* (garbage people)—were now ostensibly 'in need of reforming'.[7] 'Reforms are no longer an unqualified good', cried the *Kaysare Hinda*, noting that 'instead of *sudhārā* (reform) we now have

R. D. Nicholson, *The Colonial Public and the Parsi Stage*, Transnational Theatre Histories,
https://doi.org/10.1007/978-3-030-65836-6_7

kudhārā (retrogession)'.[8] Likewise, the erstwhile reformist *Rāst* provocatively declared, 'if the complaints regarding Parsi deterioration are true all our previous tools for reform, our schools, organizations, educational curriculum, books and plays should be brought to an end'.[9] The time had come, according to the vernacular press, to pursue 'local' social models: the unchanged, traditional, bucolic customs of the Hindus who followed the astute ways of their prudent forefathers.[10] Articles in the press railed against anti-Hindu aspersions from the English, casting Hindu norms as the new antidote to the problems of the now too-Western Indian world. The article 'Boots and Stockings from a Hindu Point of View', for example, defended the age-old Hindu custom of wearing slippers during the monsoons.[11] Concurrently, efforts were underway to reformulate the 'Parsi full dress', which was seen as 'far too English'.[12] These new Parsi declamations on the ills of colonial education, ideals, and footwear (as empty, alienating, or pernicious) were paradigmatic of a broader and rapidly growing ideological shift across the Indian subcontinent, from liberal reform to religious revivalism. While modernity—and, as a corollary, Victorian virtue—was previously viewed as the panacea to all evils, it was now considered to be the root cause of economic and spiritual deprivation. A consciousness that colonialism was legitimized through a dubious moral superiority and that Indians would never be able to reach these foreign standards emerged, propelling geographically disparate yet ideologically interrelated, subtly anticolonial nativist movements.

This sweeping transition from reformist self-criticism to introspective conservatism had a significant impact on the subcontinent's theatre world. Following multiple signs of Britain's decline in centrality—the 'disloyal' *Indu Prakāś* pronounced that Britain was not a paramount power as it had merely obtained its dominance through a series of wars and conquests, the statesman Raja Sir Dinkar Rao Rajwade ceased to speak in English after reading the *Wealth of Nations*, and the vernacular press began arguing that 'free trade (was merely) for free countries'—the Victoria, returning from its three-month tour of Poona, announced the performance of its Hindu-themed *Gopīcand* in imitation of the Marathi Sāṅglīkar Nāṭak Maṇḍalī.[13] In so doing, the company anticipated the development of the soon-to-be-paramount genre of the Hindu mythological play. The variety performers Grace Egerton and George Case, the first English actors of the Parsi stage, performed the Hindu comic parts of Loṭan and Jogan to the tunes of the *gorī* (white) Royal Artillery Band.[14] Egerton, whose call to fame was her performance of the 'Wizard of the East', was well-known for parodying 'orientals'.[15] Her presence was contentious: while she was praised for her acting, she was rebuked by the Gujarati press for the 'immorality' of her performance. Egerton thus exemplified not only the complex reverse orientalism at work in the Parsi theatre, which began to employ European actresses for non-European roles, but also normative bourgeois prejudice against actresses for their purported sexuality.[16]

The Society for the Amelioration of the Drama

Tracy C. Davis persuasively argues that Victorian actresses' conspicuousness and notoriety in the public space of the theatre propelled social bias, objectification, and sexualized readings by audiences conversant in the visual grammar of pornography.[17] Similarly, although material evidence of the correlation between acting and prostitution is deficient, actresses' employment propelled the stigmatization of the Parsi stage as a breeding ground for lewd thoughts and carnal desires.[18] It was, as the *Times of India* declared, 'the opinion of many that the Gujerathi drama in its present infancy ought to receive the guidance and supervision of men of education and position, in order that it may be carried on within reasonable limits without lowering the dignity of the stage'.[19] Itching with the desire to transform the theatre back to a righteous, decorous forum for the social benefit of the 'respectable' classes, Kekhuśro Kābrājī assembled a committee of venerated Hindu and Parsi 'well-wishers of the theatre'—including Maṅgaldās Nathubhai (secretary), Sohorābjī Jamśedjī Jījībhāi, Kharshedji Nusserwanji Cama, Pherozeshah Merwanjee Mehta, Dhīrajrām Dalpatrām, Jamśedjī Cama, Dhanjībhāi Farāmjī Paṭel, Raṇchoḍbhāi Udayrām, Mehervānjī Fardunjī Marajbān, and Mansukhrām Surajrām—to supervise a group of amateur actors.[20] Thereafter, in March 1875 the Nāṭak Utejak Maṇḍalī (Society for the Amelioration of the Drama) was established, 'with an eye to the prevention of the manifold evils that have lately multiplied in native theatricals'.[21] Kābrājī, stung by the moral ruin of his Victoria, was unsparing with the society's bylaws, implementing exacting rules such as the examination of the script and rehearsals, as well as prohibitions on child actors (unless express permission was granted by the parents and committee), troublemakers, children below the age of seven, food and drink, and shoddily dressed individuals. Domestic help were also barred from the first-class seats, indicating the central importance of upholding class divisions in the society's performances.[22]

Bombay's expanding rail and marine networks had brought in their wake swift growth in trade and industrialization, precipitating the 'mill mania' of the late nineteenth century. By 1875, Bombay possessed twenty-seven mills, a figure that increased to ninety in fifteen years, and with this growth came the demand for labour. As a growing industrial hub, Bombay began to draw penniless workers from the rural areas of Konkan, Bengal, and present-day Tamil Nadu, with Bombay's industrial population increasing to 8.4% of the total population according to the census of 1881.[23] This change in demographics affected the theatrical trade as the city's new labour force flocked to the now inexpensive theatre, which was one of the few sources of amusement and solace after the drudgery of the exploitative working day.[24] By 1878, theatre managers such as Jahāṅgīr Khambātā followed the established, illicit practice of bribing policemen to control the 'lower orders' of spectators in the pit (Khambātā paid Rs 5 per day in Lahore for the services of twenty-five policemen).[25] Consequently, middle-class disquiet vis-à-vis the 'lower orders' had a significant bearing on the society's workings. As the English press declaimed in the context of the society's inauguration:

> Dramatic performances by school-boys and other illiterates are the mania of the day, and the ruin already effected of two respectable families, as well as the impending ruin of two more, impress on us at once the necessity of taking some steps to check the growing evils of the mania. … With little urchins … occupying the stage, with an unruly mob of low class Mahomedans, Hindoos and Parsees forming an audience, with disturbances going on both on the stage and in the seats, with loud conversation going on in the midst of the performances between people from one class of seat to another, with coarse and vulgar jokes and tits for tats exchanged between the occupiers of the stage and the stalls; and lastly, with a shower of copper coins, shoes, broken bottles and soda-water corks falling upon the stage, these native performances reminded one of a fish market than a theatre.[26]

The society's first production, Kābrājī's *Śurī Vace Śopārī athvā oratnā kolnī kaśoṭī* (*A Nut in the Nutcracker, or The Test of a Woman's Promise*), premiered at the old Victoria Theatre on 27 March 1875. This performance followed a grand rehearsal at Maṅgaldās Nathubhāi's bungalow and the committee's conferral of approval on the production.[27] Described as 'a vindication of woman on the stage', this Gujarati adaptation of Susanna Centlivre's 1714 comedy *The Wonder: A Woman Keeps a Secret*,[28] was, according to 'True Lovers of the Drama',

> quite different from ordinary Guzerathi dramas of the present day. These are generally heavy pieces, with some pretensions to historical representations, in which tedious Court scenes and rigmarole speeches and dialogues enacted generally in a dull, indifferent way, in sitting postures, form the chief burden of the plays. The performance of Saturday night last was quite a relief to the theatre going-public. This was a regular five-act comedy, sparkling with fun and with wit, a highly attractive plot, full of incidents, some of which may be called thrilling, in which the scenes were laid not in gilded palaces and courts, but in domestic domains, and in which the characters are not kings and princes, demons and fairies of the unreal regions, but are men and women introduced to represent the passions and emotions of ordinary worldly life, and the various conflicts of worldly and family interests. ... The comedy of "A Woman Keeps a Secret," as performed on Saturday last, was characterised by much attention paid to real modern acting, and I can say, without fear of contradiction, that this is the first native performance in which the different positions, the groupings, the crossings, and gestures, &c., were rigidly attended to.[29]

The Parsi stage of 1874 thus witnessed a significant transition from scenes 'laid ... in gilded palaces and courts' to scenes set in 'domestic domains'. With the ninety-two-page *Śurī Vace Śopārī*, Kābrājī, previously the inventor of the Persian epic, had thus written the first *Pārsī sansārī nāṭak* (Parsi social drama), bringing the Parsi theatre from the thunder and lightning of the Persian mythological play to the realist polemics of the drawing room.[30] The *Rāst* responded positively to this shift:

> There is no end to the madness for Iranian plays based on the *Shahnama*, which is why instead of showing plays regarding our homeland, Ancient Iran, the playwright has chosen to adapt a light yet brilliant *kāmeḍī* [comedy] or *hāsyaras nāṭak*. Although there is an Iranian play in our society's program next season, we believe that the majority of our plays should portray contemporaneous subjects. Historical plays may elicit patriotism for the ancients, but this is where their effect ends. However, *kāmeḍī* that portrays everyday subjects instructs in a way that depictions of magnificent palaces and courts as in *Bejan ane Manījeh* or *Śīāvakhś* cannot.[31]

Thus, along with the prohibition on poorly dressed individuals, actresses, and children, theatrical realism was an integral component of Kābrājī's attempt to restore 'the dignity of the stage'.

However, this turn to realism is not the only reason why *Śurī Vace Śopārī* constitutes a watershed moment in the development of the Parsi theatre. Two tropes that would be prominent in subsequent Parsi plays stand out in the play text. The first of these is *nazar* (sight). In the preface, Kābrājī claims that his principal objective was to depict the unreliability of superficial observation: that what was perceived with the senses was usually false and therefore could not necessarily be equated with reality or 'truth', an idea that was similarly articulated in the play[32]:

> *Khuśro*: Woman by her very name is disloyal. Who will ever remember a woman that is never disloyal!
> *Behrām*: Come, Khuśro. ... Don't make me think badly of our Manījeh, who I consider as my sister. ... I think you are falsely suspecting her.
> *Khuśro*: No, I told you that I witnessed her with my own eyes and heard her with my own ears.
> *Behrām*: But sometimes things that you have seen with your own eyes also turn out to be false.[33]

Khuśro subsequently declaims, 'With all that has happened to me I believe that you, Manījeh, are honest. ... I know now that what one sees with one's own eyes can be false', even as another character exclaims to Behrām, 'Are your ears true, or are our eyes wrong?'[34] These passages offer evidence of a growing consensus first articulated in the secular mythological play that superficial ocular perception was distinct from true cognition. According to the play's dramaturgy, seeing was not equivalent to knowing.

The second conspicuous motif in the text is loyalty. Kābrājī played with several permutations and combinations of the inversion and subsequent righting of hierarchies—parents and children, masters and servants, and husbands and wives—in order to bring the theme into sharper focus. While a superficial reading of the play would attribute these role inversions to middle-class anxieties regarding possible shifts in the colonial patriarchal and class-based pecking order, the title of the play indicates that there was more to the depictions of marital infidelity and disobedient helpers than proverbially meets the eye. In the 1884 published edition of the text, the title of the play was changed from *Śurī Vace Śopārī athvā oratnā kolnī kaśoṭī* (*A Nut in the Nutcracker, or The Test of a Woman's Promise*) to *Suḍī Vace Sopārī. Athvā Be Vacnī Kharī Paṇ Bevacnī Nahī* (*A Nut in the Nutcracker. Or Being True to Two Loyalties as Opposed to Being Disloyal*), indicating that momentous change was on the horizon.

The First Hindu Mythological Play

But the turn to domestic settings was not the only significant transition to the Parsi theatrical repertoire ushered in by Kābrājī in the 1870s: he was also foundational to the rise of the Hindu mythological play. After a brief run of *Śurī Vace Śopārī*, the society announced that it intended to stage the Parsi theatre's first *śuḍh* (pure) Gujarati play, Raṇchoḍbhāi Udayrām's *Hariścandra*, on 3 November 1875 at the respectable Framjee Cowasjee Institute, which had hitherto primarily been used for scientific lectures and exhibitions.[35] Three years prior, when Udayrām, the first non-Parsi playwright of the Parsi theatre, published *Hariścandra*, the Gujarati press praised the play's language while questioning why the Parsi theatre (which now performed in Parsi Gujarati, Hindustani, Farsi, and English) was incapable of performing a single play in *śudh hīndu Gujrātī* (pure Hindu Gujarati).[36] With these criticisms in mind, Kābrājī adapted this 'uncorrupted' text for the stage.[37] The play was the first 'perfect' literary specimen of both ancient Hindustan ('the birthplace of theatre') and 'pure' Gujarati (with its liberal use of Sanskrit words and letters such as ળ [ḷa] as opposed to લ [la]). According to Dhanjībhāi Paṭel, the society's Parsi amateur actors Hormasjī Modī (as Hariścandra), Farāmjī Dalāl (as Viśvamitra), and Ardeśar Hīrāmāṇek (as Tārāmatī) quaked with fear at the prospect of studying this alien language with 'unsullied grammar and pronunciation' under a Hindu teacher, and of performing in this strange tongue before possibly disgruntled Parsis and condescending Hindus.[38] After a protracted period of training in pronouncing ડ (ḍa) and ટ (ṭa), 'the first instance of the Parsees with their poor Guzerathi appearing in a vernacular much more correct as well as difficult than their own, and in styles and fashions as regards dress and manners quite foreign to them' took place to great fanfare.[39] Spectators were continually turned away from this 'respectable' play (purportedly the first such play in five years), which would, amazingly, be performed one hundred and fifty times.[40]

Why was the play, shorn of spectacular effect and elaborate costume, the object of such immense and widespread public esteem, appealing to Bombay's reformist elite, European residents, sizeable working-class population, and housewives? What episteme had Udayrām inadvertently tapped into in writing this landmark Hindu mythological play? Why was a process now underway 'to revive ancient Hindoo literature and rescue it from the ravages of time'?[41]

The play consists of a story within a story, beginning in the court of the Hindu god Indra with a squabble between the two sages Vīśvamitra and Vasishṭha. The sages debate whether the legendary King Hariścandra is indeed 'the most righteous, honest, and *dharmī* (moral) of all'.[42] A bet is laid, and the wily Vīśvamitra subjects Hariścandra to a series of examinations, unbeknownst to him. Vīśvamitra tricks Hariścandra into an enormous debt, which drives the king to sell his wife (Queen Tārāmatī) and child to a rich Brahmin, even as he sells himself to a low-caste undertaker. The royals therefore lose their much-privileged caste. Thereafter, the boy is bitten by a snake sent by Vīśvamitra and dies. Hariścandra and his wife then meet at the cremation ground where the king now works. Tārāmatī, too poor to cremate their son, is compelled by Hariścandra to seek permission to do so from the owner of the ground. While she is on her way to make this request, Vīśvamitra throws the murdered body of the Prince of Benares at her feet. She is found, accused of the murder, and doomed to a death that must be carried out by her husband. Hariścandra, unswerving from his *dharma*, lifts his hand to strike the blow—but the gods stall the heinous deed and commend the king for his unswerving devotion and righteousness.

Dharma, one of the most important conceptual frameworks of Hinduism, comprising a multiplicity of meanings including laws, ethics, and societal obligations, was revived in the late nineteenth century. The term became a signifier not only of the power to penetrate and overcome all worldly illusions but also of Hindu difference and superiority. Despite the complete reversal of caste hierarchies, Hariścandra prevails in the play due to his awareness of the illusive character of his trials and his allegiance and subservience to a seemingly ageless (but in reality wholly modern) indigenous set of rules and ideals that implicitly contested the post-Enlightenment European precedence in the realm of knowledge. According to Tanika Sarkar, the complex oppositional vocabulary between colonial and indigenous moral frames that permeated the vernacular public sphere in the late nineteenth century obliquely articulated disquiet and resentment over foreign rule. The reformist movement was established on the principle that colonial morality, virtue, and reason were axiomatically superior, prompting self-doubt, self-critique, and attempts at self-transformation. As demonstrated in Chapters 5 and 6, this movement gave way to an inquisition on the nature of truth in the theatre, but by the late 1870s, a new awareness of Indians' derivative identity under colonialism blossomed, stimulating a vehement indigenism, a return to roots.[43] Within a few decades, indigenous customs were thus subjected to two contrarian interpretations: while for the reformists they were corruptions of pure religious doctrine and evidence of societal degradation, for a new group of religious revivalists they constituted an intimate realm uncontaminated by colonial rule.

Like the secular mythological play, *Hariścandra* asked whether perceptual experience was flawed, while propelling an alternative sociopolitical leaning that would gain prominence in the late 1870s. If the plays of the 1860s asked whether fairies, demons, and monsters were 'illusion or reality', reinscribing 'the real' to a 'remote spectrum of belief',[44] Hindu epic plays correspondingly, intuitively, asked whether authentic knowledge was elsewhere, distinct from education, science, law, and chronological history. However, the symbolic universe of the Hindu mythological drama further averred that colonial education and history in hegemonic linear time had no monopoly on conceptualizing reality. Even as the locus of truth shifted from text to performance, beliefs in secular magic and technological enchantment were rerouted to convictions in the shared ethics and ideals of a Hindu mythological past. As noted by Partha Chatterjee, in the place of 'outer' colonial reason, tradition, and domesticity—the unaffected, virtuous, 'inner' temple of the home—became the source of universal, transcendental meaning and the sphere of cultural distinction, authority, and sovereignty.[45] In the face of political subjection, the defence of this inner realm was viewed as paramount as it held the potential for political change, a cultural nationalism, and imminent freedom. The 'adoring eye' of religious revivalism would thus replace the 'critical eye' of reform. Hindu gods and goddesses revealed lyrical, poetic truths, enabling audiences to view plays through precolonial viewing practices analysed by scholars such as Dipesh Chakrabarty and Kathryn Hansen as *darshan* (viewing, beholding).[46] For the price of a ticket, spectators experienced psychic contact through the mutual exchange of vision and divinity, a seeing beyond the mundane that was subsequently displaced onto the aesthetic project of seeing the nation into being. The medium of this exchange—the play—was sacralized, transformed into a mystical act of deep devotional viewing, a modern sanctuary that made possible a near daily encounter with heavenly spirits. Through the mythological drama, a reconfigured corpus of Hindu religious enchantments that drew on the illusory dramaturgy of scientific performances inserted itself into people's quotidian habits, duties, and consumption practices, eventually merging into religious rituals and festivals, political assemblies, and anticolonial demonstrations. In so doing, the theatre organized, articulated, and disseminated a new idea of the past, a new understanding of nonchronological time, and a new regime of knowledge, thereby constituting the site for the confluence in rhetoric of the popular-religious and the national.

Significantly, the Parsi theatre's propagation of a Hindu episteme through its mythological plays 'worked' because scripture was officially equated with religion, and because the colonial state strategically perpetuated the 'Hindu' as an essentialized, monolithic whole. As seen in Part I, the colonial state determined personal laws according to 'authentic' scripture, thereby fostering among Indians a more acute feeling of membership to a homogenous religious group. The legal identity of an individual was no longer about sub-caste; rather, a uniform, clearly circumscribed symbolic universe—Hindu, Muslim, or Christian—legitimated assertions to morality, social control, and belonging.[47] Hinduism, initially the site for reforming or disciplining 'irrational' customs, had now become an intimate, autonomous realm of sovereignty, one where the colonial state and its bourgeois-rationalist conception of knowledge were denied intervention.[48]

According to Habermas's conceptualization of the public sphere, print enabled hitherto disconnected peoples to imagine themselves as interconnected in homogeneous, empty time. In British India, however, the national public emerged in the 'inner' cultural domain, where, as Christopher Pinney notes, precolonial faith in the power and permanence of gods and religious scriptures assumed new intensities.[49] While print capitalism supported rational-critical debate among the indigenous elite and colonial officials, a performative capitalism (disseminated through chromolithographs, pulp fiction, and above all else the ubiquitous Parsi theatre) situated the anticolonial movement in the messianic temporality of Hindu mythology, transforming the national struggle for independence into an ethical war of cosmic proportions. Through staged religious displays, a populist, anti-imperial politics was formulated, enacted, and propagated parallel to the 'official' nationalism developing in elite political associations for spectators who did not or rather could not partake in the conception of the world as novel. The political imaginary being shaped in the kairotic time of the ancient Hindu mythological play suggested a different temporality and meaning of the present than the self-reflexive bourgeois subjectivity produced by English and vernacular reformist print media. Consequently, and as Arvind Rajagopal has posited, the Indian public was fissured by two types of political language: an official, secular nationalism that was desired by modernizing elites and actuated through negotiation within colonial juridical and administrative frameworks; and an unofficial, more heterogeneous, popular nationalism that emerged, in my view, primarily through the standardized, cohesive visual realm of the Parsi theatre.[50]

For the first time in the subcontinent, long before cinematic or televised broadcasts of Hindu epics such as the *Ramayana*, the confoundingly diverse linguistic and ethnic constituencies of India were concurrently acquainted with an idealized, mythic, oral tradition in modern garb that made meaningful a complex, fractured polity. In addition to the geographically and temporally ambiguous secular magic epitomized by the theatre's fairies and monsters, a corpus of Hindu dramatic signs traversed the boundaries between private and public realms, ideological propaganda and technological pleasure. The theatre's Hindu mythological plays thus produced a strong feeling of kinship across geographic and language divides, facilitated the growth of extensive webs of information and interaction, diffused a new populist political grammar, and circumvented more protracted, elite discourses of anticolonial rebellion and national awakening. The Parsi theatre became a living library; through every subtly stylized gest, glittering trident, and Sanskritized syllable, its plays provided the visual and aural vocabulary for an authoritative anti-imperialist discourse, steadily collating the 'truths' of the history of the nation. As a form of 'archiving'—a performed, processual, dynamic, and continuous practice not dissimilar from the colonial state's compulsive compilation of demographic records—the Parsi theatre legitimated a contrarian episteme by mapping, preserving, and making possible the recovery of a deep, heavily inflected network of symbols, allegories, and rituals.[51] Through the reordering of classifications of true and false knowledge, religion thus generated not only the colonial public sphere but also the concepts of anticolonial resistance and nationhood. The *tour du monde* of the spectacular Parsi theatre was pared down, as mythological protagonists began to be grounded in a space whose fuzzy contours, shaped by increasingly standardized language, revealed traces of a unitary, self-contained whole. Progressively, Hindu mythological plays exhumed mythic worlds that were conflated with an imagined pan-Hindu geographic imagination. 'Hindu' costume and habit, 'Hindu' turn of phrase and pronunciation held the keys to a common nativist essence, racial difference, and political emancipation, animating the country into existence. The Parsis, chief intermediaries between the rulers and the ruled, had thus unwittingly created the space for a different kind of network, one predicated on 'cultural artefacts of a particular kind'.[52]

Women and/as Nationhood

On 3 December 1876, the *Rāst* announced the production of the society's third play, Udayrām's *Naḷ Damayantī*, adapted for the stage by Kābrājī. According to the press, while '*Harīścandra* demonstrated the significance of *satya* [truth], this [next] play portrayed *patīvratā*' (duty/devotion of a virtuous wife) in a manner reminiscent of the woman-centric *Sonānā Mulnī Khorśed* and *Pākdāman Gulnār*.[53] In an effort to set itself apart from the mainstream Parsi theatre on Grant Road, the company erected a stage in a temporary wooden playhouse on the Esplanade opposite Crawford Market.[54] After a grand rehearsal at Nathubhāi's residence, *Naḷ Damayantī* had its first performance on 16 December. Like *Hariścandra*, the show enjoyed an exceptional response, which prompted the *Rāst* to rebuke the audibly weeping spectators, the frivolous, inordinate clapping, and the unremitting encores.[55] Similarly, Paṭel describes the boundless enthusiasm that the play induced among Bombay's Hindus, who allegedly sent their domestic help hours before curtain to occupy the house's best seats.

Paṭel attributes the 'Hindu' craze for the play—which was performed a hundred and eight times—to its depiction of *dhārmik* incidents.[56] The word *dharma* occurs no fewer than twenty-two times just on the first page of the playbook. 'Rājprajānā [political] dharma, strīpurūshnā [marital] dharma, vaṇāshramnā dharma, dharma ane dharma, jyā̃ tyā̃ [everywhere] dharma', cries Dvāpar in tremendously convoluted, Sanskrit-heavy Gujarati. The play follows Damayantī, who pursues her *dharma* of remaining loyal to her husband in the face of numerous trials and tribulations inflicted by the gods, particularly a personified *Kalyug*. *Kalyug*, the dystopic 'Age of Downfall', was, according to Hindu conceptualizations of cyclical time, the final and most debased age in an everlasting four-yug rotational sequence, a time when caste and patriarchal hierarchies are overturned. *Kalyug* functioned from the 1870s onwards as a potent metaphor for colonial rule, slipping into the public sphere through vernacular chapbooks, farces and melodramas, autobiographies, religious treatises, and the opinion columns of newspapers.[57] Sumit Sarkar describes how nineteenth-century popular culture cherry-picked from *Kalyug's* copious catalogue of evils, emphasizing despotic, foreign kings and excessive, rational arguments as to the perversions of the modern world.[58] Through the rhetorical device of *Kalyug*, Parsi plays such as *Naḷ Damayantī* sutured together myth, history, and the present, constructing a singular chronological frame within which anticolonial nationalist historiography first emerged: the tribulations of the couple Naḷ and Damayantī are indistinguishable from those of the present day. The couple's eventual victory over *Kalyug* exemplified the growing consensus, incubated in the vernacular public sphere, that the illusion of the ordeals of the present day would give way to a shared awakening towards a better reality. This idea was especially powerful in the late 1870s, at the time of the play's production, due to several historic occurrences: the 1877 proclamation of the queen as Kaiser-i-Hind (empress of India), allegations of 'native disloyalty', and a proliferation of public censorship, including the notorious 1876 Dramatic Performances Act and the 1878 Vernacular Press Act (known as the Black Act).[59]

Furthermore, in the chaste, devoted, self-sacrificing Damayantī, a female icon popularized in the vernacular theatre, lithographs, and vernacular prose, the play indexed another important development in the Hindu public sphere: the reinvention of mythical Vedic and Puranic women as symbols of willing suffering. This new 'Hindu' female iconography of voluntary affliction, which would become central to the nonviolent Satyagraha and the Swadeshi and Hindu militant nationalist movements,[60] is thrown into particular prominence in a subsequent play performed by the society, Kābrājī's *Nand Batrīsī*, based on a short poem by Shamalbhat.[61] The play focuses on Padmini, a virtuous married woman who resists the advances of the king even when doing so brings enormous hardship.

In the play, Nandsen, the king of Nandnagri, learns of Padmini, 'the sweetest lady of the time', a woman who is 'so richly endowed by nature that even the scent of her sweat attracted hordes of wasps and flies, *fig.* gallants young and gay'. Because Padmini is the wife of Nandsen's faithful dewan (minister), the king sends his dewan to a distant land to purchase war horses and then surreptitiously proceeds to Padmini's quarters. He finds the entrance bolted and the drowsy keeper uncooperative, although the gatekeeper submits when Nandsen gifts him a pair of his own earrings. Padmini, baffled and distressed at the king's arrival, arranges a rich supper to distract him from her beauty. She prepares several dishes of rice of multiple hues with milk from 'vary-coloured' cows. These dishes, though differing in their appearance, taste almost the same. She uses the rice to indirectly moralize that superficial appearance has no effect on innate nature. This speech brings Nandsen to repent his deeds; he gifts Padmini his ring and departs.

Eventually the dewan returns and sees his guard wearing the king's famous earrings. After questioning the keeper, the dewan learns of the king's visit: consumed with rage, he enters Padmini's chamber, becoming further incensed when he sees the king's ring on her finger. He sends Padmini to her parental home and, many days later, kills the king. Padmini returns after the dewan, on trial for killing the king, reveals the ostensible duplicity of the ruler and his wife. Padmini attempts to prove her virtue, but the dewan does not believe her tale. She is forced to prove her innocence by way of supernatural means and submits to killing herself, but her spouse wants no less a miracle than the revival of Nandsen to persuade him of her guiltlessness. In despair, she summons the ground to swallow her. The earth yawns, however, not to consume her, but to send forth a magician who gives Padmini an elixir to bring the dead king to life. Thus 'Padmini's truth and chastity and Nandsen's honour are vindicated'.[62]

The virtuous, loyal woman who weathers the travails inflicted on her, first by a lustful king seeking to rob her chastity and subsequently by her disbelieving husband, was thus seamlessly transplanted from Dādābhāi Paṭel's landmark 1871 *Sonānā Mulnī Khorśed* to *Nand Batrīsī*. However, while Khorśed had symbolic significance without clear local referent, Padmini was elaborately marked—in appearance, language, and diction—by unequivocally Hindu signs and symbols, from her ornate headpiece to her marigold wreaths evocative of daily votive offerings to the neighbourhood temple. Religion therefore lay at the core of the dramaturgy of the Hindu mythological play, even as it remained a peripheral consideration in the secular mythological, whose powerful transregional appeal functioned as a template for the development of more localized, explicitly anticolonial revivalist genres wherever it travelled. Subtle allusion was giving way to unambiguously legible imagery: Hindu women, altruistic, noble, and faithful, willing to subject themselves to hitherto barbaric but now celebrated customs such as *sati*, dominate Parsi plays of the 1880s, providing models for the archetypal freedom-fighter, facilitating forms of history-making and the imagining of the nation in her image, and, at the most basic level, reinventing the Indian moral economy in opposition to the dominant colonial order.

Crucially, this proto-nationalist recovery of tradition through the heroic, chaste, and ever tormented sacred female figure not only supplied symbols for the motherland or *Bhāratmātā* but also socialized women into their familial roles of pure, loyal, dedicated wives and all-sacrificing doting mothers, the new social signs of divine strength and national power. The Parsi theatre thus joined numerous other organized events—mass *pujas* (ceremonial worship), religious celebrations, and lectures—in disseminating the desired ideal of spiritual femininity as a passive form of resistance. According to Paṭel, Hindu women came in droves to see the society's plays, 'causing bedlam when the wails of their crying infants reverberated throughout the playhouse'.[63] Under Kābrājī's supervision, cots were arranged in the theatre's compound, watched over by the doorkeeper, so that pious mothers could partake in this new form of religious consumption. Paradoxically, therefore, while the society stimulated the growth of an entirely new demographic of spectatorship in Bombay's middle-class Hindu women, who thronged the playhouse to worship their gods and goddesses, it also reinforced existing patriarchies, as well as class and caste divisions that distinguished 'high' from 'low' women on the basis of access to particular kinds of public space. Theatrical depictions of self-sacrificing Hindu women not only functioned as a conceptual response to colonial rule but also derived their effectiveness and power from orientalist, racialized, ultimately patriarchal understandings of scripture, caste division, and Aryan supremacy.

Communalism and the Theatre

The new Parsi theatrical vision of an 'inherently limited and sovereign', fraternity of Hindu-Aryan brothers extending from Bombay to Benares,[64] facilitated both the consolidation of an imagined unified nation of hitherto stratified peoples as well as a violent vision of 'insiders' and 'outsiders', the majority and minorities. In contrast with the Vedic period—which, according to the dramaturgy of the Hindu mythological play, was the golden age, the classical period of Indian civilization—both colonial and Islamic periods were cast as dark medieval interludes that contributed to the irrevocable decline of Indian power. Consequently, while emphasizing the 'Hindu-ness' of the cultural nation as comprising a variety of perspectives—including generalized anticolonial politics, religious devotion, and racialized self-identification—the visual grammar of epic plays such as *Hariścandra* and *Naḷ Damayantī* concurrently circumscribed an essentialized Hinduism on the basis of what it was not. Tacit in the incipient ideological imagining of the motherland *Bhārat* on the Parsi stage was the contestation between legitimate and illegitimate Indianness and, relatedly, the exclusion of non-Aryans or 'lower-castes' and communities that did not 'emerge' from India (Muslims, Christians, and Parsis), who began to be viewed as fundamentally alien to the emerging nation.[65]

Unsurprisingly, then, Udayrām progressively questioned his reliance on Parsi companies for the staging of his Hindu religious plays.[66] In January 1878, he established the Gujrātī Nāṭak Maṇḍaḷī for the express benefit of Gujarati-speaking Hindus. Patrons of this company, which performed at the Original Victoria Theatre, were served pious refreshments such as milk by a Brahmin.[67] The company's first production was Udayrām's *Lalitā Dukh Darśak*, the first realist 'operā' of the Parsi stage, which portrayed the travails inflicted on a dutiful Hindu wife by her mother-in-law, her husband, his mistress, and friends; at one point in the narrative, these others attempt to kill her only to be killed themselves. The Parsi press criticized the company's Bania actors, who allegedly lacked the experience, talent, and self-assuredness of their Parsi peers.[68] Simultaneously, the Hindu press began to issue complaints about the *nāṭaknũ ceṭak* (theatre mania) among the 'gāṇḍī gujrāt nā āria putro' (the mad Aryan sons of Gujarat)—that is, Gujarati Hindus. The *Nureelam* warned of the dangers of following the Parsi theatre's example—prostitutes appearing onstage, bankruptcy, actors dying on tour—albeit to little heed.[69] Despite these fears and criticisms that they were not as good as the Parsis, Hindu troupes proliferated, among them the Ārya Gurjar Nāṭak Maṇḍalī, the Ārya Nāṭako Tkarsh Maṇḍaḷī, the Nītīdarśak Nāṭak Maṇḍaḷī, the Āryagurjar Harīścandra Nāṭak Maṇḍaḷī, and the Ārīya Saṅgītotejak Maṇḍaḷī. Observing Parsi techniques of stagecraft, management, and plot, these companies significantly shifted sociocultural prestige and power and consolidated inter-communal boundaries in public space, patronage, and forms of consumption—with ripple effects extending back to the Parsi theatre.[70] Thus, for example, on 27 October 1878, the Society for the Amelioration of the Drama advertised that its first- and second-class seats for its production of *Sītāharaṇ* would be reserved exclusively for Hindus.[71]

Notably, the chosen names of these new 'Hindu' companies foregrounded notions of Aryanism, in line with Dayānand Sarasvatī's declaration that Hindus should be termed as *Āryo* and Hindustan as *Āryavrut*. The conception of Aryanism, too, had thus been transformed, from an ill-defined region that denoted a pan-continental union of Europe and Asia to a specific, landlocked area, the 'original' home of an 'original' Aryan people.[72] This turn in Aryan theory is manifest in an 1878 production of Kābrājī's last Persian-themed play, *Faredun* (1874) by the Society for the Amelioration of the Drama. In contrast with its first production, the evil Zohak was now no longer an Arab (as legend would have it) but rather a Punjabi or Kashmiri Hindu (as the orientalist 'scholarship' of George Rawlinson, James Fergusson, and Michael Laird supposedly found).[73] Likewise the *Jāme* in its description of the play went to great lengths to describe correspondences between the Persian Jamśed and his Hindu equivalent Yama, Faredun and the Vedic 'Thretno'.[74] In the wake of a rising tide of Hindu nationalist rhetoric, Parsis' claims to a primordial relation with the Hindus (and to being a part of the Hindu nation) were thus bolstered by the growing fields of 'comparative philology', 'comparative sphagiology', and 'comparative mythology'.[75] Consequently, whereas previously the booming field of orientalism was used to link a long-lost Persian past to European antiquity, spatial links and loyalties had now reversed, and the Hindu Aryan had become the common denominator of cultural, social, and racial exchange. After this brief Iranian turn, the society reverted to its Hindu mythological repertoire with *Sītāharaṇ*, another female-centric play. So too did *Sītāharaṇ*, the first Gujarati play from the *Ramayana* (adapted by Narmadāśaṅkar Lālśankar and modified for the stage by Kābrājī), enjoy great success: it offered not only 'a bird's-eye view of the epic' but also, in the form of Sītā, a key visual pivot for the gendering of Hindu nationalism.[76]

However, the society not only set the stage for the progressive popularization of Hindu epic plays and the shifting of cultural and ethnic allegiance but also fomented tensions between religious communities. Hindu religious consumption—the aesthetic currency of a novel, belligerent form of national archiving—stimulated not only inter-religious competition over the proprietorship of language, rituals, and modes of affiliation but also sweeping unrest. This turmoil came to the fore after the production of *Hariścandra* with the 1874 Parsi–Muslim riots and subsequent interfaith squabbles surrounding the Victoria, as discussed in Chapter 5. However, it was not only Muslims that the Parsis conflicted with. In 1883, the Parsi press declared:

> We used to have a number of plays such as *Ghareṇā Pehrāvvānā Gerfāydā*, *Sāvakśānā Lagan*, *Pantujīnī Nīśāḷ*, *Dhanjī Garak*, and *Nīmhakīm kaṭlehān* ... that successfully portrayed through humour lessons regarding our domestic affairs. In those days the Parsi theatre comprised Parsi actors alone, and its plays were expedient to Parsi matters. The speeches of Śīrīn and Bacū, Śāvakśśāh and Kāvlā, were familiar tools for communal reform. The Parsi theatre should not lose those edifying characters and representations. ... Those troupes that have foregone these domestic subjects for tales of gods and godesses and fairies and monsters as these are popular amongst veśyo Hīndu prajā [Vaishya Hindu public] and therefore yield greater profits should be strongly castigated. The Hindus themselves are sick of this theatrical madness for gods and goddesses.[77]

The Parsi public sphere of the 1880s was thus intensely equivocal in its artistic, ideological, and communal commitments, demonstrating both the creation, dissemination, and advocacy of a 'Hindu' ethnonationalism and a resentment of 'Hindu' culture and publics. This fissured discourse parallels the emergence of majoritarian and minoritarian group sentiment, the conflicting allegiance of Parsis to (on the one hand) the developing project of nationhood and (on the other) attempts to preserve collective identity against what was perceived as the growing menace of a Hindu monocracy. Moreover, it evinces the multiply segmented character of the colonial public sphere, which lacked a common language of debate as it was fashioned to an extent by the colonial state's methods of divide and rule. Critically, this same 1883 article also noted that Parsis were, like Hindus, 'sick of this theatrical madness for gods and goddesses', indicating the dawning age of the social drama (as was heralded in Kābrājī's 1874 *Śurī Vace Śopārī*).

The Social Drama

Even as the Parsi theatre inverted the dominant Victorian vision of India as a damsel in distress to be rescued by the valorous, masculine Englishman through its depiction of fearless Hindu-Aryan women—the symbol of the cultural glory of a classical Vedic age—plays policed the prescriptive assumptions of the gendering of the colonial project in other, more conspicuous ways. Writing of 1880s Bengali theatre, Sarkar notes how the model of voluntary hardship experienced by Hindu mythological women subsequently transformed so that women's roles went beyond self-sacrificing fortitude to include the possibility of intervention and agency while remaining submissive.[78] In a new genre of plays set in the contemporary period, women protected or re-established the authority of custom and tradition, to which they were consistently subservient, by restoring their wayward companions to the path of righteousness. This dramaturgical transition in the Bengali theatre was anticipated in the Parsi theatre in the 1870s in social plays such as *Vināś kāḷe Viprīt Budhī* (*To Lose One's Head during Turbulent Times*).[79] Performed by the Society for the Amelioration of the Drama at the Esplanade Theatre in 1879, the play, adapted by Kābrājī from an English source, portrayed the travails faced by the wife of a gambler.[80] *Jugār* (gambling) was by then a key concern in print media, which used the term to denote a variety of illicit 'modern' evils, from 'pin money' to billiard competitions and share speculation.[81]

> These clubs are a new sign of deterioration. ... Our youth are unemployed *harāmkhors* [cheats] who merely seek money to support their philandering ways. ... It is a sign of our impending destruction that our youth wish to obtain a lump sum in one stroke instead of untiringly working and saving the fruit of their labours.[82]

According to the *Yajdā̃ Parast*, the play *Vināś kāḷe Viprīt Budhī* offered 'two important moral lessons regarding our present day: the need to destroy the evil practice of gambling and that the true *dharma* of a wife is to steadfastly follow her husband, in good or bad times'.[83] The play accordingly depicted the moral crisis of the unruly husband, who, in contrast with the virtuous Hariścandra, Rām, and Lavkuś of the Hindu mythological, was a philanderer afflicted by imported, modern vices, in need of guidance towards the right *dhārmik* path.

This theme was echoed not only in novels such as *Nīrdoś Juliā ane teno Vehmī Bharthār* (*Innocent Julia and her Suspicious Husband*) but also in scores of other plays such as Nāhānābhāi Rāṇīnā's acclaimed *Kāḷā̃ Meṇḍhā̃ athvā Sansār Sukhnā Śatru* (*Black Sheep or Social Pests*), performed by the Alfred Nāṭak Maṇḍalī in 1885 (see Chapter 8).[84] As the *Times of India* wrote,

> The drama is of a highly didactic and moral character. It lays bare without fear or favour some of the social evils under the cloak of civilization [that] have been gradually gaining ground among the native communities. … Although it has only been placed on the stage a short time, the drama has caused a sensation in the native community, and large numbers flock to witness the performance of the piece by actors who are not quite unknown to them. It may be fairly said that few dramas that have been put on the stage by natives are more spirit-stirring and laughter-inducing than 'Black Sheep or Social Pests'.[85]

As with the plot of such plays as *Sonānā Mulnī Khorśed*, *Nand Batrīsī*, and *Vināś Kāḷe Viprīt Budhī*, in this play the two black sheep—the 'civilized', married Sapal and Mehlī—have their eyes set on Śīrīn, the wife of their friend Solī. Eventually, the humble yet witty Śīrīn, through a convoluted game of hide and seek, exposes their wicked intentions to their wives.[86]

Rāṇīnā's next social drama, *Akarmī Varnī Sakarmī Bairī* (*Model Wife of a Wicked Husband*), which premiered in 1885, similarly portrayed an evil husband's attempts to extract money and jewellery from his noble wife.[87] Jehangeer Jogha, the play's purported hero, is a 'depraved and a dissipated character'. As he needs money for his gambling habit, he decides to marry a rich girl who comes with Rs 5,000 as dowry. Jehangeer's accomplice, a villainous priest, tricks the bride's father into believing that Jehangeer is a desirable husband and that the dowry must be paid before the marriage. The father reluctantly hands over the money, but the priest, who was assured substantial compensation if he could extort more money, announces that the groom requires a second sizeable sum before marriage. The bride's family, its worst fears realized, refuses this ultimatum. Although Jehangeer relents his call for a second sum and weds the girl, the marriage is loveless. The girl, who is of high moral standing, attempts to help her husband relinquish his vices, but to no avail. He squanders his dowry and eventually becomes a pauper dwelling in the streets. The loyal wife does not yet lose hope. Having inherited a sizeable fortune from her father after his death, she persuades her husband's closest friends to rescue him from his life of wickedness. 'The young reprobate is once more restored to the bosom of his loving wife, and like a true penitent, having had the worst experiences of life, proves to be a kind and loving husband'.[88]

The metonymic implications of the motif of the traditional wife, the saviour of the wayward, Anglicized, cash-strapped husband that dominates this new crop of plays, novels, newspaper articles, and paintings are palpable. Although no direct mention is made of colonial rule, the jingoistic subtext of such plays—that foreign creature comforts and forms of amusement had emasculated the indigenous male body—expressed the ideological injury suffered by Indians through capitulation to the dictates of colonial capital.[89] The villain is the educated, westernized colonized man, who is to be liberated through the healing spirit of a domestic, feminine, metaphysical power, a storehouse of deep-seated, subconscious inner strength. The social play, like its Hindu mythological counterpart, thus emphasized the figure of woman as the vessel of a core set of redeeming 'Indian', 'Hindu', or 'Parsi' values, even as the rhetorical device of *Kalyug* (Age of Downfall) was relocated from a hoary Hindu antiquity to the present day.[90] The home thus became an index of historical development, shaping initially the discourse of colonial 'civilization and progress' (through the social reformist women's question), but also, subsequently and conversely, the discourse of a superior, indigenous, communalist or nationalist revivalism.

Consequently, in outlining a developing genealogy of female characters in the Parsi theatre and the configurations of power that shape these representations, we find a shift from the 1860s to the 1880s. In the earlier era, Parsi reformists depicted the necessity of reforming Parsi women, beliefs, and law. In contrast, two decades later, melodramatic representations of unspoiled, conservative, ritual-abiding women (symbols for indigenous moral superiority and power) evince widespread ideological insurrection. In 1871, Khorśed of *Sonānā Mulnī Khorśed* had neither the agency nor the discursive capacity to speak up against her many lustful suitors, running from palace to forest to town in order to safeguard her chastity. In 1883, however, the erstwhile subaltern figures of Lalitā and Padmini, Julia and Śīrīn began to challenge the malignant male 'of the material world',[91] flying to arms against the ideological rudiments of a foreign power through self-sacrifice—a mnemotechnic exercise in voluntary suffering to prepare for anticolonial struggle and nationhood. From communal affliction to national or communal glory, women thus incarnated the conceptual claims and conflicting concerns of a heaving social order that was on the verge of metamorphosis, even as their own voices in popular discourse were completely elided. Implicitly, through an anticapitalist, anticolonialist nativism, the social drama invoked the reciprocal and symbiotic polarities of private, traditional, natural woman and public, modern, artificial man. In so doing, it consolidated an image of redemptive femininity as conventionally subordinate yet morally superior, a timeless, quasi-divine norm that transcended historical development and recovered destroyed virility for the community.

The Parsi Girl of the Period

Significantly, Parsi themed plays such as *Akarmī Varnī Sakarmī Bairī* exemplify the segmentation of the colonial theatrical public as well as the division of the hitherto composite Parsi theatrical repertoire along communal lines. The moral universe and modes of religious consumption of the Hindu mythological play had mobilized feelings of alienation, isolation, and uncertainty among non-Hindu 'minority' communities, who in turn developed vernacular genres such as the Parsi social drama as a defence against what was coming to be perceived as a Hindu 'majoritarian' response to colonial rule. By articulating ethnicized forms of address, familiar cultural references, and local idiom that was relatively illegible to 'outsiders', the social drama engendered historically unprecedented feelings of social intimacy, communal solidarity, and self-reflexivity, a form of kin fetishism.[92] This evolution of the Parsi social drama as an epistemic counterpoint to Hindu nationalism is particularly pronounced in the Society's production of Kābrājī's landmark Gujarati adaptation of the *School for Scandal*, *Nindākhānũ*. First performed on 31 December 1884, the play was immediately a hit.[93] While the *Kaysare Hinda* tellingly described the melodrama as a striking novelty for theatregoers whose 'eyes were strained from persistently watching Hindu subjects', and as something 'much more beneficial to the public than the usual Parsi theatre repertoire of monsters and demons', it criticized the inclusion of Hindu Gujarati terms (such as *trut* and *kā̃*) in a Parsi domestic play, vocabulary that rendered it 'half Hindu and half Parsi'.[94] The Parsi press had thus begun not only to develop more exacting standards for theatrical realism but also to patrol the boundaries between 'Hindu' and 'Parsi' culture.

While the play was praised by Hindu and Parsi luminaries such as Nānābhāi Harīdās, Khānbāhdur Mancerjī Kāvasjī Marajbān, Rāvbāhdur Vāman Ābājī Modak, Dāmodhardās Tāpīdās Vrajdās, Pestanjī Vāḍīyā, and Kharśedjī Māṇekjī Śeṭhnā as an attempt to ameliorate the deteriorating condition of Parsi society,[95] the playwright Rāṇīnā averred,

> To call this ... sansārī nāṭak [domestic play] a 'sansār darpaṇ' [domestic portrayal] reveals its aims as well as its qualities. ... The Parsis may believe they have reason to be gratified by the condition of their social state, we on the other hand deem that they have no grounds to be proud, that there is a rot growing in the community's midst. One result of this is the rise of gossip and *nindā* [slander].[96]

Press reportage indicates that the production's marked emphasis on slander stemmed from 'a series of malignant libels' by Muncherjee Cowasjee Lungra (alias Munsookh), editor of the *Satya Mitra*, who in 1882 denounced Kābrājī's advocacy of reforms:

> What should be the method of extorting money? (1) To act the jester and pretender in order to lure the hearts of simple or credulous people is a method to extort money. (2). To establish 'clubs' or societies and exhibit women, that is a way to extort money. (3). To cause Parsee females to leave off their white head-bands and to make them put on Jewish females' gold or silver embroidered brocade skull-caps and Portuguese females' *polkas* and English ladies' dresses, and to make them go from street to street, to make them exhibit their faces at the windows of houses, is a way to get money. (4). To get up theatrical performances and dancing and singing and other kinds of parties, and to get up gatherings of males and females, is a way to make money. (5). A small drum (*tablo*) in the hands of the master, a three-stringed guitar (*tamboro*) in the hands of the father, and the gestures of the hands and swaying motions of the bodies of the daughters and female friends ... by getting together such gatherings money can be extorted in a refined manner.[97]

The article referred to such reforms as mixed gatherings, European clothing, the disposal of the *mā̃thũbānũ* (ladies' calico headband), and public music recitals such as those of the Gāyan Utejak Maṇḍalī's (Society for the Amelioration of Music's) concerts, where the playwright sang in the company of his children.[98] However, when Munsookh subsequently alluded to an *agharṇī* (ceremony performed in the seventh month of pregnancy for the newborn's prosperity) that was purportedly performed for Kābrājī's not-yet-married eldest daughter, the only Parsi woman who had entirely divested herself of her *mā̃thũbānũ*,[99] Kābrājī was unable to satisfy his appetite for revenge merely through the arm of the law.[100] *Nindākhānũ*, according to the playwright, was an ethical treatise against the scourge of gossip promoted by miscreants such as Munsookh.

Yet a cursory reading of the play indicates that slander was merely a rhetorical pivot to expound on a more complex cultural development vexing communities across the subcontinent. Munsookh's disparagement of Portuguese polkas and English dresses pre-empted a controversy known as the 'Parsee Girl of the Period', which rocked Bombay's public sphere during *Nindākhānū*'s production. An 1884 letter on the subject by Nasarvānjī Sohrābjī Jīnvālā, which circulated extensively both nationally and internationally, illuminates the gravity of the terms of the debate:

> She is leaving the manners, the traditions, the costumes of her ancestors behind her. She is advancing rapidly. She can already sue for breach of promise and divorce. But ... she is still only a parody upon her English sister. It is 'Her ambition to look and act every bit an English lady'. She dresses in a semi-English fashion, in English shoes and stockings and a waistcoat. ... She plays a little music, talks a little English, spells a little out of a trashy fifth-rate English novel, can draw a little, knit a little, and do a little embroidery. In a word, she can do a little of many things, and nothing more. She drives down to the bander and the bandstand, and looks, or thinks she looks, as Anglicised as possible. 'Her first care is her dress and face; her next, gaieties, pleasures, and agreeable friends.' Ostentatious out of doors, she is extravagant within, and contrives to revolutionise domestic life. The morning cup of tea has developed into coffee cups, chocolate, and cocoa, with creams, jams, and jellies. ... It was agreed that in England people should not marry on less than £300 a year. Here the Parsee fine lady says, 'Can't possibly marry, you know, on less than £20 a month.' The men consequently remain single, and the 'selfishness of bachelors, as bearing on the marriage question, has become the chief topic of discussion among the Parsees of late'.[101]

Nindākhānū involuntarily condemned the spoilt, conceited Parsi girl of the period, someone who was wrought in the same mould as the wayward, gambling men 'of the material world'.[102] Audiences of all religious, ethnic, and class denominations were already acquainted with the dramaturgical design behind Kābrājī's 'Jarbāi Juhāk' or 'Jarī Juhāk' (a play on Zohak), 'the Parsee "Lady Teazle,"' who screeched at her wealthy, much older husband (who, in turn, would soon repent of his choice for a spouse):

Beju: (the clock strikes 2 a.m.) Ohho it is two a.m. let me see if I can get some sleep. (Bejubāvā attempts to enter his bedroom when Jar arrives, bumping into Beju.)

Jar: Oh! What are you doing Bejanji? Can't you see where you are going? Did you bump into me intentionally? Is this how you express your anger?

Beju: Oh bother … I happened to come here of my own accord, I changed my clothes … I was thinking of you, sleepily … at that very moment you came in from the back door and bumped into me and yet it's my fault. Did you come just now?

Jar (looking at her watch): What is the time? Only 2 a.m.? It's still early. Usually guests stay until 4 a.m. at weddings these days and we were thrown out merely at 2.

Beju: arrrrrrrrrrr what is this mistake? Go back, go back. Don't miss out on the fun […]

Jar: You're swearing at me […]

Beju: Of course, I'm telling you Jarī, I'm not going to bear your torment.

Jar: And I am telling you that I am not going to bear you tormenting me.

Beju: If you want to, bear it, if you don't want to, don't.

Jar: I am going to behave the way I want … I am not your servant but your wife and I've been brought up in a village but I enjoy the same rights as any woman of the city.

Beju: Rights? Heh rights? So the husband doesn't have rights anymore does he?

Jar: Husband's rights? What is that? There is a husband's love, his money, house and carriage, what are husband's rights? If you wanted rights why did you get married to me? If you wanted rights over me then you should have bought me … you are old enough to do that.

Beju: Really, truly. I am a donkey, I am a donkey. At an old age I lost my senses. But listen Jarī you can make me unhappy with your bickering but you won't make me bankrupt with your spending.

Jar: What do you mean? What is this? I can't eat and spend? I don't spend more than others do. […]

Beju: Enough, enough woman stop your squabbling. Recall your previous village life … Do you remember your patchwork sari and poor blouse … the ones that you even wore at weddings? Do you remember how you would fold your sari to put cow dung on the floor, do you remember that? And when you would go out you would wear those village shoes, do you remember that? When you had to go for weddings from one village to another you had to sit in a bullock cart and suffer the bumpy ride, do you remember that?

Jar: Yes, yes I remember everything yet if God has blessed me why shouldn't I eat and spend? Ahha I hope weddings continue all year long and that I can wear embroidered clothes all year long, how nice that would be.

Beju: Now you need a two horse fenton to return home, you wander around until midnight, you want a foreign tailor sitting at home day in and day out, now you want striped and embroidered blouses and petticoats, you want pointed boots and silk stockings.

Jar: But I have been reformed so I need to do all this.[103]

This last statement is especially suggestive. If, in 1858, Kābrājī had been quick to discount the *Jāme Jamśed*'s fears that the reform movement was advancing too quickly, that Parsi women were not adequately equipped to enter into the public eye, and that Parsi men did not possess the courage required for defending their women against calumny, then the revered playwright now, consciously or unconsciously evinced a change of heart.[104] As a reviewer in the *Kaysare Hinda* noted:

> Reform has been taken to an extreme. Take for example the portrayal by the witty writer of *Bejan Manījeh* [Kābrājī] of the characters … 'Nājā̃māy Naśkorā̃' and 'Jarī Juāk' in contrast with the village damsel in his *Nindākhānũ*. The latter had poor clothes, she ate dry bread, curd and milk after a hard day's work, she helped support her family, she had no knowledge of wickedness and tantrums, and was fulfilled with working all day. On the other hand Jarī Juhāk is a reformed woman of boots and stockings, she wears Chinese silk, carries a fan in the afternoon and an umbrella in the evening, wears diamonds and pearls in her ears and around her neck, partakes in high society, socializes at the bandstand or at the Victoria Gardens with her peers and male friends and enjoys icecream and pastries … The purported motive of *Nindākhānũ* was to condemn slander but instead its Jarī Juhāk is an accurate portrayal of today's reformed Parsi women.[105]

The editor of the *Rāst*, hitherto the biggest advocate of unmitigated female reform, had, in his Gujarati adaptation of *The School for Scandal*, inadvertently verbalized the cultural war between 'the Parsee Girl of the Present and [that of] the Past'—or *Junī Bāi Vīrudh Navī Bāi* (*The Old Woman against the New Woman*).

This phenomenon of the new woman versus the old woman bore more than a passing resemblance to musings, debates, and disputes in novels, editorial columns, treatises, household manuals, and not least melodramas and farces across South Asia.[106] English-educated women, who two decades prior were necessary to 'prevent the machinations of the evil-disposed',[107] were now markers of the self-absorption, nihilism, and spiritual estrangement of colonial modernity. Their socializing in public, expensive habits, and berating of men were perceived as a challenge to conventional ideals of masculinity and femininity and to the order and foundation of society itself. Samita Sen notes that the contrast between the 'new', educated yet immoral woman of the city (who flouted domestic duties) and the ideal 'past' housewife from the village (who upheld familial responsibility and transmitted religious knowledge) articulated an epistemological dilemma in late nineteenth-century India of the perception of the colonial experience.[108] The villain of the plot had transmogrified from the westernized scoundrel to the new urban Indian woman, a 'parody upon her English sister', who, along with the vulgar, lower-class woman of the street, was constructed in contradistinction to the pure, spiritual, loyal, nurturing pastoral woman, the metonym of the community and/or nation. The reformed Jarī Juhāk, who had abandoned her simple sari and village shoes for embroidered blouses and petticoats, was an allegory, scrupulously cross-referenced across the subcontinent, of the abhorrent, unnatural influence of market over domestic and communitarian values. The insubordinate and disorderly modern woman, a product of industrialism, capitalism, and bourgeois thought, not only was parasitic, depraved, and monstrous—responsible for the crisis of civilization due to her incongruous disconnect from nature—but also, according to Sarkar, exemplified a commodification linked to the theme of oppressive, time-bound colonial employment.[109] The *junī* (old) 'traditional' woman and the *navī* (new) 'modern' woman were passive signs of oppositional concepts: self-sacrificing indigeneity and the shackles of foreign colonial rule.

The Parsi social drama thus depicted the traditional woman as the sign of the immutable ahistorical nature of human existence and the modern woman as her deviant other, even as the home functioned as a synecdoche of the ideological fractures of colonial modernity. The domestic sphere was not so much a theatrical setting as an archive, a foundation of history, as Antoinette M. Burton explains.[110] India's economic drain through colonialism is symbolically recorded, schematized, and documented in plays such as *Nindākhānũ* that present a 'cultural' drain from the authentic, rustic, traditional domestic sphere to urban hotbeds of moral ruin, 'citadel[s] of foreign power ... where family morality is pulled out of joint, wives lord it over hapless mothers-in-law, and prostitutes are given priority over wives and the cash nexus rules over all'.[111] A shared dramaturgical structure of loss thus binds the theatrical depiction of private moral impairment and the metatheatrical movement of anti-colonial political struggle, together forcing closure around the symbol of womanhood as a register of historical truth. It was, as the *Rāst* declaimed, 'the fashion with some people to say that the nett result of English education in India is that the native has lost whatever religion or morality he once had, and that the Government have given him nothing to replace the loss'.[112]

Education—the cause for this loss—became (as Sen notes) fundamental once again to the 'women's question'.[113] Both print and performance media increasingly contended that skills in literature, music, and the arts were inferior to the simple, honest knowledge of housekeeping, religious ritual, and familial devotion, the 'natural' responsibilities of women that pre-empted societal breakdown.[114] Despite Kābrājī's pronouncements to the contrary,[115] female education thus began to be redirected to the home and the kitchen, the natural or biological realm, even as the reformist movement increasingly converged with that of the sceptical, antimodern orthodoxy.[116] The modest woman and humble peasant, the future flagbearers of the communal and national polity, embodied 'true', inborn wisdom and freedom in contradistinction to metropolitan higher education, which bred bourgeois, materialist individualists servile to the colonial market economy. The normative image of traditional feminity thus articulated ideals of male superiority and virility as well as anti-imperial discourse. Yet the Parsi social drama in the quaint language of Parsi Gujarati—now a dialect of standardized Sanskritized Gujarati—was not uniformly critical of colonial rule and its attendant sociocultural order. Even as the Parsi social drama evoked thick material feelings of anti-imperialism through a valorization of rural life and domesticity, as a fundamentally minoritarian discourse and as a vernacular of the dominant Hindu repertoire of the stage, it began to effect feelings of communal isolation and (as the final chapter delineates) demographic imperilment and racial degeneration.

Notes

1. 'Distress Among Parsees', *RG*, 13 September 1874, 608–9; 'The Wonders of King Cotton', *RG*, 15 November 1874, 751; and 'Tāḍī uparnā kar sāme arjī karvā malelī sabhā', *RG*, 7 January 1875, 42.
2. 'The Shettias', *RG*, 28 May 1876, 365; 'Education and Occupations', *RG*, 15 April 1883, 281–82; 'Parsee Master Builders–A Retrospect of 150 Years', *RG*, 15 April 1883, 282–83; 'Inherited Callings', *RG*, 22 April 1883, 301–2; 'Public Services of Past Parsee Master-Builders', *RG*, 22 April 1883, 302; and untitled, *RG*, 6 May 1888, 526.
3. 'The Parsees', *RG*, 18 June 1876, 419–20.
4. 'Ek javān pārsīno āpghāt', *RG*, 6 August 1876, 534; 'Increase of Suicide among the Parsees', *KIH*, 25 June 1882, 435; 'Ek Kholāso', *RG*, 23 July 1882, 518; 'Pārsīoe Bāhergām̃ dhandho karvā bābe. kaysare hindnā adhīpatī jog', *KIH*, 27 August 1882, 615; 'Further Thoughts About Parsee Emigration', *KIH*, 3 September 1882, 628; and 'Suicide Among Parsees', *RG*, 25 June 1882, 485–86.
5. 'Parsi Infidelity', *RG*, 5 February 1882, 83–84.
6. 'The Parsees', *RG*, 18 June 1876, 419–20; 'Extravagance Among Parsee Females', *RG*, 14 May 1882, 333–34; 'Extravagance among Parsees', *RG*, 21 May 1882, 357–58; and 'Pārsīomā̃ Lakhluṭpaṇū', *KIH*, 30 September 1883, 772–73.
7. 'Pecuniary Distress among Parsees', *RG*, 27 September 1874, 641–43; 'An Old Adage Curiously Verified', *RG*, 9 April 1876, 247; 'Gāyan ūtejak Maṇḍalīno femīlīone māṭe karelo jalso', *RG*, 23 April 1876, 283–84; 'Gāyan Ūtejak Maṇḍaḷī', *RG*, 30 April 1876, 301–2; 'A Distinction without a Difference', *RG*, 14 May 1876, 335; 'Thanks to Our Detractors', *RG*, 21 May 1876, 349; and 'An Old Adage Curiously Verified', *RG*, 9 April 1876, 247. For calls to reform the reformers, see: 'Reform the Reformers', *RG*, 20 December 1874, 832; 'Reform Your Reformers', *RG*, 22 August 1875, 564; 'Reform Your Reformers', *RG*, 29 August 1875, 583; and 'Resuscitation of the Parsee Revivalists', *RG*, 12 September 1875, 612.
8. Ek Deśhītkārī, 'Carcā Patro', *KIH*, 26 March 1882, 210; 'New Evil amongst the Parsees', *KIH*, 16 April 1882, 255–56. For the Hindu critique of Parsi reforms, see Bhā̃ṇābhaṭ, 'Śū Pārsīo Sudhrī Gayā?', *RG*, 7 November 1886, 1225.
9. 'The Parsees', *RG*, 4 June 1876, 384–85.
10. See 'Fashions in Dress—An Explanation', *RG*, 30 September 1883, 782–83; 'Ancestral Dress of the Parsees', *RG*, 7 October 1883, 802; 'Parsi Fashions', *RG*, 23 November 1890, 1316–17; 'The Follies and Frolics of Fashions', *RG*, 30 November 1890, 1345; and 'Parsee Anglo-cism', *KIH*, 8 April 1883, 248.

11. 'Boots and Stockings from a Hindu Point of View', *RG*, 18 January 1880, 36–37; and 'Indian Prejudices against Boots and Stockings', *RG*, 25 January 1880, 52.
12. 'Thirty Years Ago', *RG*, 20 November 1881, 817–18; 'The Parsees, The Shettias and the Missionaries', *RG*, 11 December 1881, 871–72; 'Clubdom—Public Opinion', *RG*, 14 August 1881, 556; 'How to Destroy Ourselves', *RG*, 28 March 1880, 201; 'Parsi Full Dress', *RG*, 14 March 1880, 167; and 'The Dress Question in India', *RG*, 23 May 1886, 548–49.
13. 'Free Trade for Free Countries', *RG*, 25 July 1875, 502; 'Why Did Sir Dinker Rao Give Up the Use of the English Language', *RG*, 25 July 1875, 502; 'A Defense of the Native Press', *RG*, 25 July 1875, 502–3; 'Parsee Guzrati', *RG*, 26 September 1875, 646; and 'Respectable Native Theatricals', *RG*, 17 October 1875, 696.
14. Untitled, *RG*, 27 September 1874, 651; untitled, *RG*, 4 October 1874, 666; untitled, *RG*, 11 October 1874, 683; untitled, *TOI*, 7 October 1874, 1; and untitled, *TOI*, 3 October 1874, 1. The Case couple initially became renowned during their Australian tours in the 1860s and 1870s.
15. Untitled, *Illustrated London News*, 27 February 1864, 207.
16. 'Gopīcand', *RG*, 18 October 1874, 695.
17. Tracy C. Davis, *Actresses as Working Women: Their Social Identity in Victorian Culture* (London and New York: Routledge, 2002), xv.
18. 'Abuse of the Stage', *RG*, 17 October 1875, 696; 'Behind the Scenes in Bombay', *RG*, 17 October 1875, 697–98; 'Behind the Scenes in Bombay', *RG*, 24 October 1874, 715–16; and 'Mī. Kuvarjī Sohorābjī Nājar', *RG*, 21 November 1875, 790–91.
19. 'Revival of the Parsee Drama', *TOI*, 26 March 1875, 3; and 'The Guzrati Drama', *TOI*, 14 March 1875, 177.
20. 'The Guzrati Drama', *RG*, 14 March 1875, 177; and untitled, *RG*, 11 April 1875, 269.
21. 'Revival of the Parsee Drama', *TOI*, 26 March 1875, 3; and 'The Guzrati Drama', *TOI*, 14 March 1875, 177.
22. The Guzrati Drama', *RG*, 14 March 1875, 177; untitled, *RG*, 11 April 1875, 269; and Dhanjībhāi Na Paṭel, *PNTT* (Bombay: 'Kaysare-Hind' Paper Printing Press, 1931), 161. Food and refreshments were usually provided by the Grant Road Hotel, which still exists today: untitled, *RG*, 13 February 1876, 116.
23. Stephen Meredyth Edwardes, *The Gazetteer of Bombay City and Island* (Bombay: Times Press, 1909), 2:182; 'Mill Mania at Bombay', *KIH*, 4 May 1884, 368; and 'Chawls for Workmen in the Mills', *KIH*, 4 May 1884, 369.
24. 'Mill Mania at Bombay', *KIH*, 4 May 1884, 368; and 'Chawls for Workmen in the Mills', *KIH*, 4 May 1884, 369.

25. See also Khambātā's descriptions of how Bombay's commissioner Frank Souter caught Indian policemen taking bribes in return for controlling audiences in the pit: Jahāṅgīr Pestanjī Khambātā, *NA* (Bombay, 1913), 79–82.
26. True Lovers of the Drama, 'The Natuck Ootejuk Mundlee', *TOI*, 3 April 1875, 2. This regulation was subsequently copied by other Parsi theatre troupes such as the Victoria, which prohibited children under the age of ten in the pit: untitled, *RG*, 24 November 1878, 807.
27. Untitled, *RG*, 14 March 1875, 198; and untitled, *RG*, 21 March 1875, 221.
28. 'Revival of the Parsee Drama', *TOI*, 26 March 1875, 3. For the Gujarati description of Centlivre's play, see 'Women Vindicated by Women', *RG*, 25 May 1884, 481.
29. True Lovers of the Drama, 'The Natuck Ootejuk Mundlee', *TOI*, 3 April 1875, 2.
30. Theatrical realism, a trend first inaugurated by Raṇchoḍbhāi Udayrām's *Lalītā Dukh Darśak* in 1866, thus gained a further foothold in Bombay's theatres through this first Parsi social play. For a description of *Lalītā Dukh Darśak*, see Hemendra Nath Das Gupta, *The Indian Stage*, vol. 3 (Calcutta: Metropolitan Printing, 1944), 178.
31. 'Light Comedies', *RG*, 4 April 1875, 242.
32. Kekhuśro Navrojjī Kābrājī, *Suḍī Vace Sopārī. Athvā Be Vacnī Kharī Paṇ Bevacnī Nahī* (Bombay: Nha. Rū. Rāṇīnā's Union Press, 1884), preface.
33. Kābrājī, *Suḍī Vace Sopārī*, 37.
34. Kābrājī, *Suḍī Vace Sopārī*, 85.
35. 'Harīścandra Nāṭak', *RG*, 31 October 1875, 734; and untitled, *RG*, 31 October 1875, 739. The choice of location at the Framjee Cowasjee Institute may have been primarily due to the fact that Parsi theatre managers were angered by Kābrājī's attacks in the press: Paṭel, *PNTT*, 288. The institute, however, was not the best place for theatrical representations, as indicated by the *Times of India*: 'Considering the difficulties under which the stage arrangements had to be made at the south end of the hall, it was not to be wondered at that these were not quite so effective and satisfactory as could be wished.' Untitled, *TOI*, 6 November 1875, 3.
36. 'Gujrātī Nāṭakonī Tapāś', *RG*, 21 April 1872, 248–49.
37. Untitled, *RG*, 24 October 1875, 723. Udayrām was consistently praised by the *Rāst*: 'Mr. Runchordbhai's New Play', *RG*, 9 July 1876, 465–66.
38. 'Parsee Guzrati', *RG*, 14 November 1875, 766; and Paṭel, *PNTT*, 290.
39. 'A Hundred Years Ago: "Harischandra" at the Framjee Cowasjee Institute', *TOI*, 3 November 1975, 8.
40. '"Harishchandra" at the F. C. Institute', *RG*, 2 January 1876, 5; Paṭel, *PNTT*, 290; and untitled, *TOI*, 22 January 1876, 3. See also Rashna

Darius Nicholson, 'What's in a Name? The Performance of Language in the Invention of Colonial and Postcolonial South Asian Theatre History', in *The Methuen Drama Handbook of Theatre History and Historiography*, eds. Claire Cochrane and Jo Robinson (London: Bloomsbury, 2019), 204.

41. Untitled, *TOI*, 12 April 1881, 3.
42. Rā. Rā. Raṇchoḍbhāi Ūdayrām and Kābrājī, Kekhuśro Navrojjī, *Hariścandra Nāṭak* (Bombay: Daftar Āśkārā Press, 1876), 2.
43. See T. Sarkar, *Hindu Wife, Hindu Nation*, 198, 253, for a discussion of how this development transpired in Bengal.
44. Tracy C. Davis, 'What Are Fairies For?', in *The Performing Century*, eds. Tracy Davis and Peter Holland (London: Palgrave Macmillan, 2007), 41.
45. Partha Chatterjee, 'The Nationalist Resolution of the Women's Question', in *Empire and Nation: Selected Essays* (New York: Columbia University Press, 2010), 121–22.
46. Dipesh Chakrabarty, 'Nation and Imagination', *Studies in History* 15, no. 2 (1999): 200–1. For an analysis of *darshan* in the Parsi theatre, see Kathryn Hansen, 'Ritual Enactments in a Hindi "Mythological" Betab's Mahabharat in Parsi Theatre', *Economic and Political Weekly* 41, no. 48 (2006): 4985–91; and see also Diana L. Eck, *Darsan: Seeing the Divine Light in India* (Chambersburg, PA: Anima Books, 1981). For an analysis of perspectival illusion in the Parsi theatre see Anuradha Kapur, 'Impersonation, Narration, Desire, and the Parsi Theatre', in *India's Literary History: Essays in the Nineteenth Century*, eds. Stuart Blackburn and Vasudha Dalmia (Delhi: Permanent Black, 2004).
47. See T. Sarkar, *Hindu Wife, Hindu Nation*, 71.
48. Partha Chatterjee, *The Nation and Its Fragments: Colonial and Postcolonial Histories* (Princeton, NJ: Princeton University Press, 1993), 6.
49. For a comprehensive analysis of the development of a new scopic regime in colonial India, see Christopher Pinney, 'The Nation (Un)Pictured? Chromolithography and "Popular" Politics in India, 1878–1995', *Critical Inquiry* 23, no. 4 (1997): 834–67; and Christopher Pinney, *'Photos of the Gods': The Printed Image and Political Struggle in India* (London: Reaktion Books, 2004).
50. Arvind Rajagopal, *Politics After Television: Hindu Nationalism and the Reshaping of the Public in India* (Cambridge: Cambridge University Press, 2001), 24–26, 151–52.
51. For a discussion of the archiving of Hindutva as a living practice, see Sahana Udupa, 'Archiving as History-Making: Religious Politics of Social Media in India', *Communication, Culture & Critique* 9, no. 2 (2016): 212–30.

52. Benedict Anderson, *Imagined Communities* (New York: Verso Books, 2006), 4.
53. 'Nal-Damayanti', *RG*, 10 December 1876, 836.
54. 'Nāṭak Utejak Maṇḍalī', *RG*, 3 December 1876, 822; untitled, *RG*, 10 December 1876, 849; and Paṭel, *PNTT*, 291.
55. 'Nāṭak Utejak Maṇḍalī', *RG*, 3 December 1876, 822; untitled, *RG*, 10 December 1876, 849; 'The New Play at the New Theatre', *RG*, 24 December 1876, 872; and 'The Actors and the Audience', *RG*, 24 December 1876, 872–73.
56. Paṭel, *PNTT,* 291–292.
57. See S. Sarkar, 'Renaissance and Kaliyuga', 99.
58. S. Sarkar, '"Kaliyuga", "Chakri" and "Bhakti"', 1549.
59. 'The Era of the Empress', *RG*, 31 December 1876, 886–87; 'Justice to the Vernacular Press', *RG*, 13 February 1876, 105–6; 'The Dramatic Performances Bill', *RG*, 10 December 1876, 837; 'The Rumoured Restraint on the Indian Press', *RG*, 5 March 1876, 160–61; 'The Proposed Gag on the Native Press', *RG*, 12 March 1876, 173; 'Censorship of the Native Press', *RG*, 17 March 1878, 173; and 'A Farewell to Fallen Greatness', *RG*, 24 March 1878, 186–87. See also 'The Dramatic Performances Bill', *TOI*, 8 May 1876, 3, which describes the bill as, 'dangerous to the liberty of the subject, and deal[ing] a serious blow at the rising dramatic literature of the country, and vexatiously interfer[ing]with the innocent amusement of the people'.
60. See Shakuntala Rao, 'Woman-as-Symbol: The Intersections of Identity Politics, Gender, and Indian Nationalism', *Women's Studies International Forum* 22, no. 3 (1999), for an analysis of how women became the symbolic representations of community and the Indian nation.
61. Untitled, *RG*, 31 October 1880, 720; 'Recitals from "Nand Batrisi"', *RG*, 6 March 1881, 157; and 'Popular Guzerati Recitals', *TOI*, 18 April 1881, 3. The play enjoyed much success amongst Bombay's Gujarati Hindus: 'A New Gujerati Play', *RG*, 2 January 1881, 5–6.
62. 'Guzeratee Music Recital', *TOI*, 5 March 1881, 2A.
63. Paṭel, *PNTT*, 291–92.
64. Anderson, *Imagined Communities*, 6.
65. See Partha Chatterjee, 'History and the Nationalization of Hinduism', *Social Research* 59, no. 1 (1992): 148.
66. Untitled, *RG*, 17 December 1876, 867.
67. Untitled, *RG*, 5 May 1878, 301.
68. Untitled, *RG*, 6 January 1878, 14; and 'Drama among Guzrati Hindus', *RG*, 6 January 1878, 5–6. The troupe subsequently performed *Okhā Haraṇ*, which was criticized for being immoral. Consequently, Udayrām wrote *Bāṇāsur Madmardan*.

69. 'Like Causes—Like Effects', *RG*, 7 July 1878, 446–47. See also 'Our Native Theatrical Companies', *KIH*, 28 January 1882, 63–64.
70. 'The Hindu Theatre', *RG*, 25 January 1885, 87.
71. Untitled, *RG*, 27 October 1878, 735. Subsequently, the Zoroastrian Dramatic Society advertised its performances exclusively for the benefit of the Parsi community. Public space thus increasingly became regimented according to religious denomination. Untitled, *RG*, 3 April 1881, 236.
72. Untitled, *RG*, 11 June 1876, 412; untitled, *RG*, 13 October 1878, 702; untitled, *RG*, 27 October 1878, 736; untitled, *RG*, 3 November 1878, 752; untitled, *RG*, 8 December 1878, 843; untitled, *RG*, 21 November 1880, 772; and '"Aryans"—Not "Hindus"', *RG*, 10 September 1882, 680.
73. Untitled, *RG*, 6 January 1878, 14; '"Fredoon"', *RG*, 13 January 1878, 20; and 'Faredun', *RG*, 17 February 1878, 106.
74. 'An Indo-Persian Play', *RG*, 27 January 1878, 54. According to the lectures given by the Society for the Diffusion of Knowledge the Vedic Sūr was the equivalent of the Avestan Hvare, Soam of Hom, Mitra of Mithra, Vāyu of Vayu and Aryaman of Airyaman. 'Dnyān Prasārak Maṇḍaḷī', *RG*, 30 May 1886, 584–86. So also was Jartośt (Zoroaster) now the vedic Jarūth. '"Jaruthas" and Zoroaster', *RG*, 27 February 1881, 137–38; and 'Śū "jarūth" nām jartośtnūche?', *RG*, 6 March 1881, 159.
75. 'Dnyān Prasārak Maṇḍaḷī', *RG*, 30 May 1886, 584–86.
76. Untitled, *TOI*, 26 March 1879, 2; 'Native Entertainment at the Esplanade Theatre', *TOI*, 28 March 1879, 2; and *The Nátuck Uttejak Mandali* (Bombay: Education Society's Press, 1879), 3; '100 Vār thaylo nāṭak', *RG*, 28 April 1878, 274; untitled, *RG*, 19 May 1878, 334; 'The Ramayana on the Stage', *RG*, 9 June 1878, 375–76; 'A Bird's-Eye View of the *Ramayana*', *RG*, 16 June 1878, 394; and 'Nāṭak Utejak Maṇḍalī', *RG*, 6 October 1878, 678.
77. 'Social Plays', *RG*, 25 February 1883, 142.
78. S. Sarkar, 'Renaissance and Kaliyuga', 114.
79. Untitled, *RG*, 4 January 1878, 15.
80. 'Pārsīomā̃ Bīlīyarḍno śok', *RG*, 22 February 1880, 123; and 'Parsee Youths of the Period', *RG*, 27 February 1876, 140–41.
81. 'Parsi Pin-Money', *RG*, 12 December 1880, 809–10; untitled, *RG*, 20 May 1888, 582; 'Parsi Dowries', *RG*, 12 March 1882, 171–72; 'A Lame Apology for the New Parsee Custom of Dowries', *RG*, 21 June 1885, 647–48; 'The Parsee Social Evil of the Day. II', *RG*, 5 June 1887, 631–32; 'Money Making Matrimony', *RG*, 10 July 1887, 774–75; 'Jugārīo', *RG*, 10 October 1880, 664; Pārsī Jugārīo, *RG*, 5 October 1884, 976; and 'Speculation', *RG*, 19 June 1881, 417–18.

82. 'Gambling Among Parsees', *RG*, 20 March 1881, 190.
83. Untitled, *RG*, 4 January 1880, 15. See also 'Vīnāskāḷe vīprīt budhī', *RG*, 22 February 1880, 120.
84. Untitled, *RG*, 14 December 1884, 1247; and untitled, *RG*, 21 December 1884, 1274.
85. 'Local: To-Day's Engagements', *TOI*, 27 December 1884, 3. For praise of the play in newspapers such as the *Times of India*, *Bombay Gazette*, *Gujarātī*, and *Akhbare Sodāgar*, see untitled, *RG*, 1 November 1885, 1186; 'Local: To-Day's Engagements', *TOI*, 10 January 1885, 3; and untitled, *BG*, 10 January 1885, cited in untitled, *RG*, 18 January 1885, 73. See also 'Kāḷā̃ Meṇḍhā̃', *RG*, 4 January 1885, 9–10; and the review written by a Parsi woman in Ek Pārsī Bānū, 'Kāḷā̃ Meṇḍhā̃', *RG*, 28 March 1886, 334.
86. 'Local: To-Day's Engagements', *TOI*, 27 December 1884, 3; Ek Pārsī Bānū, 'Kāḷā̃ Meṇḍhā̃', *RG*, 28 March 1886, 334.
87. Untitled, *RG*, 25 January 1885, 101.
88. 'The Alfred Dramatic Company', *TOI*, 7 February 1885, 3.
89. T. Sarkar, *Hindu Wife, Hindu Nation*, 113.
90. For a description of this motif in Bengali literature, see T. Sarkar, *Hindu Wife, Hindu Nation*, 202–3.
91. Chatterjee, 'The Nationalist Resolution', 122.
92. See Thomas Blom Hansen, 'Whose Public, Whose Authority? Reflections on the Moral Force of Violence', *Modern Asian Studies* 52, no. 3 (2018), for a description of kin fetishism in the Hindutva movement.
93. Untitled, *KIH*, 17 February 1884, 148.
94. 'The School for Scandal', *KIH*, 23 December 1883, 1014–15; and 'The "School for Scandal" in Gujarati', *KIH*, 17 February 1884, 135–36.
95. Untitled, *RG*, 6 January 1884, 17; and untitled, *RG*, 20 January 1884, 62. The *Rāst* and *Kayasare Hinda* described how scores of people were turned back due to a shortage of tickets. 'Nāṭak Utejak Maṇḍaḷī', *RG*, 13 January 1884, 28; 'The "School for Scandal" in Gujarati', *KIH*, 17 February 1884, 135–36; and 'Nāṭak Utejak Maṇḍaḷīno', *RG*, 10 February 1884, 116. See also 'Nīndākhānā', *RG*, 4 May 1884, 413; 'Nāṭak Utejak Maṇḍaḷī', *RG*, 11 May 1884, 427; and Nāṭak Utejak Maṇḍaḷī', *RG*, 15 June 1884, 548.
96. Nhā. Rū. Rāṇīnā, 'Nindākhānū', *RG*, 24 February 1884, 172–73. See also untitled, *TOI*, 25 June 1884, 4; and *Graphic*, 19 January 1884, cited in 'Nāṭak Utejak Maṇḍaḷī', *RG*, 17 February 1884, 140.
97. 'The Police Courts', *TOI*, 21 March 1882, 3. See also 'The Police Courts', *TOI*, 28 March 1882, 3.
98. 'Musical, Recital at the Framjee Cowasjee Institute', *TOI*, 8 February 1882, 3. For the *Rāst's* attacks on the use of the *māthābānu*, see 'A Hideous Head Dress', *RG*, 6 September 1885, 946; 'Pārsī Strīonū

Māthubānū. 1', *RG*, 13 September 1885, 978–79; 'The Hideous Head-Dress of Parsee Ladies', *RG*, 20 September 1885, 1002–3; 'An Ugly White Bandage for a Head-Dress', *RG*, 4 October 1885, 1062; and 'Sense Sacrificed to Forms', *RG*, 4 October 1885, 1062. See also its praise of a Parsi woman who attended a play (presumably of the Victoria's) at the Gaiety theatre—that is, in public—without the controversial head piece. 'Exemplary Moral Courage', *RG*, 6 September 1885, 946–47.

99. 'The Police Courts', *TOI*, 17 April 1882, 3; 'The Police Courts', *TOI*, 24 April 1882, 3; 'The Police Courts', *TOI*, 27 April 1882, 3; 'The Police Courts', *TOI*, 8 May 1882, 3; and 'The Bombay Libel Case', *KIH*, 30 April 1882, 296–300.
100. 'The Bombay Libel Case', *KIH*, 5 March 1882, 157; 'Charges of Defamation, Criminal Intimidation and Insult against Muncherji Cawasji Langra', *RG*, 21 May 1882, 355–57; 'The Bombay Libel Case', *KIH*, 4 June 1882, 389; 'The Recent Parsi Editors' Libel Case', *KIH*, 9 July 1882, 479–80; and 'A Convicted Parsee Editor', *RG*, 9 July 1882, 510–11; 'The Police Courts', *TOI*, 5 July 1882, 3.
101. 'The Parsee Girl of the Period', *New Zealand Herald*, 9 August 1884, 2.
102. Kābrājī also published essays criticizing extravagant Parsi women as, for example, 'āglā vakhatnī bāyḍīo ane hālnā vakhatī chokrīo', 'paisā! paisā! paisā!!!', 'dukhīārī bacūnā pāhāḍ', and 'solīne sudhārnārī sunī'. Untitled, *KIH*, 10 August 1884, 689.
103. Kekhuśro Navrojjī Kābrājī, *Nindākhānū* (Bombay: Jāme Jamśed Steam Press, 1885), 23–25.
104. 'Astrīone mardonī majlasmā̃ ā̃mej karvā̃ bābe jā̃me jamśed patranā ek lakhnār tathā hamo vace takrār', *RG*, 3 October 1858, 493–94; and 'Mumbai Samācārne Hamoe paḍtū śū karvā mukīo?,' *RG*, 3 October 1858, 489–90. Jarī Juāk's name rapidly acquired currency in Bombay as the 'Parsee Girl of the Period', even as Kābrājī attempted to refute the association by insisting that the Parsi girl of the present day was better epitomized by the character of 'Nīrdoś [innocent] Gulā̃'. 'Jarī is not the outcome of female reforms nor are the complaints that there exist only half a dozen Nirdoś Gulā̃'s true', he cried: '"The Better Educated Class" of Parsee Girls', *RG*, 13 July 1884, 646–47.
105. 'The Parsee Girl of the Period', *KIH*, 22 June 1884, 509–10. See also 'The Parsi Girl of the Present and Past Periods', *KIH*, 29 June 1884, 531–32; '"Jumsoo" & "Solee" of the Present Period', *KIH*, 13 July 1884, 581–82; 'Parsee Girl of the Period', *KIH*, 13 July 1884, 577–78; 'Parsi Girl of the Period', *KIH*, 27 July 1884, 624–25; 'A Word to Criticisers on the Parsi Girl of the Period', *KIH*, 27 July 1884, 626–27; 'Strange Vindication of Parsee Girls of the Period', *KIH*, 3 August

1884, 647–48; and 'A New Phase in the Controversy', *KIH*, 3 August 1884, 648–49.

106. 'Parsee Girl of the (Past) Period', *RG*, 15 June 1884, 548–50; and untitled, *RG*, 4 April 1886, 372. Complaints of the spoilt Parsi girl of the period were not new. See criticisms of her *fiśīyārī* (arrogance) due to her purported unwillingness to marry poor boys who could not afford butlers, carriages, and jewellery: 'Parsee Girl of the Period', *RG*, 23 June 1878, 413; and Sī. Es. I., 'Pārsī Chokrīone Parṇāvāmā naḍtī ek aḍcaṇ', *RG*, 23 June 1878, 416.
107. Geraldine Forbes, 'Education for Women', in *Women and Social Reform in Modern India: A Reader*, eds. Sumit Sarkar and Tanika Sarkar (Bloomington, IN: Indiana University Press, 2008), 73–74.
108. Samita Sen, 'Motherhood and Mothercraft: Gender and Nationalism in Bengal', *Gender & History* 5, no. 2 (1993): 234.
109. Sumit Sarkar, *Beyond Nationalist Frames: Postmodernism, Hindu Fundamentalism, History* (Bloomington, IN: Indiana University Press, 2002), 2.
110. Antoinette M. Burton, *Dwelling in the Archive: Women Writing House, Home, and History in Late Colonial India* (Oxford: Oxford University Press, 2003), 5–9.
111. Tanika Sarkar, 'Nationalist Iconography: Image of Women in 19th Century Bengali Literature', *Economic and Political Weekly* 22, no. 47 (1987): 2013.
112. Untitled, *RG*, 16 June 1889, 679.
113. Sen, 'Motherhood and Mothercraft', 234.
114. Śohrābjī Pestanjī Bāṭhā, 'Hālnā vakhatnī strī keḷavṇī', *RG*, 13 July 1884, 655–56; C., 'ājnī pārsī abḷā tathā sudhāro', *RG*, 27 July 1884, 704; Śohrābjī Pestanjī Bāṭhā, 'Pārsīnī śīkhelī ablāo', *RG*, 27 July 1884, 704; 'Female Reform', *RG*, 10 August 1884, 742–43; 'Our System of Female Education', *RG*, 19 October 1884, 1019–20; 'Alleged Flaws in Female Education', *RG*, 26 October 1884, 1045–46; and 'Modern Female Education', *RG*, 2 November 1884, 1079. For a description of how the women's question transpired in Bengal, see Sen, 'Motherhood and Mothercraft', 234–35.
115. 'Mr. Ginwalla's Exaggerations', *RG*, 27 April 1884, 386. For a defence of the Parsee girl of the period, see 'Character of the Criticisms on Parsee Fashions of the Day', *RG*, 25 May 1884, 477–78; 'Extravagant Fashions', *RG*, 8 June 1884, 524–25; 'Parsee Girl of the (Past) Period', *RG*, 15 June 1884, 548–50; and 'Parsee Girl of the Period', *RG*, 22 June 1884, 572–73.

116. Nānābhāi Navrojjī Kātrak, 'Pārsīonū Bhavīane teno sudhāro', *RG*, 1 March 1885, 222; and '"State of Crime" among Parsee Females', *RG*, 26 July 1885, 779. See also the Victoria Opera Troupe's play on the same theme, entitled *Śudhrelī śīrīn ākhre ṭhekāṇe āvī*, which was translated from the *Lady of Lyons* by A. B. Patell: untitled, *RG*, 19 July 1885, 771; Untitled, *Gujarātī*, 23 August 1885, cited in 'Scandalous Dramas—A Nuisance', *RG*, 30 August 1885, 924; and 'The Parsees, Past and Present', *RG*, 29 August 1886, 938–39.

CHAPTER 8

Race-Thinking and the Parsi Social Drama

Apeing

With the widespread cultural valorization of the innocent village damsel in contrast to her evil, conniving sister in the city, larger wheels were set in motion. In the late 1880s, Bombay's presses would declaim,

> The love of Western civilization has also manifested itself in not a few of our young men, and young women delighting in a mere imitation of its outward superficialities and trivialities. … And so it has produced a band of cads, stiff and starch like their own high collars,—of tailor-made gentlemen and milliner-made ladies.[1]

> Having a remarkable aptitude to adapt themselves to the outward forms and symbols of refinement, their rising generation has been rather fruitful in the production of cads who, while too closely imitating what they conceive to be the ways and manners of English gentlemen, are entirely wanting in a capacity to understand and appreciate the qualities which go to form the better type of English character.[2]

The repeated use of the term 'imitation' is significant.[3] The critique of Western mimicry decisively permeated vernacular discourse, giving rise to such expressions as 'monkey-mimicking' and 'Parsee monkeyism'. For example, in an article provocatively entitled 'Apeing', the *Rāst* denigrated the Parsi obsession with Western dress, which it denoted as 'vāndar-nakal'

R. D. Nicholson, *The Colonial Public and the Parsi Stage*, Transnational Theatre Histories,
https://doi.org/10.1007/978-3-030-65836-6_8

(monkey-mimicking).[4] This discursive turn was indicative of a new social development. In April 1880, Edaljī Jamśedjī Khorī, the celebrated playwright of the Parsi theatre and assistant editor of the *Mumbai Samācār*, published a then little known book entitled *Prāṇī Vidhā* (*The Science of Animals*), a Gujarati-language translation of Charles Darwin's 1859 *On the Origin of Species*.[5]

The book marked the advent in the subcontinent of Darwin's influential thesis that man originated from animals. Comparative philology and orientalist methods of historical scholarship exemplified by Max Müller's 1866 *Lectures on the Science of Language* had given way in the vernacular press to social Darwinism and technical deliberations on the relationships between language, society, and race, as exemplified by such texts as Dr Charles W. Cathcart's 1883 *Health Lectures for the People*.[6] The study of the body through orientalism was thus usurped by the burgeoning field of biology, heralding the dawn of race thinking in South Asia, a framework that would become endemic to the development of its history.[7] The implementation of the first complete census in British India in 1881 further reinforced this sweeping ideological shift. Theories of the increase, decrease, and biological character of religious groups began to occupy a prime place in the Indian imagination, stimulating an awareness of Hindus' position as the majority and, by contrast, Muslims', Christians', and Parsis' relative positions as minorities.

In the Parsi press, this new blueprint of the emerging nation's peoples prompted deliberations on how best to increase or safeguard the community's population, which was now perceived as infinitesimal in comparison to other religious groups.[8] The Parsis' diminutive size, which had a profound impact on communal self-definition, was attributed to the increase in spinsters (due to a rise in divorce) as well as a steady decrease in Parsi marriages—a trajectory that was blamed on the exorbitant demands of *eskī* (fashionable) Parsi boys (for dowries) and girls (for maintenance).[9] 'The number of Parsi weddings that used to take place in a single season now take place in an entire year. … It is an outcome of both a number of reforms as well as a certain deterioration', the *Rāst* decried.[10] Within this shifting microphysics of power, the controversy of the Parsi girl of the period evolved. The 'civilized world'—with its lack of fresh air, good food, pure water, healthy exercise, and the regular infusion of 'new blood' from the countryside—was, according to the press, the cause for the degeneration of the Parsi race.[11] Urbanization and industrialization had resulted in a social, cultural, and ethnic deterioration that debilitated the foundations of the community itself.

Little by little, the Parsi public sphere began to look for sources of demographic vitality and renewal, a divine cure for the evils that modernity had brought in its wake. Accordingly, global ideas of the necessity of physical exercise, modern child-bearing facilities, and fresh 'blood' for the development of 'a strong, fresh population' increasingly came under the communal radar.[12] Gradually, Parsis began to attribute the decline in Parsi marriages, the concomitant population decrease, and the impending demise of the Parsi community to the mixing of 'pure' and 'impure' blood.[13] The oppositional terms 'pure' and 'impure' thus became a rhetorical frame, continually shifting in its legibility, to explain the Parsi community's physical, financial, and moral problems, inadvertently conditioning the ethnicized idea of a distinct Parsi nation. In a range of print media, Parsi writers began to correlate racial intermixing—as exemplified by the children of Parsi fathers and '*ghāṭaṇ*' (a slur for Maharashtrian) mothers—with social degeneracy.[14] In 1883, a 'Brittanicus' in the *Englishman* went so far as to describe the existing Parsi community as the illicit offspring of 'low caste Hindu women'. The Parsis went to great lengths to disprove the article, citing James Campbell's 1882 *Gazetteer of the Bombay Presidency*, which described the Parsis as 'easily known by their fairness and robust vigour' and thus not mixed with the local population.[15]

The ripple effect of the transnational intellectual movement of Darwinism and racial thinking that instigated seemingly petty yet portentous squabbles in Bombay's presses also had a direct bearing on the Parsi theatre. In 1882 Kekhuśro Kābrājī first articulated the themes of *lohī* (blood) and *jatī* (race) in his *Saṅgīt Rustam-Sohrab*. The heartrending tale of a father who unwittingly kills his son functioned as an ideal backdrop for Kābrājī's enunciation of a new racial theme in the theatre. Through a constellation of phrases—'tears of blood', 'pool of blood', 'the earth flowing with blood', 'eyes filled with blood', 'sea of the enemies' blood', 'dipping one's sword in blood', 'blood-drenched', 'the ground filled with blood', and 'the raining of blood', an ethnicized vocabulary was elaborated as endemic to communal identity.[16] Significantly, two actors, who would eventually come to rule the subcontinent's entertainment industry, embodied onstage the racialized words that littered the pages of Kābrājī's script: the starry-eyed, 'mixed-race' couple Kāvasjī Pālanjī Khaṭāu and Mary Fenton.

The Parsi Theatre's First Actress

The English actress Grace Egerton, who briefly portrayed a Hindu woman in the Victoria's *Gopīcand* (1875), was followed by a second English 'Madam', an actress whose name would eventually be recognized in cities and cantonments across India. Mary Fenton's life in the Parsi theatre began when Jahāṅgīr Khambātā, embroiled in rehearsals for his newly founded Empress in Delhi, was informed by the theatre's custodian that a 'memsahib' wished to speak to him. A 'young, beautiful, tall and slender white girl about twenty years of age' greeted him, asking for permission to use his theatre for her father's (an Irish military pensioner) magic shows. As she was fluent in Hindustani, she also asked Khambātā for two tickets to see that evening's performance of *Indra Sabhā*. That night, Fenton witnessed Khambātā's star actor, Khaṭāu, onstage for the first time. A whirlwind romance followed, and Khambātā, vexed by this 'white woman's' influence on his lead actor, interrogated Khaṭāu (who was already married to a Parsi in Bombay) about his new dalliance. In his autobiography, Khambātā describes at length the plans that he made to take the company from Delhi to the cantonment town of Meerut, in the hope that the romance would die a natural death.[17] However, his schemes were dashed as Fenton accompanied Khaṭāu to Meerut, taking up residence in a bungalow adjacent to the company's guesthouse. After a brief yet mercurial confrontation with her father, Fenton remained with Khaṭāu and the company.[18]

The Empress subsequently left Meerut for Lahore, where it became the first Parsi theatre troupe to tour what is today Pakistan. The company performed in an enormous tent at Heera Mandi to great public acclaim for five months—that is, until the actors' one-year contracts expired. Many of the actors absconded to form their own company, albeit with little long-term success; an article published in the *Civil and Military Gazette* described a group of Parsi performers in Lahore that were so destitute that they did not have enough money to buy bread.[19] Khambātā and Khaṭāu were only marginally more successful. Together, they set up a joint-stock company bankrolled by a Parsi; this company failed after a brief stint in Amritsar and Delhi.[20]

Fortuitously, Khambātā found a second Parsi benefactor, and on 27 November 1881, the *Rāst* published an advertisement of the Empress's performance at Bombay's newly established Gaiety Theatre. While the announcement carried no note of the play to be performed, it publicized in bold letters a 'vakhṇāelī maḍam nāṭakkār' (famous madam actress).[21] Thus, although Khambātā in his autobiography stresses that he 'rejected Khaṭāu's suggestion that Fenton perform on Bombay's stages' due to middle-class animosity towards actresses, newspapers of the time suggest otherwise. When Fenton first graced the Parsi stage as a member of the Empress this same year, her presence fed the theatrical rumour mill that Khaṭāu had been thrown out of his house by his mother, even as Parsi presses severely censured the couple. The *Kaysare Hinda* castigated the management of the Framjee Cowasjee Institute for permitting actresses to perform at their 'honourable' premises.[22] 'They perform as late as 2–3 at night. … It is appalling to see respectable Parsi men and women patronize these plays. … This "Madam" knows nothing about singing yet Parsi boys and girls throng to the theatre to see her perform.'[23] Similarly an 'A.' condemned Parsi women who remained in the playhouse in the company of 'Muslims and Khojas' until daybreak to witness the 'maḍamvālī nāṭak tolī' (Madam's theatre troupe), thereby 'injuring the reputation of the entire Parsi community'.[24] Fenton thus embodied the social constructs of both the actress as the epitome of all civilizational evils and the deteriorating racial character of the Parsi community, prejudices that she was powerless to refute.

Like their Victorian counterparts, Indian actresses constituted a threat to a paternalistic culture that enforced prescriptive guidelines of social conduct, employment, and sexuality for wives and mothers. In Bombay, however, the stigma against actresses' occupational skills of disguise, pretence, and coquetry melded with broader apprehensions of interracial contamination.[25] Women's bodies thus came to represent the site for expressing fears of the contamination of the communal body politic. A pure, thriving Parsi race needed pure, thriving Parsi women, and Fenton embodied the dangers of societal pollution at best and obliteration at worst. As noted by 'A', Fenton gradually began to draw scores of Parsi ladies to the theatre. The combination of her growing influence on Parsi women and speculation that she had destroyed the conjugal bliss of a happily married Parsi couple prompted not only calls for theatre licences following the English model (which would proscribe the hiring of prostitutes as performers) but also fears that Parsi women would follow Fenton's example in taking up the acting profession—the ultimate omen of moral deviancy and racial collapse.[26] For example, in 1883, Kuvarjī Nājar was compelled to quash rumours from Madras that he had hired six

Parsi actresses in his dramatic company.[27] The actresses, he swiftly clarified, belonged to other (non-Parsi) communities from Calcutta, Madras, and Bombay. Therefore, although Parsi women were encouraged to perform in public in socially upright, morally immaculate, sterile venues such as the concerts of the Gāyan Utejak Maṇḍalī, the 'disreputable' Parsi theatre—which was watched by publics of all religious, caste, and class denominations—was unequivocally out of bounds. Actresses such as Fenton not only breached normative middle-class divides between public and private spheres but also incarnated the possibilities of racial intermixing and ethnic contamination.[28] As the *Kaysare Hinda* declaimed, it was unacceptable that the respectable, scientific Framjee Cowasjee Institute permitted Fenton, 'the illicit, illiterate child of a relationship between a white man and a Muslim woman', to perform.[29]

It was, uncoincidentally, at this pivotal juncture that the question of the inclusion of Parsi *juddins* (half-castes) in the community was debated for the first time in the Parsi press.[30] The question of whether 'others' could be 'admitted as Zoroastrians' pertained to two families living in Mazgaon, Bīlīmorīyā and Ganḍevīā, who followed Parsi customs but did not wear the sacred vest and thread due to their 'mixed ancestry'. After a fund of Rs 2000 was raised by the Parsi public, the *navjote* (baptism) was performed on ten people from these two families, a sign according to the *Kaysare Hinda* of 'the effect of public opinion among Parsees'. Simultaneously, however, several writers condemned the *navjote* on the grounds that the inclusion of 'half-castes' signified the adulteration of the community's *nirmaltā* and *pavītrāi* (purity).[31] The term *lohī* (blood) was deployed in this context to describe the infiltration and infection of the communal body politic: *sāru* (good) blood was distinguished from the *halku* (low) blood of the 'low-caste' Hindu 'māhār, māṅg, ḍheḍā̃ and ḍubrā̃', even as the previously progressive *Rāst* attempted to downplay its new orthodox stance by arguing that 'low-caste children' could potentially grow to be virtuous adults.[32] Noteworthy here is the conservative stance of the erstwhile reformist *Rāst*; the newspaper delineated not only the laws drafted by merchant leaders of the community fifty years prior, prohibiting *juddins* born to prostitutes from wearing the *sadra* (sacred vest), but also the 'fact' that the *anjuman* (Parsi public) had not been included in the deliberation process regarding the *navjote*.[33]

In response to criticisms by 'Fair Play' and the *Jāme Jamśed* that the newspaper was propagating *jātībhed* (caste/race distinction), the *Rāst* unsuccesfully attempted to distinguish between *jātībhed* and *pratibhed* (class distinction):

> If Christians convert the lower castes to their fold it makes little difference due to their enormous population, but the Parsis are an entirely different matter. According to our census for every one Parsi there are 16,000 persons of other faiths, and so to accept halkī varṇanūj lohī [low-caste blood] is to perpetuate the degeneration of our offspring and the destruction of our community.[34]

The taxonomies of writing about the community had thus shifted: class, caste, and race had fused together in a unified semantic field. A different kind of evidence—fair skin, hooked noses, and unadulterated blood—was now brought to bear in the community's construction of truth regimes and its archiving of self-knowledge. In addition to social tradition, religious duty, and household chores, the notions of racial purity and intra-ethnic reproduction had now become fundamental to societal regeneration and redemption, interracial mixing having supplanted capitalist modernity as the harbinger of the community's decadence and destruction. If in prior decades the primary sites for the disciplining of the 'irrational masses' had been the realm of written law (in the 1850s) and the body (in the 1860s and 1870s), then in the 1880s the emerging science of biology made blood the object of social anxiety and the archetype for the conservation of the social order through the 'Juddin Question'. A pronatalist, palingenetic idea of social development thus became the solution to restoring the strength of a depraved, effeminate, infertile, demographically deteriorating Parsi community, becoming the burden of its women and the anchor of its self-identity and conceptual rhetoric in ways hitherto neither fully examined nor vocalized.

The Pārsī Nāṭak Maṇḍaḷī (Parsi Theatrical Company)

Paradoxically, this complex, late nineteenth-century tapestry of morality, religion, race, and blood gradually began to work in Fenton's favour. The physical markers of her fair skin and blue eyes and her attempts to perform 'modest' roles enabled Bombay's increasingly class- and race-conscious public to distinguish her as a woman of high pedigree in comparison to the customarily deplored 'low caste' nautch girls that had hitherto performed on the Parsi stage. Eventually Fenton and Khaṭāu left Khambātā's company to establish their own troupe, known as the Pārsī Nāṭak Maṇḍalī. This company, owned by Māṇekjī Māsṭar, Kāvasjī Khaṭāu, and a Bohra Muhammad Alī, catered to 'Parsi as well as other communities'.[35] The troupe was supported by the famous reformist lexicographer and playwright Rāṇīnā, who provided it with moral credibility and social standing.[36] Although newspapers were quick to condemn Rāṇīnā for collaborating with an actor who lived with a white woman of questionable repute instead of his lawfully wedded Parsi wife,[37] they were eventually obliged to admit that Fenton's dress, mannerisms, and Gujarati and Hindustani pronunciation were impeccable.

This transformation in public opinion was effected by the 1883 production of *Sāvitrī*, Rāṇīnā's Gujarati adaptation of the Italian orientalist Angelo de Gubernatis's 1878 text of the same name.[38] Replete with bucolic references to a Sanskritized Brahminic Aryan India, the pastoral idyll, part of an elaborate attempt to 'uplift the native drama', was performed at the plush Gaiety Theatre for the Baronet Sir Jamsetjee Jejeebhoy and a 'crowded house of respectable native families'.[39] Although the play did not succeed at the box office, it launched Fenton (who had only just given birth to her son Jehangir, the future actor-manager) as the epitome of the virtuous female icon of the motherland. With her conservative clothing, orthodox mannerisms, white skin, and flawless pronunciation of 'classic' (heavily Sanskritized) Gujarati, Fenton kept 'the Guzerati-speaking audience spell bound' as she incarnated all the conceptual claims of the authentic sphere of Hindu nationalist discourse.[40]

The prescriptive set of assumptions of an emerging cultural nationalism thus granted novel subject positions to actresses such as Fenton, who exploited and was exploited by the hegemonic, class-conscious, male-dominated viewing practices of the Parsi theatre. By embodying the archetypal traditional Indian woman, an emblem of antimodernism, anticolonialism, and social, cultural, and racial supremacy, actresses occupied a double position of ethical superiority and social subordination. Consequently, the modern, respectable actress was a paradox in terms: inhabiting the boundaries of modern female professional self-sufficiency and publicity on the one hand, and of time-honoured social propriety on the other. Through gesture, costume, and language, Fenton embodied an authoritarian yet attractive conservatism and thereby occupied the grey area between 'base' nautch girl and spoilt Anglicized shrew. As the first 'respectable actress' of the Parsi theatre, Fenton thus experienced heavily circumscribed representational power within the oppressive gendered discourse of nation building, setting a standard for the scores of other actresses that followed in her footsteps.

The Alfred Nāṭak Maṇḍaḷī (Alfred Theatrical Company)

Between 14 and 21 September 1884, the Pārsī Nāṭak Maṇḍalī was renamed the Alfred Nāṭak Maṇḍalī, indicating that Kābrājī's Society for the Amelioration of the Drama had been bought by the Khaṭāu syndicate.[41] Although the society had enjoyed limited success with its 1884 *Nindākhānũ*, a series of failed productions forced its owners to close their doors and sell their properties for a pittance to Khaṭāu.[42] Hence, on 27 September 1884, the Alfred Nāṭak Maṇḍalī performed along with the three owners of the society at the latter's theatre at Crawford Market.[43] Subsequently the Alfred took possession of the society's premises for its Urdu performances of *Alādīn*, *Tīlesame Jamśed*, *Tīlesame Sulemān ūrf aksīre ājam*, *Alībābā ane Cālīs Cor*, *Nacrange Iśk*, *Humāyun Ajīj*, and *Māhmudśāh Ādīl ūrf Sītāre Gajnī*, as well as its Gujarati repertoire of *Lalītā* and *Nīndākhānũ*.[44]

But the theatre building and properties were not the only things that the Alfred took over from the society: it also gained the moniker of 'Bombay's sole respectable Parsi theatre troupe'.[45] This turnaround was conclusively achieved with Fenton's landmark 1884 performance of Gul in the Parsi social drama *Dukhī Gul* (*Pained Gul*, subsequently titled *Bholī Gul yāne Gulnī Bhūl*).[46] The play was tailored for the stage by Bahmanjī Navrojjī Kābrājī, the younger (and, at the time, less famous) sibling of Kekhuśro Kābrājī (Fig. 8.1).[47] The stage text was based on his older brother's Gujarati novel *Dukhīyārī Bacũnā Dukhnā Pāhāḍ*, which was itself an adaptation of Ellen Wood's *East Lynne* (1861). The production was hailed as a turning point in the Parsi theatre's history.[48] Both Dhanjībhāi Paṭel and Bahmanjī's daughter Śīrīn Vācchā describe the production's unparalleled success, with the latter writing that '*Bholī Gul* was far more popular than *Hariścandra* despite being under copyright. … Families would buy their tickets through money order as it was impossible to get tickets on the same day'.[49] But why was this innocuous social play about the miniscule Parsi community more popular than the Hindu mythological *Hariścandra* (1875), which had been performed a hundred

Fig. 8.1 Photograph of the Kābrājī family with Bahmanjī standing at centre (Courtesy: Rusi Vaccha)

and fifty times? What episteme had the younger Kābrājī inadvertently tapped into in writing this landmark Parsi play? Why was a process now underway to bring the theatre from the storm and thunder of fairies and demons, Hindu gods and goddesses, to the daily travails of Parsi society?

Contrary to every Indian dramatic convention, and unlike all Parsi theatre productions previously staged, Bahmanjī's *Bholī Gul* ends tragically. Like *East Lynne*, *Bholī Gul* portrays the tale of a woman (Isabel Carlyle/Gul) who leaves her child (Falī) and husband (Lavjī) after suspecting her spouse of infidelity with another woman (Barbara Hare /Śīrīn). In contrast with Wood's original text, Gul soon realizes that she had been duped by the evil Dīno into falsely suspecting her loyal husband. The realization, however, comes too late. As Lavjī declares to their son, 'Falī … She lives, but despite being alive, from here on and forever she will be dead to you, me and the entire community'.[50] Disguised as an English woman named Margarett, Gul eventually returns to her previous home to care for her ailing son, only to find her husband now married to Śīrīn.

Lavjī: … (Seeing Gul) But who is this? (Bringing Śīrīn close to him.) Oh Madame Margarett, are you here already? Glad to see you. (They shake hands.) You have been so strongly recommended that I have no doubt as to my only child being well looked after by you.
Gul: Thank you. You may rely upon it, sir, I will care for the darling as if he were my own.
Lavjī: But, by the bye, have you seen the child?
Gul: No sir, I haven't yet.
Lavjī: He couldn't have been put to bed yet. Be seated; make yourself quite at home; we will have him brought to you that you may make friends with him at once. (Śīrīn and Lavjī leave.)
Gul: (Seeing them leave in sadness) That you may make friends with him at once! [In Gujarati] Oh god! This house, this sitting room, this furniture that I knew since my youth! Everything in my former home when I was loved by my parents and husband has remained loyal to me but I, I the unlucky disloyal one had lost it all and ruined my name.[51]

Bahmanjī's text, notably, thus constitutes the first Parsi play to evince a liberal use of English. Fenton, an Englishwoman performing as a Parsi wife who in turn was disguised within the play as an English mistress, was both near and far, epitomizing all that was weak in the innocent yet foolish Anglicized Parsi woman through a bewildering series of movements between her embodied and appropriated linguistic and racial identities (Fig. 8.2). The play ends with the death of Falī, who, as he lies dying onstage, has not recognized Gul in her disguise and thus does not realize that she is his rightful mother:

Falī: Madam, father used to tell me that good people go to heaven, do you think I will see my mother there?
Gul: (crying aloud) You will meet her, of course you will! …
Falī: But why are you crying? If my real mother was here she would cry, but you are not my mother and I am not your son. Oh, how I wish to see my mother. If she was here she would not have left me all alone. Madam, when will father come? If I die before father comes, tell him that I said goodbye.

Fig. 8.2 Portrait of Mary Fenton in Parsi dress (*Source* Paṭel, *PNTT*, 308. Courtesy: The Trustees, The K. R. Cama Oriental Institute, Mumbai)

Gul (striking her head): Oh this is the result of my sins! (To Falī) You must be thirsty, would you like something to drink?
Falī: No Madam, I don't want anything anymore. I only want to meet my true mother. All the life left in me is within her. (Lamenting) Oh, someone, bring my mother to me! Someone show me my true mother! (Shrieking) Oh mother, oh my mother, where are you?
Gul (embracing him): Here, I am here, my son! I am your mother—your true mother—I am here in your presence as your servant; look!
(Gul reveals herself.)
Fali (overcome and screaming): Mother! (His head falls in her hands, and he dies.)[52]

Shortly thereafter, Lavjī discovers his dead son and the now exposed Gul in his house. On her deathbed, Gul gasps to her penitent husband, 'it is [he] who has been disloyal, not her'.[53] With Gul's climactic death, the first on Western India's stages, tragedy entered Parsi playhouses, and Fenton was memorialized for posterity by her Parsi name, Meherbāi.[54]

Kābrājī's landmark play is paradigmatic of a growing ambivalence of allegiance among minoritarian communities that was prowling on the boundaries of the developing realm of cultural nationalism. On a wider scale, it also evokes the ideological ruptures along ethnic, religious, and linguistic lines that were progressively deepening within the South Asian vernacular public sphere. His play signifies an important development, the severing of the social drama from the popular Parsi theatre and its Hindu-national moral economy. Although the false accusations of Gul's infidelity and her eventual death demonstrated the superiority of Parsi womanhood, the play averred that all relationships that were seemingly indestructible, true, and immemorial were now susceptible to a premature passing. Even the staunchest loyalties and deepest blood lines—motherhood itself—no longer ran clear. Who embodied disloyalty: Gul or her husband, both or neither? Who or what was she disloyal to? Her family, home, community, ethnic identity, or nation? Mothers and sons, husbands and wives, ostensibly imperishable relationships that formed the cornerstones of healthy society, were, from *Bholī Gul* onwards, no longer clearly recognizable in the Parsi social drama. If women's bodies were the sites onto which political imaginings such as nationalism and ideological concepts such as race-thinking were articulated—if explicitly faithful, chaste, spiritual women signified an essentialized 'Indianness' or 'Parsiness'—then the new feminine subject in the Parsi social drama responded to a complex

Parsi communal problematic. By occupying the nebulous ground between fidelity and infidelity, Gul and her successors suggested fears of an ideological uncertainty of allegiance between British colonialism and what was coming to be perceived as an exclusionary Hindu nationalist movement.

'Is a Parsi a Native of India?'

The play *Bholī Jān athvā Dhannū Dhān* by Kekhuśro Kābrājī, Bahmanjī's brother, further centred this conflict. An adaptation of the 1860 play *The Colleen Bawn* by Irish playwright Dion Boucicault, the play told the story of Dhan, 'a village damsel of priestly extraction from Nowsaree…'[55] Performed by the Victoria at the Gaiety Theatre on 12 February 1887 under the patronage of Jamshedji Jeejeebhoy, the production struck a deep chord with Bombay's Parsis, particularly due to the recent imposition of the Abkari Act of 1886, which had ruined the livelihoods of many of the community's toddysellers by banning the local production of alcohol.[56] Kābrājī's tearjerker, replete with secret marriages, debts, dowries, and disguises, portrayed, in brief, the true wealth (*dhan*) of the poor daughter of a priest and toddyseller living on the outskirts of Surat in contrast with the superficial, material wealth of her 'reformed' husband and his family in the city.[57] Kābrājī's Dhan, despite being lawfully wedded to the cowardly cad Jahāṅgīr, was willing to sacrifice her marriage and reputation due to both her upper-class mother-in-law's disapproval of the alliance and her husband's impending poverty (as he had not married a wealthy wife). Kābrājī thus contrasted the villains of city life with the virtuous heroes from the village: 'If the wealthy cityfolk laugh at the villagers for their simple means, the villagers laugh at the urban gentry for their false, so-called reformed ways', said Rāṇīnā in his lengthy review of Kābrājī's work.[58] The community's rural roots in India were thus equated by Kābrājī with a nostalgia for a lost golden age, communal prosperity, and relatedly a lost purity. The oppositional frame of the decadent, urban, bourgeois materialist against the exalted, poverty-stricken, honest villager suggested the Parsis' appropriation of global ideas, not only of the moral crisis resulting from capitalism and industrialization, but also of rural populations as an ethically and biologically purer nucleus of a distinctive nation. As Sandro Bellassai notes, the populist myth of the rural man in Europe was the outcome of a wholly modern, paternalistic, anti-plebeian discourse; he was not only the guardian of authentic spiritual values but also the archetype of 'natural', undomesticated masculinity.[59] What then did the village girl Dhan symbolize in the Parsi theatre? What, as Elizabeth K. Helsinger asks, was a deeply conservative nostalgia conserving—and for whom?[60]

Dhan's innocence, her purported moral 'purity', occupied the same discursive terrain of racial 'purity', a rhetorical correspondence that would, subsequently, be explicitly articulated in the realms of Parsi literature and journalism.[61] In a sense *Bholī Jān*'s propagation of ruralism as a regenerative process that would rebuild the community's lost moorings anticipated what the reader of a Parsi newspaper was thus informed in 1889:

> the rural districts have long supplied the Bombay Parsee community with a stronger and healthier race than the permanent population produced amongst themselves. Parsee females, shrewd and observant as they are, have long since made the discovery that whether in matters of maternity, or household labours or endurance of any kind, their sisters in the mofussil are of superior physique to themselves, and better fitted for improving and prolonging the race. ... The mofussil Parsee females have not yet cast aside their working or labouring domestic implements in favour of the piano and crewl work, and hence they are more fitted to become the mothers of a thriving Parsee race. As long as the mofussil can be the best breeding place of the Parsee race, it will increase in numbers and maintain its vigour. It is quite certain that marriages of Parsees amongst themselves in Bombay, unmixed by new blood from the mofussil, must impoverish the race and lead to its extinction in process of time.[62]

Treatises on racial degeneration and pastoral life as the cure for moral, social, and racial evils pervaded Parsi literary circles in the late nineteenth century, melding organicist, neo-romantic, nostalgic motifs with conservative ideas of racial reinvigoration and rural vitality. The conception of communal regeneration through a return to the mofussil, 'the best breeding place of the Parsee race', was essentially premised on the idea of the healthy, 'fitted' female body, a microcosm of the healthy community and the sole defence against its 'extinction in process of time'. Parsi women thus came to be viewed as mothers responsible for preserving the race or, alternatively, deviants culpable of racial decline, their fertility and body becoming once again the site of public surveillance and deliberation. Racial atrophy, formulated through themes such as ethnic defilement and hygiene, purity of blood, virility, and demographic strength, haunted Parsi plays, novels, and journal articles, reorganizing private and public realms and generating a new biopolitical understanding of the past, present, and future of society.

This new vision of a racialized Parsi pastoral utopia was not disconnected from the community's ambivalence towards the Hindu nation. While Bengali plays that depicted the weakening of the bourgeois urban Hindu male body signified the ills weathered by indigenous society under colonial rule,[63] in the Parsi social drama of the late 1880s, an ideologically charged ruralist nostalgia with woman in centre became both redemptive and destructive, disturbing while allowing for the possibility of emancipation from dominant colonial and Hindu understandings of memory and history, of the past and truth, the past and duty, and the past and political affiliation. This conflict is thrown into relief in the character of the loyal servant Hījo (Myles-na-Gopaleen in Boucicault's original) in *Bholī Jān*, whom the *Times of India* described as 'the real hero of the play'.[64] Hījo, who tries to murder Dhan for the sake of his master's future happiness, portrays how one staunch loyalty (between masters and servants) cannot take precedence over other loyalties (between husbands and wives).

Although Kābrājī was attempting to formulate a hierarchy of loyalties, *Bholī Jān* (like *Bholī Gul*) was an epistemological exercise that deliberately confounded a clear reading of Parsi allegiance. The pastoral—with its dramaturgical design of Parsi villagers triumphing against urban blackguards while obviating any clear fealties to lords, spouses, or children—thus became the site for the articulation of not only the ideological fractures of colonial modernity but also a deep-seated ambivalence towards the Parsis' place within the project of nationalism. While condemning urbanity and modern living (the metaphor for colonial rule), the Parsi social drama—as performed in Parsi Gujarati and hence culturally isolated from both English and Hindustani print and performative media—began to formulate a parallel archive that interrogated blind communal fidelity to a hegemonic Hindu nationalism, thus registering a significant transition in Parsi discourse and its claims to truth and power. By distorting the dominant discursive and ideological frames and functions of the Hindu social drama (which articulated a majoritarian moral economy distinct from that of colonialism), the Parsi theatre enunciated for the first time a unique, competing, and fractured understanding of indigenous communal culture, racial identity, and national polity. In this regard, the Parsi social drama, which was increasingly performed in private Parsi parties and amateur clubs, was essentially creating a parallel culture separate from that of the 'Indian' nation, a separate public sphere that increasingly reflected troubled and disoriented aspirations to a distinct self- and nationhood.[65]

The Alfred's *Gamrenī Gorī* (1890), written by Bahmanjī Kābrājī, similarly depicted anxieties of racial contamination and communal and national identity through its depiction of a nostalgia for a lost, pre-industrial, pastoral past and interrogation of seemingly impervious familial relationships.[66] By contrasting members of the same family living in rural and urban settings, Kābrājī sought to portray, in the words of the Iranian servant Behrām, the real savages as those who resided in Bombay.[67] Once again, the village belle (Gul) and her humble father (Meherjībhāi Mehtā) were juxtaposed against a fashionable, quick-talking youth from the city (Meherjī's nephew Kāus). The wicked Kāus steals from his poor family in the village and wishes the death of his well-heeled uncle Ardeśar in order to claim a substantial inheritance. This oppositional frame between modernity and tradition was reflected in the play's language itself, which interspersed Gujarati and English with commentary on both:

> *Kāus*: [in Gujarati] Why would I be irritated? [in English] Not a bit.
> *Ardeśar (aside)*: [in Gujarati] What is this nonsense nata bit fata bit. He's anything but an Englishman…
> *Kāus*: [in Gujarati] Tsk tsk, Uncle why do you say these things? [in English] I don't like it at all.
> *Ardeśar*: [in Gujarati] Brother, please do speak in Gujarati so that I can understand. How can we old men understand this Got Pit Sot Pit.[68]

Audiences would have found Kābrājī's mockery of Western-educated Parsis' Anglicization of their mother tongue hysterical. Yet it was also indicative of the Parsis' desire to see, voice, and listen to their own world in their own language.[69] The now delegitimized colloquial dialect of Parsi Gujarati with its substitution of ca with śa and o with ā̃ furnished Parsi audiences with sonic guarantees of their distinctive communal identity uncorrupted by modern civilization and external influence. In the end, Gul wins the inheritance, and Kāus is stalled by Ardeśar, who, like the audience, sees, hears, and knows all that takes place in the narrative as he disguises himself as a pauper to determine who should be the rightful beneficiary of his fortune. Ardeśar—and, correspondingly, the audience—thus assumes the position of God-figure, appraising the dramas' characters as good or evil, loyal or disloyal. Through asides, disguises, and monologues, the audience sharing Ardeśar's position of all-knowing judgement, adjudicated from their theatre seats on the punishment to be meted to a nephew who wished the death of his own uncle. This last theme reverberated deep in the subconscious of the comprador Parsi community—the connecting link between the rulers and the ruled. Unwitting old uncles and disloyal tyrant nephews, dying fathers hoping in vain for the retribution of their profligate sons, servants who played as masters: these figures had become the principal dramaturgical design of the Parsi social drama and its farces for reasons obvious to the discerning spectator.[70]

These ideas of multiple competing loyalties and of a separate Parsi culture and *deś* (community/race/nation) subtly articulated in *Bholī Jān* and *Gamrenī Gorī* gained further traction in the press when a section of the Parsis sought to distinguish themselves from the 'natives' of India on the grounds that the community possessed a distinctive 'nationality'. For instance, at a public meeting convened at the town hall to discuss the Ilbert Bill, handbills were circulated that proclaimed that the Parsis were not *deśī* (natives) and therefore had no reason to oppose English rule.[71] 'So what is our *deś* [country] if not India? It certainly isn't Iran', blasted the *Rāst*.[72] Soon after, the central government officially declared that Parsis were both residents and natives of Hindustan, in response to a series of appeals by a surgeon Keḷā̃vāḷā, who attempted to apply for a public post at a higher, European rate of pay.[73] The question, however, showed few signs of dying down. As the *Rāst* initially argued, writing in 1888:

> Are the Parsees foreigners in India? … Does the distinguishing mark of the foreigner consist in a distinct nationality or a distinct religious creed from that of the Hindus? If so, the Mahomedans are no less foreigners than the Parsees in India. But that, we presume, does not constitute a fair test in the case. Again, should the Parsees be regarded as foreigners, because they originally came to this country from Persia? If so, the Parsees are more the natives of the country than the Mahomedans, for the Parsees landed in India some centuries before the Mahomedans … Why, then, are they regarded as more foreigners and less natives than the Mahomedans? Is it that the Parsees, though they first landed in India many centuries ago, have no settled habitations like the Mahomedans in the country, that they reside only for a few years for commercial or other pursuits like Europeans and then return to Persia which they call their native country, their 'home'? This, however is not the case. The home of the Parsee population is Bombay and Guzerat and not Persia, where their co-religionists number about give or take six thousand souls. They go to China, England, America, Australia and other parts of the world in pursuit of commercial or other

objects and return to India and not Persia as their 'Home'. Their every thing is in India. Persia has now only an historical interest for them.[74]

Two years later the *Rāst* reiterated its stance, albeit with a key revelation:

'Is a Parsi a native of India?' It is surprising that this question should crop up periodically in the papers. There is not the least doubt that a Parsi is a native of this country. He has been here now for hundreds of years. ...True, of all the races of India, the Parsis have naturally taken most kindly to English institutions and, in the opinion of competent European judges, of all the races of India, the Parsis come nearest to Englishmen. But their superiority to the other natives does not raise them above being themselves natives. If they are not the natives of India, what country are they natives of? Of old Iran? No. Or are they houseless wanderers, like nomads, owning no country as their own? The idea of being mixed up with the other children of the soil may be galling to the pride of some Parsis. But that which is the fact cannot for that reason be no-fact.[75]

The article, a baroque oxymoron, sought to validate the claim that the Parsis were natives and that India was 'home' while affirming that the community was superior 'to the other natives' thereby voicing for the first time the deep equivocality that lay at the core of every Parsi social drama. Where did the community's loyalty lie? With India, England, or Iran? Who were the Parsis? Natives or 'houseless wanderers, like nomads, owning no country as their own'? The antibourgeois sentiment cultivated by the Parsi public sphere thus propagated two converging attitudes: on the one hand the feeling of a 'distinct nationality', and on the other a revulsion at 'being mixed up with the other children of the soil', an ideological position that had a knock-on effect on the sign systems and modes of production of the Parsi theatre with the female performer at centre stage.

Actresses

In February 1890, a few years after Fenton's landmark admittance on the Parsi stage, the *Kaysare Hinda* castigated the Victoria's management for engaging boy-actors despite the many ills of child labour.[76] A month later, Dilārām's part in the Victoria's *Diler Dilśer urfe corī aur sarjorī* was performed, according to the press, by a 'respectable woman'.[77] Advertisements dating to this time indicate that Khurśedjī Bālīvālā, now the sole owner of the Victoria, had hired two actresses, Mujhaiyan and Jharīnā, for the company's productions (Fig. 8.3).[78] Subsequently, two 'Hindī actresses', sisters from Punjab by the names of Buddhā and Śuddhā, were employed to sing for the Victoria at the newly built Novelty Theatre.[79]

Fig. 8.3 'Scene in a tragedy by Famous Troup[e] [Bālīvālā's company]', H. C. White Company, 1996.0009.WX25692, Keystone-Mast Collection, UCR/California Museum of Photography, University of California at Riverside

The vernacular press pointedly elaborated on the women's journey to Bombay with their families and their exceptionally high wages of Rs 400 a month. As the *Kaysare Hinda* described,

> We are informed on reliable authority that an interesting experiment is to be tried next week in connection with the native stage. ... It is, in short, to introduce a female to play the part of a female on the native stage. Looking to the rather anomalous conditions of native society, and the manifold difficulties in the way of an efficient stage proprietor of finding a respectable lady to play upon his stage, the experiment appears to us to be a daring one. We are however assured that the *artiste*, whose services the Victoria Company have been fortunate enough to secure, and who hails from Northern India, is a respectable married lady, who has come down to Bombay under the protection of her husband, and her parents, and will be performing upon the stage under their special care and supervision. ... we may say that it is certainly a welcome thing to witness the part of a Tehmina or a Bakàvali, a Gûl or a Shirin, played by the sweet, tender lips of a lady, than to sit yawning and listening to the hoarse, croaking utterances of a rough-bearded youth, whose female garments on the stage, stand but in ghastly contrast to his every-day male attire beyond it. ... On our part we shall await with great anxiety the result of an innovation which is calculated to lead the native stage one step forward towards the goal of perfection.[80]

The result of the innovation, according to the following week's newspapers, was unmistakeably positive.[81] In a dumbfounding reversal of opinion, both the *Rāst* and *Kaysare Hinda* heralded the sisters' performances as worthy of emulation, praising their engagement as a necessary measure to uplift the Parsi stage, which had deteriorated due to the enactment of female roles by young men and children. 'The immoralities that may come from employing actresses cannot possibly be more than the appalling sins that arise from the enforced feminization of young boys playing female roles', the *Rāst* proclaimed.[82]

The *Rāst* was inadvertently propagating normative ideals of masculinity and femininity, articulating globalist desires for the social and ethnic restoration of the individual and communal body, and ventriloquizing transregional anti-modernist anxieties of the moral and racial emasculation of men due to industrial development. Bellassai describes how in the last decades of the 1800s, a perceived civilizational decay was attributed to the feminization of men. That women were biologically inferior to men was implicit in this thesis, feminization marking a retrogression of humans on the evolutionary spectrum.[83] The antidote to this modern, urbanist pathology was to resurrect an age-old natural masculinity; corporeal discipline, paramilitary exercise, and the purification of men from female sociocultural influence would revert inactive, feeble, domineered men to their pure, natural manly state. The Parsis' denigration of boy-actors was part of this global conceptualization of prescriptive gender ideals, as evinced by the *Rāst*'s declarations that illiteracy, ill health, and feminization were rampant among Muslim and Hindu child actors, who were compelled to perform at the tender age of eight or ten, even as the journal revealingly disclosed that the Parsis had been spared from these particular afflictions.[84] Soon after, an 'experienced thespian' wrote into the newspaper to condemn the 'immoral effects of boys being made into girls, a practice that, fortunately, had spared the Parsis ... but that was rampant among the lower classes of other communities':

> Whether Sohlī or Rūstam, Rāmo or Gaṇu, Kāsam or Kādar, the lower classes no longer identify these poor boys according to their real names. Instead they are now famous as 'Solī śīrīn', 'Rūstam Gohar', 'Rāmo Sītā' or 'Kāsam Bakāvalī'. They are not only praised for having become women but have also managed to gather a clique of lovers who are abnormally attracted to them. These men are so besotted with these boys that they often come to blows, breaking one anothers bones.[85]

A week later a letter writer 'Gulfām' similarly argued that boys had become the unwitting objects of debauched male fantasies.[86] Thereafter, a 'Hindu writer' echoed Gulfām's homophobic rhetoric, calling for an official ban on all child actors in Bombay's theatres.[87] The Indian stage, according to these letter writers, now required reputable, morally upright actresses to assume female parts.[88] Respectable actresses thus assumed the social function of restoring the virility, indigenous values, and moral superiority of men that had been 'lost' as a result of industrialization, the rise of professional working women, and the confusion of gender roles.

Yet the calls for respectable actresses on the stage apparently did not extend to hiring Parsi women. When a 'Ka' asked the *Rāst* whether its advancement of the cause of 'native' actresses was an indirect insinuation that Parsi women take to the stage,[89] the *Rāst* rushed to clarify that it had never made such a claim and that, following the examples of boy's schools and lodges, it were preferable to produce public theatricals that contained no female parts at all.[90] Seared into the consciousness of the Parsis was an exalted vision of Parsi women as wives and mothers, the nucleus of the *volk* and nation. The possibility of their employment as actresses prompted not only the resurfacing of immemorial prejudices about female performers' sexuality but also new, apocalyptic fears of the future state of the cosmic racial order. The widespread objectification of actresses—at the intersection of moral righteousness and sexual commerce—here once again met late nineteenth-century conceptualizations of the female body as an interpretive grid of racial purity or racial pollution. Parsi actresses (unlike Parsi actors), the press insinuated, posed the threat of being 'mixed up with the other children of the soil', and therefore they carried the burden of a different kind of authenticity than that of the Indian nation.

Consequently, although the Victoria would set the precedent of introducing actresses on the Asiatic stage (through Dādābhāi Paṭel) and of making the practice publicly tolerable (through Bālīvālā), its employment of 'Hindu and Muslim women' and the *Rāst*'s disconcerting stance of promoting 'native', that is, non-Parsi actresses evinced not only a restructuring of discursive patterns of women as metonym of community but also the profound ambivalence of the Parsi position in Indian society.[91] From the social reformist symbol of woman as the body of law of a barbaric indigenous culture to her image as a storehouse of inner strength for the gestation of the nation to her embodiment of the purity and impurity of the larger social organism, empire, nation, and community implemented in the name of the women's question, a violent politics of the body onto which political desires were cyclically mapped. The public sphere functioned as a mirror and agent of these evolving visions of womanhood, interpreting, indexing, and archiving in her name multiple converging and diverging registers of historical truth, empyrean pipe dreams, and future (im)possibilities of home.

Notes

1. 'The Parsi New Year. A Lay Sermon', *RG*, 14 September 1890, 1030–31.
2. 'The Progress of the Parsees', *RG*, 16 September 1888, 1071.
3. 'Parsee Monkeyism', *KIH*, 19 March 1882, 188; 'New Evil Amongst the Parsees', *KIH*, 16 April 1882, 255–56; and 'Parsee Anglo-cism', *KIH*, 8 April 1883, 248.
4. 'Apeing', *RG*, 7 December 1890, 1375.
5. Untitled, *RG*, 24 January 1875, 65; 'Light on Light', *RG*, 4 July 1880, 453–54; and untitled, *RG*, 25 April 1880.
6. Charles W. Cathcart, 'Physical Exercise', in *Health Lectures for the People. Delivered in Edinburgh During the Winter of 1882–83* (Edinburgh: Macriven & Wallace, 1883), 17–36.
7. 'Zoology in the Vernaculars', *RG*, 30 May 1880, 350; untitled, *RG*, 6 June 1880, 381; and 'The Late Dr. Darwin', *KIH*, 30 April 1882, 301–2.
8. For descriptions of the Parsi census of February 1881, see 'The Parsees', *KIH*, 25 December 1881, 909–10; 'The Parsi Population of Bombay', *KIH*, 25 December 1881, 911–12; 'The Last Census—The Parsees', *KIH*, 22 October 1882, 758; 'Parsees! Beware!', *KIH*, 1 April 1883, 231; 'Parsee Marriage Statistics', *RG*, 15 January 1882, 37–38; and 'Parsee Marriage Statistics', *RG*, 22 January 1882, 55–56.
9. Nakhrā̃, 'Vadhī Paḍelī Pārsī Kũvārīo', *RG*, 29 May 1887, 611.
10. 'The Parsee Social Evil of the Day', *RG*, 29 May 1887, 603–4; and 'The Parsee Social Evil of the Day. II', *RG*, 5 June 1887, 631–32.
11. C., 'Ājnī Pārsī ablā tathā sudhāro. nā. 2', *RG*, 3 August 1884, 726. See also 'Female Reform', *RG*, 10 August 1884, 742–43; and Nānābhāi Navrojjī Kātrak, 'Pārsīonũ Bhavīś ane teno sudhāro', *RG*, 1 February 1885, 118.
12. C., 'Ājnī Pārsī ablā tathā sudhāro. nā. 2', *RG*, 3 August 1884, 726. On the issue of Parsi women marrying at a late age, see 'The Paramount Question for the Parsees', *RG*, 19 February 1882, 128. For a call for better child-bearing facilities to mitigate the decline in the community's numbers, see 'Mortality Among Parsees', *RG*, 27 November 1881, 837–38.
13. 'The Parsi Social Evil of the Day', *RG*, 19 December 1880, 829–30; 'Parsi Marriages by Auction', *RG*, 26 December 1880, 847; 'Strange Misgivings of Parsi Parents', *RG*, 2 January 1881, 5; 'Will Late Marriages Prevent the New Social Evil among Parsis?', *RG*, 6 February 1881, 87–88; and 'Parsis Fifty Years Hence', *RG*, 13 February 1881, 101–2.
14. 'Divorces in Civilized Nations', *KIH*, 29 April 1883, 301–2; 'Anītīvān koṇ?', *RG*, 24 December 1882, 978; 'Pārsīone māṭe guṇkārī salāh', *RG*, 24 December 1882, 978–79; 'Social Evils II', *RG*, 31 December 1882; 'A Word to the Parsees', *RG*, 31 December 1882, 1003; and 'Commotion Among Parsees!', *RG*, 17 December 1882, 958.

15. 'The Early Parsi Settlers in India', *RG*, 17 June 1883, 467–68. See also James M. Campbell, *Gazetteer of the Bombay Presidency Thana Originally Printed in 1882*, Volume XIII, Part I (Bombay: Government Central Press, 1984), 258.
16. Kekhaśru Kabrajī, *Saṅgīt Rustam-Sohrab* (Bombay: Sañj Vartaman Press, 1906), 13, 18, 20, 24–25, 27, 36, 37. See also Rashna Darius Nicholson, 'Corporeality, Aryanism, Race: The Theatre and Social Reform of the Parsis of Western India', *South Asia: Journal of South Asian Studies* 38, no. 4 (2015): 627.
17. Jahāṅgīr Pestanjī Khambātā, *NA* (Bombay, 1913), 79–82.
18. One day, after the company had retired, Fenton's father abruptly appeared in a two-horse carriage and took his daughter away, much to Khaṭāu's consternation. Khaṭāu allegedly sped to catch the next train for Delhi, which was at 5 a.m., promising to return in time for the night's production. True to his word, the actor returned at 6 p.m. with Fenton by his side to play Tājul Mulk in *Gule Bakāvalī*. Khambātā, *NA*, 79–82.
19. *Civil and Military Gazette* cited in 'Ek Pārsī Nāṭakīnī Kāhāṇī', *RG*, 8 December 1878, 838. Khambātā found himself in the eye of the storm when the *Rāst* suggested that the dissolute company in question was the Empress. Khambātā was quick to put down the allegation in a letter to the editor, declaring that he was not the errant director and that his troupe had earned well on its last tour. The latter was a lie: Jāhāṅgīr Peśtanjī, 'Ek Kholāso', *RG*, 15 December 1878, 854; and Khambātā, *NA*, 79–82.
20. Matters took a turn for the worse when Khambātā fell sick on his way to Bombay, putting off theatrical activity for four months. Although, after recovering, Khambātā found a Parsi businessman to buy into his next undertaking, his previous spat with the Victoria made it difficult for him to rent a theatre in Bombay.
21. Untitled, *RG*, 27 November 1881, 849.
22. Dhanjībhāi Na Paṭel, *PNTT* (Bombay: 'Kaysare-Hind' Paper Printing Press, 1931), 214–15; and 'A Madam (!!!) Actress in the Institute', *KIH*, 29 January 1882, 67–68.
23. 'The Dramatic Folly of Parsi Boys', *RG*, 13 June 1880, 388–89.
24. A., 'Nāṭaknū Ceṭak', *RG*, 20 June 1880, 406.
25. Tracy C. Davis, *Actresses as Working Women: Their Social Identity in Victorian Culture* (London and New York: Routledge, 2002), xiv–v.
26. 'Ramat Gamatnā̃ majānone bandh karvānī araj', *RG*, 7 November 1880, 732.
27. 'Pārsī Orat khelāḍīo', *KIH*, 27 May 1883, 397; 'Atrenā', *KIH*, 3 June 1883, 412; and 'Cha Pārsī Strīo Nāṭakkār', *RG*, 27 May 1883, 415. Additionally, Nājar was not by any means the only manager to hire actresses. Insolvency records certify that a Soondrabai (*alias* Tarabsi)

Naikunji worked for the Elphinstone Theatrical Club. Untitled, *TOI*, 26 June 1885, 3.

28. Similarly, the press noted, 'The *Jame* is disgusted with the very unseemly sight presented at one of Chiarini's performances by Parsee women scrambling up and down regardless of the "roughs" of every class, who seemed to have come there only to annoy them. The *Jame* sees no hope for the woman who will "bear the touch" of a strange man.' Untitled, *TOI*, 12 April 1881, 3. So also did the *Satya Mitra* strongly object to what it regarded 'as an exhibition of women when females of their community are permitted to sit side by side with persons of other races': 'The Police Courts', *TOI*, 5 July 1882, 3.
29. 'A Madam (!!!) Actress in the Institute', *KIH*, 29 January 1882, 67–68; and 'The Use of the Framji C. Institute', *KIH*, 7 May 1882, 317.
30. 'A New Parsee Creed at Mazagon', *KIH*, 4 June 1882, 388–89.
31. 'Can Others Be Admitted as Zoroastrians?', *RG*, 2 July 1882, 458–59; 'Majgāmvālā pelā "juddīn"', *KIH*, 25 June 1882, 444; 'The Effect of Public Opinion Among Parsees', *KIH*, 9 July 1882, 479. See also 'Force of Public Opinion', *KIH*, 9 July 1882, 478; 'Juddīn pārsīo māṭenī arjī māṇḍī valāi', *KIH*, 30 July 1882, 536; 'Can Others Be Converted in the Zoroastrian Religion?', *KIH*, 24 September 1882, 684–85.
32. 'A Caution to the Parsees', *RG*, 9 July 1882, 508–9; and 'Much Ado about Nothing', *RG*, 2 July 1882, 486–87.
33. 'Fifty Years Ago', *RG*, 9 July 1882, 509. See also 'A Parsee Problem Solved', *RG*, 24 September 1882, 720–21; 'Parsee Ceremonials for Proselytes', *RG*, 1 October 1882, 742–43; and 'Proselytism among Parsees', *RG*, 22 October 1882, 803–4.
34. 'The Question of Proselytising among Parsees', *RG*, 16 July 1882, 526–27. See also 'Growth of Parsee Population', *RG*, 13 August 1882, 602–3.
35. Untitled, *KIH*, 15 April 1883, 279. The *Times of India* referred to the company's proprietor as Appoo a.k.a. Farāmjī Apu, and so the proprietorship of the troupe is unclear. 'Parsee Dramatic Company', *TOI*, 3 March 1883, 3.
36. Paṭel, *PNTT*, 216–17; and Khambātā, *NA*, 77–78. See also the advertisement of an unnamed troupe that highlighted the performance by a 'Famous Madam Actress' in its Gujarati play *Khodābakhs*: Untitled, *RG*, 16 April 1882, 292.
37. 'A Madam (!!!) Actress in the Institute', *KIH*, 29 January 1882, 67–68; and 'The Use of the Framji C. Institute', *KIH*, 7 May 1882, 317.
38. See Rashna Darius Nicholson, 'From India to India: The Performative Unworlding of Literature', *Theatre Research International* 42, no. 1 (2017): 5–19.
39. 'Parsee Dramatic Company', *TOI*, 3 March 1883, 3.

40. 'Parsee Dramatic Company', *TOI*, 3 March 1883, 3. Similarly, a reviewer in the *Rāst* commended the play's *rasīlā and caḍhtā bhāśā* (sparkling and superior language). 'Now that the Parsis are learning *śuḍh* [pure] Gujarati, dramatists such as Raṇīnā make not only Parsi but also Hindu writers green with envy with [their] superior language', the writer proclaimed. 'Social Plays', *RG*, 25 February 1883, 142; 'Sāvītrī Nāṭak', *RG*, 25 February 1883, 148; and 'Savitri—A Play', *RG*, 28 October 1883, 865.
41. The Society, like the Victoria, could not be managed according to Kābrājī's exacting standards for an indefinite period. On 8 May 1881, the Society published an uncharacteristically long program that followed the model of the *cavcav* (pantomime) while issuing an advertisement for actors offering salaries of Rs 40 per month to work in its new day club that would begin touring the subcontinent. The advertisement indicates not only that the Society had presently transformed into a professional touring company but also that its three previous owners, Kāvasjī Kohīdārū, Hormasjī Modī, and Farāmjī Dalāl had fallen out, largely due, according to Paṭel, to the latter's hot-tempered character. Untitled, *RG*, 8 May 1881, 320; and Paṭel, *PNTT*, 285–86, 300.
42. Untitled, *RG*, 4 September 1881, 629; and Paṭel, *PNTT*, 217, 300–2.
43. Untitled, *RG*, 21 September 1884, 924.
44. Untitled, *RG*, 28 September 1884, 942; untitled, *RG*, 5 October 1884, 979; untitled, *RG*, 12 October 1884, 1009; untitled, *RG*, 26 October 1884, 1064; untitled, *RG*, 2 November 1884, 1091; and untitled, *RG*, 16 November 1884, 1143.
45. 'Vernacular Theatricals', *RG*, 16 November 1884, 1130. See the *Rāst*'s and the *Times of India*'s praise of Rāṇinā and the Alfred after the production of *Tīlsame Jamśed* before 'honourable' patrons such as James Gibbs and Lord and Lady Reay. 'The Native Drama', *RG*, 3 May 1885; 'The Alfred Dramatic Company', *TOI*, 20 March 1885, 3; 'Dramatic Performance in Honour of Mr. Gibbs', *TOI*, 1 May 1885, 5; 'Ālfreḍ Nāṭak Maṇḍalīno khās khel', *RG*, 28 February 1886, 228; and 'Fareb-e-Efrid', *RG*, 7 March 1886, 252.
46. 'Geiṭī Thīyeṭarmā̃', *KIH*, 5 October 1884, 915. See also untitled, *KIH*, 21 September 1884, 861; and untitled, *KIH*, 28 September 1884, 887.
47. The name Bahmanjī Navrojjī Kābrājī is also spelled Bamanjī Navrojī Kābrājī.
48. For a description of *Dukhīyārī Bacū*, see untitled, *TOI*, 7 April 1886, 5.
49. Śīrīn Vācchā, foreward to *Kaḷjug!*, by Bahmanjī Navrojjī Kābrājī, *Kaḷjug!* (Bombay: Jamśedjī Naśarvānjī Pītīt Parsi Orphanage Captain Printing Works, 1950), 18; see also Paṭel, *PNTT*, 221–22.
50. Bahmanjī Navrojjī Kābrājī, *Bholī Gul yāne Gulnī Bhūl* (n.p.: n.d.), 74.
51. Kābrājī, *Bholī Gul*, 92.
52. B. Kābrājī, *Bholī Gul*, 98–99.

53. B. Kābrājī, *Bholī Gul*, 102.
54. Paṭel, *PNTT*, 221.
55. 'Mr. Kabraji's Parsee Adaptation of "Colleen Bawn"', *TOI*, 19 February 1887, 3.
56. For a description of the act, see Abkari Act, Madras Act I of 1886; 'Toddy Shops in Surat and Broach', *RG*, 13 March 1887, 295; and 'The Abkari Policy', *RG*, 5 June 1887, 632–33.
57. Kekhuśro Navrojjī Kābrājī, *Bholī Jān athvā Dhannū Dhān* (Bombay: Sāñj Vartamān Electric Printing Press, 1907); 'Parsee Adaptation of "Colleen Bawn"', *RG*, 6 February 1887, 149; untitled, *RG*, 6 February 1887, 164; '"Bholī Jān" athvā "Dhannū Dhān"', *RG*, 19 February 1888, 219–20; 'Bholī Jān', *RG*, 1 April 1888, 395; and untitled, *TOI*, 19 February 1887, 2.
58. Rāṇīnā Nhā Rū, 'Bholī Jān', *RG*, 3 April 1877, 381–83. For further reviews see Rāṇīnā Nhā Rū, 'Bholī Jān', *RG*, 10 April 1887, 410–11 and abhyāsī, 'Bholī Jān', *RG*, 17 April 1887, 439.
59. Sandro Bellassai, 'The Masculine Mystique: Antimodernism and Virility in Fascist Italy', *Journal of Modern Italian Studies* 10, no. 3 (2005): 314–35, 320.
60. Elizabeth K. Helsinger, *Rural Scenes and National Representation: Britain, 1815–1850* (Princeton, NJ: Princeton University Press, 2014), 7.
61. 'Gumāstānī Gulī Garīb', *RG*, 20 March 1887, 327.
62. 'Town and Country Life', *RG*, 12 January 1889, 31.
63. T. Sarkar, *Hindu Wife, Hindu Nation*, 29.
64. 'Mr. Kabraji's Parsee Adaptation of "Colleen Bawn"', *TOI*, 19 February 1887, 3.
65. Bahmanjī's plays would usually be performed at parties, festivals, and amateur clubs, thus becoming popular as parlour entertainment: untitled, *RG*, 21 October 1888, 1231.
66. Amrit Keshav Nayak, the first Hindu star actor of the Parsi theatre, received his break in this play under Khaṭāu's watchful eye: Harish Trivedi, 'Amrit Keshav Nayak: Actor', *TOI*, 14 July 1968, 7.
67. Bahmanjī Navrojjī Kābrājī, *Gāmrenī Gorī 3rd edition* (Bombay: The Royal Printing Press, 1894), 16.
68. B. Kābrājī, *Gāmrenī Gorī*, 21–23.
69. Similarly, in *Bholī Gul*, Parsi audiences felt a strong affinity to characters such as Gul's father, the toddy seller Tehemuldārū, who spoke in rural Parsi Gujarati: B. Kābrājī, *Bholī Gul yāne Gulnī Bhūl*, 6.
70. These themes were also evinced in Kābrājī's other works, including the play *'Kācā Kānnī Kharābī' Jhabnejhar ane Śīrin*, which was performed by the Amateur Zoroastrian Nāṭak Maṇḍaḷī, and the one-act farce *Behrā Behelākākā!*, which was performed by Naśarvānjī Rustamjī Vācchā's Ripon

Music Club for the benefit of the Parsi Lying-In hospital on 7 June 1888: Untitled, *RG*, 29 March 1885, 339; and untitled, *RG*, 3 June 1888, 660.

71. The Ilbert Bill was a controversial amendment proposed in 1883 that sought to permit local judges to try British subjects in India. The Parsis' response (or lack of) was severely critiqued by the *Kaysare Hinda*, which went to great lengths to describe how Parsis had consistently been treated as second-class citizens compared to the English and were an important part of native society: 'Pārsīo deśī tarīke gaṇāy ke?', *KIH*, 29 April 1883, 306–7; and 'Are Parsees Natives of India?', *KIH*, 6 May 1883, 320–21.
72. 'Parsees as Natives', *RG*, 27 May 1883, 404–5.
73. 'Pārsīo Deśī ke pardeśī?', *RG*, 4 November 1883, 896.
74. Untitled, *RG*, 24 June 1888, 724.
75. Untitled, *RG*, 9 February 1890, 152.
76. 'Vīkṭorīyā Nāṭak Maṇḍaḷīno "Alībābā"', *KIH*, 16 February 1890, 10–11.
77. Untitled, *RG*, 23 March 1890, 339. For a review of the play, see 'Dīler Dīlśer', *KIH*, 23 February 1890, 9–11.
78. Untitled, *RG*, 30 March 1890, 368. The age of the journalist-playwright had by now given way to that of the actor-manager. Even as Mogal and Ghaḍīālī handed over the reins of the Victoria to Khurśedjī Bālīvālā (by 1890), Khaṭāu and Ṭhuṭhī became sole owners of the Alfred and of the Mumbai Nāṭak Maṇḍalī, respectively. This transition in turn heralded a subcontinental celebrity culture, which centered on figures such as Khaṭāu and Bālīvālā in their travels to the far ends of Asia and Africa.
79. For a description of Buddhā's acting, see the *Kaysare Hinda*'s description of the Victoria's performance of *Saṅgīn Bakāvalī*. 'Saṅgīn Bakāvalī', *KIH*, 7 September 1890, 12–13.
80. Untitled, *KIH*, 23 March 1890, 2. See also 'Deśī Nāṭak takhtā upar ajmāvvāmā̃ āvnāro ek navo akhatro', *KIH*, 23 March 1890, 9–10; and untitled, *KIH*, 23 March 1890, 17. This is not to say that child-actors stopped performing entirely; the Victoria, for example, continued its performances of *Laylī Majnū*, where the title roles were played by boy actors (Dādābhāi Navrojjī Sacīnvālā and the Punjabi Maṅgu): Untitled, *KIH*, 23 March 1890, 17.
81. For a description of the performance, see 'Vīkṭoryā Nāṭak Maṇḍaḷīnī strī kheläḍīo', *KIH*, 6 April 1890, 9–10.
82. 'Female Actresses on the Native Stage', *RG*, 13 April 1890, 408.
83. Bellassai, 'The Masculine Mystique'.
84. 'Female Actresses vs. "Boy-Actresses"', *RG*, 20 April 1890, 436; Śokīn Tamāśgīr, 'Strī Nāṭakkāro', *RG*, 20 April 1890, 440; and 'Evils of Boys Personating Female Characters on the Native Stage', *RG*, 18 May 1890, 551–52. The *Kaysare Hinda* was the first to condemn the evils of child labour in the theatre: 'Vīkṭorīyā Nāṭak Maṇḍaḷīno "Alībābā"', *KIH*, 16 February 1890, 10–11.

85. '"Boy-Actresses" on the Native Stage—A Source of Evil', *RG*, 29 June 1890, 722–23. Additionally, the 'experienced thespian' reported instances of *bhavāiā* (singing) boys being kidnapped by fans. See also the *Rāst*'s calls for the criminalization of the practice: 'The Art of Making Youths Effeminate', *RG*, 28 December 1890, 1465; and 'The Evils of Boys Acting as Females on the Native Stage', *RG*, 18 January 1891, 65–66. And see 'Males Personating Females on the Stage', *RG*, 14 December 1890, 1406.
86. Gulfām, 'Deśī Nāṭakomā̃ strī bannārā bāylā chokrāonī badī', *RG*, 6 July 1890, 756. See also Tamāśgīr, 'Nāṭakkār chokrāone bāylā̃ banāvvānī badī', *RG*, 13 July 1890, 784.
87. 'Boys as Actresses', *RG*, 20 July 1890, 809. Fuel was added to the fire when a Parsi thespian Navrojjī Dhanjībhāi was accused of kidnapping a fourteen-year-old boy named Mahmadśāh and absconding with him to Jabalpur. 'Ek Pārsī Nāṭakkār upar nānī vaynā chokrāne fuslāvī javāno ārop', *RG*, 9 November 1890, 1260.
88. Ek Anubhavī Nāṭakkār, 'Deśī Bāṭakomā̃ bairī bannārā chokrāo', *RG*, 29 June 1890, 728.
89. Ka, 'Pārsī Āmecyur Drāmāṭik Klab', *RG*, 21 December 1890, 1440.
90. 'The Art of Converting Youth into Effeminacy', *RG*, 21 December 1890, 1434–35.
91. Hence, for example, in March 1892 Ṭhuṭhi joined the fray of hiring actresses with his new Mumbai Nāṭak Maṇḍalī, a move that was commended by the *Rāst*: 'Strī Nāṭakkāro', *RG*, 6 March 1892, 273.

CHAPTER 9

Conclusion

In the final months of 1888, the Parsi press first began to articulate the contentious idea that the Indian National Congress, founded in 1885 as the foremost organizing body of the Indian nationalist movement, could not adequately represent the Parsis and their interests. Parsi public opinion, according to the press, had become averse to the Congress after its leaders Jamshedji Jeejeebhoy and Dosabhai Framji resigned from the organization and after the wealthy entrepreneur Dinshaw Petit began advocating for its boycott.[1] On 12 May 1889 in an article entitled 'Pārsīo ane Kongres' ('Parsis and the Congress'), the *Rāst* asked its readers whether the community ought to boycott the Congress:

> We now have only three Parsis in the Congress, Dādābhāi Navrojjī, Fīrojśāh Mehtā and Dīnśāh Edaljī Vachā. … However the Parsi community cannot

The original version of this chapter was revised: The chapter has now been published with supplementary material. The correction to this chapter is available at https://doi.org/10.1007/978-3-030-65836-6_10

Electronic supplementary material The online version of this chapter (https://doi.org/10.1007/978-3-030-65836-6_9) contains supplementary material, which is available to authorized users.

R. D. Nicholson, *The Colonial Public and the Parsi Stage*, Transnational Theatre Histories, https://doi.org/10.1007/978-3-030-65836-6_9

> possibly be deemed to be represented by these three persons. ... The Muslims have already boycotted the Congress across Hindustan and if the Parsis follow their example the Congress will become an unmistakeably Hindu organization.[2]

The Parsis, the *Rāst* argued, 'are so different from the Hindus in matters of race, religion, custom, nature, behaviour, thought, affections and political aspirations that to unite with the Hindus in the Congress would not advance Parsis' interests, it would have the opposite effect'.[3] These feelings of exclusivity, imperilment, and the need to safeguard Parsi political interests were compounded by the demographic game playing out on the colonial stage. In the previous 1888 congress in Allahabad that involved 1248 total delegates (including 965 Hindus), one Hindu represented 160,200 of his co-religionists in India. If the Parsis were to abide by the concept of political representation based on the size of their population, then half a Parsi, the press averred, would have sufficed to stand on behalf of the community of 85,000, rather than the seven Parsi delegates present.[4] Accordingly, as cries for the right to self-rule grew increasingly louder, all 'minorities' began to fear the consequences of stewardship by the 'majority'—or, in other words, a Hindu nation-state. The Congress, hitherto a vehicle for sociopolitical discussion between Indians and government, had become a 'death trap [not only] for Mahomedans' but also for Parsis[5]:

> Mr. Munshi Abdul Kareem, secretary to the Anjuman-i-Habab, referred to the valuable and enduring services rendered by Mr. K. N. Kabraji by continually warning in his *Rast Goftar* the members of the Parsee community from joining a movement, in which his keen eyes saw the germs of future disaffection among the contented population ... Why should, he asked, the Congress be called the 'National Congress'; it had better be called the 'Hindoo Congress', because none but the Hindoos had joined it, and it appeared that there was a difference of opinion even among them.[6]

Kābrājī, the venerable editor of the *Rāst* and purported 'Father of the Parsi theatre', had thus become the strongest Parsi advocate against the Congress, as well as against the project of anticolonial nationalism. The consensus that the Congress was in fact a 'Hindoo Congress' opposed to Parsi concerns had been steadily indexed, organized, and legitimized by the speculative metaphorical vocabulary of Kābrājī's and his peers' plays over the course of two decades. The Parsi press's declamations that 'Hindus' had monopolized the primary indigenous political organ for the representation of Indian public opinion, were essentially the fruits of the culturally intimate, ethnicized vernacular idiom of insular cultural forms such as the Parsi social drama. Functioning as deep archive, the Parsi theatre had thus assumed an authorial and curatorial role, concurrently imagining the future Indian nation while also casting the Parsis as a thick yet diminished and isolated public from an essentialized seemingly hostile Hindu-Indian nationalist sphere proper. Profound fissures within a seemingly multilingual, multi-ethnic, and multireligious polity that Kābrājī had initially symbolically addressed in his plays had now surfaced into explicit political precept; religious myths and sensitivities here defined not only the differences between publics but also the conception of imminent nationhood itself.

Between 1888 and 1889 the register of the particular narrative of social, cultural, and racial insiders and outsiders had thus transitioned from the aesthetic and allegorical to the political and literal, with the Parsis now wrestling for the legitimization of their polity before the putative audience of empire. For the Parsis and Muslims the National Congress was a 'misnomer', as its compositional structure, cultural grammar, and moral universe—its very 'politicized community identity'—were 'Hindu' and hence illegible, unacceptable, and lacking in representational authority[7]:

> Is the Congress' aim to run its own Raj? Even if they do not yet have the knowledge to do so isn't it their ultimate ambition to learn the same? Even if they are incapable of doing so now, isnt it their aim to become capable of doing so in the future? ... What will be the result of this? ... No, they do not want to destroy the British Raj but to retain it nominally. All rights all rule is to be handed over to the Hindus. In short to ask as Ireland did, of 'Home Rule'. To make a Hindu Parliament in Hindustan—To elect Hindi Governors and collectors and Judges—To rule the country with a Hindi army—to give Hindis weapons—to make Hindis volunteers—to make everything Hindi and only Hindi. Then to tell the English to get lost and to give these bickering Parsis allowances according to their tiny numbers. ... It is the Congress' wish to belittle the English Raj in India, to make it a mere token but the Parsis cannot wish this. The Parsis want the British to rule Hindustan for ever and for its power to never abate. As a result there is a huge gap between the Parsi community's loyalty and the

> Congress and the Parsis refuse to join the Congress due to their unabiding, pure and irresistible loyalty.[8]

The oft-repeated term 'loyalty' is critical. Kābrājī's doomsday predictions of a Hindu Parliament, Hindi Governors, and a Hindi army served to reshuffle the discourse of demographic power and inter-religious competition into the narrower interpretative frame of loyalty and disloyalty so fundamental to Parsi theatrical repertoire. Drawing on the lexicon of the Parsi social drama, the Parsi press rejected the 'spirit of discontent and disaffection' that now prevailed against British rule through an elaborate metatheatrical staging of the community's 'loyalty'. Echoing the proclamations delivered and plays performed in the aftermath of the Indian Rebellion, the *Rāst* cried:

> as soon as these children of the soil begin to imagine that they are able enough to govern their country and strong enough to enforce their wishes on the Government, there will be an end to the loyalty which is based upon self interest ... it is not in the power of the Congress leaders to guarantee that 'the dormant and unsuspected forces' which it is their object to galvanize into activity will act just in the manner they desire. Who knows but that they might only succeed 'in due course of time and by the irresistible logic of events', to quote their own favourite expressions, in calling into being a Frankenstein who may rise in rebellion against its creators![9]

The conception of 'a Frankenstein who may rise in rebellion against its creators' was, as seen earlier, not unique to the Parsi press. The Parsi social drama had long decried profligate sons, wicked nephews, and treacherous servants. Yet so also had it critiqued injudicious fathers, foolish mothers, and abusive masters. The *Kaysare Hinda*, the Parsi organ of the Congress, increasingly began to counter the *Rāst*'s attacks on the Congress by delineating other notions of fidelity. Citing the English democrat Charles Bradlaugh's speech from the fifth Indian National Congress (in Bombay on 2 December 1889), the *Kaysare Hinda* proclaimed: 'We are here loyal to one rule with the best of loyalty. That is no real loyalty which is only blind submission. Real loyalty means that the governed help the governors by leaving little for the Government to do'.[10]

The perception of the imminent demand for 'Home Rule' had thus given the Parsis 'food for studying and knowing their proper position in the confusion of races and denominations inhabiting India'.[11] Rejected by the colonizers who considered them 'natives' and rejecting the colonized who they considered their inferior, the Parsi social body that hitherto had been indelibly marked by painful and constant ambiguity thus fissured in line with competing political allegiances, geographic imaginations, and ethnic assertions. Simultaneously, however, these exceptionally polarized Parsi musings were legible to adjacent publics, who increasingly vilified the Parsis as imperial sympathizers opposed to the nationalist cause. Articles such as 'Race Animosity against the Parsis' described how the 'Hindus and Muslims' of Surat and Ahmedabad despised the Parsis for usurping all the higher posts in public office.[12] Additionally, several 'anti-colonial' Hindu newspapers including the *Gujarati* mobilized a political movement known as 'Anti-Parsee Attitude', which denounced the Parsis' blind loyalty to the Crown.[13] The movement gained momentum in 1889 when the inspector-general of police, H. T. Ommanney, accused 'the whole Parsi community from Sir Jamshedji Jijibhai himself down to Mr. Merwanji, a pleader' of fraud during the official investigation into the misconduct of Bombay's first municipal commissioner, Arthur T. Crawford.[14] In the midst of this 'most notorious case of corruption in Victorian India', the Parsis did all they could to vindicate 'the character of the nation from the false, cruel and unjust aspersions made against them in an official document laid on the table of the Houses of Parliament'.[15] The damage, however, had been done. In the aftermath of the Crawford case, the community's character assassination by the vernacular press amplified beyond measure as the Parsis were framed as corrupt traitors to their poorer Indian brethren, capable of turning a blind eye to English atrocities when the need suited them.[16]

In this tug of war of allegiances, the Parsis would therefore find themselves as they had historically been, betwixt and between. However, this time the political current was working against the community's benefit. The shunning of the Parsis as stewards of the *pax Britannica* rippled out from the realm of politics, affecting education, literature, linguistics, and the theatre. For example, in the watershed year of 1888, Bombay witnessed not only a series of disputes between the reformist Rāv Sāheb Mahīpatrām Rūprām and the *Rāst* (the former accused the Parsis of ruining the Gujarati language)[17] but also the rise of 'Hindu' troupes such as the Ārya Subodh Nāṭak Maṇḍaḷī who castigated Parsi theatre companies for imitating the English.[18] Subsequently, the *Pakhvāḍiyānī Majhā* (*Weekly Entertainment*) averred,

> The Parsi thespians act like Muslim servants in order to earn a living. … Although they are Parsi by race, language and custom, these poor souls have to wear Muslim costumes each night to visit Parīstān [fairy lands] and Kabrastān [funeral grounds]. … The theatre is a tool for reforming the idiot, instead it has now become a tool to make idiots of the reformed.[19]

At play in these examples of the Parsis' cultural ostracism are two fundamental characteristics of the late colonial vernacular public sphere: the segmentation of publics on communal, religious, caste, and linguistic lines; and, more significantly, the 'ubiquity of highly performative violence'.[20] In Habermas's original adumbration, the presence of religion in the public sphere was to fade away in the course of the development of a fully rational constitutional state. Westphalian states ostensibly experienced the secularization and democratization of political power as they no longer required religion for legitimation.[21] In colonial India, however, as scholars have pointed out, 'the colonial state was haunted by the persistent reminder of its "externality"', a foreign transplantation rather than a natural autochthonous development that was conscious of its normative framing and limits.[22] As demonstrated in Part I, the vernacular public sphere as a disciplinary space for rational debate arose from disputes between missionaries and local elites on indigenous religious custom and tradition—the primary site for the operation of colonial power. Through a practical yet aggressively disruptive coordination of the administration of communities, religion, overdetermined by textuality, became an essential component of public life and violence a constituent part of the incipient bourgeois public sphere. Gradually, the appropriation of the language of Victorian morality and virtue by local elites gave way to broader populist introspection, indigenism, and meditative conservatism. Nationalist discourse, as shown in Part II, reworked the social reformist conception of religion as a sphere of societal transformation to generate a new, 'authentic', performative moral economy, undergirded by 'figural affective intensities' that implicitly opposed the interventions of colonial rule.[23] Divergent understandings of the present, past, and future, of social imaginaries, historical development, and common fate, of modes of debate and demands for justice, and of the spatio-temporal positioning of political claims were thus brought to bear on the vernacular public sphere, which was, as a consequence, highly fissured. Between the (homogeneous, empty) clock time of elite, English-educated groups and the kairotic, mythological time of crowds who did not share the self-reflexive bourgeois vision of the world, there existed no one overarching narrative of the modern and the nation.[24] Rather, through endorsements and invalidations, the pillaging of rediscovered myths and ideals, the meeting of peoples through words, thoughts, and performative gestures, a great inexact web of unique yet intersecting discourses of spirituality, civil society, and citizenship surfaced of whose breadth no one had a clear idea. As such, the project of nationalism in the nineteenth century was archival rather than deliberative, and the public sphere—with the Parsi theatre in the lead—was its primary tool. The drama connected disparate peoples through the hazy silhouette of the proscenium, accumulating, indexing, and articulating sacred symbols and codes and engraving in the minds of people abstractions of labyrinthine excess, thereby stirring up hitherto dormant political forces into tempests. Consequently, even as indistinct values of a more composite public were suggested through the secular mythological repertoire of the Parsi theatre, the sensational success of vernacular Hindu mythological and Parsi social idioms consolidated the development of Hinduism and Zoroastrianism as 'fully formed discursive totalit[ies]'.[25] The dramaturgical choice of a glittering crown or temple arch, of colloquial Parsi vowel or white-laced, Gujarati-draped sari, became naturalized as a particular society's memory, preserving and privileging cultural frameworks that were central to understanding the collective present and future.

Crucially, at the heart of the relationship between the archive and the societies that establish and draw on it, as Joan M. Schwartz and Terry Cook note, is power: to record and exclude events, ideas, and names; to preserve, mediate access, and destroy collective remembrance and identity; to amplify or marginalize voices, narratives, and forms of meaning; and to reveal and rebuild power relations.[26] As Part III demonstrates, new revivalist idioms of religious consumption and mythic populist visions of the Indian past so fundamental to the production of thick emotions of intimacy, solidarity, and militant belonging generated not only a primordial animosity towards 'outsiders'—Muslims, Christians, and Parsis—but also power struggles over cultural property. Imbricated in the theatre's composition of knowledge, truths, memory, and identity was a decisive contestation over the ideological contours of the nation, a universalizing category necessary for the legitimization of the state. Which community belongs, why, and to what it belongs were questions that profoundly influenced the constitution and character of the theatre and relatedly of forms of national cohesion, marginalization, and remembrance. The Indian public sphere, fundamentally characterized by the 'segmentation of publics' from its beginnings thus came to be marked as much by the performance of religious group feeling as of violent exclusion, becoming the site for not only territorial imaginings but also ethnic competition, chauvinist assertion, the routinization of outrage, and the re-feudalization of publicity.[27]

Violence, as Thomas Blom Hansen notes, is endemic to political life across contemporary South Asia as it is legible across profoundly fissured, often hostile, public worlds. According to him, crowd violence—a mode of public performance imbricated in official, mediatized forms of communication such as the press—as well as its agonistic vocabulary of righteous outrage stemming from perceived injury, was, and is, considered as legitimate as a sardonic editorial.[28] Yet, in answering how this 'predominant modality of public violence' as performance in postcolonial India came to be, it is difficult to look away from the Parsi theatre, the most pivotal battleground in the late nineteenth century for the assertion of cultural authenticity and social authority and the wresting of control and power over the archive.[29] On 17 March 1889 the Alfred, under Khaṭāu's ownership, first publicized *Khalīf Hārūn Raśīd*. The play, adapted from an *Arabian Nights* tale of a wealthy emperor who wandered in his kingdom in disguise after sunset, was performed in Bombay to little critical notice.[30] The next year, the company, now a *tour de force* in the subcontinental theatre world, toured Poona, Ahmednagar, and Hyderabad, performing its spectacular repertoire including this play before Hyderabad's dewan and nawabs.[31] The company returned to Bombay in October 1891, unaware or unmindful of the rapidly growing tensions in the city.[32] As early as January 1890, the *Rāst* described how Parsi actors had to '"mouthe it" before a chilling array of empty benches' because Bombay's Muslims- 'the majority of the patrons of the Grant Road theatres'-had boycotted the drama: 'the Mahomedans of the East and the West, of Turkey, Persia and India', the newspaper averred, were outraged by Henri de Bornier's *Mahomet, drame en 5 actes*, which dramatized the Prophet Muhammad's life and was censured by the Ottoman caliphate. Christopher Balme notes that by the end of 1889 the controversy had left the French public sphere and internationalized to a remarkable degree. Particularly in India the news of the impending production caused massive protests'.[33] According to local newspapers, the secretary of an organization known as the 'Vāejhe Islām' (Vision of Islam) established vigilance committees and decreed that any transgressors caught entering Bombay's theatres would be charged a 5 Rs fine, with repeat transgressions subject to a fine of 10 Rs and then expulsion from the *jamāt* (community) and denial of appropriate burial rites.[34]

The Parsi press, seemingly unconcerned with the effects of this first mammoth transregional protest against a theatrical production, argued, 'The solemn covenant will not last long ... the Mahomedans, especially of the lower classes, in whom love of the theatre is very strong, will again flock to it, as before'.[35] Nevertheless, the quizzical *Rāst* wondered, 'why Bombay's Muslims were boycotting Bombay's theatres [which were primarily Parsi owned] instead of directing their energies at the French Government?'[36] The *Rāst*'s musings were, in fact, forebodings. A year later, on 10 November 1891, half an hour before the opening of the Alfred's *Khalīf Hārūn Raśīd* at the Novelty Theatre, the night's performance was abruptly cancelled as Khaṭāu had been informed by police superintendents Harry Brewin and Joseph McDermott that its staging would prompt 'a serious affray' due to its portrayal of the khalif. Brewin and McDermott threatened Khaṭāu with the implementation of Section 10 of the 'Dramatic Performances Act', which entailed the prohibition of all dramatic performances in Bombay except those that received a licence. Consequently, although the khalif was 'anything but a religious character' (as 'a Disappointed Spectator' noted),[37] and although the play had been performed in Hyderabad before the nawab and his ministers, Khaṭāu, acutely aware that his fanciful visions of oriental splendour could now spark violence between Sunnis and Parsis, swiftly withdrew the performance.

In addition to fostering the development of a transregional public sphere and pan-Islamic identity, the 'Muslim' boycott of Bombay's theatres demonstrates a new colonial response to assertions of cultural proprietorship and feelings of perceived injury to an intimate sphere of belief. Though denigrated as irrational hooliganism by local officials and the Parsi press,[38] the boycott raised a salient issue: the primacy of religious signs in the public sphere and the perceived need for their protection, control, and defence.[39] Religious feelings, considered only as an afterthought in 1874 once the damage to property and life had been done, had become a significant force in imperial (and subsequently national) policy that sought to pre-empt any disturbance of the peace. Moreover, in contrast with the riots of 1874, the boycott was scarcely reported in the *Kaysare Hinda* and the *Rāst*, as the British Government's increasingly precarious position in India percolated down to its comprador subjects, the Parsis' enactments of economic, political, and cultural authority giving way to one of diplomacy and concession.

Crucially, even as Khaṭāu was grappling with a new pan-Islamic force in colonial politics, he would find himself caught in the middle of a virulent crossfire between Parsis, Muslims, and Hindus.[40] On 8 February 1890, the Alfred Dramatic Company's play *Śrī Krushṇa Vijay*, written by the playwright Śokhar Bāpujī and based on Hindu *danta kathā* (legend), was shut down during the play's second rendition in Bombay.[41] Despite facing a police presence, 'Hindus' gathered outside the Gaiety Theatre to call for the play's prohibition due to the portrayal of their god Krishna. According to the Parsi press, at a subsequent public meeting where the Muslim embargo on Bombay's theatres was deliberated, several Bhatias decried, 'if such a representation [as that of Lord Krishna] of the Muslim Prophet was performed, what would they have done?' Consequently, Khaṭāu unhesitatingly took the play off the boards, despite multiple mitigating factors: the mythological drama's authorship (Bāpujī was a '*dhārmik* [pious] Hindu'), a defence of the play voiced by many Hindus, and the Alfred's own history of performing plays based on the *Bhagvad Gita* in 'pure' Gujarati for its 'Hindu brothers'.[42] Subsequently, the *Rāst* 'condemned conniving Hindus that were inciting their more susceptible brethren to arms'.[43] Yet conniving Hindus, conniving Parsis, and conniving Muslims were now issues to contend with. The South Asian modern theatre that performed religion had undeniably become imbricated in claims to cultural property, and outrage—its new *lingua franca*—reconfigured the ground on which politics was imagined, performed, and comprehended. Who could write what, who could produce what, and who could enact what had become central questions in the colonial theatrical public sphere, which was grappling with a potent meta-performance of power.[44] Thus not unexpectedly, shortly after the Parsi theatre's raging religious waters appeared to have calmed, Bombay witnessed its most significant communal outbreak, Bombay's riots of 1893 caused due to the Prabhas Pattan affair, the cow-killing agitation, and the feeling among the Muslims that they were suffering under the Hindus.[45] The scope of this riot was unmatched: 530 were wounded, eighty murdered, and its effects were long felt.[46]

Against this backdrop of the deepening of ethnic, cultural, and linguistic cleavages, the complex tapestry of morality, religion, race, and blood as first articulated in these early years of Indian Nationalism, gained in strength in the years to come. In the famous Parsi Punchayet Case of 1909, the judgement laid down by judges Dinshaw Davar and Frank Beaman stated that a Parsi could only be so termed if he or she was born of a Parsi father. Subsequently, the Parsis, following the example of other religious communities, began to consider possibilities for the establishment of military schools and eugenic programs, the exclusion of 'half-castes' from the community, the castration of 'mentally defective' community members, and the renewal of ties to Iran (Persia) and the creation of a separate state of Parsistan.[47] The Parsi theatre in its second phase (1893 and 1933) would therefore not only function as the stimulus for and target of the new political era of high nationalism but also became a lasting threshold of thought, governing for years to come enunciative possibilities or the terms of what could be understood and said of the past and relatedly, the historical evidence that could be displayed, provisionally preserved, or destroyed. Although the theatre eventually conceded to film, which inherited its repertoire, modes of address, personnel, and record-building and -keeping function,[48] its thick, interpretative legacy of archiving had a lasting effect, reverberating in the very meanings, truths, histories, and discourses that it connected or attempted to exclude. Through a syncopation of irruptions, insertions, blurrings, and exorcisms, the colonial Parsi drama as archive bore witness to a specific regularity of events, words, and ideals yet as an embodied, evanescent form not dissimilar to collective memory, it was also constituted by its own self-effacement, making history by forgetting it. The spectralization of impossible, failed, or repressed dreams thus becomes as much the basis for self-definition as the highlighting of stories that absolve shame and grant cohesion, glory, and meaning. As this book has attempted to show, beneath the ranks of Parsi freedom fighters, nation- and city-builders, and philanthropists lay the tangential rumour of playwrights such as Kābrājī, whose almost lost last words express a history composed by the erasure of its own memory:

> If the educated Parsi begins to feel and think with those who made the Political Liberty of a people their life-work, if he fondly hopes that his country and his people may also achieve that liberty some day I ask him to consider for a moment what it is that he can call his country or his people. With the exception of his 1,00,000 co-religionists, the millions of India will not eat or drink with him, will not take him into their house and

treat him as a brother. How many in a thousand will understand his ways, wants and language, and as to country, what part of it will he be pleased to call his country? Let an educated Parsi honestly answer the question. India cannot be his country and he cannot be the patriot that he has read of in English books ... he has no love for India and its people. On the other hand, he must confess that, notwithstanding his curt treatment as a subject race, his sympathies are all English. He apes the English in their dress and manners, and he writes, thinks and speaks in English. ... In what way, then, can he advance the object of the Baboo Congress, composed of people who, compared to him, have a real stake in the country, who have their ancient traditions, their history, their laws, their literature and social institutions? ... Higher intellectual education has been the thin end of the wedge of the ruin of the Parsis, and the Congress will be the death-knell. The programme of the Congresswallas has been simply chimerical, and, like little children, they ask for edged tools which can only cut them. ... Let us have nothing to do with the Congress. It has everything to take away from us, nothing to give us. Let the Parsis take the example of the Jews. There are many points of similarity between us. We are, like them, wanderers from our father-land. They have made themselves famous as merchants. Until now we were doing the same. They have steered clear of politics. We ought to do the same, for in that alone is our salvation. It has been written in the Book of Fate that India can never be a country nor its people a nation. The dream is in vain.[49]

Notes

1. 'Should the Parsis Retire from the Congress Movement?', *RG*, 18 November 1888, 1331–32.
2. 'Parsees and the Congress', *RG*, 12 May 1889, 542–44.
3. 'Parsees and the Congress', *RG*, 12 May 1889, 542–44.
4. 'Only "Half a Parsee" Would Suffice', *RG*, 23 June 1889, 711–12. The increasing disaffection between Parsis and Hindus was purportedly the reason behind the Parsi boycott of the fifth national congress: Śamśer Bahādur, 'Pārsīo ane Kāngres', cited in *RG*, 19 January 1890, 68–69; and untitled, *RG*, 27 April 1890, 457. See also George Yule, 'Early Official Obstruction to the Congress and Incitement to Muslims', Allahabad Session, 1888. https://cultural.maharashtra.gov.in/english/gazetteer/VOL-II/INDIAN_NATIONAL_CONGRESS_II.pdf.
5. 'The Mahomedans and the Indian Congress', *RG*, 12 August 1888, 925.
6. 'The "National Congress" and the Mahomedans', *TOI*, 27 December 1889, 6.

7. Sandria B. Freitag, *Collective Action and Community: Public Arenas and the Emergence of Communalism in North India* (Berkeley: University of California Press, 1989), 6.
8. 'Parsee Loyalty vs. Congress Loyalty', *RG*, 2 June 1889, 626–27.
9. 'The Tendencies of the "National" Movement', *RG*, 16 June 1889, 681. See also 'Pārsīo ane Kāṅgres', *RG*, 16 June 1889, 690; 'A Partial Convert to the Parsee View of the Congress', *RG*, 30 June 1889, 743; 'Moral Objections of Parsees Against the Congress', *RG*, 7 July 1889, 768–69; 'Parsees and the Congress', *RG*, 3 November 1889, 1254–55; and 'The Congress and the Parsees', *RG*, 15 December 1889, 1429.
10. 'What Is True Loyalty', *KIH*, 8 June 1890, 8.
11. 'The Congress and the Parsis', cited in *RG*, 17 November 1889, 1309–10.
12. 'Race Animosity against the Parsis', *RG*, 17 April 1887, 434–35.
13. 'Anti-Parsee Attitude Growing among Hindu Writers', *RG*, 18 November 1888, 1332; 'The Prevailing Tone of the Hindu Press', *RG*, 2 December 1888, 1393; and 'Sectional vs. National Interests', *RG*, 2 December 1888, 1393.
14. Stephen M. Edwardes, *Memoir of Sir Dinshaw Manockjee Petit, First Baronet (1823–1901)* (London: Oxford University Press, 1923), 47.
15. 'Supposed Want of Unanimity among the Parsis', *RG*, 25 August 1889, 969–70; and Knut Aukland, 'Connecting British and Indian, Elite and Subaltern: Arthur Crawford and Corruption in the Later Nineteenth Century Western India', *South Asian History and Culture* 4, no. 3 (2013): 314. See also 'A Foul and False Slander of the Parsees in a State Document', *RG*, 14 July 1889, 795–96; 'Demands of Parsee Feeling', *RG*, 21 July 1889, 824–25; 'Mr Ommanney's Libels on Parsees', *RG*, 21 July 1889, 825–26; 'The Next Step for the Defense of the Parsee Community', *RG*, 28 July 1889, 854; and 'Mī. Omānīnā Humlā sāmenī pārsīonī jāher hīlcālnũ ek bacũ', *RG*, 2 February 1890, 125–26.
16. According to the *Rāst*, only the *Subodh Patrikā* defended the Parsis; all other Hindu newspapers were apathetic or critical of the community: 'Increasing Antipathy of Hindu Writers Against Parsees', *RG*, 21 July 1889, 826–27.
17. 'Uncharitable Attack on Parsee Authors', *RG*, 19 February 1888, 217; 'Mr. Mahipatram Rupram and the Parsees', *RG*, 19 February 1888, 217; 'What Constitutes Incorrect Gujarati!', *RG*, 19 February 1888, 217; 'Gujrātī Bhāshānā ūpsargo vishe rāv sāheb mahīpatrāmnũ adnānpaṇũ', *RG*, 19 February 1888, 219; 'Parsee Authors and Their So-Called Hindu Critics', *RG*, 26 February 1888, 243–44; and 'Pārsī Lakhnārāonī khāmī Kāhāḍvā', *RG*, 26 February 1888, 248–49.

18. 'Native Drama in Bombay', *RG*, 27 May 1888, 615–16; 'Pārsī ane Hindu Nāṭako', *RG*, 3 June 1888, 646–47; and 'Bhartruhari Nāṭak', *RG*, 10 June 1888, 677.
19. 'Pārsī-Musalmān Nāṭako', *Pakhvādiyānī Majhā*, cited in *RG*, 24 March 1889, 343.
20. Thomas Blom Hansen, 'Whose Public, Whose Authority? Reflections on the Moral Force of Violence', *Modern Asian Studies* 52, no. 3 (2018): 1076.
21. Jürgen Habermas, 'Religion in the Public Sphere', *European Journal of Philosophy* 14, no. 1 (2006): 1–25.
22. Sinha Mrinalini, *Specters of Mother India: The Global Restructuring of an Empire* (Durham, NC: Durham University Press, 2006), 7.
23. Christopher Pinney, *'Photos of the Gods': The Printed Image and Political Struggle in India* (London: Reaktion Books, 2004), 113.
24. See Kimberly Hutchings, 'Time, Politics and Critique', 107.
25. Shakuntala Rao, 'Woman-as-Symbol: The Intersections of Identity Politics, Gender, and Indian Nationalism', *Women's Studies International Forum* 22, no. 3 (1999): 318.
26. Joan M. Schwartz and Terry Cook, 'Archives, Records, and Power: The Making of Modern Memory', *Archival Science* 2, no. 1–2 (2002): 5.
27. Arvind Rajagopal and Anupama Rao, eds., *Media and Utopia: History, Imagination and Technology* (Abingdon and New York: Routledge, 2017), 304.
28. Hansen, 'Whose Public'. For a description of agonism as a form of expression in the theatrical public sphere, see Christopher B. Balme, *The Theatrical Public Sphere* (Cambridge: Cambridge University Press, 2014), 9–12.
29. Hansen, 'Whose Public', 1084.
30. Untitled, *RG*, 17 March 1889, 327.
31. 'Ālfreḍ Nāṭak Maṇḍaḷī', *RG*, 10 August 1890, 904.
32. Untitled, *RG*, 15 March 1891, 310; 'Ālfreḍ Nāṭak Maṇḍaḷī', *RG*, 22 March 1891, 321; Untitled, *RG*, 19 April 1891, 451; Untitled, *RG*, 9 August 1891, 932; and Untitled, *RG*, 25 October 1891, 1242.
33. Balme, *The Theatrical Public Sphere*, 117.
34. For an analysis of the Muslim boycott of Bombay's theatres and pan-Islam see Rashna Darius Nicholson, 'The Picture, the Parable, the Performance and the Sword: Secularism's Demographic Imperatives', *Ethnic and Racial Studies* 41, no. 12 (2018).
35. Untitled, *RG*, 26 January 1890, 88. Instead the *Rāst* patronizingly chose to focus on how Bombay's 'intelligent and appreciative public' could reap the injunction's benefits as managers would, 'have to work in the direction of the higher and better class of dramas, in order to draw the more intelligent and appreciative public, which has for years been scared away

by so-called operas, reaching far into the small hours of the morning and calculated neither to instruct nor elevate…' n.t., *KIH*, 19 January 1890, 3.

36. 'Mehomedans and the Drama', *RG*, 26 January 1890, 93. A few months later, on 9 November 1890, a public meeting of all the 'esteemed Muslims residents of Bombay' was convened to protest a second play, Hall Caine's adaptation of de Bornier's *Mahomet* for production at the Lyceum. See 'The Play of Mehomed', *RG*, 9 November 1890, 1261–62.
37. A Disappointed Spectator, 'A Theatrical Performance Stopped', *TOI*, 11 November 1891, 6. Although the playbook is currently untraceable, the songs of the play (as indicated in the songbook) appear to conform to the standard Parsi theatre repertoire of Urdu love songs: Unknown, *Khalīf Hārūn Raśīd* (Bombay: Rising Star Printing Press, 1889).
38. 'Nāṭak vishe mumbainī polīse ek navāi jevũ paglũ', *RG*, 15 November 1891, 1327.
39. Freitag, *Collective Action and Community*, 94.
40. Untitled, *RG*, 15 March 1891, 310; 'Ālfreḍ Nāṭak Maṇḍaḷī', *RG*, 22 March 1891, 321; Untitled, *RG*, 19 April 1891, 451; Untitled, *RG*, 9 August 1891, 932; and Untitled, *RG*, 25 October 1891, 1242.
41. See also untitled, *KIH*, 2 February 1890, 21; Untitled, *KIH*, 9 February 1890, 20. For an analysis of the relationship between the Hindu boycott of the Parsi theatre and disputes on the Gujarati language see Rashna Darius Nicholson, 'What's in a Name? The Performance of Language in the Invention of Colonial and Postcolonial South Asian Theatre History' in *The Methuen Drama Handbook of Theatre Historiography*, eds. Claire Cochrane and Jo Robinson (London: Bloomsbury, 2019), 206–7.
42. Untitled, *RG*, 20 December 1885, 1380; 'Ālfreḍ Nāṭak Maṇḍaḷī', *RG* 27 December 1885, 1403; Untitled, *RG*, 27 December 1885, 1409; and Untitled, *RG*, 3 January 1885, 22. The Alfred subsequently performed the Hindu mythological *Shrīyāl Rājā*: Untitled, *RG*, 9 October 1887, 1156; 'Ālfreḍ Nāṭak Maṇḍaḷī', *RG*, 16 October 1887, 1169–70; and 'Rājā Shrīyāl', *RG*, 18 December 1887, 1429.
43. 'The Drama under Difficulties', *RG*, 23 February 1890, 210. The *Rāst* continued: 'Just as the Muslims boycotted Bombay's theatres due to the representation in Paris of their prophet, the Vaiśṇav Hindus have followed suit in making a ruckus'. The play would go back on the boards after these tensions had subsided: Untitled, *RG*, 16 March 1890, 311; Untitled, *RG*, 23 March 1890, 340; and Untitled, *RG*, 30 March 1890, 366. See also a statement issued by the troupe's actor Dhanjībhāi Māsṭar against the boycott: 'Ālfreḍ Nāṭak Maṇḍaḷīvālāoe', *KIH*, 16 February 1890, 4.
44. Uncoincidentally, it was at this pivotal juncture that the Parsi press began to cite the contributions of such Muslim playwrights as Marhum Munśī

Miyā̃ Raunak and Munśī Vināyak Prasād Tālib in the Parsi theatre: Untitled, *RG*, 5 October 1890, 1137; untitled, *KIH*, 9 Feb 1890, 21; and untitled, *KIH*, 16 February 1890, 21.

45. See Shashi Bhushan Upadhyay, 'Communalism and Working Class: Riot of 1893 in Bombay City', *Economic and Political Weekly* 24, no. 30 (1989): PE69–PE75.
46. Statement forwarded with Government of India (Home Dept.) to secretary of state, 26 September 1894, British Library, Oriental and India Office Collection cited in Matthew Groves, 'Law, Religion and Public Order in Colonial India: Contextualising the 1887 Allahabad High Court Case on 'Sacred' Cows', *South Asia: Journal of South Asian Studies* 33, no. 1 (2010): 90.
47. Jamśedjī Māṇekjī, 'Pārsīo māṭe ek "mīlīṭarī skul" bābe sucnā', *RG*, 16 March 1890, 301. This period also witnessed the first official contact between Parsis and the Persian consul: 'The Parsees and the Persian Consul General', *RG*, 25 March 1888, 364 Kha. For a description of the deepening ties between the Parsis and the Shah of Persia, see 'The Parsees and the Shah of Persia', *RG*, 24 June 1888, 727; 'The Parsees and the Shah of Persia', *RG*, 21 October 1888, 1216; and 'Irā̃nnā śāhne pārsīo tarafnū̃ mānpatra', *RG*, 28 July 1889, 858–59. At this juncture, the Victoria Nāṭak Maṇḍalī under Bālīvālā announced its intention to go to Persia on the recommendation of the consul to perform for Shah Nasarūddīn: 'Vikṭoriyā Nāṭak maṇḍalī', *RG*, 8 April 1888, 416. See also the attempts being made to cultivate 'a taste … among Parsi females for the Persian Language': 'Wanted a Persian *Cercle Litteraire* in Bombay', *KIH*, 25 May 1890, 5.
48. Jamśedjī Farāmjī Mādan set up the Elphinstone Bioscope Company, screening Pathé films in a tent on Calcutta's *maidan*. Madan would soon become the pioneer of film production in South Asia, progressively recruiting Parsi theatre personnel for the burgeoning Indian film industry, which would in turn herald the mainstream Parsi theatre's ultimate demise.
49. 'The Congress and the Parsis', *RG*, 17 November 1889, 1309–10.

Correction to: The Colonial Public and the Parsi Stage

Correction to:
R. D. Nicholson, *The Colonial Public and the Parsi Stage*, Transnational Theatre Histories,
https://doi.org/10.1007/978-3-030-65836-6

The original version of this book was inadvertently published without an ESM and with the word "West Africa" instead of "East Africa" at the end of the first paragraph in Chapter 1. This has now been corrected.

The updated version of these chapters can be found at
https://doi.org/10.1007/978-3-030-65836-6_1
https://doi.org/10.1007/978-3-030-65836-6_9

R. D. Nicholson, *The Colonial Public and the Parsi Stage*, Transnational Theatre Histories,
https://doi.org/10.1007/978-3-030-65836-6_10

Bibliography

Newspapers

Baldwin's Monthly
Bataviaasch handelsblad
Bombay Gazette (BG)
Bombay Times and Journal of Commerce (BT)
Devon and Exeter Daily Gazette
Dundee Courier and Argus
Era
Golden Era
Illustrated London News
Kaysare Hinda (KIH)
Morning Post
Northern Echo
New York Times
Pall Mall Gazette
Rāst Goftār and Rāst Goftār tathā Satya Prakāś (RG)
South Australian Register
South China Morning Post
Standard
Straits Times
Straits Times Overland Journal (STOJ)
Times of India (TOI)

R. D. Nicholson, *The Colonial Public and the Parsi Stage*, Transnational Theatre Histories, https://doi.org/10.1007/978-3-030-65836-6

Books and Articles

Aguiar, Marian. *Tracking Modernity: India's Railway and the Culture of Mobility*. Minneapolis: University of Minnesota Press, 2011.

Allen's Indian Mail, and Register of Intelligence for British and Foreign India, China, and All Parts of the East. Vol. 12, January–December 1854. London: Wm. H. Allen, 1854.

Anderson, Benedict. *Imagined Communities*. London: Verso, 2006. First published 1983.

Asad, Talal. *Formations of the Secular: Christianity, Islam, Modernity*. Stanford: Stanford University Press, 2003.

Aukland, Knut. 'Connecting British and Indian, Elite and Subaltern: Arthur Crawford and Corruption in the Later Nineteenth Century Western India.' *South Asian History and Culture* 4, no. 3 (2013): 314–35.

Balme, Christopher B. *The Theatrical Public Sphere*. Cambridge: Cambridge University Press, 2014.

Banaji, Khoshru Navrosji. *Memoirs of the Late Framji Cowasji Banaji*. Bombay: Bombay Gazette Steam Printing Works, 1892.

Bandekhodā. *Barjo ane Meheršīmīnojār*. Bombay: Reporter's Press, 1871.

Bellassai, Sandro. 'The Masculine Mystique: Antimodernism and Virility in Fascist Italy.' *Journal of Modern Italian Studies* 10, no. 3 (2005): 314–35.

Bengalee, Sorabjee Shapoorjee. *The Parsee Marriage & Divorce Act 1865: Act No. XV of 1865; the Parsee Chattels Real Act: Act No. IX of 1837; the Parsee Succession Act: Act No. XXI of 1865; and the Indian Succession Act 1865; Act No. X of 1865; with an Appendix & Guzerattee Translation*. Bombay: Parsee Law Association, 1868.

Bengallee, Nowrozjee Sorabji. *The Life of Sorabjee Shapoorjee Bengallee*. Bombay: Times of India, 1920.

Benjamin, Walter. 'The Work of Art in the Age of Mechanical Reproduction.' In *Illuminations*, translated by Harry Zohn, 217–51. New York: Schocken Books, 1969.

Berncastle, Julius. *A Voyage to China: Including a Visit to the Bombay Presidency; the Mahratta Country; the Cave Temples of Western India, Singapore, the Straits of Malacca and Sunda, and the Cape of Good Hope*. London: W. Shoberl, 1850.

The Bombay Riots of 1874. Bombay: Bombay Gazette Steam Press, 1874.

The Bombay Riots of February 1874. Re-Printed from the Times of India. Bombay: Times of India Printing Works, 1874.

Briggs, Henry George. *The Pársís: Or, Modern Zerdusthians: A Sketch*. Edinburgh: Oliver and Boyd, 1852.

Browne, Victoria. 'Feminist Historiography and the Reconceptualisation of Historical Time.' PhD diss., University of Liverpool, 2013.

Burton, Antoinette M. *Dwelling in the Archive: Women Writing House, Home, and History in Late Colonial India*. Oxford: Oxford University Press, 2003.
Campbell, James M. *Gazetteer of the Bombay Presidency Thana Originally Printed in 1882*. Vol. 13, Part 1. Bombay: Government Central Press, 1984.
Cathcart, Charles W. 'Physical Exercise.' In *Health Lectures for the People. Delivered in Edinburgh During the Winter of 1882–83*, 17–36. Edinburgh: Macriven & Wallace, 1883.
Chakrabarty, Dipesh. '"In the Name of Politics": Sovereignty, Democracy, and the Multitude in India.' *Public Culture* 19, no. 1 (2007): 35–57.
———. 'Nation and Imagination.' *Studies in History* 15, no. 2 (1999): 177–207.
———. 'Postcoloniality and the Artifice of History: Who Speaks for "Indian" Pasts?' *Representations* 37 (1992): 1–26.
Chatterjee, Partha. 'Colonialism, Nationalism, and Colonialized Women: The Contest in India.' *American Ethnologist* 16, no. 4 (1989): 622–33.
———. 'History and the Nationalization of Hinduism.' In *Representing Hinduism: The Construction of Religious Traditions and National Identity*, edited by Veena Dalmia and Heinrich Von Stietencron, 103–28. New Delhi: Sage, 1995.
———. 'The Nationalist Resolution of the Women's Question.' In *Empire and Nation: Selected Essays*, 116–35. New York: Columbia University Press, 2010.
———. *Nationalist Thought and the Colonial World: A Derivative Discourse?* London: Zed Books, 1993. First published 1986.
———. *The Nation and Its Fragments: Colonial and Postcolonial Histories*. Princeton, NJ: Princeton University Press, 1993.
Cochrane, Claire. *Twentieth-Century British Theatre: Industry, Art and Empire*. Cambridge: Cambridge University Press, 2011.
Cohen, Matthew Isaac. 'On the Origin of the Komedie Stamboel: Popular Culture, Colonial Society, and the Parsi Theatre Movement.' *Journal of the Humanities and Social Sciences of Southeast Asia and Oceania* 157, no. 2 (2001): 313–57.
Cohn, Bernard S. 'Representing Authority in Victorian India.' In *An Anthropologist Among the Historians and Other Essays*, 632–82. Delhi: Oxford University Press, 1987.
Dalal, Hormazdyar Shahpurshah. *Adi Marzban—A Gentle Genius*. Bombay: R. K. Anklesaria.
Dās, Aśok Kumār. 'Jaypur mẽ Pārsī Thiyeṭar.' In *Pārsī Thiyeṭar Sampādak*, edited by Raṇbīr Sinha, 131–51. Jodhpur: Sangeet Natak Akademi, 1990.
Das, Sisir Kumar. *History of Indian Literature: 1911–1956, Struggle for Freedom: Triumph and Tragedy*. New Delhi: Sahitya Akademi, 2005.
Das, Veena, and Deborah Poole. 'State and Its Margins: Comparative Ethnographies.' In *Anthropology in the Margins of the State*, 3–33. Oxford: Oxford University Press, 2004.

Das Gupta, Hemendra Nath. *The Indian Stage*. Vol. 3. Calcutta: Metropolitan, 1944.

Davar, Sohrab P. *The History of the Parsi Punchayet of Bombay*. Bombay: New Book, 1949.

Davis, Tracy C. *Actresses as Working Women: Their Social Identity in Victorian Culture*. London and New York: Routledge, 2002.

———. 'What Are Fairies For?' In *The Performing Century*, edited by Tracy C. Davis and Peter Holland, 32–59. London: Palgrave Macmillan, 2007.

Dharwadker, Aparna Bhargava. *Theatres of Independence: Drama, Theory, and Urban Performance in India Since 1947*. Iowa City: University of Iowa Press, 2009.

Dickens, Charles, ed. *Household Words*. Vol. 17. London: Bradbury and Evans, 1858.

Dobbin, Christine E. *Asian Entrepreneurial Minorities: Conjoint Communities in the Making of the World-Economy 1570–1940*. Richmond: Curzon Press, 1996.

Douglas, James. *A Book of Bombay*. Bombay: Bombay Gazette Steam Press, 1883.

Dube, Saurabh. *Enchantments of Modernity: Empire, Nation, Globalization*. London: Routledge, 2012.

Eck, Diana L. *Darsan: Seeing the Divine Light in India*. Chambersburg, PA: Anima Books, 1981.

Economist Office. *The Economist, Weekly Commercial Time*. Vol. 23. London: Economist Office, 1865.

Edwardes, Stephen M. *The Gazetteer of Bombay City and Island*. 3 vols. Bombay: Times Press, 1909–10.

———. *Memoir of Sir Dinshaw Manockjee Petit, First Baronet (1823–1901): Late Member of the Legislative Council of the Governor-General of India and Pioneer of the Textile Industry in Bombay*. London: Oxford University Press, 1923.

Forbes, Geraldine. 'Education for Women.' In *Women and Social Reform in Modern India: A Reader*, edited by Sumit Sarkar and Tanika Sarkar, 83–112. Bloomington: Indiana University Press, 2008.

Foucault, Michel. *Discipline and Punish: The Birth of the Prison*. Translated by Alan Sheridan. New York: Vintage Books, 1995.

Fraser, Nancy. 'Transnationalizing the Public Sphere: On the Legitimacy and Efficacy of Public Opinion in a Post-Westphalian World.' In *Transnationalizing the Public Sphere*, edited by Kate Nash, 8–42. Cambridge: Polity Press, 2014.

Freitag, Sandria B. *Collective Action and Community: Public Arenas and the Emergence of Communalism in North India*. Berkeley: University of California Press, 1989.

———. *Culture and Power in Banaras: Community, Performance, and Environment, 1800–1980*. Berkeley: University of California Press, 1992.

———. 'The Realm of the Visual: Agency and Modern Civil Society.' *Contributions to Indian Sociology* 36, no. 1–2 (2002): 365–97.

Green, Nile. *Bombay Islam: The Religious Economy of the West Indian Ocean, 1840–1915*. Cambridge: Cambridge University Press, 2011.

Groves, Matthew. 'Law, Religion and Public Order in Colonial India: Contextualising the 1887 Allahabad High Court Case on "Sacred" Cows.' *South Asia: Journal of South Asian Studies* 33, no. 1 (2010): 87–121.

Guha, Amalendu. 'The Comprador Role of Parsi Seths, 1750–1850.' *Economic and Political Weekly* 5, no. 48 (1970): 1933–36.

———. 'Parsi Seths as Entrepreneurs, 1750–1850.' *Economic and Political Weekly* 5, no. 35 (1970): M107–15.

Gulfām. *Bhamto-Bhut*. Bombay: Fort Printing Press, 1913.

Habermas, Jürgen. 'Religion in the Public Sphere.' *European Journal of Philosophy* 14, no. 1 (2006): 1–25.

———. *The Structural Transformation of the Public Sphere: An Inquiry into a Category of Bourgeois Society*. Translated by Thomas Burger and Frederick Lawrence. Boston: MIT Press, 1989.

Hansen, Kathryn. 'The Birth of Hindi Drama in Banaras, 1868–1885.' In *Culture and Power in Banaras: Community, Performance, and Environment, 1800–1980*, edited by Sandria B. Freitag, 63–93. Berkeley: University of California Press, 1992.

———. 'Languages on Stage: Linguistic Pluralism and Community Formation in the Nineteenth-Century Parsi Theatre.' *Modern Asian Studies* 37, no. 2 (2003): 381–405.

———. 'Parsi Theater, Urdu Drama, and the Communalization of Knowledge: A Bibliographic Essay.' *Annual of Urdu Studies* 16 (2001): 43–63.

———. 'Ritual Enactments in a Hindi "Mythological": Betab's Mahabharat in Parsi Theatre.' *Economic and Political Weekly* 41, no. 48 (2006): 4985–91.

Hansen, Thomas Blom. 'Whose Public, Whose Authority? Reflections on the Moral Force of Violence.' *Modern Asian Studies* 52, no. 3 (2018): 1076–87.

Headrick, Daniel R. *The Tools of Empire: Technology and European Imperialism in the Nineteenth Century*. New York: Oxford University Press, 1981.

Helsinger, Elizabeth K. *Rural Scenes and National Representation: Britain, 1815–1850*. Princeton, NJ: Princeton University Press, 2014.

Hinnells, John. 'Anglo-Parsi Commercial Relations in Bombay Prior to 1847.' *Journal of the K. R. Cama Oriental Institute*, no. 46 (1978).

———. 'Bombay Parsi Panchayat.' *Encyclopædia Iranica*, online edition 4, Fasc. 4, 349–50. https://www.iranicaonline.org/articles/bombay-parsi-panchayat-the-largest-zoroastrian-institution-in-modern-history.

Hutchings, Kimberly. *Time and World Politics: Thinking the Present*. Manchester: Manchester University Press, 2013.

———. 'Time, Politics and Critique: Rethinking the "When" Question.' In *Transnationalizing the Public Sphere*, edited by Kate Nash, 98–111. Cambridge: Polity Press, 2014.

Jeejeebhoy, J. R. B. 'Historical Survey of Bombay Journalism.' In *Jāme Jamśed Centenary Memorial Volume*, 272–87. Bombay: Messrs Jehāṅgīr Be. Marajhbānnī, 1932.

Kābrājī, Bahmanjī Navrojjī. *Bholī Gul yāne Gulnī Bhūl*. n.p.: n.d.

———. *Gāmrenī Gorī*. 3rd ed. Bombay: Royal Printing Press, 1894.

Kabrājī, Kekhaśru. *Saṅgīt Rustam-Sohrab*. Bombay: Sañj Vartaman Press, 1906.

Kābrājī, Kekhuśro Navrojjī. *Bholī Jān athvā Dhannū Dhān*. Bombay: Sāñj Vartamān Electric Printing Press, 1907.

———. *Jamśed*. Bombay: Daftar Āśkārā Press, 1870.

———. *Nindākhānū*. Bombay: Jāme Jamśed Steam Press, 1885.

———. *Suḍī Vace Sopārī. Athvā Be Vacnī Kharī Paṇ Bevacnī Nahī*. Bombay: Nha. Rū. Rāṇīnā's Union Press, 1884.

Kapur, Anuradha. 'Impersonation, Narration, Desire and the Parsi Theatre.' In *India's Literary History: Essays on the Nineteenth Century*, edited by Stuart H. Blackburn and Vasudha Dalmia, 87–118. Delhi: Permanent Black, 2004.

Karaka, Dosabhai Framji. *History of the Parsis, Including Their Manners, Customs, Religion, and Present Position*. Vols. 1 and 2. London: Macmillan, 1884.

Karanjia, B. K. 'Parsi Pioneers of the Press (1822–1915).' In *A Zoroastrian Tapestry: Art Religion & Culture*, edited by P. J. Godrej and F. Punthakey Mistree, 479–82. Ahmedabad: Mapin, 2002.

Kaviraj, Sudipta. 'Modernity and Politics in India.' *Daedalus* 129, no. 1 (2000): 137–62.

Kember, Joe, John Plunkett, and Jill A. Sullivan, eds. *Popular Exhibitions, Science and Showmanship, 1840–1910*. London: Pickering & Chatto, 2012.

Khalīf Hārūn Raśīd. Bombay: Rising Star Printing Press, 1889.

Khambātā, Jahāṅgīr Pestanjī. *Ek Jāṇītā Pārsī Ekṭarno Ardhī sadī Uparno Nāṭakī Anubhav*. Bombay, 1913. Unpublished manuscript.

Khorī, Edaljī Jamśedjī. *Jālem Jor*. Bombay: Mumbai Vartamān Press, 1876.

———. *Sonānā Mulnī Khorśed*. Bombay: Daftar Āśkārā Press, 1871.

Kidambi, Prashant, Manjiri Kamat, and Rachel Dwyer, eds. *Bombay Before Mumbai: Essays in Honour of Jim Masselos*. Oxford: Oxford University Press, 2019.

Kulke, Eckehard. *The Parsees in India: A Minority as Agent of Social Change*. Bombay: Vikas, 1974.

Kumkum, Sangari, and Sudesh Vaid, eds. *Recasting Women: Essays in Indian Colonial History*. New Brunswick, NJ: Rutgers University Press, 1990.

Luckhurst, Roger. 'W.T. Stead's Occult Economies.' In *Culture and Science in the Nineteenth-Century Media*, edited by Louise Henson et al., 125–35. Aldershot: Ashgate, 2004.

Māḍagāvakara, Govinda Nārāyaṇa. *Govind Narayan's Mumbai: An Urban Biography from 1863*. Translated by Murali Ranganathan. New Delhi: Anthem Press, 2008.
Mani, Lata. 'Contentious Traditions: The Debate on Sati in Colonial India.' *Cultural Critique* 7 (1987): 119–56.
———. *Contentious Traditions: The Debate on Sati in Colonial India*. Berkeley: University of California Press, 1998.
Mathur, Saloni. *India by Design: Colonial History and Cultural Display*. Berkeley: University of California Press, 2007.
Mehta, Kumudini A. 'Bombay's Theatre World 1860–1880.' *Journal of the Asiatic Society of Bombay* 43–44 (1970): 251–78.
———. 'English Drama on the Bombay Stage in the Late Eighteenth Century and in the Nineteenth Century.' PhD diss., University of Bombay, 1960.
Menant, Delphine. *The Parsis in India*. Bombay: M. M. Murzban, 1917.
Metelits, Michael D. 'Background to a Scandal.' In *The Arthur Crawford Scandal: Corruption, Governance, and Indian Victims*. Oxford: Oxford University Press, 2019.
'Missionary Efforts in India.' In *The Asiatic Journal and Monthly Register for British India and Its Dependencies*, vol. 21, 441–50. London: Cox and Baylis, 1826.
Mitchell, John Murray. *In Western India: Recollections of My Early Missionary Life*. Edinburgh: D. Douglas, 1899.
Modī, Śamsul Olmā, and Jīvanjī Jamśedjī. 'Jāme Jamśed, tenā e nām māṭenā sababo.' In *Jāme Jamśed Centenary Memorial Volume*, 39–44. Bombay: Messrs Jehāṅgīr Be. Marajhbānnī, 1932.
Morus, Iwan Rhys. 'Seeing and Believing Science.' *Isis* 97, no. 1 (2006): 101–10.
Mrinalini, Sinha. *Specters of Mother India: The Global Restructuring of an Empire*. Durham, NC: Duke University Press, 2006.
Munśī, Ek Mahmadīyan. *Śīrīn Farhādno Gāyanrūpiī Operā*. Bombay: Oriental Press, 1882.
Nandy, Ashis. *Intimate Enemy*. Oxford: Oxford University Press, 1989.
Naoroji, Dadabhai. *The Manners and Customs of the Parsees: A Paper Read Before the Liverpool Philomathic Society, 13th March, 1861*. London: Pearson, 1862.
The Nátuck Uttejak Mandali. Bombay: Education Society's Press, 1879.
Nicholson, Rashna Darius. '"A Christy Minstrel, a Harlequin, or an Ancient Persian"?: Opera, Hindustani Classical Music, and the Origins of the Popular South Asian "Musical".' *Theatre Survey* 61, no. 3 (2020): 331–350.
———. 'Corporeality, Aryanism, Race: The Theatre and Social Reform of the Parsis of Western India.' *South Asia: Journal of South Asian Studies* 38, no. 4 (2015): 75–91.
———. 'From India to India: The Performative Unworlding of Literature.' *Theatre Research International* 42, no. 1 (2017): 5–19.

———. 'Italian Impresarios, American Minstrels and Parsi Theatre: Sonic Networks and the Negotiation of Opera in Colonial South and Southeast Asia.' In *Italian Opera in Global and Transnational Perspective: Reimagining ITALIANITÀ in the Long Nineteenth Century*, edited by Axel Körner and Paulo M. Kühl. Cambridge: Cambridge University Press, forthcoming.

———. 'The Picture, the Parable, the Performance and the Sword: Secularism's Demographic Imperatives.' *Ethnic and Racial Studies* 41, no. 12 (2018): 2197–214.

———. 'Troubling Englishness: The Eastward Success and Westward Failure of the Parsi Theatre.' *Nineteenth Century Theatre and Film* 44, no. 1 (2017): 75–91.

———. 'What's in a Name? The Performance of Language in the Invention of Colonial and Postcolonial South Asian Theatre History.' In *The Methuen Drama Handbook of Theatre History and Historiography*, edited by Claire Cochrane and Jo Robinson, 199–209. London: Bloomsbury, 2019.

Numark, Mitch. 'Translating *Dharma*: Scottish Missionary-Orientalists and the Politics of Religious Understanding in Nineteenth-Century Bombay.' *Journal of Asian Studies* 70, no. 2 (2011): 471–500.

Osterhammel, Jürgen. 'Semi-colonialism and Informal Empire in Twentieth-Century China: Towards a Framework of Analysis.' In *Imperialism and After: Continuities and Discontinuities*, edited by Wolfgang J. Mommsen and Jürgen Osterhammel, 290–314. London: Allen and Unwin, 1986.

Palsetia, Jesse S. *Jamsetjee Jejeebhoy of Bombay: Partnership and Public Culture in Empire*. Oxford: Oxford University Press, 2015.

———. 'Parsi and Hindu Traditional and Nontraditional Responses to Christian Conversion in Bombay, 1839–45.' *Journal of the American Academy of Religion* 74, no. 3 (2006): 615–45.

———. *The Parsis of India: Preservation of Identity in Bombay City*. New Delhi: Manohar, 2008.

Paṭel, Dhanjībhāi Na. *Pārsī Nāṭak Takhtānī Tavārīkh*. Bombay: 'Kaysare-Hind' Paper Printing Press, 1931.

Patel, Simin. 'The Great Persian Famine of 1871, Parsi Refugees and the Making of Irani Identity in Bombay.' In *Bombay Before Mumbai: Essays in Honour of Jim Masselos*, edited by Prashant Kidambi, Manjiri Kamat, and Rachel Dwyer, 57–76. Oxford: Oxford University Press, 2019.

Pinney, Christopher. 'The Nation (Un)Pictured? Chromolithography and "Popular" Politics in India, 1878–1995.' *Critical Inquiry* 23, no. 4 (1997): 834–67.

———. *'Photos of the Gods': The Printed Image and Political Struggle in India*. London: Reaktion Books, 2004.

Postans. 'The Brightest Jewel of Our Dependencies.' In *The Charm of Bombay, an Anthology of Writings in Praise of the First City in India*, edited by R. P. Karkaria, 191–94. Bombay: D. B. Taraporevala, 1915.

Rajagopal, Arvind. *Politics After Television: Hindu Nationalism and the Reshaping of the Public in India*. Cambridge: Cambridge University Press, 2001.

Rajagopal, Arvind, and Anupama Rao, eds. *Media and Utopia: History, Imagination and Technology*. Abingdon: Routledge, 2017.

Rao, Shakuntala. 'Woman-as-Symbol: The Intersections of Identity Politics, Gender, and Indian Nationalism.' *Women's Studies International Forum* 22, no. 3 (1999): 317–28.

Rocha, Esmeralda M. A. 'Imperial Opera: The Nexus between Opera and Imperialism in Victorian Calcutta and Melbourne, 1833–1901.' PhD diss., University of Western Australia, 2012.

Said, Edward W. *The World, the Text, and the Critic*. Cambridge, MA: Harvard University Press, 1983.

Sarkar, Sumit. *Beyond Nationalist Frames: Postmodernism, Hindu Fundamentalism, History*. Bloomington: Indiana University Press, 2002.

———. '"Kaliyuga", "Chakri" and "Bhakti": Ramakrishna and His Times.' *Economic and Political Weekly* 27, no. 29 (1992): 1543–66.

———. 'Renaissance and Kaliyuga: Time, Myth, and History in Colonial Bengal.' In *Between History and Histories: The Making of Silences and Commemorations*, edited by Gerald M. Sider and Gavin A. Smith, 98–126. Toronto: University of Toronto Press, 1997.

Sarkar, Sumit, and Tanika Sarkar, eds. *Women and Social Reform in Modern India: A Reader*. Bloomington: Indiana University Press, 2008.

Sarkar, Tanika. *Hindu Wife, Hindu Nation: Community, Religion, and Cultural Nationalism*. New Delhi: Permanent Black, 2017. First published 2001.

———. 'Nationalist Iconography: Image of Women in 19th Century Bengali Literature.' *Economic and Political Weekly* 22, no. 47 (1987): 2011–15.

Schwartz, Joan M., and Terry Cook. 'Archives, Records, and Power: The Making of Modern Memory.' *Archival Science* 2, no. 1–2 (2002): 1–19.

Scott, J. Barton, and Brannon D. Ingram. 'What Is a Public? Notes from South Asia.' *South Asia: Journal of South Asian Studies* 38, no. 3 (2015): 357–70.

Sen, Samita. 'Motherhood and Mothercraft: Gender and Nationalism in Bengal.' *Gender & History* 5, no. 2 (1993): 231–43.

Sharafi, Mitra. *Law and Identity in Colonial South Asia: Parsi Legal Culture, 1772–1947*. Cambridge: Cambridge University Press, 2014.

Sheppard, Samuel Townsend. *The Byculla Club, 1833–1916, a History*. Bombay: Bennett, Coleman, 1916.

Smith, Adam. *Theory of Moral Sentiments*. 2nd ed. London: A. Miller, 1761. First published 1759.

Soneji, Davesh. *Unfinished Gestures: Devadasis, Memory, and Modernity in South India*. Chicago: University of Chicago Press, 2012.

Stock, Eugene. *One Hundred Years: Being the Short History of the Church Missionary Society*. London: Church Missionary Society, 1899.

Tetens, Kristan. 'The Lyceum and the Lord Chamberlain: The Case of Hall Caine's *Mahomet*.' In *Henry Irving: A Re-evaluation of the Pre-eminent Victorian Actor-Manager*, edited by Richard Foulkes, 49–63. Farnham: Ashgate, 2008.

Thapar, Romila. 'The Theory of Aryan Race and India: History and Politics.' *Social Scientist* 24, no. 1/3 (1996): 3–29.

Udayrām, Rā. Rā. Raṇchoḍbhāi. *Naḷdamayantīnāṭak*. Bombay: Nirṇaysāgar Mudrāyantra, 1883.

Ūdayrām, Rā. Rā. Raṇchoḍbhāi, and Kekhuśro Navrojjī Kābrājī. *Hariścandra Nāṭak*. Bombay: Daftar Āśkārā Press, 1876.

Udupa, Sahana. 'Archiving as History-Making: Religious Politics of Social Media in India.' *Communication, Culture & Critique* 9, no. 2 (2016): 212–30.

Upadhyay, Shashi Bhushan. 'Communalism and Working Class: Riot of 1893 in Bombay City.' *Economic and Political Weekly* 24, no. 30 (1989): PE69–PE75.

Usmānī, Abul Faiz. 'Urdū Ḍrāmā aur pārsī thiyeṭar.' In *Pārsī Thiyaṭar Sampādak*, edited by Raṇbīr Sinha, 18–26. Jodhpur: Rajasthan Sangeet Natak Akademi, 1990.

Van der Putten, Jan. 'Bangsawan.' *Indonesia and the Malay World* 42, no. 123 (2014): 268–85.

Van der Veer, Peter. *Imperial Encounters: Religion and Modernity in India and Britain*. Princeton, NJ: Princeton University Press, 2001.

———. *The Modern Spirit of Asia: The Spiritual and the Secular in China and India*. Princeton, NJ: Princeton University Press, 2014.

Viswanathan, Gauri. *Masks of Conquest: Literary Study and British Rule in India*. New York: Columbia University Press, 2014.

Vitalis, Robert. 'On the Theory and Practice of Compradors: The Role of Abbud Pasha in the Egyptian Political Economy.' *International Journal of Middle East Studies* 22, no. 3 (1990): 291–315.

Wacha, Dinshaw Edulji. *A Financial Chapter in the History of Bombay City*. 2nd ed. Bombay: A. J. Combridge, 1910.

———. *Premchund Roychund: His Early Life and Career*. Bombay: Times Press, 1913.

———. *Shells from the Sands of Bombay; Being My Recollections and Reminiscences, 1860–1875*. Bombay: K. T. Anklesaria, 1920.

Weber, Max. *The Sociology of Religion*. Translated by Talcott Parsons. London: Methuen, 1971.

Williams, Richard David. 'Songs Between Cities: Listening to Courtesans in Colonial North India.' *Journal of the Royal Asiatic Society* 27, no. 4 (2017): 591–610.

Wilson, John. *The Parsi Religion as Contained in the Zand-Avastá*. Bombay: American Mission Press, 1843.

Yajnik, R. K. *The Indian Theatre, Its Origins and Its Later Developments under European Influence with Special Reference to Western India*. Woking: Unwin Brothers, 1933.

Yang, Anand A. 'Whose Sati? Widows Burning in Early Nineteenth-Century India.' *Journal of Women's History* 1 (1989): 8–33.

Yelle, Robert A. *The Language of Disenchantment: Protestant Literalism and Colonial Discourse*. Oxford: Oxford University Press, 2013.

Yule, George. 'Early Official Obstruction to the Congress and Incitement to Muslims.' Allahabad Session, 1888.

Zachariah, Benjamin. 'Travellers in Archives, or the Possibilities of a Post-post-archival Historiography.' *Práticas da História*, no. 3 (2016): 11–27.

Ziter, Edward. *The Orient on the Victorian Stage*. Cambridge: Cambridge University Press, 2003.

Index

A

accidents, 116, 181, 191, 197–198, 207

actors, 93–95, 152–153, 176, 198
  child, 148, 223, 277, 279, 280, 287, 288
  English, 57, 222–223
  Iranian refugees, 115–116
  male, of female parts, 181, 206, 207, 212, 277, 279–280
  schoolteachers as, 147
  women, 161–162, 262–267, 278

adaptations, 145, 162–163, 225, 267, 272

Ahmad, Śekh Mohammad (Raunak Banārasī), 181

Ahmednagar, 197, 296

Aladdin, or the Wonderful Lamp (play), 199

Ālādīn (play), 144, 157

Albert Edward, Prince of Wales, 184–187

Alchymist, The (play), 46

Alexandra School for Girls, 62

Alfred Nāṭak Maṇḍalī (theatre company, active 1870s), 109, 121, 137, 146, 149, 168, 207

Alfred Nāṭak Maṇḍaḷī (Alfred Theatrical Company, active 1880s-90s), 267–272

American Civil War, 72, 75

Anglicization, 55–56, 57, 62, 244, 269

anticolonialism, 10–12, 155, 218, 222, 230, 231, 233, 234, 236, 241, 248, 266, 290, 293

Āpakhatyār (newspaper), 50, 70

Āpakhatyār, Naśarvānjī Dorābjī, 50, *51*, 64, 74, 85, 86, 91, 98, 198

Apu, Farāmjī Dādābhāi, 168, 188, *190*, 194, 208, 210, 284

Aryanism, 108–113, 112, 114, 237

Atkinson, James, 112

audiences
  class of, 148–151, 224
  development of, 194, 196–197

R. D. Nicholson, *The Colonial Public and the Parsi Stage*, Transnational Theatre Histories,
https://doi.org/10.1007/978-3-030-65836-6

misbehaviour of, 148–149, 153
mixed, 26–27, 65, 119, 139–140
Muslim, 160–161
reception, 194, 199–200, 232
risks to, 197–199
royalty in, 185, 186–187, 194–196, 201–202
segregation, 26–27, 237
in Southeast Asia, 199–200
women as, 62, 63–64, 93, 149, 184, 235, 263, 284
authenticity, 230
of customs, 66–67, 69

B

Bad ilat no Gofo (play), 46
Badkārokī Maktab (The School for Scandal) (play), 46
Bālīvālā, Khurśedjī Mervānjī, *152*, 170, 181, 188
Bāl Vīvā (Child Marriages) (play), 46
Banārasī, Raunak (Śekh Mohammad Ahmad), 178, 181
Bandekhodā (Dādābhāi Edaljī Pockhānāvālā), 74, 185
Bāpujī, Śokhar, *Śrī Krushṇa Vijay*, 297–298
Baronet Theatrical Club, 74
Batavia, 199, 200, 203
Baṭlīvaḷa, Pestanjī Jījībhāi (Pesu Pokhrāj), 196
Bejun Soortee (Ūṭhāūgīr Śurtī) (play), 46
Benares (Varanasi), 181, 184, 228, 235
Bengalee, Sohrabjee Shahpurjee, 43, 59, 84, 98
Bengal Tiger (play), 57
Bennee, Mr and Mrs, 57, 133
Bharatmātā (motherland), 12, 155, 235
Bhāu (set designer), 176
Bhavnagar, 177–179, 184, 185
Bholey Mia, or Half a Face for 50 Rupees, 200
Bhul Cuknī Hasāhas (Comedy of Errors) (play), 93
Bīlīmorīyā, Kāvasjī Ho., 47, 264
bodies, 91–93
discipline of, 92, 110
masculine, 91, 110–113
of women, 11–12, 15, 273–274
Bomanjee, Hormusjee, 26
Bombastes Furioso (play), 57
Bombay Amateur Theatre, 23–25, 29
Bombay Association, 44
Bombay Gazette (newspaper), 25, 46, 48, 50, 52, 70, 71, 79, 86, 107, 115, 116, 148, 255
Bombay (Mumbai), 3, 4, 23–27. *See also* Grant Road Theatre; New Victoria Theatre
economy, 72, 74–75
Elphinstone College, 43, 47
Elphinstone Theatre, 198
Framjee Cowasjee Institute, 132, 227, 251, 263, 264
Gaiety Theatre, 198, 203, 262–263, 266, 298
Gateway of India, 191
Hīndī Theatre, 176, 177, 207
Mulla Firoz Library, 35
Novelty Theatre, 278
Parsi migration to, 4
population, 72, 224
railways, 129–130
Victoria Museum, 132
Victoria Theatre, 103, 162, 188
Bombay Theatre Company, 103
Bombay Vartaman (newspaper), 33–34
Bombe, Bishop H.A., 159
Bornier, Henri de, *Mahomet, drame en 5 actes*, 296

boundaries
cultural, 179, 242
disruption of, 196
ethnic, 298–300
between real and imaginary worlds, 143–145
boys
actors, 277, 279, 280, 287
schools for, 30
Burma (Myanmar), 201–202
Burmese language, 201
Bushell, Professor, 133–137, 143
Busvān, Professor, 92

C
Cābuk (newspaper), 34, 50, 52, 64, 70
Calcutta (Kolkata), 27, 77, 130, 167, 181, 184, 196, 198, 200, 203, 264
Cama, Byramjee Hormusjee, 75
Cama, Kharshedji Nusserwanji, 45, 54, 98, 223
Cama, Kharshedji Rustomji, 98, 108
Cāndāru, Navrojī Dorābjī, 33
capitalism
collaboration with, 29–30
Carson, Dave, 63, 75–76, 85, 133, 170
Case of the Fraud at Hyderabad by the Poona Thugs, The (play), 57
caste, 7, 10, 33, 71, 140, 158, 228, 233, 235, 264–265, 294
Cathcart, Charles W., 260, 282
Cavcavno Murabo (play), 179
censorship, 159, 233, 297–298
charity, 72–74, 113, 114–115
child marriage, 50–52
children
actors, 148, 223, 277, 279, 280, 287, 288
mixed heritage, 264–265
Church Missionary Society, 30
Cīcgar, Edaljī Berāmjī (Bhaglā Hajām), 194
Cicgar, Hormasjī Mancerjī, 93
Cijgar, Dārā(b)śāh Ratanjī, 93
class, 63
of audiences, 148–151, 224
elite, 29, 34, 73
lower, 149, 160
and race, 264–265
clothing, 59, 101
headscarves/bands, 66, 243
colonialism
collaboration with, 5, 29–30, 56–57, 73
governance, 7–8, 29
and religion, 8, 31–32, 36–37
values, transmission of, 29–30, 31
comedy, 149–151, 200. *See also* farces
skits (*ḍhong*), 92
communalism, 15, 165, 235–238
community
consciousness, 114–115
scrutiny of, 43
compradors (collaborators), 5
cultural, 178
conservatism, 9, 12, 89, 222, 266–267, 294
copyright, 171, 180–181
corporeality, 91–93
discipline of, 92, 110
masculine, 110–113
of women, 11–12, 15, 273–274
corruption, 90, 146, 293
cosmopolitanism, 14–15, 165, 178–179, 184–185
costume, 59
English, 99, 200
Hindustani, 151
Italian, 93, 98
Persian, 100–101, 107, 115

cotton, 5, 24, 28, 34, 72, 75, 178
Crawford, Arthur T., 293
crime, 146, 293. *See also* riots
Cursetjee, Manockjee, 26, 47, 64, 68–69, 79
customs, 44, 46, 68, 205
  authenticity of, 66–67, 69
  child marriage, 50–52
  critique of, 50–53

D
Dādābhāi, Edaljī, 181, *182*, 196
Dāde Darīāv (Pericles, Prince of Tyre) (play), 137–139, *138*
Dāhāyābhāi, Dalpatrām, 107, 168
Daji, Dr Bhau, 98
Dājī, Jamśedjī Kāvasjī (Jamsu Manījeh), 103, 176, 179, 207, 208
Dalāl, Farāmjī Gustādjī, 85, 93, *95*, 98, 161, 227
Dalāl, Jamśedjī, 59
Dārūvālā, Kāvasjī Naśarvānjī (Kāu-Rodābe), 176, 203, 207
Darwin, Charles, *On the Origin of Species*, 260
Dāvar, Farāmjī, 161
Dāvar, Naśarvānjī Jīvājī, 109
Dāvar, Ratanśāh Jīvājī, 188
Deacle, Mrs (actress), 27, 76
Delhi, 181, 192–194, 262
Deśī Pantujīo (Native Teachers) (play), 46
Dhanji Garak (play), 45–46, 48, 55, 67
ḍhong (skits), 92
Diamond Cut Diamond (play), 57
directors, 98, 139, 196. *See also* Paṭel, Dādābhāi Sorābjī Farāmjī
drop scenes, 101, 202
Duff, Alexander, 186

E
East India Association, 90, 99
East India Company, 23, 29
education, 90–91
  through entertainment, 132–133
  evangelical schools, 30–31
  of girls, 62
  schools, 43, 47, 62
  of women, 93, 248
ek "dhutārā" athvā "jādugar" (play), 55, 62
Elīaṭ (Eliot), Dādābhāī, 47
Elliot, A.W., 26
Elphinstone College (Bombay), 38, 43, 47, 57, 68
Elphinstone Nāṭak Maṇḍalī (Theatrical Club/Company), 57–59, *58*, *60*, *61*, 74, 137, 146, 158, 162
Elphinstone Theatre (Bombay), 188, 198
Empress Nāṭak Maṇḍalī (theatre company), 193, 194, 207, 262–263
English language, 222
  and education, 55
  in Parsi drama, 269
  in Parsi press, 57
  performances in, 57

F
fairies, 3, 9, 55, 133–135, 139, 141–143, 157, 161, 194, 200, 229, 231, 268
farces, 45–46, 47, 55, 56, 137
Fardunjī, Dastur, 112
Fardunji, Naoroji, 43, 68, 89, 159
Farebe Fītnā (play), 203
Farrokh Sabhā (play), 191, 200
femininity, 91, 162, 235, 242, 279–280
feminization, of men, 279–280

Fenton, Mary, 261–264, 265–267, 269–271, 277, 283
Ferdowsi. *See* Firdausi
finances, 103, 193, 204
  bankruptcy, 203
  debt, 23
  losses, 206
  speculation, 72–73
  ticket prices, 159, 161, 171
Firdausi, *Śāhānāmā (Book of Kings)*, 99, 107, 111, 112
fires, 197–198, 207
Forbes, Naśarvānjī, 74
Framjee Cowasjee Institute, 132, 227, 251, 263, 264
Framji, Dosabhai, 289
Framji, Sorabji, 26
Frāmnā, Rūstamjī N. Rūstam, 196, 210
Frere, Bartle, 57
Furrokh Sabha (play), 200

G
Gaiety Theatre (Bombay), 198, 203, 262–263, 266, 298
Gandhī, Kāvasjī Mancerjī, 201
gas lighting, 130
Gāyan Utejak Maṇḍalī (musical society), 243, 264
Gentlemen Amateurs Club (theatre group), 74, 85, 98
Ghaḍīāḷī, Dhanjībhāi Kharśedjī, 188, 192, 199
Gobineau, Arthur de, 108, 112
Going to the Derby (play), 57
Grant Road Theatre (Bombay), 26, 27, 103, 146, 188
Gubernatis, Angelo de, 266
Gujarati language, 26, 162, 185, 225, 236–237, 242–246
  Parsi, 15, 274
Gule Bakāvalī (play), 158–159, 175, 188, 200, 283
gymnastics, 63, 91–93, 110, 135

H
Habermas, Jürgen, 6–7, 10–11, 17, 37, 41, 230, 294, 301
Hajām, Bhaglā (Edaljī Berāmjī Cīcgar), 194
Halkārū (newspaper), 33, 34. *See also* Cābuk
Hāṇḍo, Kāu (Kāvasjī Mīstrī), 194
Hataria, Manekji Limji, 113
Hāthīrām, Rū. Ho., 47
Haug, Martin, 31, 69, 112
Hīndī Nāṭak Maṇḍalī (theatre company), 160, 207
Hīndī Theatre (Bombay), 176, 177, 179, 207
Hīndu ane Fīraṅgī Rāj vace Tafāvat (The Battle between the Hindu and Foreign Raj) (play), 56
Hinduism, 33, 236
  Hindu-Muslim riots, 2
  mythological plays, 9–10, 12, 222–223, 227–238
Hindustani language, 151–153, 160, 181, 199–200, 203
Holcroft, Thomas, *The Road to Ruin*, 23
Honeymoon, The (play), 57, 150
Hong Kong, 201, 203
Horājī ane Andhīārūjī (play), 99
Hormajjī, Jāhāṅgīr, 147
horses, on stage, 115, 116
Hyderabad, 160, 161, 177, 178, 184, 185, 296, 297

I
Illustrious Stranger, The (play), 57
imperialism. *See* colonialism

Indian Mutiny (1857), 72
Indian National Congress, 289, 292
Indian Theatrical Club, 56
Indra Sabhā (play), 161–162, 184, 188, 194, 200, 208, 262
Irānī Nāṭak Maṇḍalī (Persian Theatrical Club), 115–117
Iran, 66–67, 100, 109, 113–116, 145, 177, 225, 276, 298
Islam, 113, 151
  boycott of theatres, 296–297
  Hindu-Muslim riots, 2
  Parsi–Muslim relations, 160–166, 296–297
  Parsi–Muslim riots, 162–166

J
Jāfar ane Keśar (play), 178
Jālbhāi, Rūstamjī Hormajjī, 162–163
Jāme Jamśed (newspaper), 107, 112
Jamsetjee, Rustomjee, 74
Jamshed (mythological king), 110–113
Jardine Matheson and Co, 24, 28
Jeejeebhoy, Sir Jamsetjee (1st Baronet), 24, 28, 29, 32, 57, 62, 74
Jeejeebhoy, Sir Jamsetjee (3rd Baronet), 266, 272, 289
Jehangir, Cowasjee, 73
Jhansi, 198
Jījībhāi, Jamśedjī. *See* Jeejeebhoy, Sir Jamsetjee
Jījībhāi, Rūśtamjī J., 74
Jones, William, 107
Jośī, Farāmroj Rūstamjī, 93, *96*
Jośi, Kharśedjī Mancerjī, 93
journals. *See* press
juddins ('half-castes'), 264–265
Junī Pārsī Nāṭak Maṇḍalī (Old Parsi Theatrical Club/Company), 56, 63

K
Kābrājī, Bahmanjī Navrojjī, 268, 286
Kābrājī, Kekhuśro, 75, 96, *97*, 98, 102, 103, 129, 153, 170, 223–227, 237
Kalyānīvālā, Bhīkhājī (Bhīkhu Śyavakṣ), 109, 176, 188
Karaka, Dosabhai Framji, 93, 98
Karṇī tevī pār ūtarṇī (play), 203
kaśrat (gymnastics), 92–93
Kean, Charles, 101, 132
Kekāuś ane Rūstam (play), 160
Kerāvālā, Dhanjībhāi Rūstamjī, 103, *104*, 161, 170
Khambātā, Hīrjībhāi, 146
Khambātā, Jahāṅgīr Pestanjī, 46, 98, 115, 191–194, 224, 262, 283
Khan, Sir Mir Turab Ali (Salar Jung I), 160
Khānsāheb, Naśarvānjī Mervānjī, 176, 181
Khaṇvo Ḍungar ane Kāhāḍvo Undar (Much Ado about Nothing) (play), 98
Khaṭāu, Kāvasjī Pālanjī, 194, 261, 266
Khodābakś (play), 139–140
Khorī, Edaljī Jamśedjī
  Hajambād ane Ṭhaganāj, 149–151
Kohīdārū, Kāvasjī Naśarvānjī, 47, 63, 93, 98, 103, *105*, 161
Kolkata (Calcutta), 27, 184

L
Lahore, 194, 200, 262
Lalu Mehetānī Nīśāḷ (Master Lalu's School) (play), 93
Lāṅgḍā, Mancerjī, 112
laws and legislation
  Abkari Act, 1886, 272
  English Education Act, 1835, 55
  for Parsis, creation of, 67–69
Layard, Austen Henry, 101–103, *102*

Layelī Majnu (play), 188
lighting, 198
Limji, Banaji, 27
Living too Fast (play), 57
London, 2, 72, 77, 132, 204, 206
Love's Quarrels (play), 57
loyalty, 73, 226–227, 271, 277, 291–292
Lucknow, 181, 184
Lucky Hit, A (play), 57
Lying Valet, The (play), 57

M
Mādan, Jamśedjī Farāmjī, 167, 171, 188, *189*, 304
Mādan, Naśarvānjī Farāmjī (Naslu Tehmīna), 176, 203
Mādan, Pestanjī Farāmjī, 137, 152, 167, 176, 203
Mādan, Pestanjī Kharśedjī, 194, 202, 206
Madon, Cursetji Framji, 203
Madras (Chennai), 130, 186, 188, 190–191, 196–198, 200, 211, 263
magazines. *See* press
magic, 131, 142
  and religion, 31
Majgāmvāḷā, Edaljī Naśarvānjī (Edaljī Prussia), 47
Malcolm, John, 112
Marajhbān, Behrāmjī Fardunjī, 151
Marzban, Fardunji, 32
masculinity, 91, 107, 272
Māśtar, Māṇekjī Jīvaṇjī, 149, 266
Māsṭar, Pestanjī Dhanjībhāi, 47, 93, 98
mechanical scenery, 9, 140, 143, 158, 176–177, 205
media. *See* press
Meerut, 194, 262
Meharhomjī, Mancerśāh Be., 47
Mejar, Barjorjī Farāmjī, 93
men. *See also* masculinity
  boys, 30, 277, 279, 280, 287
  in female roles, 181, 206, 207, 212, 277, 279–280
  warriors, 91, 92–93, 107–108, 109–110
mesmerism, 133–137
mimicry (*nakal*), 100, 101, 259
  blackface, 148
  whiteface, 178, 179, 200, 205
minstrels, 63, 133, 148
missionaries, 30–31, 33, 35–36, 36, 66, 131, 155, 294
Mīstrī, Kāvasjī (Kāu Hāṇḍo), 194, 210
Modī, Hormasjī Dhanjībhāi, 93, 98, 161, 170, 227
Mogal, Ḍosābhāi Fardunjī, 181, *183*, 188, 193, 209
Molière, *Mock Doctor*, 57
Moor Tragedy, The (play), 74
Moos, Ardeshir Framji, 45, 98
morality, 46–47
Mulla Firoz Library (Bombay), 35
Müller, Max, 108, 162, 260
Mumbai. *See* Bombay
Mumbai Samācār (newspaper), 32, 34, 64–65, 112
munśīs (playwrights), 179–181, 208
  Śīrīn Farhādno Gāyanrūpī operā, 145
Mus (Moos), Bhīkhājī Kha., 47
music, 95
  and gymnastic performances, 92, 110
  songs, 56, 75, 98, 107, 109–110, 111
Myanmar (Burma), 201–203
Mysore, 192
mythological plays, 9–10

Hindu, 9–10, 12, 222–223, 227–232
Persian, 9, 49–50, 112, 116, 137, 140–145, 156

N

Nādarśānā Lagan (The Marriage of Nādarśā) (play), 50
Naik, Anandrao Sabaji, 203
Nājar, Kuvarjī Sorābjī, 57, *58*, 172, 181, 187–188, 208
Nānā Sāhebno Natak (The Play of Nānā Sāheb) (play), 56
Naoroji, Dadabhai, 43, 45, 89, 159
Nāṭak Utejak Maṇḍalī (Society for the Amelioration of the Drama), 223–227, 267, 285
nationalism, 3, 10–11, 230–231, 289, 295
nautch (dances), 12, 54, 63, 80, 162, 186–187
Nav Naval Neāedhīśo (play), 98
nazar (observation/vision), 43–44, 144–145
newspapers. *See* press
New Victoria Theatre (Bombay), 110
Novelty Theatre (Bombay), 278, 297

O

observation, 43–44
and power, 66
of women by men, 65–66
Ogrā, Sorābjī Farāmjī, 176, 207
Old Parsi Theatrical Club, 70
opera, *Benajhīr ane Badremunīr*, 160, 176–177
opium, 5, 24, 28, 32, 34, 44, 46, 54, 178, 191
Oriental Christian Spectator (journal), 31, 32
orientalism, 260
and knowledge, 101–103
reverse, 178
Original Victoria Nāṭak Maṇḍalī (theatre company), 176, 188–190, 207

P

Padmāvat (play), 188
Pakistan, 262
pan-Zoroastrianism, 113–117
Pārakh, Dhanjīśāh Navrojī, 59, *60*
Pārakh, Naśarvānjī Navrojī, 59, *61*, 171, 188
Parsi Gymnasium and Music Company (Pārsīonī kaśrat ane Gujrātī Gāeṇ Maṇḍalī), 91–93, 96
Pārśī Nāṭak Maṇḍalī (Parsi Theatrical Club/Company), 46, 74, 265–268
Parsi Panchayat (governing body), 29, 34, 39, 51, 69–72, 92
Parsi people, 1, 4–5. *See also* Zoroastrianism
clothing, 44, 59
in colonial trade, 27–29
communal identity of, 142–145
as compradors, 5, 28–31, 178
criticism of, 292–293
and education, 30–31
employment, 90
identity, 276–277, 292, 298–300
Indianness of, 276–277
as minority, 260–261, 274–277
Parsi–Muslim relations, 160–166
priesthood, 34
śeṭhs, 24–28, 29, 54, 73, 221
Parsi Punch (journal), 91
Parsi Punchayet Case of 1909, 298
Pārsī Stage Players (theatrical group), 70, 74, 91
Parsi Theatrical Club/Company. *See* Pārśī Nāṭak Maṇḍalī

Parsi Theatrical Committee, 45, 47
Pārsīonī kaśrat ane Gujrātī Gāeṇ Maṇḍalī (theatrical group), 104
Paṭel, Dādābhāi Sorābjī Farāmjī, 103–105, *106*, 107, 159, 170, 181
Paṭel, Dhanjībhāi, 74, 103, 115–117, 181
periodicals. *See* press
Persian language, 115
Persian Theatrical Club (Irānī Nāṭak Maṇḍalī), 115–117
Persian Zoroastrian Nāṭak Maṇḍalī (Theatrical Club), 117, 144
Petit, Dinshaw, 289
philanthropy, 72–74, 113–115
Pizarro (play), 56
playwrights, 99, 103–107
  anonymous, 145, 179–181
Pleader, Jehangir Merwanji, 98
Pockhānāvālā, Dādābhāi Edaljī, *Khuśru Śīrīn*, 109, 121
Pokhrāj, Pesu (Pestanjī Jījībhāi Baṭlīvaḷa), 196
Poona (Pune), 45, 140, 176, 184, 186, 222, 296
Premkuvarnā Premno Peālo (Premkuvar's Love Goblet) (play), 101
press, 31–35, 50. *See also* Cābuk; Rāst Goftār
  and theatre, imbricated relationship with, 70–72
  Āpakhatyār, 50, 70
  Bombay Gazette, 25, 71
  Bombay Vartaman, 33–34
  disputes among, 70
  English language, 57
  Jāme Jamśed, 34, 50, 65, 70, 107, 112
  Mumbai Samācār, 65, 112
  Oriental Christian Spectator, 31
  Parsi Punch, 91
  private life, scrutiny of, 43
  Strī Bodh (Female Instructor), 59, 93
  for women, 59, 93
Prince Edward Parsi Theatrical Company, 203
prostitution, 223
public sphere, 6–9. *See also* press
  antidisciplinary, 149
  gendering of, 149
  influence of, 158
  inter-communal, 164–166
  Parsi, 33–35
  and religion, 31–32
  and self-representation, 71–72
  vernacular, 7–11, 293–295
  women in, 63–66

Q

Quack Doctor, The (play), 200, 201

R

race
  of audiences, 25–26, 27, 261
  and class, 264–265
  intermixing, 261
  and mixed heritage, 264–265
  purity of, 272–273, 281
race theory, 108–109, 260–261
Ramprakash Theatre (Jaipur), 196
Ram Singh II, Maharaja Sawai, 194–196
Rām Sītā (play), 202
Rawlinson, Henry, 100, 107, 111
re-enchantment, 163–164
reform, 3, 52, 89
  religious, 8, 32–34, 44–45, 52–53
  social, 43, 256
    and anticolonialism, 221–222
    failure of, 77, 221–222

opposition to, 50–53
theatre as disruptor of, 159
and women, 59–66, 151–153, 154–155, 248, 256
refugees, 113–115, 115–116
regulation
censorship, 159, 233, 297–298
of theatre, 197–199, 263, 297
religion, 8–11, 294
and colonialism, 8, 31–32, 36
conversions, 32–34, 35
missionaries, 30–31, 35–36
and mythology, 31–32
and public sphere, 31–32
rationalized, 131
reform of, 32–34, 44–45
Religious Reform Association (Rāhnumāi Mājdayaśnī Sabhā), 44, 113
respectability, 63, 160–161
of actresses, 280–281
riots, 2, 165–166, 297–298
Roostum Zabooli and Sohrab (Ruśtam Jabulī) (play), 45, 48
Rūprām, Rāv Sāheb Mahīpatrām, 293
Rūśtam ane Barjor (Roostum and Burjor) (play), 115
Rūstam ane Sohrāb (play), 160
Ruttonjee, Dady, 140

S
Sacīnvālā, Dorābjī Navrojī, 194
Saef-us-śulemān (play), 202
Śāhānāmā̃ (Shahnama, Book of Kings), 101
Saklātvāḷā, Farāmjī, 188
Salar Jung I (Khan, Sir Mir Turab Ali), 160
San Francisco Minstrels, 63, 75
San Souci (theatre, Calcutta), 27
Sarkārī, Naśarvānjī Ratanjī, 194, 210
scenery. *See* set design
schools, 30–31, 43, 47, 62, 147
science, 131, 133–137, 142–143
Scott, Sir Walter, *Ivanhoe*, 99, 119
scripture, 66, 230
scrutiny. *See* vision
set design, 115, 137
criticism of, 153
drop scenes, 101–103, 202
mechanical scenery, 158, 176–177
stage effects, 125
technological development, 140–141
sexuality, 149–151, 222–223, 280
Shakespeare, William, 55–56
Shankarsheth, Jagannath, 26, 57, 98
Sheridan, Richard Brinsley
The Rivals, 26
Shroff, Meheribai Hormusjee, 62
sight. *See* vision
Singapore, 2, 199–203, 206
Siṅgh, Lālā Lāl, 193
Śīrīn Farhādno Gāyanrūpī operā (play), 145
social Darwinism, 108, 260
Society for the Amelioration of the Condition of the Zoroastrians in Persia, 113
Society for the Amelioration of the Drama. *See* Nāṭak Utejak Maṇḍalī
Society for the Diffusion of Knowledge (Dnyān Prasārak Maṇḍalī), 44, 108, 132
Śohrābjī, Dārāśāh, *Kekāuś ane Rūstam*, 160
songs, 56, 75, 98, 107, 109–110
Sosan Rā̃mesga (play), 177
Souter, Frank, 162–165, 251
sovereignty, 3, 6, 7, 9, 71, 144, 229, 230
spectacle, 3, 8–9, 116, 132–133, 135
critique of, 137–139

and Parsi identity, 142–145
technological development, 140–141
state, construction of, 13
Strī Bodh (Female Instructor) (pamphlet), 59, 93
Student's Society's Girls School, 62
Students Amateur Club, 56, 70
Sunkersett, Jugonnathjee, 74
superstition, 8, 9, 46, 47, 55, 62, 133, 134

T
Tabelāvālā, Ardeśar Pīrośāh (Ado), 196
Tagore, Satyendranath, 54
Taming a Tiger (play), 57
Tātā, Kekāus, 149
technology, 129–131
electricity, 134
flight, 130
railways, 129–130
telegraph, 130
theatrical, 9, 132–133, 158, 176–177
tents, as theatres, 93, 188, 190, 192, 193, 197–198
theatre
amateur, 23–24, 26, 53, 223, 227
commercial, 147–151, 156–159, 47–48
professional, 9, 26, 27, 93–98
regulation of, 197–199, 263, 297
technological development, 132–133, 140–141
Thibaw Min (King of Burma), 201
Ṭhuṭhī, Dādābhāi Ratanjī (Dadi Christ), 93, *94*, 98, 118, 287
Benajhīr ane Badremunīr, 160
Dāde Dariāv, 137
Hīndī Nāṭak Maṇḍalī, 176–177, 179
tours, 177, 196
Victoria Nāṭak Maṇḍalī, 188, 193
time, 294
conceptualizations of, 35
regulation of, 29–30
Tīrīrām (play), 46
toddysellers, 272
tours/touring, 190–206
in England, 204–206
in India, 176–184, 188, 190–199
in Southeast Asia, 199–203
traditionalism, 50–53, 59, 64, 66, 68, 73
traditions. *See* customs
translations, 93, 98–99, 119, 151, 201
Turan, 48, 109
Twelve Months' Honey-Moon (play), 57

U
Unvālā, Jamśedjī, 59
Upstairs and Downstairs (play), 57
urbanization, 272–276

V
Vaccha, Jehangir Burjorji, 43, 45
Vāḍīyā, Pestanjī Naśarvānjī, 93
Varanasi (Benares), 184
Veer, Peter van der, 32–33, 131
Velātī, Pestanjī Farāmjī, 116
Victoria Museum (Bombay), 132
Victoria Nāṭak Maṇḍalī (Victoria Theatrical Company), 179–181, 193
Victoria Theatre (Bombay), 103, 152, 160–162, 188, 200
Vīktorāinā or Bandīkhanethī Bāpne Chodāvnār ek Beṭī (A Daughter Releasing Her Imprisoned Father) (play), 99
Village Lawyer (play), 57

violence, 295–296. *See also* riots
vision, 43–44, 144–145
  unreliability of, 134–135, 140, 142–145, 226
  of women by men, 65–66
Viswanathan, Gauri, 33, 55

W
Wacha, Dinshaw Edulji, 130
Wadia, Bomanjee Hormusji, 24, 25
warriors, 91–93, 107–110
whiteness, performance of, 179, 200, 205
Wilson, John, 30–33, 35
wives, 238–242
women, 11–13, 154, 162. *See also* femininity
  actors/performers, 13, 54, 161–162, 262–267, 278
    criticism of, 186–187, 222–223
    praise of, 277–278
  agency of, 12, 239, 241–242, 266
  Anglicized, 62, 244, 269
  as audiences, 62–64, 93, 149, 184, 235, 263, 284
  bodies of, 11–12, 15, 273–274
  clothing of, 66, 67, 243
  and degeneration, 273–274
  girls, 30, 244–246
  legal rights of, 68
  mothers, 235, 267–272
  observation of, 65–66
  publications for, 59, 93
  in public sphere, 63–66
  representations of, 12–13, 154, 156–157, 185, 241–242, 248, 266–267, 271–272
  roles, traditional, 235, 238–242, 263–264, 281
  sexualized, 149–151
  and social reform, 59–66, 151–155, 244, 256
  subjectivity of, 154, 162
  subjugation of, 11–12, 62
  traditional, 246–247, 266–267
Wood, Ellen, *East Lynne*, 267–269
Writer, Farāmjī Bamanjī, *Śāhājādā Sīāvakhś*, 109, 121

Z
Zoroastrian Nāṭak Maṇḍalī (Theatrical Club), 56, 64, 68, 69, 74, 109, 114, 117, 139, 144, 168, 177, 212
Zoroastrianism, 8
  'authentic', 67–69
  Hindu influence on, 68–69
  Jijibhoy Dadabhoy Parsi Madressa, 35
  Kalgīr Torānā songs, 109–110
  muktād, 109, 121
  Mulla Firoz Library, 35
  pan-Zoroastrianism, 113–117
  reform of, 32–34, 44–45, 52
  scholarship, 108
  Vendidad, 31
  Western accounts of, 31
  Zend Avesta (prayer book), 31

CPSIA information can be obtained
at www.ICGtesting.com
Printed in the USA
LVHW080815200922
728806LV00006B/434

9 783030 658359